MAN OF REASON

THOMAS PAINE

FROM THE PORTRAIT BY JOHN WESLEY JARVIS

ALFRED OWEN ALDRIDGE

MAN OF REASON
The Life of
THOMAS PAINE

J. B. LIPPINCOTT COMPANY
Philadelphia & New York

❧ *Contents* ❧

ᏗᎾ *Introduction* ᏗᎾ

Thomas Paine stands out in the literature and history of the eighteenth century as one of the luminaries of both the American and the French revolutions. He served in America as a soldier, diplomat and journalist; in France, as a legislator and constitution-maker; then became in both countries, as well as in his native England, a symbol of the rights of man and the struggle for democracy. In a third great revolution—that in the realm of theology—he became the most notorious champion of deism the world has ever known and is still a symbol of the rationalistic spirit of his age.

Though born of the people, his manners rough and ungracious, Paine was consulted by presidents in America: caressed by the rich and titled in Europe; and alternately loved and hated by the simple folk to whom he devoted his tireless intellectual energies. Having tasted only the rudiments of formal education, he developed his innate scientific ingenuity with such zeal that he became one of the foremost bridge engineers of his time. Although boasting that he almost never read the works of other authors, he developed a vigorous literary style which influenced the political and religious ideas of millions. He rose to fame as the literary-politico guide of the American nation. His contribution to the propaganda of its Revolution equaled that of Franklin to its diplomacy and that of Washington to its military strategy. He passed his middle years amid the turmoil of the succeeding Revolution in France. After defending its principles in England against the attack of Burke, he was elected to the French Assembly. Here he collaborated with Condorcet and other leaders in creating a constitution for the new society. Like most moderates, however, he fell victim to the suspicion and ani-

7

mosity of the radicals. Narrowly escaping the guillotine, he passed
ten dreary months in the Luxembourg prison, where he conceived
part of his apologia for deism, *The Age of Reason.* After his release through the efforts of the American Minister, James Monroe,
he remained in France for several years, attempting to serve as
an unofficial liaison agent between the French and American governments. Although on close terms with Napoleon and other
leaders, he played his subsequent political role entirely behind the
scenes, never again attaining official rank in public affairs. On
his return to America, during the last decade of his life, he was
known primarily as the author of *The Age of Reason,* the most
calumniated book of the epoch. A revolutionary in politics and
religion, he was neither communist nor atheist, although he is
sometimes described as such by those who do not understand his
writings—both his extreme foes and his extreme partisans. Many of
his opinions have gradually won general acceptance, and in the
twentieth century his thought seems for the most part entirely
respectable.

It is no accident that Paine should have written both the most
influential book on deism and the most influential tracts in English
on the revolutions in America and France. The same impulse
which made him question the role of privilege in society made
him doubt authority in religion.

There are two types of revolutionary reformers—the idealist and
the agitator. Paine was both. The idealist can be happy by retreating to a haven of dreams and creating a future utopia in
imagination. But the agitator—who is of the people and a dweller
among them—cannot retreat from reality. Only when the reforms
he seeks are realized can he attain a momentary contentment. But
when these reforms are delayed, defeated or ridiculed, he has no
peace of mind.

Paine never stopped working for political and social reform,
and only during and immediately after the American Revolution
did he attain a measure of success sufficient to afford him personal
satisfaction. Nearly every cause which he afterwards espoused
ended in checkmate or defeat. In this sense, the life of Paine was
a tragedy—although a tragedy on a sublime scale, embracing mon-
umental revolutions on two continents. Unlike Voltaire and Swift,
who were also agitators, Paine lacked a cushion of inner cynicism.

A philosophic lover of humanity, he suffered because his fellow men ignored his appeals. He sensed that the masses of people to whom he devoted his talents and energies were, by and large, indifferent—sometimes hostile—to the causes he espoused. His propaganda for the American Revolution is, of course, the one great exception. Here—and only here—his writings had the effect he wished. On other subjects he was ahead of his age. A few grains of cynicism would have made Paine a happier man, but the world might thus have been deprived of his fervent pen, and the cause of democratic political action and religious liberty considerably retarded. Despite his disappointments at the ingratitude and irrationality of his fellow men, he enjoyed a sufficient fund of inner pride—or vanity—to feel satisfied with his life. Throughout the most eventful part of it he had considered "the world as his home, and the good of it in all places as his object." At the end he wrote in his will, "I have lived an honest and useful life to mankind; my time has been spent in doing good, and I die in perfect composure and resignation to the will of my Creator."

One may ask why a new life of Paine should be undertaken at this time. In a sense Joel Barlow's statement in 1809, the year of Paine's death, is still applicable: "His own writings are his best life, and these are not read at present." In recent years, however, a large number of new letters and essays by Paine have been discovered, and the present work is based on a considerable number of documents unknown to any of Paine's editors or his previous biographers.

Man of Reason is in part favorable to Paine; in part it exposes his human frailties. Its intention is not to please either Paine's idolators or his enemies, but to gather and present documentary evidence.

A word is needed concerning previous biographies of Paine. The first of these, in 1791, was *The Life of Thomas Paine, the author of Rights of Man, With a Defense of his Writings,* by Francis Oldys, a pseudonym. Ostensibly a vindication of Paine, it was actually an unscrupulous assault, commissioned by the Pitt administration to undermine confidence in Paine and his writings. The author, George Chalmers, in order to give an air of veracity to his fulminations, made a painstaking search for authentic documents concerning Paine's private life. Apart from a few references in Paine's own writings, nearly everything that is known about his life before his emigration to America has its source in this book. As a contemporary author pointed out, although Chalmers's interpretations are colored by prejudice and party malice, neither Paine nor any of his numerous admirers ever contradicted the details of Chalmers's account. The next major life, published in New York in 1809, the year of Paine's death, is equally violent and prejudiced, the first muckraking biography in American literature. The author, James Cheetham, a fellow Englishman and publisher of a Jeffersonian newspaper in New York to which Paine had contributed many essays, changed his political affiliations in 1807. Paine immediately denounced him, and they became bitter enemies. Cheetham held his fire until Paine's death, and then discharged his blunderbuss of spite and malice. The book is especially rich in details concerning Paine's last years in New York, most of which can be verified from other sources. In 1819 and 1820 three favorable biographies appeared in England, by Richard Carlile, Thomas Rickman, and William Sherwin, only the last two of which are important. Rickman knew Paine before his migration to America in 1774, and after his return to England Paine lived in Rickman's house for several months. Sherwin was too young to be personally acquainted with Paine, but had the assistance of a political friend in the United States who sent him some Paine manuscripts.

An American freethinker, Gilbert Vale, published a complete life toward the middle of the nineteenth century, and finally Moncure D. Conway at the very end of the century published a biography in English and a few years later an expanded version in French. Conway is the only previous biographer of Paine to investigate the original documentary sources of Paine's career in France. There have been a number of biographies since Conway's, but not a single one adds anything of importance concerning Paine's French period, and very few contain new factual material of any kind. Conway's *Life,* an admirable example of research and devotion to principle, is impaired by prejudices in Paine's favor. His partiality, for example, leads him to portray Gouverneur Morris as a detestable villain, who deliberately plotted to keep Paine confined in the Luxembourg prison, and Robespierre as a benevolent administrator, unwittingly misled by the wicked Morris. In describing this and other affairs, I have tried to be fair to all concerned. I have also had the aid of documents (French, English and American) not known to Conway. The best known book on Paine is an adulatory novel by Howard Fast, which in its own way gives a view of Paine as false as Chalmers's. But whereas the latter takes relatively few liberties with historical fact, Fast's *Citizen Tom Paine*, even as a novel, is filled with fantastic episodes based on nothing but the author's imagination.

As we follow Paine's influential career in the formation of the new American nation and in the reconstruction of the French social order, we shall see that he was intimately concerned with the most important political events in the United States, England and France during his residence in each of these countries. He came into contact with leaders in government wherever he went; Franklin was the only American to have a wider acquaintance among the great in Europe. Although Paine was at times short-sighted, at times vain, he made an imposing contribution to the foundation of the United States. As James Monroe wrote to the French government in claiming him as an American, "the citizens of the United States cannot look back to the æra of their revolution, without remembering, with those of other distinguished patriots, the name of Thomas Paine. The services which he rendered them in their struggle for liberty have made an impression of gratitude which will never be erased, whilst they continue to merit the character of a just and generous people."

I

A Civil Servant

Thomas Paine during his essentially proletarian existence cared little for questions of titles, birth and family prestige. Undoubtedly he would have had little interest in any attempt to trace his humble lineage beyond the modest household of his father and mother in Thetford, England, where he was born, 29 January 1737, an only child, except for a sister born the next year, who died in infancy.

In his writings Paine mentions his father, Joseph, with great affection, but has little to say concerning his mother, Frances, who, several years older than her husband, suffered from a severe and desiccated character. Paine's father followed the trade of staymaker—a trade which the young Thomas naturally learned and which he practiced for a time later in life. More important, Paine's father belonged to the small sect of Quakers in the village, a group which seems to have been much farther removed from orthodoxy than was William Penn. Paine may well have acquired from the Thetford Quakers his habits of nonconformity—his ease in rejecting accepted ways and opinions. Although it is by no means true that the Quakers of the eighteenth century adopted deistical principles, the direction of Paine's mature thought may have been derived from his Quaker background. He said in *The Age of Reason* that the Quakers resembled true deists in the moral part of their religion, but that they "contracted themselves too much by leaving the works of God out of their system." True enough, philanthropy is essential to both deists and Quakers, but Paine gives a false impression when he affirms that Quakers, like deists, "do not believe much about Jesus Christ; . . . they call the Scriptures a dead letter."

13

Paine respected the Quakers for their humanitarianism, but deplored their lack of esthetic sense. He amused himself with the conceit "that if the taste of a Quaker could have been consulted at the Creation, what a silent and drab-colored Creation it would have been! Not a flower would have blossomed its gayeties, nor a bird been permitted to sing."

Paine's mother, however, belonged to the Established Church; had been married with the rites of the Church; and saw to it that her children were baptized in the Church. She sent Thomas to her sister, to recite his catechism and prepare for confirmation, which he received at the hands of the Bishop of Norwich. Despite this indoctrination, Paine did not lose his early distaste for orthodoxy. On one occasion at the age of seven or eight after his aunt or some other relation had read to him a sermon on redemption, he went out into the air to meditate. "Going down the garden steps," he wrote later in life, "I revolted at the recollection of what I had heard, and thought to myself that it was making God Almighty act like a passionate man who killed His son when He could not revenge Himself in any other way, and, as I was sure a man would be hanged who did such a thing, I could not see for what purpose they preached such a sermon."

Paine attributed to his father and his father's Quaker profession his own "exceedingly good moral education, and a tolerable stock of useful learning." Though he went to the grammar school, he did not learn Latin, not only because he had "no inclination to learn languages, but because of the objection the Quakers have against the books in which the language is taught." But this did not prevent him from being acquainted with the subject matter of all the Latin books used in the school.

The natural bent of his mind was to science, Paine remarked, an inclination which remained with him throughout his life. Paradoxically he made his first voyage to America principally to seek a career in science and teaching, but found it exclusively in journalism; he returned to England primarily to pursue his peaceful scientific interests (to construct an iron bridge he had himself invented), but found himself hounded from the country because of his defense of the French Revolution. Along with his scientific aptitude, he possessed a liking and talent for poetry, but this he rather repressed than encouraged, "as leading too much into the field of imagination." Nevertheless, he continued to write verse through-out every period of his life. At the age of eight, he is said to have written the following elegy on the death of a favorite pet:

> Here lies the body of John Crow,
> Who once was high, but now is low;
> Ye brother Crows, take warning all,
> For as you rise, so must you fall.

Paine left grammar school at the age of thirteen for a three-year apprenticeship in his father's shop. Here he learned the trade of staymaking—and learned also some of the facts of life; particularly, that to earn one's daily bread was an uncertain enterprise for a young man in his social position. He saw around him "age going to the work-house, and youth to the gallows." Like most young lads, he also experienced wanderlust. While still at school he had picked up a "pleasing Natural History of Virginia," which gave him his first desire to visit the western side of the Atlantic.

One of his masters at the grammar school, the Reverend William Knowles, imbued with a false sense of heroism from having once served on a man-of-war, gave Paine the zest for a life of adventure at sea. At the age of sixteen, according to *The Rights of Man*, he went so far as to sign aboard a privateer, the *Terrible*, which had a captain named Death, but "from this adventure . . . was happily prevented by the affectionate and moral remonstrance of a good father." The effects of his father's remonstrance soon wearing off, he allegedly signed on another privateer, the *King of Prussia*, and actually went to sea. There exists no corroborating evidence for this romantic tale.

At the age of twenty, we find a record of Paine practicing his father's trade in the shop of a certain Morris in London. It was during this period that he began a serious study of Newtonian science. He tells us in *The Age of Reason*: "As soon as I was able, I purchased a pair of globes, and attended the philosophical lectures of Martin and Ferguson, and became afterward acquainted with Dr. Beers, of the society called the Royal Society, then living in the Temple, and an excellent astronomer." Paine's sojourn in the capital was brief, however, for in the next year he was employed by another staymaker in Dover. In April 1759, he set up for him-self as master staymaker in the town of Sandwich (Kent). On

27 September 1759, almost as soon as he was established in business, he married an orphan, Mary Lambert, who died within a few months. Mary Lambert's father had been a customs officer, and Paine soon took steps to enter the excise service, although it was a poorly paid profession, for which the populace entertained antipathy rather than respect, and one ridden with nepotism. Another famous customs officer, the poet Robert Burns, advised one of his acquaintances:

The way of getting appointed, is just the application of GREAT FOLKS to the Commissioners of the CUSTOMS. . . . The EXCISE is a superiour object, as the salary is fifty Per annum. . . . To apply there, is the same business as at the Customs. . . . Find out, among your acquaintances, who are the private friends of the Commissioners of the particular BOARD at which you wish to apply, & interest them—the more the better.

Records of the Excise Board, in the Customs House Library, London, indicate that Paine was first admitted to the service as a supernumerary, or unattached officer, 1 December 1762 on the motion of Frederic Falkland, presumably one of the "Great Folks" to whom Paine applied. A supernumerary had to wait for a vacancy which usually occurred only when a station officer died. On 8 August 1764, Paine was appointed to the Alford Out-Ride, Grantham Collection. An out-ride was a country station requiring a horse, and normally an officer was expected to pass from a country out-ride to a town division or "walk" before he was promoted to examiner or supervisor.

Excise officers because of their low rate of pay were subject to great temptation to submit dishonest reports. As Paine himself remarked, "scarce a week passes at the office but some detections are made of fraudulent and collusive proceedings." Paine apparently indulged in one of these equivocal practices, but one which seems to have been commonplace and without financial advantage to the customs officer involved. This was "stamping," which consisted in approving a consignment of merchandise before inspecting it, solely on the basis of the invoice and the good name of the tradesman receiving the shipment. After this approval, the subsequent inspection was a mere formality. Paine freely admitted this generally-condoned practice, for which he was dismissed from office, 29 August 1765, after an experience of about two and a half years in the service and one year in his station. The minute of the board declares:

Thomas Pain, Officer of Alford O[ut] R[ide], Grantham Collection, having on July the 11th *stampt his whole Ride* as appears by the *specimens* not being signed in any Part thereof, tho' proper entry was shewn in Journal and the victuallers stocks drawn down in his Books as if the same had been surveyed and the Collector's Report thereon, also by said Pain's own Confession by Letter of the 13th instant. *Ordered* that he be discharged.*

With the loss of his customs post, Paine had been forced to revert to his former trade of staymaker, which he practiced for a time with a certain Gudgeon in Diss, Norfolk, where, allegedly, his irascible temper frequently led him into disputes with his fellow workmen. The next trace we find of him is in Lincolnshire "about the year 1766." In an essay "Forgetfulness," written many years later, he describes a summer visit to the home of a widow lady in a small village in that county. While walking with his hostess at nightfall in the garden, he encountered a young lady about to drown herself because of a disappointment in love. She at first appeared as "a white shapeless figure, without head or arms, moving along one of the walks." Paine wondered whether it could be a phantom. As he reached out to touch it, an idea came to him: "Will my hand pass through the air, or shall I feel anything?" When his hand actually rested on a human shoulder, he discovered that the young lady was attired in a white petticoat with an apron over her head. Through gentle usage and adroit conversation, Paine was able to reconcile her to a continued existence.

The greater part of 1766 Paine passed in London, teaching English at an academy conducted by a certain Noble at Goodman's Fields.

On 3 July 1766, he petitioned to be restored to his former employ, writing from London:

In humble obedience to your Honours' letter of discharge, bearing date August 29, 1765, I delivered up my commission, and since that time have given you no trouble. I confess the justice of your Honours' displeasure, and humbly beg leave to add my thanks for the candour and lenity which you at that unfortunate time indulged me with. And though the nature of the report and my own confession cut off all expectations of enjoying your Honours' favour then, yet I humbly hope it has not finally excluded me therefrom; upon which hope I humbly presume to entreat

* All quotations follow original spelling, punctuation, etc.

your Honours to restore me. The time I enjoyed my former commission was short and unfortunate—an officer only a single year. No complaint of the least dishonesty, or intemperance ever appeared against me; and if I am so happy as to succeed in this, my humble petition, I will endeavour that my future conduct shall as much engage your Honours' approbation, as my former has merited your displeasure.

The next day, the order was given to reinstate Paine on the occasion of the next vacancy. The promptness with which Paine's request was granted suggests that some "off the record" influence had been exerted in Paine's behalf, perhaps by Falkland or by another of his patrons, George Lewis Scott, who was also a member of the board. The official minute reads:

Thomas Pain, . . . having petitioned the Board, praying to be restored, begging Pardon for the offense for which he was Discharged, and promising diligence in future: *Order'd* that he be restored on proper vacancy. He has had notice.

In January of the next year he accepted another teaching position in a school conducted at Kensington by a Mr. Gardiner.

Although Paine had been promised the next vacancy in the excise service in August 1766, he was not reappointed until 29 February 1768, this time to the district of Lewes. Earlier, a vacancy had opened up in Cornwall and Paine was offered the post 15 May 1767, a station in a town division. He must have felt confidence in the good will of his patrons, for on the twenty-sixth of the month he declined the Cornwall vacancy. On 18 February 1768, Paine was appointed to an anticipated vacancy in Somerset, but, the vacancy not accruing, he was finally appointed to Lewes.

Here he took up lodgings with Samuel Ollive, a tobacconist, and his wife and daughter. In July of 1769, Samuel Ollive died. Paine moved to other lodgings—no doubt to respect the proprieties, but soon after, while still acting as an exciseman, joined the widow in conducting the business, which had been expanded to include groceries. On 26 March 1771, he married the Ollives' daughter, Elizabeth. Although Paine seems to have been accepted in a form of partnership, Mrs. Ollive retained in her own name legal title to the tobacconist shop, part of a property known as Bull House, immediately adjoining a nonconformist chapel. Paine was considered tenant; Mrs. Ollive, landlord. In a letter to neighbors, 18 July 1772,

Paine replied to complaints concerning "the filling up" of a doorway on his premises. Paine argued that the affair concerned only Mrs. Ollive, the landlord, not himself, the tenant, and he added, "As I have not even the Right of objecting should Mrs. Ollive fill it up immediately, I cannot have any power to give any kind of Answer in a case which is entirely her's not mine." In another document of the same date, however, Paine accepted certain responsibilities of the property. He acknowledged himself "under an Obligation of Paying the sum of One shilling yearly to the Trustees of the dissenters' Meeting House situated in the Parish of St. Michael, Lewes, as an Acknowledgment for their suffering the droppings of Rain which fall from a New Building lately erected by me, to fall into a Yard belonging and adjoining to the North side of the said Meeting House." A lovely image to describe the precincts of an outhouse.

These meager documents, along with the excise minutes, support the contention of Chalmers that Paine originally spelled his family name "Pain" without the final "e." Spelling practice was, of course, rather erratic in the eighteenth century. The name is spelled "Paine" in the church register of his parents' marriage and "Payne" in the record of his sister's birth. Thomas, however, seems to have adopted "Pain" consistently until after the publication of *Common Sense*. In the church registers of both his marriages the name is recorded "Pain." Thus it appears also the first time he is mentioned in the Pennsylvania press.

Paine was thirty-four years old at the time of his second marriage, "tall and slender," and, if not handsome, at least pleasing in appearance. It is impossible to give details of his manner of dress, although nearly all historians of the American Revolution, even his admirers, have had occasion to picture Paine's coat as unkempt, soiled, worn and shabby. Yet in his many portraits he seems uniformly neat, and in one by Laurent Dabos, he has the appearance of a dandy. The only physical description of Paine at Lewes is that of William Carver, who knew Paine in England and then lived with him in New York shortly before Paine's death. According to Carver, Paine in his youth was about five feet eight inches tall. A lover of sport, literature, good talk, oysters and wine, he was doubtless an ideal companion. His boldness in the water, his daring on the ice were so remarkable that he was given the name,

The Commodore. He lived in the intimacy of a circle of warm friends, a group of highly respectable citizens, who were at the same time jolly companions. These he amused by his witty sallies and instructed through serious conversation. In politics he was said to have been a confirmed Whig, noted for the obstinacy and independence of his opinions, which he supported with ardor, elegance and clear logic. He aired his political views habitually at the local tavern, the White Hart, which served also as meeting place of a social-literary club of which Paine was a leading spirit. To keep disputes within bounds and tempers under control, the members in fun devised what they called their Headstrong Book. This was an ancient Greek Homer, sent the morning after a particularly warm argument to the most obstinate participant in the debate. An inscription in the book implies that Paine most frequently deserved and obtained this distinction: "The Headstrong Book, or Original Book of Obstinacy Written by ––– of Lewes, in Sussex, and Revised and Corrected by Thomas Paine."

A local printer with a poetic vein, William Lee, wrote of his friend at this time:

> Immortal Paine! while mighty reasoners jar,
> We crown thee General of the Headstrong War;
> Thy logic vanquish'd error, and thy mind
> No bounds but those of right and truth confined.
> Thy soul of fire must sure ascend the sky,
> Immortal Paine, thy fame can never die;
> For men like thee their names must ever save
> From the black edicts of the tyrant grave.

Paine's name is spelled with an *e* because the poem was published by Rickman many years after the American Revolution.

Paine also cultivated the muse for his own amusement and for the pleasure and instruction of the habitués of the White Hart. According to tradition, he recited at one of the inn meetings his most famous poetical composition, an elegy on the death of General Wolfe, which he later published in the *Pennsylvania Magazine*. One of Paine's closest friends at this time was his biographer, Thomas "Clio" Rickman, then a young poet, who later wrote songs in praise of political liberty and the French Revolution.

During the six impecunious years of his residence in Lewes, Paine continued to serve His Majesty's government as excise collector. Even with a good horse, he must have had rough going in traveling around the country, if we may judge from Daniel Defoe's tour of Great Britain some fifty years before. "Going to church at a country village, not far from Lewes," Defoe "saw an ancient lady, and a lady of very good quality . . . drawn to church in her coach with six oxen; nor was it done in frolic or humour, but mere necessity, the way being so stiff and deep that no horses could go in it." An exciseman received fifty pounds a year, but keeping a horse and other expenses reduced his net income to about thirty-two pounds—the insufficiency of which may be judged by the storm of indignation aroused by Goldsmith's complacent line describing the financial lot of a country curate as

. . . passing rich with forty pounds a year.

After four years in the service, Paine was forced to sell his personal and family possessions to satisfy his creditors. Placards on the Lewes hoardings announced the sale by auction, 14 April 1772, of all his household furniture, stock in trade and other effects; "also a horse tobacco and snuff mill, with all the utensils for cutting tobacco and grinding off snuff; and two unopened crates of cream-coloured stone ware." In proportion to the share he took in conducting the affairs of the Ollive estate, Paine was personally responsible for its insolvency. He was no businessman, as he freely admitted in America: "Trade I do not understand."

Other agents besides Paine suffered from underpayment, and he initiated a plan to appeal to Parliament for an increase in their salaries. Following his scheme, a petition was circulated early in 1772 through every part of the kingdom and signed by all of the officers. Each subscribed three shillings, producing a total of over five hundred pounds for expenses. Paine set forth in detail their plight in a pamphlet, *Case of the Officers of Excise*. He had four thousand copies printed in 1772 and arranged the delivery of a copy to each member of Parliament prior to the presentation of the petition. He is said also to have written at the same time a folio sheet, *A Letter concerning the Nottingham Officers*, but no trace of this work has survived. In the *Case of the Officers of Excise*, Paine's first printed work, he demonstrated with clarity and logic that a task poorly remunerated would be poorly carried out, and that an increase in the salary of the customs agents would immediately bring about greater efficiency and a tremendous increase in the revenue of the state. A service which fails to provide a competent maintenance for its officers, he argued, attracts only the ill qualified and breeds corruption, collusion and neglect. "An augmentation of salary sufficient to enable them to live honestly and competently would produce more good effect than all the laws of the land can enforce." Paine had already developed the plain, forthright style and proverbial vigor which characterize his revolutionary pamphlets. Warning against the evils arising from inadequate salaries, he declared:

Poverty, in defiance of principle, begets a degree of meanness that will stoop to almost anything. A thousand refinements of argument may be brought to prove that the practice of honesty will be still the same, in the most trying and necessitous circumstances. He who never was ahungered may argue finely on the subjection of his appetite; and he who never was distressed, may harangue as beautifully on the power of principle. But poverty, like grief, has an incurable deafness, which never hears; the oration loses all its edge; and *"To be, or not to be"* becomes the only question.

Despite Paine's style and convincing arguments—comprising, by the way, a forceful presentation of the hardships consequent upon fixed incomes during inflationary periods—his tract and his lobbying had no influence whatsoever upon Parliament. As others have cynically observed, a rebellion of excise officers, who rarely have the good will of the people, is little to be feared by their superiors.

As might have been expected, the chief result of the pamphlet for Paine was to draw the unfavorable attention of his superiors to himself. It was also to draw the charge of untruthfuness upon him later in America, for in a report to a committee of the Continental Congress in October 1783, he declared roundly "in England I never was the author of a syllable in print." John Adams reported that Paine "declared again and again that he had never written a line nor a word that had been printed, before *Common Sense*," and when Chalmers' *Life* appeared in 1791 with an account of Paine's custom-house publication, Adams confirmed his already-existing doubts of Paine's veracity. Apologists for Paine have argued that his declaration to Congress covered only his "public works"—that his *Case of the Officers* was printed only for private distribution in 1772 and that it was not sold to the public until 1793 (at which time an enterprising publisher brought out a new edition undoubtedly to capitalize on the notoriety of Paine's *The Rights of Man*, which had appeared in the previous year). This defense hardly exonerates Paine completely, for he had made no distinction between private and public circulation in his denial.

Paine sent a copy of *Case of the Officers of Excise* to Oliver Goldsmith and, despite his alleged impecuniousness, invited the convivial author to join him in "a bottle of wine, or anything else." In this epistle to a brother man of letters concerning the debut of his literary career, Paine remarked that he had received so many letters of thanks and approbation for his performance that, were he not rather singularly modest, he "should insensibly become a little vain." (Paine's vanity far exceeded his sensitivity, a characteristic which remained with him and grew throughout his life.)

Paine must have been rather lenient as an exciseman, for he affirmed twenty years later: "The name of Thomas Paine is not to be found in the records of the Lewes justices, in any one act of contention with, or severity of any kind whatever towards the persons whom he surveyed." Whether his lenient disposition or a zeal to reform working conditions led him to neglect his duties, or whether his superiors decided that his penchant for agitation constituted a pernicious influence in the service, Paine was once more discharged, 8 April 1774. The minute reads:

Thomas Pain, . . . having quitted his Business without obtaining the Board's Leave for so doing, and being gone off on Account of the Debts which he hath contracted, as by Letter of the 6th instant from Edward Clifford, Supervisor, and the said Pain having been once before Discharged: *Order'd* that he be again Discharged.

The eccentric journalist William Cobbett, in tracing how small causes may have tremendous effects, argued that this dismissal of Paine was the real cause of the American Revolution. Even though libertarian principles may have been ingrained in the American people, Cobbett maintained, it was Paine alone who put these principles into action.

Two months after his dismissal from the excise, Paine and his wife parted company, 4 June 1774. One can only guess at the reasons for the separation, but certainly the loss of Paine's customs post coming on the heels of the sale of their common property for debt had much to do with it. Elizabeth probably considered

Thomas a hindrance rather than a help as a family man. Clio Rickman says that Paine always spoke tenderly and respectfully of his wife and that he several times rendered her pecuniary aid without ever revealing its source.

The subsequent attitude of Mrs. Paine toward her husband is a subject of some mystery. Conway discovered a legal document dated 14 October 1800, signed by Mrs. Paine and other members of the Ollive family in which it is affirmed that Paine had long ago left the realm and that, if living, he resided beyond the seas; also that Elizabeth had not heard from him since his leaving and did not know whether he were living or dead. Conway was astounded that neither Mrs. Paine nor any of her relations should have heard some tidings of Paine, particularly in view of the tremendous publicity given in England to his *Rights of Man*. The probable answer is that Mrs. Paine in order to enjoy maximum legal freedom in questions of property had found it to her interest to disavow all knowledge of her husband. When Mrs. Paine died, 27 July 1808, her obituary immediately appeared in an English magazine. In it, her marital relations were fully discussed—and abuse of her husband was called "needless, ungenerous, unjustifiable." This seems good evidence that the Ollive family knew right along of Paine's activities, for if they had been living in such great seclusion in 1800 that they did not even know that Paine had written two or three best sellers, it is hardly probable that they would have been so well known in 1808 that Elizabeth's death would have come to the attention of a monthly magazine. Gilbert Vale, on the authority of an intimate English friend who was at one time apprenticed in the house where Mrs. Paine lived, indicated that Mrs. Paine remained constantly aware of her husband's career. After the appearance of *The Age of Reason*, she habitually left the room without a word if anyone spoke disrespectfully of Paine in her presence. "If, too, she was questioned on the subject of their separation, she did the same."

All biographers agree that the relations between Paine and Elizabeth Ollive were from the first entirely Platonic—that absolutely no cohabitation took place. Clio Rickman professed to have documents proving that Paine's separation from Elizabeth arose from no physical defect. We can be reasonably sure, moreover, that there was nothing disgraceful to Paine attached to his separation, for had there been, his wife, surrounded as she was by his bitter enemies, would undoubtedly have exposed the circumstances.

The whole subject of the romantic interests or the loves of Thomas Paine is completely veiled in obscurity. There is reason to wonder whether such concerns figured at all in his life—even though his poetry reveals a literary interest in gallantry, and a French acquaintance records that he sometimes "recited the love letters he had written during his youth, letters written in a bizarre style which were worthy of Mascarille." Certainly he was not insensitive to feminine charms, for he once said that there was nothing in the world as fine as his bridge "except a woman," no faint praise considering Paine's vanity. He also addressed some poems to the wives of one or two friends, but the chief characteristic of these is a good-natured coyness. Eminently safe, they were obviously written to be read in public. In America in 1787, he was acquainted with two teen-aged sisters, Hannah and Catherine Nicholson, daughters of a naval captain. Paine, about thirty years their senior, engaged in a semi-playful, semi-sentimental correspondence with both girls, but this can hardly be taken seriously. Later, in France, he knew a Belgian baroness of his own age, who at least once sent him a rather affectionate note.

Cheetham's accusation that Paine had taken a French mother of three children as his mistress during his old age was retracted after a libel suit.

Yet Paine was not a recluse, certainly not a misogynist, and not the victim of a physical handicap. It may even be that he accepted the old-fashioned notion, apart from religious sanctions, that a married man—even though separated—owned fidelity to his wife, and Elizabeth Ollive did not die until 1808. His respect for the institution of marriage he expressed almost lyrically in 1789, congratulating Catherine Nicholson on her marriage to Colonel Few, Senator from Georgia:

Though I appear a sort of wanderer, the married state has not a sincerer friend than I am. It is the harbor of human life, and is, with respect to the things of this world, what the next world is to this. It is home; and that one word conveys more than any other word can express. For a few years we may glide along the tide of youthful single life and be wonderfully delighted; but it is a tide that flows but once, and what is still worse, it ebbs faster than it flows, and leaves many a hapless voyager aground. I am one, you see, that have experienced the fate I am describing. I have lost my tide; it passed by while every thought of my heart was on the wing for the salvation of my dear America, and I have now, as contentedly as I can, made myself a little bower of willows on the shore that has the solitary resemblance of a home. Should I always continue the tenant of this home, I hope my female acquaintance will ever remember that it contains not the churlish enemy of their sex, not the inaccessible cold hearted mortal, nor the capricious tempered oddity, but one of the best and most affectionate of their friends.

Why then, at least from his thirty-fourth year on, date of his second marriage, did Paine apparently maintain a complete sexual abstinence?

The hostile Chalmers suggested that sexual impotence was responsible for the break-up of Paine's marriage to Elizabeth Ollive. But apart from this hypothesis of impotency, several other conjectures have been ventured concerning it. Conway suggests that Elizabeth's religious scruples may have been responsible since it was customary among some Quakers of the time that when a young couple were espoused, that they were to be kept apart for a season to "mourn." Not only does this counter another theory of Conway's that the Quakers of the time were much like deists, but it fails to explain the three years during which the marriage actually lasted, a rather long period of "mourning." It has also been suggested that Paine married Elizabeth entirely from philanthropic motives—that he felt compassion for the difficult circumstances of the widow and daughter of Samuel Ollive. Were this the reason for the marriage, it would hardly explain a separation at the moment that the family's affairs had degenerated almost to destitution.

Clio Rickman once asked Paine why the separation had taken place, and Paine replied merely: "It is nobody's business but my own: I had cause for it, but I will name it to no one."

At the end of his thirty-seventh year, therefore, the life of Paine would have seemed to the ordinary observer—and perhaps also to himself—a record of a dismal series of false starts, failures in his profession, in commerce, and in domestic relations. Apart from his literary amusements at the White Hart and the Excise pamphlet, there had been absolutely nothing in his inconspicuous career to forecast his subsequent role as the pamphleteer-philosopher of two revolutions.

The question, therefore, naturally occurs: why was it that Paine rose like a rocket, to use one of his own metaphors, from these inauspicious beginnings to become one of the most influential intellectual forces in three countries? The answer is that Paine's literary gift of clear, forceful statement, his proletarian origin, and his inherent sympathy for the common man fitted him to become the literary dynamo of the American Revolution. His rise coincided with the development of popular journalism and the outbreak of the American Revolution, the first great political and social movement based in theory and in practice on the consent, support and power of the common man. Paine, himself a child of the people, addressed his appeals primarily to the man of ordinary understanding rather than to the man of taste or learning, following the example of Benjamin Franklin rather than that of the unidentified author of the *Letters of Junius*, the latter perhaps the most influential political journalist before Paine. From the moment of the printing of *Common Sense*, his fame was established as a man of letters—his subsequent careers as man of science, political theory, economics and deism can all be considered normal developments from his first striking literary success.

It may be that without the stimulus of the great events of the American Revolution he would have remained in the mediocrity of his early life. He himself said that it was the cause of the Revolution which inspired his pen; that "he was at a loss to know whether he was made for the times or the times made for him."

We shall see in the next chapter, however, that he inspired the confidence of the astute Franklin and that he turned professional man of letters even before the battles of Lexington and Concord. Obviously Paine's intellectual endowments were the basis of his literary success. He was "evidently the child of nature from the beginning." There were many pamphleteers during the American Revolution, but only one Thomas Paine. As Joel Barlow pointed out: "He had a surprising memory and brilliant fancy; his mind was a storehouse of facts and useful observations; he was full of lively anecdote, and ingenious original pertinent remark, upon almost every subject." The power of memory, the fertile spark of imagination, and the great events of the American Revolution working together produced the career of Thomas Paine.

"The Summer Time of Wit"

Practically nothing is known of Paine's movements between June 1774, when he and his wife separated, and October of the same year, when he left for America, bearing letters of introduction from Franklin. Paine apparently went directly from Lewes to London, where, free from domestic troubles and responsibilities, he indulged his interests in politics and science.

Among his scientific friends was George Lewis Scott, member of the Excise Board and a former sub-preceptor during the childhood of King George III. From Scott, Paine acquired his knowledge of the personal character of the King, perhaps one of the reasons for the effectiveness of *Common Sense*, which owed much of its vigor to the fact that Paine addressed himself to a personal villain, unlike other agitators who had limited themselves to abstract political principles. Paine himself considered his insight into English political affairs of inestimable value in his subsequent career. As he wrote in 1780: "It was in a great measure owing to my bringing a knowledge of England with me to America that I was enabled to enter deeper into politics, and with more success than other people."

A meeting which Scott arranged with Benjamin Franklin, then serving in England as agent for Pennsylvania and other colonies, changed the whole course of Paine's life. Franklin liked Paine's ideas and felt that he could find a career in Philadelphia. Paine's particular design in going to America was, as he himself stated, "to establish an academy on the plan they are conducted in and about London, which I was well acquainted with." Franklin gave Paine a letter of introduction to his son-in-law, Richard Bache, stressing his pedagogical capacities.

The bearer, Mr. Thomas Paine, is very well recommended to me, as an ingenious, worthy young man. He goes to Pennsylvania with a view of settling there. I request you to give him your best advice and countenance, as he is quite a stranger there. If you can put him in a way of obtaining employment as a clerk, or assistant tutor in a school, or assistant surveyor, (of all which I think him very capable,) so that he may procure a subsistence at least, till he can make acquaintance and obtain a knowledge of the country, you will do well, and much oblige your affectionate father.

This time at least we are sure that Paine put to sea—and as a cabin passenger. During the nine weeks' voyage on the *London Packet*, an epidemic of typhus broke out among the 120 indentured servants. Only five of the latter and two of the cabin passengers escaped the disease. Paine suffered so violently that he gave up hope of living to see America. When the ship docked in Philadelphia, 30 November 1774, Dr. John Kearsley, learning that a passenger recommended by Dr. Franklin was on board, immediately sent two of his men with a stretcher to bring him on shore, to a lodging which he provided, for Paine at the time could not even turn in his bed without help. It was six weeks before he could call on Richard Bache and the others to whom Franklin had recommended him. Thanks to Franklin's warm approbation, a number of gentlemen engaged him as tutor to their sons, and he soon acquired a literary reputation.

In January 1775 one of Paine's admirers, Robert Aitken, a printer, launched a monthly periodical with six hundred subscribers under the title of *The Pennsylvania Magazine; or, American Monthly Museum.* For the first issue Paine wrote an introductory essay on the "Magazine in America," a commentary remarkable for its vigorous support of the new world and modern times against the old world and antiquity. In verses paralleling this essay, Paine announced that "the summer time of wit" was at hand in the coming issues of the magazine.

Aitken was so impressed with Paine's journalistic talent that he engaged him as editor for subsequent numbers. By March the subscription list had increased to fifteen hundred.

In that same month, Paine published in a Philadelphia newspaper (*Postscript to Pennsylvania Journal*, 8 March) a moving essay against the slave-trade, the first of the hundreds of humanitarian pieces on which his fame was to be built. Appealing to the light of nature and the dictates of men's hearts, Paine condemned the wickedness and inhumanity of the institution of slavery, then refuted the conventional arguments from history and the Scriptures used to support it. His chief design was not to win a debate, however, but to entreat Americans to take immediate steps to do away with a vicious institution. As a new arrival from the Mother Country, he argued that Americans could not logically complain of English attempts to enslave them politically while they themselves tolerated actual slavery and bloodshed. This essay so captured the admiration of Benjamin Rush that he expressly sought to make the acquaintance of the anonymous author and offer his congratulations.

Aitken shortly before his death confided some details of his collaboration with Paine to another printer, Isaiah Thomas. "On one of the occasions, when Paine had neglected to supply the materials for the Magazine, within a short time of the day of publication, Aitken went to his lodgings, and complained of his neglecting to fulfil his contract. Paine heard him patiently, and coolly answered, 'You shall have them in time.' Aitken expressed some doubts on the subject, and insisted on Paine's accompanying him and proceeding immediately to business, as the workmen were waiting for copy. He accordingly went home with Aitken, and was soon seated at the table with the necessary apparatus, which always included a glass, and a decanter of brandy. Aitken observed, 'he would never write without *that*.' The first glass put him in a train of thinking; Aitken feared the second would disqualify him, or render him untractable; but it only illuminated his intellectual system; and when he had swallowed the third glass, he wrote with great rapidity, intelligence and precision; and his ideas appeared to flow faster than he could commit them to paper. What he penned from the inspiration of the brandy, was perfectly fit for the press without any alteration, or correction."

This anecdote sheds light on one of the most controversial aspects of Paine's life—the extent of his drinking. His enemies have consistently pictured him as a confirmed drunkard, and his partisans have maintained that he drank only late in life and then as a result of illness contracted in the Luxembourg prison during the French Revolution. It would appear from Aitken's anecdote that his drinking had been an established habit even before the American Revolution. Although this tale may have been colored by Aitken's resentful reminiscences of unfruitful contact negotiations with Paine, Isaiah Thomas insisted on its truth because of Aitken's irreproachable character and reputation for veracity. The details regarding Paine's method of composition are confirmed by Paine manuscripts still preserved. With few corrections, additions, or cancellations, these show that Paine's ideas flowed rapidly and without effort.

Two other eminent witnesses support the testimony concerning Paine's drinking at this period. John Witherspoon, President of New Jersey College (Princeton) and a contributor to the *Pennsylvania Magazine*, asserted that Paine could not write "until he had quickened his thought with large draughts of rum and water," and Benjamin Rush wrote that "he was intemperate and otherwise debauched in private life."

Paine remained as editor until the fall of 1775, during which time he printed a number of poems and essays of his own composition. None of the pieces which can be proved to be Paine's foreshadow the zeal for humanitarian political and social concepts which motivated his subsequent career. He revealed an interest in practical science with two brisk expository articles, "Description of a New Electrical Machine" (January) and "A New Method of Building Frame Houses" (April). A more ambitious effort to popularize scientific research, "Useful and Entertaining Hints on the Internal Riches of the Colonies" (February), sprang from his visit to the fossil collection of the Library Company of Philadelphia.

In the vein of pure entertainment, Paine composed two allegorical visions, "New Anecdotes of Alexander the Great" (February) and "Cupid and Hymen" (March) as well as highly stylized "Reflections on the Life and Death of Lord Clive" (March), a combination of melodramatic imagery and rhetorical didacticism in the moralistic vein of Hervey's *Meditations*. This is more like bad poetry than good prose, and as a matter of fact Paine's verse in the *Pennsylvania Magazine* stands up at least as well as his ornamental prose. Benjamin Rush attributed in large measure the "sudden currency" of the *Magazine* to the elegy on "The Death of General Wolfe" (March) which Paine had written in Lewes and, according to legend, recited at the meetings of his social club at the White Hart. Instead of eulogizing the fallen hero by simple statement, Paine elevated his theme by personifying Britannia, mourning in a "mould-ering cave" for her fallen son, Wolfe. Mercury, sent to comfort her, reveals that Wolfe had been called to heaven to participate in a battle there between the gods and "the proud giants of old" who had broken out from their subterranean abodes. Paine used other classical deities in a semi-humorous poem in the same issue, "An Account of the Burning of Bachelors' Hall." He had recourse again to the celestial regions in a song "Liberty Tree" (July), this time to publicize the colonists' displeasure with British mercantile re-strictions. When reprinted subsequently it bore the subtitle "A Song Written Early in the American Revolution," but those who read it in 1775 were still not aware that a revolution had begun. Paine's two other poems in the *Pennsylvania Magazine* are doggerel productions concerning events in England, "Farmer Short's Dog Porter" (July) and "The Tale of the Monk and the Jew Versified" (March). The latter, a satire, reveals a decided anticlerical bias—for modern readers the chief importance of the piece. It shows that Paine had begun to entertain deistical notions before going to France, where he developed them under the influence of various *philosophes*.

During all the time that he worked on the *Pennsylvania Magazine*, Paine haggled with Aitken over financial terms, and he eventually left his employer because the pay was inadequate and because he had hopes of getting financial backing to set up a magazine of his own. There is no reason to assume with some authors that the separation was caused by any kind of ideological conflict. Paine at this time was motivated by money, not politics.

III

An Uncivil Rebel

When Paine landed in Philadelphia in November 1774, the colonies were torn by political dissent and economic dissatisfaction. As a result of the Boston Massacre, March 1770, all the colonies were alerted to the menace of red-coated slaughter—even though the danger was at that time more theoretical than real. The Boston Tea Party had taken place eleven months before Paine arrived, and the First Continental Congress had already assembled. In April 1775, while Paine, as editor, was selecting poetry and essays for the *Pennsylvania Magazine*, the battles of Lexington and Concord were producing the first heroes of the new nation. In May, the Second Continental Congress came together and in June took under its wing the armed troops in the Boston area.

These events undoubtedly stirred Paine to examine critically the political ties binding the colonies to Great Britain. By temperament at least he was a revolutionary, of a restless nature, and somewhat of an opportunist. The excitement and tense atmosphere of the rising spirit of revolution must have appealed strongly to him—even though he later wrote to Franklin: "I thought it very hard to have the country set on fire about my ears almost the moment I got into it."

First concrete evidence that Paine considered himself an American allied with other Americans against British oppression appeared in a newspaper report (22 November 1775) of experiments which he had conducted with Thomas Pryor "for the purpose of fixing some easy, cheap, and expeditious method of making Salt-Petre in private Families." The demonstration showed the feasibility of a plan, proposed by Paine, "of forming a Salt-Petre Association, for voluntarily supplying the public Magazines with Gun-powder."

This experiment reveals that Paine devoted his scientific talents to the Revolution even before he dedicated his pen.

Because of the discretion needed in compiling such documents as the *Journals of the Continental Congress* and because of the caution with which statesmen expressed themselves in public, it is difficult to know exactly when a sentiment for independence became wide-spread in America. According to one theory, based on British colonial records, the sentiment had been latent in the colonies ever since their founding. Even in England liberal Whigs had thought in terms of an independent America months before Paine landed in Philadephia. In the spring of 1774 John Cartwright published a series of essays in the London press under the title "American Independence The Interest and Glory of Great Britain." These were being reprinted in the Philadelphia papers while Paine was editing the first issues of the *Pennsylvania Magazine*.

As we look back upon the events of 1775, it seems scarcely credible that the colonies could have been in a state of open warfare against England, and yet no one have publicly uttered an appeal for independence. The Continental Congress—an unconstitutional body—reigned in the place of King and Parliament as supreme authority of the land. It directed military affairs, created a Committee of Secret Correspondence to negotiate with foreign powers (November 1775), and authorized the construction of a navy (October 1775). Yet the moderates within the Congress insisted that they aimed at nothing more than the redress of grievances, and even the radicals hesitated to call for independence lest they alienate their more conservative or timorous colleagues. John Adams had declared in 1774 that independence was "a Hobgoblin of so frightful Mien, that it would throw a delicate Person into Fits to look it in the Face." As late as December 1775, prevailing sentiment throughout the colonies still favored reconciliation, and even the extremists, rather than risk disunion by an abortive appeal, had been content to wait for British intransigence to force public opinion to accept independence.

During the three months' period before the publication of *Common Sense* in January 1776, several influential leaders were working for independence, particularly generals Washington, Greene and Charles Lee at Cambridge, and Franklin, Benjamin Rush, Samuel

Adams and Richard Henry Lee at Philadelphia. While these and other colonial statesmen had expressed a desire for independence—and there may even have been a general undercurrent of sentiment among educated and sophisticated citizens—Paine nonetheless showed himself a pioneer spirit by publishing *Common Sense*. No one before had called forthrightly in print for independence. And no one had previously appealed to the common man—to the farmers and simple merchants whose work and responsibilities kept them far removed from legislatures and public forums. These were the ones who had to be convinced and aroused before a successful war could be fought. Until Paine arrived on the scene the best known pamphleteers had been James Otis and John Dickinson, whose arguments fell short of independence and who wrote for men of education. One cannot, however, say that Paine's words came in advance of events or that his readers were unprepared for the message of defiance and independence. Indeed it is precisely because the Americans were waiting for this message that Paine's pamphlet became the rallying cry for the new nation. It appeared at just the psychological moment.

We know little about the circumstances of Paine's composing *Common Sense*. When it first appeared, identified merely as "Written by an Englishman," it was variously attributed to Franklin, John Adams, and Samuel Adams, and even much later some contemporaries asserted that Franklin had suggested the project to Paine and had furnished a large share of the materials. Benjamin Rush specifically asserts that no one gave him any assistance:

I suggested to him that he had nothing to fear from the popular odium to which such a publication might expose him, for he could live anywhere, but that my profession and connections which tied me to Philadelphia, where a great majority of the citizens and some of my friends were hostile to a separation of our country from Great Britain, forbad me to come forward as a pioneer in that important controversy. He readily assented to the proposal, and from time to time he called at my house, and read to me every chapter of the proposed pamphlet as he composed it. I recollect being charmed with a sentence in it, which by accident, or perhaps by design, was not published. It was as follows, "Nothing can be conceived of more absurd than three millions of people flocking to the American shore, every time a vessel arrives from England, to know what portion of liberty they shall enjoy." When Mr. Paine had finished his pamphlet, I advised him to show it to Dr. Franklin, Mr. Rittenhouse, and Mr. Samuel Adams, all of whom I knew were decided friends to American independence. I mentioned these facts to refute a report that Mr. Paine was assisted in composing his pamphlet by one or more of the above gentlemen. They never saw it until it was written and then only by my advice. I gave it at his request the title of "Common Sense."

Paine's only statement on the antecedents of his pioneer literary work appears in a note to the third of his series of essays (1776-83), *The Crisis:*

In October, 1775, Dr. Franklin proposed giving me such materials as were in his hands, towards completing a history of the present transactions and seemed desirous of having the first volume out the next Spring. I had then formed the outlines of *Common Sense*, and finished nearly the first part; and as I supposed the doctor's design in getting out a history, was to open the new year with a new system, I expected to surprise him with a production on that subject, much earlier than he thought of; and without informing him what I was doing, got it ready for the press as fast as I conveniently could, and sent him the first pamphlet that was printed off.

Paine's pamphlet had not been incited by any immediate event or change in British policy. The fundamental change in political relations between England and America he dated back to 19 April 1775, the commencement of hostilities at Concord and Lexington, nine months before his pamphlet was published. However, by a stroke of good fortune or by contrivance, both *Common Sense* and the King's speech at the opening of Parliament, which Paine had predicted would be bellicose and intransigent, appeared in print in Philadelphia on the same day, 10 January 1776.

Paine opens his pamphlet with a distinction between society and government. "Society in every state is a blessing," Paine argued, "but government, even in its best state, is but a necessary evil; in its worst state an intolerable one. . . . Government, like dress, is the badge of lost innocence; the palaces of kings are built upon the ruins of the bowers of paradise." This fundamental distinction—apart from scores of other concepts in Paine's writings—shows the basic difference between Paine's thought and modern totalitarianism, which assumes that government and society are identical. Much closer to Hobbes than to Locke, Paine maintained that government is "a mode rendered necessary by the inability of moral virtue to govern the world."

After this preliminary disparagement of government in general, Paine attempted to undermine faith in the British Constitution. He condemned as absurd the concept of balance of powers, for which Montesquieu had praised the British system. According to Paine, "to say that the Constitution of England is an *union* of three powers, reciprocally *checking* each other, is farcical; either the words have no meaning, or they are flat contradictions." This "much boasted" Constitution, Paine castigated as "imperfect, subject to convulsions and incapable of producing what it seems to promise."

Throughout most of the eighteenth century, it had been tacitly assumed that Parliament had the right to legislate for the colonies. A few years before the Revolution, however, public opinion in America began to make a distinction between Parliament and Crown, repudiating Parliament but reaffirming loyalty to the monarch. It was argued that the colonies, like the shires of England, owed allegiance to the Crown, but unlike the shires were not bound by Parliament since they had no representation in it. The differences appeared as a contest between Parliament and colonies, not between Crown and people. Speaking of the connection between Britian and the colonies, Benjamin Franklin insisted several years before the Revolution "that the bond of their union is not the Parliament, but the King." The Massachusetts Assembly maintained likewise in 1773 that the colonies had "been originally constituted distinct states, subject to the king, but independent of the parliament." This was the theory of colonial agents and friendly Whig politicians in England and even of the most radical agitators in the colonies. Paine, however, not only derided the British Constitution, but denounced George III as a person, terming him the "Royal Brute of Great Britain," and the "greatest enemy this continent hath, or can have." He argued that George III had undertaken "in his *own* right to support the parliament in what he calls *theirs*," a grievous oppression of the American people.

Paine attacked the institution of monarchy on the grounds of both natural rights and Scriptural authority, giving pre-eminence to the latter. He knew what would convince his readers, and since his job was to stir them, he used the arguments to which they would respond—even though he had probably already adopted his own skeptical attitude toward Revelation.

Even to the pious colonial churchgoers, Paine's rough, idiomatic language was probably as effective in undermining respect for monarchy as was his scriptural reasoning. "Of more worth is one honest man to society and in the sight of God," he declared, "than all the crowned ruffians that ever lived." In treating the evils of monarchy, he stressed the absurdity and the injustice of hereditary succession. He called on nature for proof that moral and intellectual characteristics are not inherited; for example, the heirs of a wise man might turn out to be fools. No generation, he affirmed, has the right to impose its choices upon posterity.

Paine also shattered the dream of an enlightened and glorious British Empire, the ideal to which Benjamin Franklin had devoted his political life until the outbreak of hostilities. Although Franklin probably espoused independence as early as Paine, even after the Declaration of Independence he regretted the breaking of "that fine and noble china vase, the British Empire." According to Franklin's dream, the western world was destined to participate with Great Britain and the other colonies in exalting political institutions to a level of freedom and economic activity which had never before been realized. Paine ruthlessly smashed this vision of empire, exhorting America to build her freedom and prosperity in solitude.

Examining the connection between America and Great Britain by the "principles of nature and common sense," Paine argued that America would have flourished as much, and probably more, had no European power taken notice of her. Whatever protection Britain had afforded had been given entirely from a selfish motive. As nature disproves monarchy, he reasoned, so it disproves the dependence of the continent of America upon an island kingdom. "In no instance hath nature made the satellite larger than its primary planet." Propounding a vision which has won general acceptance in America only in the twentieth century, he argued that America should forget England and "claim brotherhood with every European Christian." Paradoxically, almost immediately after this international sentiment, Paine proposed a theory which in practice has led to the isolationism of the United States—the view that "it is the true interest of America to steer clear of European connections." Paine, not Washington, is the first to have expressed this doctrine. He had in mind the series of wars between England and France during the seventeenth and eighteenth centuries—wars which had had an American phase. Paine argued that America could have avoided them had it not been for its colonial status. This is isolationism, but an isolationism directed only against a vassal status or connection with only one part of Europe. It is not an isolationism opposed to international co-operation and commerce. Indeed, elsewhere in *Common Sense*, Paine proposed the dispatching of a manifesto to foreign courts and suggested the seeking of foreign aid. In a later publication, the *Forester's Letters*, however, he was forced to emphasize the isolationist drift of *Common Sense*. The idea which it holds up, he then declared, "is to have nothing to do with the political affairs of Europe."

In addition to castigating George III and destroying the vision of empire, *Common Sense* looked toward the future political development of America. Since the British Constitution had been proved inadequate, a new American government must be erected. Independence might mean the creation of a new aristocracy—the selection of a new superior class to rule in perpetuity—but Paine unequivocally prescribed a republic. His suggestions for a new form of government were, however, scant and ambiguous. He proposed merely that assemblies—to take the place of colonial legislatures—be elected annually and have a president and that the thirteen colonies should choose delegates to a continental congress, each sending at least thirty.

More important, Paine called for the assembling of a continental conference to form a constitution which would establish a permanent form of government—on Paine's plan or another. Paine was the first to call for a constitutional convention in America; he was later to do the same in England and in France.

Shortly after the publication of *Common Sense*, John Adams published a pamphlet, *Thoughts on Government applicable to the Present State of the American Colonies*, in which he presented a detailed plan for a republican government—considering many problems and phases of government which Paine had not even mentioned. Even though Paine had suggested a single legislature and Adams laboriously detailed the advantages of a legislature of two houses, Adams's pamphlet is not in any sense an attack on Paine's, nor would any contemporary reader have imagined that it had any reference to *Common Sense*. One is primarily an appeal to throw off British sovereignty; the other a proposal for a form of government after independence had been achieved. Apart from the question of a single legislature, Adams agreed with Paine on the desirability of annual elections and admitted the feasibility of rotation in office. Adams's recollection is not to be trusted in his autobiography when he alleges that Paine reprehended him for publishing his pamphlet, saying "he was afraid it would do hurt, and that it was repugnant to the plan he had proposed in his Common Sense." In a letter to his wife two months after the publication of *Common Sense*, a more reliable indication of his attitude at the time than his later autobiography, Adams states merely that Paine's notions of continental government were not much applauded, that he had a better hand in pulling down than in building. Although admitting that he could not have "written anything in so manly and striking a style," he flattered himself that he made a more respectable figure than Paine as an architect. Paine, he concluded, seemed "to have very inadequate ideas of what is proper and necessary to be done in order to form constitutions for single colonies, as well as a great model of union for the whole."

Some writers have speculated on the sources of Paine's ideas, ascribing them variously to Locke, Burlamaqui, Beccaria, Milton and Montesquieu. The fact is that Paine never was a reader of the works of other men. Although later in life he could recite all his own works by heart, he knew little of other writing. The originality of his ideas was always one of his dearest boasts. Referring specifically to *Common Sense*, he later declared: "So far from taking any ideas from Locke or from anybody else, it was the absurd expression of a mere John Bull in England, about the year 1773, that first caused me to turn my mind to systems of government. In speaking of the then King of Prussia, called the Great Frederick, he said, '*He is the right sort of man for a king for he has a deal of the devil in him.*' This set me to think if a system of government could not exist that did not require the devil, and I succeeded without any help from anybody."

If the ideas of other men appear in Paine's works, he probably picked them up from conversation. John Adams's account of the origins of *Common Sense*, apart from its obvious prejudice, is quite plausible: Paine "came from England, and got into such company as would converse with him, and ran about picking what information he could concerning our affairs, and finding the great question was concerning independence, he gleaned from those he saw the common-place arguments, such as the necessity of independence at some time or other; the peculiar fitness at this time; the justice of it; the provocation to it; our ability to maintain it, &c. &c."

Although Paine wrote *Common Sense* as a public service without seeking profit for himself, he encountered several obstacles and annoyances in publishing it. At first he had intended to have his work printed as a series of letters in the newspapers, but had realized that most editors would not accept them. On the recommendation of Rush, he turned over his manuscript to a printer, Robert Bell. Paine agreed that if any loss should arise, he would pay it, and to make Bell industrious in circulating the work, he allowed him half the profits. The other half Paine earmarked for the purchase of mittens for the troops going to Quebec, giving a written order on Bell to two officers of the Continental Army. Bell set a price of two shillings on the pamphlet.

Within two weeks the whole edition of one thousand copies had been exhausted. Paine believed that this should have brought in a profit of sixty pounds in addition to printing expenses, but Bell maintained that there were no profits whatsoever. Paine refused to accept Bell's accounting and threatened to sue him unless he immediately turned over a just half of the proceeds for the purchase of mittens. Meanwhile, having enlarged the pamphlet with an Appendix and an Address to the Quakers, Paine paid two other printers to print six thousand more copies and gave them to another bookseller, W. & T. Bradford, for 8½d each, pledging him to sell them at one shilling so that they would be within the reach of humble purses. Although Paine had not authorized Bell to print a second edition, the latter proceeded to do so without permission. Bradford hereupon published an advertisement of his own enlarged edition in the *Pennsylvania Evening Post*, 25 January, denouncing Bell for printing an incomplete and unauthorized edition. Bell retaliated two days later by accusing Paine and Bradford of "dishonest malevolence," and a battle of advertisements continued for several days.

In 1783, when there was talk that Congress contemplated recommending to the states the passing of a law to secure literary property,

Paine wrote out a full account of his relations with Bell, specifying that Bell had kept the whole profits of the first edition and that when Paine objected to his printing a second edition, Bell had replied that it was none of Paine's business. In 1779 Paine was still thirty-nine pounds, eleven shillings, out of pocket for the enlarged edition—although he had reason to believe that Bradford had sold enough additional copies to wipe out this deficiency, and he still hoped to be reimbursed by the venal publisher.

That Paine acquired no profits from *Common Sense* was a source of pride throughout his life. He once calculated that, at the usual price of books, his profits at that time would have amounted to a thousand pounds a day in Pennsylvania alone. He believed that 150,000 copies were sold in America—"the greatest sale that any performance ever had since the use of letters,—exclusive of the great run it had in England and Ireland." There may be more self-satisfaction than truth in this declaration.

Paine's estimate of the importance and influence of the pamphlet is more plausible: "The light which that performance threw . . . gave a turn to the politics of America which enabled her to stand her ground. Independence followed in six months after it, although before it was published it was a dangerous doctrine to speak of, and that because it was not understood." There is no doubt that its vogue was instantaneous and enormous. A letter, dated 12 March which appeared in the British press reported that *Common Sense* "is read to all ranks; and as many as read, so many become converted; tho' perhaps the hour *before were most violent against the least idea of independence*." Charles Lee, English-born army officer, who was soon to become a general in the continental troops, wrote to Washington, 24 January, "I never saw such a masterly, irresistible performance. It will . . . give the coup-de-grace to Great Britain." Washington himself reported that in Virginia it was "working a powerful change . . . in the minds of many men." A vigorous appraisal, which has never been reprinted, appeared in *The American Annual Register . . . for the Year 1796.*

When the first copies arrived in the American camp at Cambridge, they were perused with transport. An officer then in that army observed lately that a reinforcement of five thousand men would not have inspired the troops with equal confidence as this pamphlet did, in the justice of their cause and the probability of their ultimate success. . . . Before the plain arguments of an obscure individual, . . . the pensioned and titled advocates of royalty sunk into forgetfulness. The greatest orators of antiquity did not more tyrannically command the conviction of their hearers than the writer of Common Sense: nor did Taliessin or Ossian, at the hand of their fellow soldiers, ever inspire more inflexible enthusiasm. Like the Draper's letters, a pamphlet of sixty pages, a pamphlet which has neither the fascination of poetry, nor the elegance of prose, irresistibly seized the helm of public opinion, and tore up resistance by the roots. The summons to liberty and to vengeance resounded from New Hampshire to Georgia. From the degraded appendage of a foreign monarchy, the thirteen United States rose to an independent existence. Thomas Paine was the Tyrtaeus of that revolution.

This does not, of course, mean that American independence would not have taken place without *Common Sense* or even that such a statement of principles was a necessary antecedent to independence. The great contribution of *Common Sense* was in preparing the minds of plain men for independence and in shifting their loyalty from the British Crown to the American republic.

Its influence later extended far beyond the continental boundaries of America. Paine himself considered it a defense of the natural rights of man and argued that many of its circumstances are universal. The cause of America, he proclaimed, was in great measure the cause of all mankind. Silas Deane reported in August 1776 that in France it had been translated and had had a greater run, if possible, than in America. And later during the Revolution of 1789 it was reissued into Spanish to vindicate the new French republic. In Latin America, where it was retranslated and circulated, it became highly influential in the independence movements of Venezuela, Mexico and Ecuador.

IV

The Modern Tacitus

From the outset of hostilities, Paine planned to write a complete narrative of the Revolution, and Franklin gave him materials for that purpose. Even the French Ministry of Foreign Affairs provided some financial backing. Although Paine never wrote the formal history which during a period of at least ten years he felt was to be his major literary undertaking, his propaganda pieces during the Revolution, particularly the *Crisis* and the *Letter to the abbé Raynal*, comprise an informal record of the conflict. Like the ancient Thucydides, Paine witnessed many of the exciting events which he chronicled. And like Tacitus, he developed a style noted for vigor, irony and terseness.

While Paine was composing *Common Sense*, the Quakers of Pennsylvania and New Jersey had affirmed their loyalty to King and Parliament in a formal address, motivated, they maintained, by the desire for peace rather than dissension. It was this which led Paine to add to Bradford's edition of his pamphlet a "seasonable and friendly admonition to the Quakers" in which he tried to convince them that the American troops wanted peace as much as the Quakers did, but were enduring the evils and burdens of armed conflict in order to gain a peace which would be endless and uninterrupted. Paine did not urge the Quakers to cooperate with the armed forces, but merely asked them, in the name of consistency, not to support the King. If they could not aid their countrymen, he argued, they should at least not hinder them. Paine concluded with the hope that the Quakers' example of mingling religion with politics might be disavowed and reprobated by every inhabitant of America. In general terms, Paine

44

argued that religion when it becomes a party in political disputes is a danger to society. This is the only principle of universal application in the addendum to the Quakers.

During February, 1776 Paine visited the troops in New York, motivated primarily by a desire to meet General Charles Lee to whom he carried letters of introduction from John Adams, Franklin and Benjamin Rush. Lee, who invited him to dine, found his conversation lively and perceived the "genius in his eyes."

In the meantime two pamphlet replies to the sentiments of *Common Sense* appeared in Philadelphia and one in New York. The most challenging answer consisted of a series of eight letters in the *Pennsylvania Ledger* under the pseudonym Cato. These were written by an aristocratic Anglican clergyman, William Smith, Provost of the College of Philadelphia. His letters were composed with such great skill that the advocates of colonial liberty recalled Paine from New York expressly to answer them. Paine unmasked and ridiculed Cato in a series of letters under a pseudonym of his own, The Forester.

Cato's most effective argument against *Common Sense* had been that its author proposed seeking ties with other European nations at the moment he sought independence from England. Smith charged that this meant substitution of an unknown foreign control for a benevolent English supervision under which the colonies had flourished for more than a century. He argued that Britain had listened sympathetically to the complaints of the colonists and was seeking measures of peaceful conciliation profitable to the colonists. Paine forthrightly replied that "conquest, and not reconciliation" was the plan of Britain. He explained that "foreign assistance" did not mean surrender of the continent to France or Spain, but merely acceptance of guns and ammunition. Smith's attack forced him to reaffirm, however, that "it is the true interest of America to steer clear of all European contentions."

Smith and his Tory partisans, aware that Paine was the Forester, then disparaged his opinions as emanating from an obscure nobody. Paine, irritated by their insinuations against his connections, tartly answered that it is "better to have none than bad ones." He disclosed that the Forester and the author of *Common Sense* were one and the same—and that he had arrived on the London packet over a year previously "bringing with him two unsealed letters of introduction from Dr. Franklin." Paine explained that he had published this vindication of his antecedents at the request of his friends and challenged Cato in turn to disclose his rank and recommendations—a challenge which Smith never accepted.

During this period Paine spent much time in the company of a patriotic Quaker, Christopher Marshall, whose radical zeal had alienated him from the timorous hearts of his co-religionists. Marshall noted in his diary that Paine had dined at his home, received him in turn at his own lodgings, and met him for political discussion at various places in Philadelphia in the company of such other patriots as James Cannon, Thomas Young, James Wigdon, Timothy Matlack and Benjamin Rush. Undoubtedly the primary subjects of conversation among such politically conscious groups were the Declaration of Independence and the state constitution of Pennsylvania, which was being drawn up in a special convention during 1776.

Until recent years it has been almost universally believed that Paine attended the convention and engineered the adoption of democratic provisions. John Adams, for example, affirmed that "it was not Franklin, but Timothy Matlack, James Cannon, Thomas Young, and Thomas Paine, who were the authors of it." Actually the democratic provisions came from Franklin, and Paine had absolutely no connection with the constitution. In a letter in the *Pennsylvania Packet*, 18 March 1777, he asserted that during the forming of the convention he had been serving as a soldier in camp. He roundly declared: "I held no correspondence with either part, for, or against, the present constitution. I had no hand in forming any part of it, nor knew any thing of its contents till I saw it published."

Paine felt that his duty lay with the fighting forces rather than with the constitution-makers. In the summer of 1776, he enlisted with the "flying camp," a mobile body of ten thousand men formed from the militia and volunteers of Jersey, Pennsylvania and Maryland. Paine served with the Pennsylvania division under General Roberdeau and was stationed at Perth Amboy and later at Bergen. When the time of the "flying camp" expired, Paine went to Fort Lee as aide-de-camp to General Nathanael Greene, the commanding officer. Paine, who held the rank of brigade major, was sometimes the victim of practical jokes. A certain Major Blodget, a young gentleman of considerable wit and humor, once asked Greene for permission to have a little diversion with Paine. Greene agreed to the fun provided that it not be carried too far. "It was so contrived among the aides that an alarm in the night should be made, which accordingly was done, and Mr. Paine rising from his bed in great hurry and confusion, could not find one of his boots and wig. . . . Consequently, the next morning, the laugh went round, and fear was substituted as the real cause of the loss." A visitor to the camp, James I. Wilmer, reported this incident to show that no man is exempt from ridicule and that "though Mr. Paine certainly possessed a strong mind in many respects, yet in his appearance and usual conversation, he scarce was up to mediocrity." Greene himself always regarded Paine with affection, reporting once to his wife, 2 November 1776, that Paine and Colonel Snarl, or Cornwell, were "perpetually wrangling about mathematical problems."

Judging by Paine's own account, he was a valiant and aggressive fighting man. One of his comrades in arms, however, Charles Biddle, later Vice President of the Supreme Executive Council of Pennsylvania, expressed a contrary view. In his *Autobiography* he charged, "Paine may be a good philosopher, but he is not a soldier—he always kept out of danger."

Paine more than once witnessed action at Fort Lee and presumably, despite Biddle's bad opinion, discovered that he could stand the whistling of a cannonball with composure. On Sunday 27 October, Lord Percy, commander of the British forces on York Island, moved his troops to a position on the Harlem plains between his and the American advance posts. Alexander Graydon, a soldier among the Pennsylvania troops, later described Percy's maneuver and rejoiced that "the celebrated Thomas Paine . . . happened to witness the proceeding from Fort Lee, and gave us an handsome puff in one of the Philadelphia papers."

Paine indeed reported the engagement in the *Pennsylvania Journal* which published other reports from the camp of General Greene—probably written by Paine. One described the loss of Fort Washington: another, which was immediately reprinted in England and attributed to Paine by Chalmers, depicted the loss of Fort Lee and Washington's retreat across New Jersey.

The army remained four days at Newark and twice marched out to meet the enemy even though the latter's numbers were greatly superior. Subsequently the Americans withdrew to Trenton and to the banks of the Delaware. Posterity, Paine concluded, would call this retreat glorious, "and the names of Washington and Fabius will run parallel to eternity." In this first of many tributes, Paine celebrated the "master stroke of generalship" by which Washington "crossed the Delaware, surprised three regiments of Hessians, and with little or no loss, took near a thousand prisoners." Washington, the American Fabius, attained much of his early celebrity thanks to Paine's journalism.

Paine had personally contributed toward preserving the morale of the weary Americans during this disheartening retreat from the Hudson to the Delaware. He had marched with the army until the crossing of the Delaware on 8 December 1776. Later he revealed that it had been Washington's intention to make a stand at Newark "could he have been timely reinforced; instead of which, near half the army left him at that place, or soon after, their time being out." At Newark Paine began writing the first number of the *Crisis*, beginning with the now famous declaration: "These are the times that try men's souls." He had it printed at Philadelphia on 19 December, six days before the first victory of the Americans, the taking of the Hessians at Trenton, a victory toward which Paine's pamphlet in some measure contributed. The need for Paine's heartening words may be judged by the note of despair in Washington's correspondence during these days. On 27 November he wrote to General Lee, "It has been more owing to the badness of the weather that the enemy's progress has been checked, than to any resistance we could make." On 13 December he wrote to Lund Washington, "Your imagination can scarce extend to a situation more distressing than mine. Our only dependence now is upon the speedy enlistment of a new army. If this fails, I think the game will be pretty well up."

Amid this heavy pessimism, extending from the Commander-in-Chief to the lowest deserter, Paine took up his pen and wrote: "The summer soldier and the sunshine patriot will, in this crisis, shrink from the service of his country; but he that stands it *now*, deserves the love and thanks of man and woman. Tyranny, like hell, is not easily conquered; yet we have this consolation with us, that the harder the conflict, the more glorious the triumph. What we obtain too cheap, we esteem too lightly." Paine praised the manly and martial spirit of the American soldiers, which had enabled them to endure the long and disheartening retreat.

After reviling the British King and the American Tories, Paine appealed to the loyalty of his countrymen, urging them not to listen to the hypocritical peace talks of British General William Howe, who sought "partly by threats and partly by promises, to terrify or seduce the people to deliver up their arms." Despite the retreat through New Jersey, Paine felt confidence in a glorious victory. The withdrawal had been slow and orderly, no signs of fear had been shown, and a new vigorous army for the next campaign was rapidly being recruited. Paine's encouraging words were distributed throughout the country under the title *The American Crisis*, first of the famous series which Paine continued throughout the Revolution.

According to tradition, this first *Crisis* was read in camp to every corporal's guard, and the flagging spirits of soldiers and officers miraculously revived. Despite James Cheetham's blanket assertion that "Hope succeeded to despair, cheerfulness to gloom, and firmness to irresolution," it is impossible to find corroborating evidence of this miraculous metamorphosis. Washington's dramatic victory at Trenton on Christmas was due primarily to the befogged minds of the Hessian commanders, who had been drinking heavily all that night, rather than to the magically invigorating power of Paine's words. Still Charles Biddle reported that Paine's opening lines "were in the mouths of every one going to join the army."

The action at Trenton and Princeton Paine considered so important that two years later he rebuked an official congressional report for slighting it. Gouverneur Morris and W. H. Drayton in their *Observations on the American Revolution*, published for Congress in 1779, ascribed little importance to this campaign. Paine forthwith charged them with reversing "the line of facts." Drawing upon his own experience, he maintained that "the insolence of the enemy after the engagement on Long Island, and their barbarity after taking Fort Washington, were far greater than their vigor at any one time of that campaign." "Truth will, and history ought to say" that British success began to ebb at Trenton and Princeton. "These two actions disabled and laid the enemy dormant for more than six months afterwards; and by throwing a spirit of joy into the continent, gave life and vigor to the recruiting service for the next campaign."

During the lull after the victory of Trenton, Paine attended Meeting in Princeton one Sunday in the company of Washington. Before entering the meetinghouse, Paine entrusted his overcoat to the care of an Irish servant, who absconded with it. When the theft was discovered, Washington said to Paine that it was necessary to watch as well as pray, but then cheered his friend by saying that he had two coats and gave him one.

After Trenton, Paine decided that henceforth his political and literary talents would be more valuable to his country than his military service.

On 13 January 1777 he published his *Crisis* No. 2, written in the form of an open letter to Richard Viscount Howe, brother of General Howe, who had been sent to America to handicap the Revolution by offering free pardon to all those who would lay down their arms. Paine taunted Howe for having no effective power as commissioner to negotiate, and ridiculed his childish faith in believing that the Americans would lay down their arms merely in response to his blustering threats or his pallid promises. Paine pointed out that the size of the continent made conquest impossible. "By the time you extended from New York to Virginia, you would be reduced to a string of drops not capable of hanging together; while we, by retreating from State to State, like a river turning back upon itself, would acquire strength in the same proportion as you lost it." Turning to the internal affairs of England, Paine charged her with virtual bankruptcy and actually threatened steps to foment a revolution there. "A few thousand men landed in England with the declared design of deposing the present king . . . would assuredly carry their point." With a mind to the negotiations for the French alliance then being carried on by Franklin, Paine concluded by advising the English to make a speedy peace, for it might not be possible later for the Americans to come to terms without consulting their allies.

A week after the date of this *Crisis*, Paine was appointed secretary to the Commissioners for an Indian Treaty to be held the following week at Easton. He set out immediately for the western frontier, where he remained until March. The conference opened

27 January in the First (German) Reformed Church. Before proceeding to negotiations, the Indians and commissioners shook hands and drank rum to the health of both groups while the organ was played. Paine fraternized amiably with the representatives of the five northern nations. He was "often pleased with the sagacious remarks of those original people," and later repeated the observations of one of them, King Lastnight, concerning British vessels on the Great Lakes and British troops on land. "The King of England is like a fish. When he is in the water he can wag his tail. —When he comes on land he lays down on his side." At another time Paine recalled the eloquence of another chief, Colonel Sampson, who "scolded the restless Delawares in a high tone, and concluded his address to them in these words: 'You dogs, if you do not be quiet, I will catch you by the hair of the head and throw you one by one over the Blue Mountains.'"

On 1 April, 1777, Paine was unanimously elected to a Committee of Correspondence of the Whig Society of Philadelphia. This band of patriots, led by its president, Charles Willson Peale, attempted to arouse public feeling against sympathizers with the British and urged that they be prosecuted. In keeping with the policy of the Whig Society, Paine devoted his *Crisis* No. 3, published 19 April, to a bitter reprobation of the Tories, whom he castigated as actual traitors. He admitted no neutral ground between citizen or traitor, Whig or Tory; and he accused the latter of opposing independence from motives of *"avarice, down-right villainy, and lust of personal power."* Since a large percentage of the Tories were Quakers, Paine resumed the denunciation of the sect that he had begun in his earlier writings, being careful this time to distinguish between the patriots, among whom were some of his own friends, and the Crown partisans. "A religious Quaker is a valuable character," he declared, "and a political Quaker a real Jesuit."

Not averse to a few strokes of completely irrelevant personal satire, he seized upon Hannah Lightfoot, alleged mistress of George III, to make the entire sect seem ridiculous. "The present king of England, who seduced and took into keeping a sister of their society, is reverenced and supported by repeated Testimonies, while the friendly noodle from whom she was taken (and who is now in this city) continues a drudge in the service of his rival, as if proud of being cuckolded by a creature called a king."

The best means of dealing with all American Tories, Paine concluded, was to make them dread the consequences of their disloyalty. Paine proposed that the sentiments of all men be brought into the open by the joint establishment of an oath of allegiance to the United States and a property tax of ten to twenty per cent annually. Those who took the oath would be exempt from the tax by virtue of their service to the cause, but those who refused the oath would be obliged to pay their quota in money. Not only would this stamp out incipient Toryism, he argued, but it would enable funds gathered from Tory estates to be used to reward loyal citizens who would turn out to repulse the enemy.

Two days before the publication of this *Crisis,* John Adams nominated Paine as secretary to the Committee for Foreign Affairs of the Congress. It was on this occasion that John Witherspoon, delegate from New Jersey, spoke out against him with amazing invective. He alleged that when Paine "first came over he was on the other side, and had written pieces against the American cause; . . . afterwards . . . finding the tide of popularity run rapidly, he had turned about." Witherspoon charged also "that he was very intemperate; . . . that he was, in short, a bad character, and not fit to be placed in such a situation." Since no one confirmed Witherspoon's allegations, and General Roberdeau testified in Paine's favor, the Congress appointed him to the post. Witherspoon's own writings give no account of this episode, the only authority for it being the autobiography of Adams. John Jay, himself rabidly conservative, however, later wrote a slanderous accusation bearing out Witherspoon. According to Jay, Paine was "made secretary to the Committee for Foreign Affairs; and when General Washington was retreating before the enemy in Jersey, . . . he was again so suspected as that Congress became uneasy lest the committee's papers in his custody should fall into the enemy's hands, and took their measures accordingly." As we have seen, Paine was not made secretary until after Washington's retreat, and Jay's insinuation is patently false. It reveals that the testimony of contemporaries, even that of respected founding fathers, cannot be accepted without scrutiny, particularly when religious or political prejudices are involved.

Paine believed that Witherspoon made his accusations through jealousy—that Witherspoon could not forgive him "for publishing *Common Sense* and going a step beyond him in literary reputation." It is worth noting, moreover, that Benjamin Rush in his autobiography says nothing about Paine's anti-American sentiment, but, on the contrary, specifically affirms that a few days after their first meeting he perceived that Paine "had realized the independence of the American Colonies upon Great Britain, and that he considered the measure as necessary to bring the war to a speedy and successful issue." Even more interesting, Paine alleged in 1802 that "Dr. Rush at the period when he [Paine] commenced Common Sense told him, that there were two words which he should avoid by every means as necessary to his own safety and that of the public,—*Independence* and *Republicanism*." Yet there is no absolute evidence that Paine held republican notions before coming to America. All that we know is that both Rickman and Sherwin considered Paine a confirmed Whig in Lewes, and he himself declared that during his residence in London he had espoused "those political notions which I have since given to the world in my *Rights of Man*." But regardless of when they came into being, the radical ideas of this humble staymaker were destined to nurture revolutions in the three continents of North America, Europe and South America.

Shortly after being named secretary, Paine wrote to his sponsor, Franklin, to express his pleasure at receiving the unsolicited honor. Franklin had been sent to France as a member of a diplomatic commission to negotiate military and economic aid. In his letter Paine referred to Franklin's safe arrival in terms showing a firm belief in the doctrine of special providence. "There has been such a wonderful and visible chain of matters without the disorder of a single link, in bringing this important affair to an issue," he wrote, "that a man must be an infidel not to think heaven has some hand in it."

On 11 September 1777, the British outmaneuvered Washington at Brandywine Creek on the road from Wilmington to Philadelphia, the action of his career in which the American General came closest to defeat. Although the Americans were forced to abandon their positions, Washington took advantage of darkness to withdraw his army and save his reputation. The army remained intact,

but the British seemed to be in control. Paine, realizing the need
of revitalizing the discouraged troops and the panic-stricken citizens
of Philadelphia, took up his pen to write *Crisis* No. 4, which he
dated "Sept 12 at noon" and published the next day. In this, the
shortest of the *Crisis* papers, Paine limited himself to exhorting
the troops to renewed efforts and praising them for their valor
and loyalty, painting an optimistic picture of the future, and
reiterating the noble aims which had inspired the American cause.
He reminded his readers that "those who expect to reap the bless-
ings of freedom, must, like men, undergo the fatigues of supporting
it." Sympathizing with their recent dejection, he predicted that
"the glow of hope, courage and fortitude" would in a little time
displace all inferior passion. Every success of the enemy, he argued,
had contributed to reduce their strength—and they had only eventual
defeat to await. The English contended entirely for mercenary
motives; whereas the Americans fought "not to enslave, but to
set a country free, and to make room upon the earth for honest
men to live in."

Because of his experience in the field with General Greene as
well as his journalistic success, Paine was engaged 10 October
1777 by the Pennsylvania Assembly to act as observer with Washington's army and to furnish regular and constant intelligence of
the proceedings of the forces. In offering Paine this post, Timothy
Matlack, Secretary of the Assembly, stressed the importance of
the task and observed that few but Paine were capable of carrying
it out. He promised Paine a reasonable compensation and—what
probably served as even more of an inducement—suggested that a
correspondence of this kind might be the best opportunity for
Paine to give important hints to the Council. For the first time
in his career, Paine's advice was being sought by an official political
organization. Hereafter he would communicate his opinions to
the government in official dispatches—as well as to the public in
his *Crisis* papers.

After Brandywine, the British forces marched northeast to Philadelphia, and on Friday 19 September, about one in the morning,
word came that they were crossing the Schuylkill. "It was a beauti-
ful still sunlight morning," Paine later recollected, "and the streets
as full of men, women and children as on a market day." On the
previous evening, Paine, fearing that the city would be taken,

had approached Colonel Bayard, Speaker of the Assembly, with a plan for defending the city. He reasoned that even an appearance of sturdy defense would deter the suspicious Howe, or at least hold him off until Washington could come to the city's assistance. He convinced Bayard that a voluntary assessment of $50,000 for defending Philadelphia would be better than deserting it, and asked General Mifflin to lead a force of three thousand men if it could be mustered. Before Paine could proceed further with his scheme, however, Mifflin had abandoned the city, and Paine was forced to do likewise, sending his chest and everything belonging to the Committee for Foreign Affairs by shallop to Trenton. On 29 September, Paine set off for Washington's camp, not knowing exactly where to find it because of its constant mobility. He "kept pretty high up the country, and being unwilling to ask questions," not knowing Tory from patriot, he took three days to find his destination. On 3 October at nine o'clock at night the body of the American troops marched for Germantown, and Paine himself set out at five the next morning.

At about the same hour Washington's troops arrived in Germantown and fell suddenly upon the British lines. Disorganized by surprise and panic, the British fell back two miles, leaving their entire camp to the Americans, according to Paine. In the midst of the retreat a party of about five hundred British regulars garrisoned themselves in a large stone house and steadfastly refused to surrender. Washington checked his advance in a vain attempt to reduce this band, losing his advantage over the remainder of Howe's forces. The later re-formed their ranks and, joined by fresh reinforcements, turned their flight into a successful counterattack. Washington and the other bewildered Americans, suddenly undeceived of an illusion that they were riding a victorious tide which would take them to Philadelphia, were forced to withdraw ignominiously from Germantown. Paine wrote that neither he nor any one else could ever learn or explain "truly the cause of that day's miscarriage." He reported that the retreat was extraordinary. "Nobody hurried themselves. Every one marched his own pace. The enemy kept a civil distance behind, sending every now and then a shot after us, and receiving the same from us. . . . The army . . . appeared to me to be only sensible of a disappointment, not a defeat."

Paine breakfasted next morning with Washington—and remained in camp two more days. Then "lest any ill impression should get among the garrison at Mud Island and Red Bank, and the vessels and galleys stationed there," he "crossed over to the Jerseys at Trenton and went down to those places." Some days later he went on an expedition as aide-de-camp to General Greene. "The occasion was—a party of the enemy, about 1500, lay over the Schuylkill at Grey's Ferry. General McDougall with his division was sent to attack them; and Sullivan and Greene with their divisions were to favor the enterprise by a feint on the city, down the Germantown road." Paine, knowing the ground well, was sent to discover the enemy's picket. "But the enemy either on the approach of McDougall, or on information of it, called in their party, and the expedition was frustrated."

Paine divided his time during these crucial months between the camp at Valley Forge and the home of his friend Colonel Joseph Kirkbride at Bordentown, New Jersey, where he stayed until the end of January. Kirkbride had formerly commanded the first regiment of Bucks County, Pennsylvania. Then after the British burned his home, he re-established himself at Bordentown. Paine compared the army at Valley Forge to a "family of beavers; every one busy; some carrying logs; others mud, and the rest fastening them together." During one of his visits to Colonel Kirkbride's, he volunteered to serve as member of a party of four to carry out his own project of burning the enemy shipping at Trenton, but the naval and military chiefs rejected his proposal.

Before the British occupied Philadelphia, the Congress had moved to Lancaster and thence to York, where Paine occasionally spent a day or two. Since there were seldom more than fifteen members of the Congress present during these days, Paine's secretaryship made little demands on his time. During February and March 1778, Paine lived at Lancaster in the house of William Henry, treasurer of the borough and pioneer scientist. He and Paine had each independently thought of applying steam power to vessels and at this time they discussed ways of carrying out the project. Henry's son John Joseph in his old age wrote out his recollections of Paine's habits during his Lancaster sojourn: "Paine would walk of a morning until 12 o'clock; come in and make an inordinate dinner. The rising from table was between two and three o'clock.

He would then retire to his bed-chamber, wrap a blanket around him, and in a large arm chair, take a nap, of two or three hours— rise and walk. These walks and his indolence, surprised my parents." As an example of Paine's excessive sloth, Henry cited the compo- sition of *Crisis* No. 5. "It was written in my father's house. Mr. D. Rittenhouse inhabited the front room, in the upper story, where was the library. . . . While that excellent man was employing his hours in the duties of his office, . . . Paine would be a snoring away his precious time in his easy chair, regardless of those in- junctions imposed upon him by congress, in relation to his po- litical compositions. His remissness, indolence or vacuity of thought, caused great heart-burning among many primary characters in those days. . . . His *Crisis*, No. V, lay on his table, dusted: to-day three or four lines would be added, in the course of a week, a dozen more, and so on." The writer, a very religious man, might be suspected of prejudice against Paine since his remarks were penned after Paine became known as an infidel, but later French diplomats in Philadelphia, who had no reason to be prejudiced against Paine, also stressed his laziness in their confidential reports.

In the first part of *Crisis* No. 5, addressed to General Sir William Howe, Paine slashed out with heavy-handed humor at the latter's recent elevation to the peerage. Passing to invective, Paine charged Howe with being "the patron of low and vulgar frauds, the en- courager of Indian cruelties," and the importer of a cargo of heinous vices, the worst of which was *meanness*.

The particular act of meanness which drew Paine's fire was the distributing in New York of counterfeit continental bills. Paine called this adding a new vice, forgery, to the military catalogue. He observed that England of all nations should have been the least willing to encourage forgery, for England had "the greatest quantity of paper currency and the least quantity of gold and silver of any nation in Europe."

Paine thereafter reviewed in detail the entire history of the American campaign, describing Howe's movements as a military jig, "the labors of a puppy pursuing his tail." Indeed if one relied upon Paine's survey of the war, one would hardly imagine that the Americans suffered a single reverse. But what Paine lacked in historical perspective he made up in invective against Howe and his superiors. "They have refined upon villainy till it wants a

name. To the fiercer vices of former ages, they have added the
dregs and scummings of the most finished rascality, and are so
completely sunk in serpentine deceit, that there is not left among
them *one* generous enemy."

In the second part of *Crisis* No. 5, devoted to the inhabitants
of America, Paine reviewed the military and political situation with
unmixed optimism. He styled the present action as "the most virtu-
ous and illustrious revolution that ever graced the history of mankind" and refused to "yield the palm of the United States to any
Grecians or Romans that were ever born." So confident was Paine
that the spirit of corruption in the British Ministry and the natural
difficulties of invading the continent would eventually defeat the
British that he argued that the loss of Philadelphia was attended
with more advantages than injuries. He exhorted his countrymen
to undertake the siege of Philadelphia as a single, immediate and
primary aim and not to diversify defense to other areas. As a means
of forwarding the undertaking, he presented a plan for recruiting
more men and supplies by a quota system.

Considering that Paine was writing during the bleak winter of
1778, when the troops at Valley Forge were suffering harrowing
privation, when Congress had been driven from Philadelphia by the
occupying enemy, and when Paine himself had been forced to
flee to Lancaster, one wonders on what grounds he based his
cheerful confidence in an American victory. Some years later
Paine explained that he had written this *Crisis* in order to defend the
reputation of Washington against Adams and others who wished
to have him removed as Commander-in-Chief on the grounds that
"he did nothing." Paine affirmed in retrospect that when writing
in 1778 he had realized that the black times of '76 were the natural
consequence of Washington's lack of military judgment, but he
"could see no possible advantage, and nothing but mischief, that
could arise by distracting the army into parties." Although it is
possible that Paine's complacency had its source in a desire to protect Washington, it is more likely a form of generalized morale-
boosting, with perhaps an element of personal optimism. There
is much less direct praise of Washington in this *Crisis* than in the
first.

A few weeks after the completion of *Crisis* No. 5, news came to
America of the conclusion of an alliance between the United States

and France, and hopes for an American victory immediately began to soar. People expected the British to evacuate Philadelphia, but Paine—much less exuberant in private than in public communications —held a contrary view, which he expressed in a note to Washington, 5 June 1778. Feeling that the General might find his opinion valuable in planning his strategy, Paine pointed out that the British, wishing to avoid war with France, would probably soon acknowledge American independence—and foreseeing an eventual peace treaty, with the usual background of bargaining, would "endeavor to hold all they can."

Five days later, Paine wrote an additional article, which could be labeled like one or two later ones an "Extraordinary" or a "Supernumerary Crisis." This piece, although published in the *Pennsylvania Gazette*, 10 June, has not been noticed by Paine's previous biographers or editors. In spite of being about one sixth the length of *Crisis* No. 5, the letter presented more specific information as well as a shrewd analysis of the state of affairs. Paine's tone was markedly less ebullient as he warned against overconfidence with the return of warm weather. He continued to abuse English leaders and politicians, but abandoned the somewhat labored rhetoric, the ingenious parallels and sardonic euphemisms of the fifth *Crisis* in favor of rapid, sharp stabs. Analyzing the trend of events, Paine found only three possible courses for England: war with France; acknowledgment of American independence, by which England could honorably avoid war; or submission to every indignity France might show, by which England could still avoid war, but would bring dishonor upon herself.

During the same month a British commission to present peace proposals arrived in Philadelphia shortly before its evacuation on 18 June. One of their number, George Johnstone, former governor of West Florida, inspired a number of publications designed to turn the people against Congress. He also attempted to bribe several of its members to desert the American cause. Johnstone's activities were immediately exposed, and Paine denounced his unscrupulous tactics in satirical verse in the *Pennsylvania Packet*, 28 July. Paine imitated the sharp precision of Alexander Pope's couplets, but reduced the vigor of his scorn by a cumbersome title: "To Governor Johnstone, one of the British Commissioners, on his later letters and offers to bribe certain eminent characters in America, and threatening after-

wards to appeal to the public." Pointing to Johnstone's public utter-
ances on virtue, Paine asked,

> Must he, Oh shame to genius! be the first
> To practice arts himself so loudly curst?
> Must he exhibit to a laughing mob,
> A turn coat patriot conquer'd by a jobb:
> And prove from under his adult'rous pen
> How few are just of all the sons of men?

One of the Congressmen whom Johnstone had attempted to sway
was Joseph Reed of Philadelphia. An enormous bribe of ten
thousand guineas had been offered "through the mediation of a
Lady." Paine denounced the procedure in the *Pennsylvania Packet*,
30 July.

Modern historians have pointed out that security measures invoked during the Revolution had much in common with certain
aspects of the modern police state generally reprobated by democratic thought. Paine in July had signed, as had others, a species
of loyalty oath or declaration promising to disclose any facts within
his knowledge concerning suspicious characters or others notori-
ously disaffected to the American cause. The purpose of the declaration was to instruct and assure those citizens who may have
been "so far misled as to suppose their appearing as witnesses against
such offenders officious and dishonorable." In other words, to
make informing on one's neighbor respectable. In the spirit of
the declaration of loyalty, Paine demanded the exposure and punishment of the treasonable lady. "I ask not," he wrote, "whether
the offer was made through the means of a man or woman. Bribery
is of neither sex; public justice knows no distinction of persons;
the moment it begins to discriminate it loses its rank and assumes the
contrary stile. We reason wrong when we put the person in
the place of the offence and consider the doer instead of the deed.
Besides which, mercy comes in character when it follows conviction, but that which precedes it has the appearance of partiality or
influence. Had we no laws we might complain: but if we execute
them not we ought to be complained against."

Because of the highly unfavorable publicity associated with Johnstone, the Crown appointed a new commission of three members.
Failing completely in their efforts to negotiate a return of Ameri-

can allegiance to the Crown, these commissioners as a last resort, on 3 October, appealed directly to the American people to lay down their arms and accept the liberal British terms of surrender. Paine replied in the name of the American people in his *Crisis* No. 6, 20 October. Repeating much that he had said to the Howes on the futility of royal pardons and proclamations, he ridiculed the commissioners for seeking to pass off military weakness as mercy. Again he threatened the possibility of carrying destruction to England itself should the British persist in their attempt to reduce the colonists and break up the alliance with France. "Can you think," he taunted, "that we, with nearly half your army prisoners, and in alliance with France, are to be begged or threatened into submission by a piece of paper?" Paine's threats of reprisals drew the approval of Conrad Alexandre Gérard, first French Minister to the United States. In an official despatch to the Comte de Vergennes, French Minister of Foreign Affairs, Gérard asserted that he had personally solicited Paine to resume his writing after the British commissioners' proclamation, and unaware of Paine's anonymous newspaper satires, he expressed satisfaction that Paine had regained his verve.

Three weeks later, Paine brought out *Crisis* No. 7, this one addressed to the people of England. The English people had in the past taken it for granted that their national armies were glorious and invincible. For their benefit Paine exposed the poor record of British troops in America and their "low, cruel, indolent and profligate" conduct. He charged that the Ministry had sought to provoke the colonies into revolt in order to annex America as a conquered country. Also he pointed out that "nothing but the whole soil and property of the country can be placed as a possible equivalent against the millions which the ministry expended," and to arouse British taxpayers, he observed that no return for this outlay could ever be hoped. "No taxes raised in America could possibly repay it." The folly of the Ministry was "to go to war for profit's sake." Addressing "the great bulwark of the nation, . . . the mercantile and manufacturing part thereof," Paine insisted that war and conquest would serve the interest of only the Crown and bureaucrats, but an independent America would be to the interest of the people as a whole.

Three days after this *Crisis,* Paine published in the *Pennsylvania*

Packet a poem "To the King of England," which subsequently enjoyed wide circulation as a propaganda piece. The work, a searing satire, accused George III of inhuman sentiments and wished for his death. Paine associated the British monarch with Satan, Cain, mental guilt, cruelty, hate and unreasoned bloodshed. In comparing the British monarch to Cain, he ingeniously referred to the recent nativity of the American nation.

> Both curs'd supremely (for the blood they drew)
> Each from the rising world while each was new.

While Paine was addressing the people and the King of England, a very strong opposition arose in Pennsylvania to the form of its state constitution. The persons then in office or hoping to be elected under the prevailing constitution became seriously alarmed and applied to Paine for aid, which he provided gratis in the form of a series of articles in the Philadelphia press. He supported the constitution on the grounds that it was an experiment and argued that tampering with it while the enemy occupied the country might be dangerous. He also pointed out that its single legislative chamber permitted maximum dispatch and dispensed with wasteful deliberation in time of war. No doubt Paine was favorably disposed to the constitution because Franklin had been one of its principal framers. Its opponents were by and large the conservative elements in society, and the changes they proposed, particularly a bicameral legislature and the appointment rather than the election of magistrates, led away from popular government. Paine argued that the democratic provisions which rendered the constitution "good for a poor man" made it good for a rich man as well. Prosperity for the poor made consumers for the merchants, and buyers, tenants and laborers for the landed interest. Paine saw in society a harmony in interests of rich and poor rather than a conflict. His principle was to "defend the freedom of the poor out of policy to the rich."

Paine's fundamental social philosophy here was the same as that of *Common Sense*, the doctrine of natural rights. "As in religion, so in civil rights, every man naturally stands upon the same plane." He considered "freedom to be inseparable from the man as a man." If freedom be "dangerous in the hands of the poor from ignorance," he argued, it is equally "dangerous in the hands of the rich from influence." If one could be affected by poverty, the other could be swayed by connection. Consequently Paine insisted that the rights of neither should be abridged. Paine opposed, among the practical measures being considered by the Pennsylvania Assembly, property qualifications for officeholding and the appointment of magistrates by the executive branch. Property cannot defend a country, he observed, nor can house and lands fight the enemy.

He argued for public election of magistrates on the ground that the public voice is impartial and that men so chosen will feel a sense of obligation to the community, not gratitude toward a special interest which appointed them.

Paine had intended to continue the discussion in still further articles, but he was sidetracked by the bursting into the public arena of the most notorious scandal of the American Revolution, the affair of Silas Deane. Paine immediately involved himself in its nasty mess of personalities and politics and, consequently, suffered the first major set-back of his hitherto felicitous career in America. The enemies he had created by defending the constitution soon found reason to rejoice at his entering the domain of foreign policy where he was to be more vulnerable to their attacks.

V

The Deane Affair

Silas Deane's *cause célèbre*, which led to an investigation of all forms of profiteering in the American war, grew out of the attempts of the Continental Congress to obtain commitments from the French government, preferably an alliance and, failing this, material aid. As early as January 1776, private groups in France had offered to furnish military supplies to America in return for trade agreements, and Silas Deane, a Connecticut delegate, was sent by Congress to Versailles in March to seek official recognition of the United States. Although received by Vergennes, French Minister of Foreign Affairs, he negotiated mainly with two men of letters, at first with Dr. Barbeu Dubourg, French editor of Benjamin Franklin's works, and later with Caron de Beaumarchais, author of *The Marriage of Figaro*. The latter had become interested in American affairs while in London where he had met Arthur Lee, who, in 1775, had succeeded Franklin as colonial agent. Lee had convinced him that the Revolution would be victorious. Beaumarchais returned to Paris determined to aid America and to make his own fortune in doing so. Since France was not yet ready for an open alliance with America or war with England, any aid to the rebels had to be kept secret. Beaumarchais therefore set up a dummy corporation, Hortalez and Company, for the channeling of supplies to America. His ingenuity and smooth talking won the confidence of both Deane and Vergennes. The kings of France and Spain each provided secretly a million livres, which Beaumarchais supervised in laying out in arms and equipment, and which Deane gratefully acknowledged receiving on behalf of the Congress.

The principal question which had not been resolved—and even

64

now remains obscure—was whether these supplies were to be a purchase or a gift. Not only were the official contributions cloaked in secrecy—they were hopelessly entangled with other transactions. In addition to handling the royal donations, the firm of Hortalez and Company acted as agent for Beaumarchais himself and other speculators who expected to make a handsome profit. These obscure transactions came into the open after Franklin and Arthur Lee had been appointed joint commissioners with Deane. In October 1777, Vergennes announced that no payment would be demanded for money or materials thus far furnished by the French government. Deane maintained in communications to Congress that this largesse did not include the supplies which had passed through the hands of Beaumarchais. Arthur Lee roundly declared that the gift comprised everything supplied. Lee, a dour, suspicious, and fanatically honest man, discovered that Deane had also been acting as a purchasing agent for a private commercial organization, that of Philadelphia's most powerful capitalist, Robert Morris. Seeing Deane involved with Beaumarchais, on one hand, and with Morris, on the other, Lee became convinced that Deane was perpetrating a fraud on his country and denounced him to his face and in letters to his American friends. He even involved Franklin in his accusations, and soon the three commissioners became mutually distrustful, resentful, and acrimonious. When the wranglings of the commissioners reached the ears of Congress, Deane was recalled, ostensibly to report on the state of affairs in Europe; actually to give an account of his contracts and engagements.

Shortly after his return to America, Deane requested an audience of Congress for the purpose of vindicating his conduct. In the midst of a hearing, granted 15 August 1778, a motion was made to require Deane to put his narrative in writing. Debate on the motion, which did not carry, showed that Congress had already been split into pro-Deane and anti-Deane factions. Henry Laurens, President of the Congress, lamented "that my fellow labourers had as absolutely taken sides as it can be supposed Gentlemen are capable of in a *pure unbiased Assembly.*"

As charges and countercharges multiplied, Congress embarked upon a full-scale investigation of all the dissensions detrimental to the public service which existed among the commissioners in Paris. This left poor Deane in a state of nervous uncertainty, and he pressed Congress to resume its inquiry into his own activities. When Congress continued to ignore his appeals, Deane took his case directly to the people by writing an open letter in the *Pennsylvania Packet*, 5 December, charging that the ears of Congress had been shut against him. This he reprinted in a thousand handbills. Apart from empty fulminations against William and Charles Lee and one or two members of Congress, Deane presented nothing specific either against his enemies or in his own vindication. But he succeeded in exposing to the world at large the disharmony and factionalism disrupting the American government. Richard Henry Lee, brother of Arthur, later asserted "that the single publication of that Libel on the 5th of December had done more injury to the American cause than a reenforcement of 20,000 men to the enemies general could have produced."

When Congress met on the Monday following Deane's outburst, Laurens deemed it "dishonorable to Congress" to have further personal dealings with the author of a libel against it, but the majority refused to go on record against Deane. On the next morning, Laurens in protest resigned as President, thinking that he could combat Deane with more success on the floor than in the chair.

Paine was personally friendly to both Laurens and Richard Henry Lee, one of the most radical of the Virginia statesmen. After waiting ten days, during which Congress still took no action against Deane, Paine addressed him in a series of newspaper letters, charging him with violating propriety in making his personal animosities public. In a sentence soon to be fraught with significance to Paine himself, he observed that "a public man, in Mr. Deane's former character, ought to be as silent as the grave; for who would trust a person with a secret who showed such a talent for revealing?" Somewhat unfairly he added that Congress had been waiting in vain for Deane's explanation of his conduct in France and charged Deane with refusing to give it.

Paine's purpose in entering the controversy can only be guessed. Certainly he must have been moved by more than disgust at Deane's whining. Perhaps he first spoke out primarily to defend his friends, the Lees. It is usually said that his main concern was to frustrate the mercenary designs of Beaumarchais and save Congress from a charge which it was not required to pay. He undoubtedly also sought to expose the monopolizing practices of Morris and other financiers, although in his initial publication he accused Deane of little more than indiscretion and poor taste. Later, as a result of a newspaper answer under the signature "Plain Truth," Paine made more serious insinuations, namely that Deane had connived at having his records stolen and that he had mercantile connections with delegates to the Congress. In connection with this charge Paine advocated that an investigation be made of all links between business and government. At the same time in a secret letter to Laurens, Paine urged him to inquire whether Deane's accounts said to be left in France had any connection with those of Robert Morris. Deane's blast in the papers, he seemed to think, may have been intended to divert attention from the settling of accounts. In another newspaper article, 21 December, Paine declared that "he has not, nor ever had, any interested connection with either Mr. Deane or Mr. Lee; . . . and whether Mr. Deane is wrong, or Mr. Lee wrong, or both wrong, is alike to him as to personal favor or interest. He *believes* the whole affair to be an inflammatory bubble, thrown among the public to answer both a mercantile end and a private pique."

Paine presumably intended to root out the financial dealings going on behind the scenes, but in so doing he exposed a diplomatic secret of international significance, which spelled disaster for him as well as for Deane. In his fourth article, 2 January 1779, he declared with show of authority that the supplies which Deane plumed himself for acquiring "were promised and engaged, and that as a present, before he ever *arrived* in France." By making this declaration Paine was revealing information known to him only because of his post of Secretary of the Committee for Foreign Affairs. When taking office he had sworn "to disclose no matter, the knowledge of which shall be acquired in consequence of such his office, that he shall be directed to keep secret." Presumably the details of French aid before the announcement of the alliance were considered top secret. Paine justified his disclosure, however, on the ground that England had been aware of the transaction for at least a year and that France and England, by January 1779, had already come to an open rupture.

The French Minister to the United States, Conrad Alexandre Gérard, concerned for the honor of his country, could not allow these facts to remain unchallenged. Gift or no gift, France could

not afford to admit that she had officially given aid to America before the alliance since the other powers of Europe would have
considered such an action dishonorable and inimical to international
peace and stability.

Gérard had to act fast. He immediately sought out Paine with
the object of persuading him to retract his assertion that the supplies
were a gift. He and Paine were on the best of terms since he had
previously offered Paine discreet financial inducements to write on
the advantages for America in the alliance with France. He now
renewed his offers of payment, and Paine grudgingly promised to
repair the damage in his next letter. When it appeared, 5 January
1779, however, Gérard discovered to his astonishment that Paine had
said absolutely nothing to modify the impression he had given
originally. Later he was told that Richard Henry Lee and Samuel
Adams had prevailed upon Paine not to alter his story. Gérard
thereupon indignantly protested to Congress that Paine's writings
had sullied the honor of France and that "all the supplies furnished
by M. de Beaumarchais . . . were furnished in the way of commerce." This declaration may have satisfied the monarchs of Europe, but to the American people it made the French King appear
as a mercenary dealer in surplus goods instead of a benevolent and
altruistic patron in the struggle for freedom. Furious and still un-
appeased, Gérard on the next day protested to Congress against
Paine's "indiscreet assertion" and asked that it "take suitable measures."

Paine, fully aware of Gérard's complaints, wrote to Congress, 6
January, offering to resign his post of Secretary if Congress so
wished. Instead of answering his letter, Congress called Paine before the bar of the House to ask merely whether he had written the
offending articles. He was not permitted to say anything but "Yes."
The next day he wrote to the Congress asking for an opportunity to
present his case. He could not, he said, in his "character as a freeman submit to be censured unheard."

For five days, 6-11 January, debate on Paine occupied nearly all
of the time of Congress. Paine's staunch friends spoke out earnestly
in his behalf, but the Deanites attacked him with every weapon at
their disposal, relevant or not. Gouverneur Morris, for example,
urged Paine's plebeian origins as sufficient reason for dismissal. He
argued that Congress had no wish to punish Paine, but merely to

turn out of office a man who "ought never to have been in it," a "mere adventurer *from England*, without fortune, without family or connexions, ignorant even of grammar."

Learning from his friend Henry Laurens that he was not to be given a hearing, he wrote again, 8 January, resigning his office as the only action consistent with his earlier declaration.

On 12 January, Congress disavowed Paine's publications on Deane and expressed the conviction that His Most Christian Majesty "did not preface the alliance with any supplies whatever sent to America," an open and obvious untruth. "Gérard . . . fairly bullied the Congress into the declaration of a falsehood"—so wrote a contemporary British observer.

Gérard protested, Congress lied, and Paine for telling the truth had his reputation besmirched. Paine might well have said as did Richard Henry Lee three months later: "A doctrine quite new in the history of politics is broached now, which is, that it becomes the dignity, and consists with the interests of Sovereign powers to consult foreign Courts, and less than that, foreign Ministers, who they first shall send to represent them abroad." Not only did Paine lose his public employment; he was accused of accepting payment from the Lees, and even received a beating from Matthew Slough, a merchant friendly to Deane.

According to John Joseph Henry, Slough in the company of Colonel Samuel J. Attlee and other drinking partners encountered Paine coming toward them on Market Street. "There comes 'Common Sense,' says Attlee to the company. 'Damn him,' says Slough, 'I shall common sense him.' As he approached the party, they took the wall. Mr. Slough tripped him, and threw him on his back into a gutter, which at that time, was very offensive and filthy."

Even before the resolution of Congress, Gérard began to worry lest Paine might turn his pen against France. The only remedy he saw was to take Paine unreservedly into his own employ. Through an intermediary he had offered Paine on the second or third of January the amount of his former salary if he would agree to publish nothing on political affairs or on the Congress without Gérard's approbation and to use his pen primarily to inspire favorable sentiments toward France and the alliance. Paine considered this "a very genteel and profitable offer,"—Richard Henry Lee had no hesitation in calling it a bribe—but as Paine's whole reputation was staked on proceeding with the Deane affair, he replied, "Any service I can render to either of the countries in alliance, or to both, I ever have done and shall readily do, and Mr. Gérard's *esteem* will be the only recompense I desire." On 8 January, Paine received an invitation to supper with an emissary from Gérard, and the offer was renewed "with considerable additions of advantage." The same invitation and offer were repeated twice more, and finally, on 14 January, Paine accepted an invitation from Gérard himself. According to Paine's account of their meeting, they both avoided as much as possible every subject which might bring up discussion of a financial recompense. Gérard once or twice alluded to the Deane publications and added that "he hoped no more would be said on the subject," but Paine immediately diverted the conversation to other channels.

Paine had already made up his mind not to accept payment from Gérard, for this would have ruined his reputation as an independent journalist, but he hoped to avoid giving any offense to Gérard by a direct refusal. At a convenient opportunity he rose to take his leave, whereupon Gérard remarked, "Mr. Paine, I have always had a great respect for you, and should be glad of some opportunity of showing you more solid marks of my friendship." Although some historians have assumed that Paine accepted Gérard's money, the formal declarations of both Paine and Gérard show that he did not.

Paine was, however, willing to make some concessions. In his next article, 16 January 1779, he affirmed that he "never *labored to prove* that the supplies *were* or *are* a present"; merely that "there was a disposition in the gentlemen of France to have made America a very handsome present." Yet, as he continued with the controversy, smarting under the injustice of the congressional resolution and the repeated barbs of the Deane faction, he abandoned all moderation by quoting compromising documents formerly in his possession, particularly a joint letter from Franklin, Deane and Lee, declaring "That for the money and military stores already given no remittance will ever be required." This new evidence of Paine's "inconsistency and obstinance" further alarmed Gérard, who told his colleague Holker, French Consul-General at Philadelphia, that he was "afraid to hire a man who writes in a frenzied manner against Congress," and charged that Paine had "defaulted on everything he promised." He would, however, "try to see him."

Meanwhile Robert Morris had replied in the newspapers to Paine's insinuations about the private business interests of government officials. He admitted frankly that while a delegate to Congress he had negotiated three private mercantile contracts with Deane, but argued that this implied no fraud or dishonesty and that he had never relinquished his right of forming mercantile connections.

Philadelphia, at this time, was suffering an acute shortage of food and clothing, and since imports of all kinds were vitally needed, prices rose and profiteering became easy. Paine continued to keep a watchful eye on Morris, particularly in his relations with Holker, who as Consul-General acted as purchasing agent for the French marine. Largely as a result of Paine's surveillance, both Holker and Morris came under the scrutiny of citizens' committees. Gérard in reporting these developments to Vergennes, charged that Paine, the "instrument of [Samuel] Adams and [R. H.] Lee, authors of popular committees, had concocted the whole conspiracy." Paine's design, Gérard felt, was to destroy the patricians, particularly Morris, the most popular among them.

Paine's suspicions of Morris came into the open with the arrival in May of a vessel, the *Victorious*, which remained for an extended period under public guard. Because of this circumstance people began to say that it belonged to Silas Deane and was being detained by Congress until he could settle his accounts. When it was learned that Morris was handling the whole cargo, a general citizens' meeting was called on 25 May to investigate the matter as well as all charges of profiteering which had grown out of the Deane affair. Resolutions aimed specifically at Deane and Morris were drawn up, and Paine was appointed to serve on a committee of investigation.

Morris replied to the committee that he had made no personal attempts to procure the cargo of the *Victorious*, but that a Baltimore citizen named Sollikoff, who had an option on the cargo, had offered to put it under his management and to give him a commission if he would provide an outward cargo for the vessel. Morris had accepted the offer, but insisted that the French merchants sell their goods at a reasonable price.

In the meantime, another connection between Morris and French commercial interests came under suspicion. It was generally known that Morris was serving as middleman for Holker in his capacity of purchasing agent for the French royal marine. A citizen of Lancaster County reported to the citizens' committee that Morris through Matthew Slough had contracted for flour at a rate far higher than the one set at the 25 May meeting. Morris was requested to lay before the committee the agreements between him and Holker, as well as an account of the quantities of flour contracted for, and of the conveyances and storing places used. Morris replied to the committee, 18 June, that Holker deemed it improper for him to divulge this information since it concerned activities of servants of the King of France. On his own account as a private citizen, however, Morris stated that Slough's orders were dated prior to the citizens' meeting, that he had been ordered not to exceed prices given by the continental army, and that he had been instructed to hire the cheapest teams available, public or private.

On 2 July, Morris received another letter from the committee informing him that it had resolved to detain a quantity of flour purchased at an excessive price by Jonathan Rumford in Delaware under the direction of Morris and Holker. In a tone of restrained indignation, Holker wrote to the committee on the same day stating that French royal agents could not give an accounting to any body except the Congress. On behalf of Morris he added the terse statement: "I am alone accountable for the purchase of the flour, he having only acted in consequence of my express orders and direction." While Paine cannot be considered the sole investigator of proceedings against the monopolizers, he took as active a part as anyone else and, as usual, took charge of newspaper propaganda.

On 21 July, two committees presented reports—one on the cargo of the *Victorious;* the other on Rumford, Holker and the flour. The first committee grudgingly admitted that Morris's account was just, but refused a complete exculpation. Their conclusion: "tho' as a merchant he may be strictly within the rules, yet when he considers the many public and honorary stations he has filled and the times he lives in, he must feel himself somewhat out of character." The other committee reported suspicions that the flour purchased by Holker may not have been intended solely for the fleet of D'Estaing, but in part for private trade. It explained that the citizens of Wilmington, sharing their devotion to fair practices, had promised to observe the minimum prices established in Philadelphia. Learning that Rumford had given amounts well in excess, the Wilmington citizens had impounded 182 barrels of flour purchased for Holker and sent it to the citizens' committee of Philadelphia. The latter wrote to Holker agreeing to deliver him 150 barrels at the legal price if he would explain the circumstances of his transactions and take his oath that all of the flour was intended for D'Estaing.

Holker immediately complained to his superior Gérard, who wrote a strong letter to the President of the State of Pennsylvania, 24 July, and another one two days later to Congress. Gérard stated that he approved and confirmed Holker's conduct and that all the orders placed by Holker had been under his own direction. He charged furthermore that the committee was hindering French officers in the pursuance of their duties by publicly imputing to them crimes and errors and calling in question their titles and powers.

On 26 July at another general town meeting it was resolved that Mr. Thomas Paine was considered "a friend to the American cause" and therefore those present would support and defend him so long as his conduct should continue to prove him to be a friend to the country. During the proceedings General Cadwalader several times attempted to address the body on behalf of the Morris faction. At length he proceeded to the College Yard with his supporters, who appointed Morris chairman and passed a number of resolutions; particularly that Holker had "acted in a most unexceptionable manner, altogether becoming his rank and office," and that Morris had "fully acquitted himself, in his late publication, of all the charges brought against him."

During the period of the Morris-Holker investigation, Paine served on another committee—of which he was also the prime mover—a committee designed to suggest means of checking inflation and raising public funds. The committee presented a plan, of which Paine and Owen Biddle were later revealed as joint proposers and projectors. Later, Paine, Biddle, David Rittenhouse and James Hutchinson prepared an address presenting the plan to the President and Council of Pennsylvania. Paine also suggested in the *Pennsylvania Packet*, 11 September, his own plan to encourage the importation of salt, West India produce and dry goods. He proposed that vessels owned by inhabitants of the state be registered and that inquiry be made to determine whether merchants had created an artificial scarcity.

On 2 August the citizens of Philadelphia elected a committee to regulate prices and prevent monopolizing. Timothy Matlack, leader of the popular ticket, fearful that Holker's defense of Morris might prevail against his slate of candidates, including Paine, had the idea of printing the arms of France on their handbills. Probably with tongue in cheek, he wrote Gérard an unctuous letter explaining the device, which "gave great satisfaction to all ranks of men, without offending a single individual." The popular ticket won 2,396 votes against 281 for the opposition.

Gérard, who had been waiting for an answer to his protests of 26 July against the behavior of the flour committee, received a letter, 3 August, from John Jay, President of Congress, transmitting from the minutes a statement approving Holker's measures to procure flour and disapproving "the several proceedings and publications" which Gérard had complained of. The Council of Pennsylvania, however, under the influence of its secretary Matlack, restored the flour, but gave Holker only half-hearted clearance, 9 August, and particularly recommended that he "employ none but persons of fair and unsuspected characters" if he should make any further purchases.

The middle-man Jonathan Rumford and his friends, making capital of the intervention of Gérard, sought to create apprehensions that France, resentful of the treatment of Holker, Morris, and himself, might break the alliance with America. This gave Paine occasion for the last mocking word in the press. He asked in which of the two groups the French Court would place most reliance— the committee, which had sought to ascertain the truth, or the commercial agents, "who, if any collusive profits were to arise therefrom, would be sharers therein." Paine marveled ironically that the Rumford faction had not discovered a plot "forming at the center of the earth, from which a mine is to be sprung to blow them up and the alliance with them." He compared Rumford's absurd supposition that the alliance could be broken up for his sake to Milton's innocent whim of placing "a number of little duck-winged angels" somewhere near the equator to shove the earth by main strength from a perpendicular position to that it now stands in, "a laughable way of effecting such a weighty affair."

The alignment of Americans on political issues tended to follow a pattern. Those who opposed Deane, opposed also the commercial activities of Holker and Morris. The supporters of Holker and Morris, on the other hand, uniformly vindicated Silas Deane. Richard Henry Lee even believed that "the Scene which opened upon the public on the 5th of December was plotted some months before" by Holker, Morris and Deane. It is not quite correct, however, to speak of radical against conservative or anti-French against pro-French alignments since allegiances sometimes became confused. Franklin, for example, was radical, a moderate Deanite, and pro-French. Paine also was in general pro-French, but in tackling another issue, that of fishing rights off the coast of Nova Scotia, he warned his readers that American and French interests are not always identical.

A writer named "Americanus" in three lengthy articles in the *Pennsylvania Gazette*, in June and July 1779, although not advocating abandoning of these rights, argued that they should not be included in the peace treaty with England. To do so, he argued would merely prolong the war. Both Paine and Richard Henry Lee believed that "Americanus" was Gouverneur Morris, although Morris disavowed the publications. Paine realized that French interests lay against maintaining American rights to the fisheries since extension of the war would drain the French treasury. In three articles in the *Gazette*, Paine denounced "Americanus" for advocating injurious peace terms. Ridiculing the "mighty bugg of peace" then circulating at "almost every tea table," he cautioned the Congress against treating Gérard "as if that gentleman was *our* minister instead of the minister of his Most Christian Majesty." They seemed to forget "that as France is the great ally of America, so America is the great ally of France."

While these matters were being debated, Paine's close friend, the artist Charles Willson Peale, drew him unintentionally into further contention with Deane. Peale, outraged by the gross abuse of Paine in an anonymous newspaper letter, thought it his duty to defend Paine since he knew from personal knowledge that Paine had "done more for our common cause than the world, who had only seen his publications could know." Paine had at one time mentioned to Peale that he had been offered $700 annually for his literary services, but did not indicate Gérard as the source of the offer or the nature of the propaganda desired. Peale came to the logical but erroneous conclusion that it was an attempt at bribery by the Deane forces, and so declared at a coffee-house on the morning of 26 July. Deane, knowing that for once he was on sound ground, sent Peale a letter demanding the names of the persons who had made the offer. This put Paine in a very awkward position. He could not reveal the truth without compromising Gérard, who would have un-doubtedly denied having made any propositions to Paine. Nor could Paine by remaining silent support a false accusation against Deane. He answered, therefore, that he had already given full particulars of the offer to Congress, that it was made both before and after his resignation, that it was urgently pressed upon him, and that it "amounted to more than twice" his salary to Congress, which would have made it $1,400. He declared that he would give further particulars to Congress if that body wanted them, but he could not reveal more to the public. The strange part of this decla-ration is the amount allegedly offered, for in his statement to Con-gress Paine had put it at exactly the figure of his salary, $700, and Gérard had reported it to Vergennes as $1,000. To carry the com-bat back into Deane's camp, Paine accused him of initiating the controversy in order to becloud the investigation of the committee for detaining the flour, and repeated his challenge for Deane to clear his own suspected name.

Eventually Paine had the final word and was able to say "I told you so" to all the Deanites.

Despite Paine's revelations Congress never took punitive action against Deane, but neither did it sift his accounts nor vindicate his record. Losing patience with Congress and American public opin-ion, Deane returned to France as a private citizen and later took up residence in England, where he lost faith in the American cause. Although he died virtually penniless, it is not so certain that this would have been his end had Paine not exposed his commercial ventures.

In 1781, when some pro-British letters of Deane to prominent Americans were intercepted and published, Gérard's successor, the Chevalier de la Luzerne, actually proposed to Vergennes that he pay Paine to renew his writing against Deane, an ironical vindi-cation for Paine. Even Gouverneur Morris by way of apology "hopped round upon one leg" and swore they had all been duped, himself among the rest. Paine reviewed the controversy in his *Crisis* No. 10, featuring the metaphor, "As he rose like a rocket, he would fall like a stick," a jibe which he was later to apply to Edmund Burke. "Every man, almost without exception," at the outset of the controversy, Paine recalled, had thought him wrong in opposing Deane. But in short time the public delusion perished, and when Deane departed for Europe he was the object of general suspicion. His letters from England brought about his final detection, and "his name, like that of Arnold, ought . . . to be forgotten among us."

So ended the episode of Silas Deane—an episode which terminated in Paine's complete vindication, but which had momentarily exposed him to the glare of unfavorable publicity and created bitter animosities against him. Some of these endured long after the events which inspired them. Although he himself soon became completely reconciled with Robert Morris and patched up his differences with Gouverneur Morris, neither the latter nor John Jay really overcame his antagonism to Paine, which was to have repercussions upon Paine's political career in France.

VI

State Clerk and Diplomatic Agent

After Paine lost his situation as Secretary of the Committee for Foreign Affairs, he had no income of any kind. To avoid running into debt he hired himself for almost a year as a common clerk to Owen Biddle at a clerk's customary wages. He may have been paid at the ordinary rate, but he was indeed an uncommon clerk, for, as we have seen, he once collaborated with his employer in framing an address to the state concerning economic policy. Paine resented his poverty as well as the neglect of Congress and the state of Pennsylvania. "I think I have a right to ride a horse of my own," he wrote to Henry Laurens, 14 September 1779, "but I cannot now even afford to hire one, which is a situation I never was in before."

At first he regarded literature as the only solution to his financial difficulties. He proposed either publishing an edition of *Common Sense* and his other pieces by subscription or compiling a history of the Revolution. The latter scheme he had projected ever since October 1775, when Franklin had given him the notion. Paine outlined these projects to Laurens in detail, and also asked Gérard for assistance on the historical venture when the latter was about to return to France. In his letter, 20 September 1779, now in French archives, Paine also indicated that he planned a trip to France to visit Franklin at the most convenient opportunity, the only extant record of this early desire to see France.

A week later Paine wrote to the Executive Council of Pennsylvania suggesting that he be given a kind of literary pension as compensation for his past services. Observing that the last four years had produced "no other signature universally known, and read here and abroad" except that of "Common Sense," he pointed out that were he forced to give up his writing it would "not be easy to establish a new signature" which would "collect and keep the sentiments of the country together should any future emergency arise."

Reed, President of the Council, sought Gérard's advice and sanction before even considering the request. Gérard told him that Paine had in the past accepted payment to write in the public interest, but had not lived up to his agreement. He damned Paine's prospects with Reed by the faint recommendation, "if you believe you are able to guide his pen for public welfare and utility, which perhaps will not be difficult for your zeal, your talent and your superior enlightenment, I shall be the first to applaud the success of an attempt in which I have failed."

While Paine was thus trying to arrange his private financial affairs, the hungry citizens whom he and other radicals had been stirring up against profiteering merchants broke out into a bloody riot in the streets of Philadelphia. Paine later described the unfortunate affair with dramatic intensity. "It was the fourth of October. The anniversary of the action at German town. A day, distinguished by perplexities and consigned to misfortune." A crowd spontaneously assembled on the Commons, and individuals began exclaiming against Tories, profiteers, and monopolists. For some reason which Paine was unable to fathom, the mob directed its rage against a conservative legal theorist, James Wilson, who had grown unpopular by defending a number of acknowledged Tories in the courts.

Even more mysterious to Paine, a group of Wilson's friends had been brought together in his house, fully armed and prepared to fight the popular forces. Paine felt sure that no one of them "had the least reason to be apprehensive of his own safety. They must, in general, have been induced by misrepresentation tho' some . . . were led by a generous intention of preventing mischief; and pity it is that their advice was not taken." Although critical of Wilson and his henchmen, Paine did not condone the mob's violence. Despite Wilson's unpopularity, "the difference is exceedingly great," he observed, "between not being in favor and being considered as an enemy."

The group barricaded in the house fired on the attacking mob

—and a real battle broke out. Several of the invaders were killed and wounded, and the besieged conservatives would have been literally torn to pieces by the infuriated mob had it not been for the timely arrival of Joseph Reed leading the Philadelphia Light Horse. The crowd immediately dispersed.

Paine felt that the Wilson forces shared responsibility for the tragedy. "That he who never armed when the country was in danger, should arm his house to provoke danger, and draw to it a number of Gentlemen at the hazard of their lives, when a timely application to the Civil Power might have prevented every thing, was at once both unconstitutional and unfriendly."

Paine published his description of the turmoil lest the British get comfort from thinking that the people of Philadelphia were divided. He wrote in the *Pennsylvania Packet*, 16 October, that "when the parties in and out of the house were known, and became known to each other, the animosity began to subside; and the whole exclusive of the imprudence, explained itself into a tragedy of errors." Characteristically Paine drew optimistic conclusions. "It generally happens that distress is the forerunner of benevolence. . . ." A subscription had been set on foot for the families of those killed or wounded, and, for Paine, this proved that "the affair . . . was not the quarrel of enemies or of parties, but the unfortunate blunder of friends."

At length, Paine's trust in the personal loyalty and benevolence of his fellow citizens was justified. The Assembly came to his assistance and named him Clerk on 2 November 1779. On the next day, the one on which he was sworn in, a committee was appointed to draw up a bill for the gradual abolition of slavery, and Paine is usually considered to be the author of its eloquent preamble although no proof for this tradition exists. The Act for the Incorporation of the American Philosophical Society, February 1780, has also been attributed to Paine since it bears his name as Clerk of the Assembly, but there is likewise no proof that he had anything to do with composing the document.

Paine found in his clerkship great relief from the "idleness, uneasiness and hopeless thinking" which had "got so much the upper hand" during the preceding three or four months. The job did not amount to much, he wrote to Laurens, but was "something like business." Charles Willson Peale reported that Paine gave great satisfaction as Clerk and expressed a wish that the House, which owed its existence in part to Paine's exertions in support of the constitution, would do something further for him.

Enjoying the prestige of his clerkship, Paine had less need to express himself in public forums. Although closely following the ups and downs of the American troops, he remained silent until 26 February 1780, when he again addressed the people of England in his *Crisis* No. 8. Here he repeated his threat of an invasion of the British Isles—made more real by a recent naval victory of John Paul Jones off the coast of Scotland—and pointed out that the interest of the other nations of Europe lay in an American victory. The last five years had shown that America could not be conquered. Why then, Paine asked, should England persist in a useless war, "pursuing self-destruction with inflexible passion."

The most important passage of the work is a denunciation of nationalistic, insular limitations, in a sense a repudiation of the isolationism of *Common Sense*. "There is something in the extent of countries," he argued, "which, . . . insensibly communicates extension of the mind. The soul of an islander, in its native state, seems bounded by the foggy confines of the water's edge; . . . while those who are inhabitants of a continent, by casting their eye over a larger field, take in likewise a larger intellectual circuit, and thus approaching nearer to an acquaintance with the universe, their atmosphere of thought is extended, and their liberality fills a wider space."

Despite Paine's continued optimism, the American cause suffered severe setbacks in 1779-1780, when the British strategy decreed a shift from the North to the South. By December 1779 all of Georgia had come under British domination, and on 12 May 1780 General Lincoln surrendered Charleston, South Carolina, together with his army of over five thousand men, the most disastrous defeat of the entire Revolution.

A few days before this calamity, the Assembly had received a gloomy letter from Washington, which Paine as Clerk read to the House behind closed doors. The General, despite his confidence in the loyalty of the army to the common cause, feared that destitution and physical distress among the soldiers had risen to such a degree that the imminent result would be wholesale desertion and defeat. When the letter was read, Paine observed a despairing silence in the House. One member even arose to assert that it was "vain to contend the matter any longer. We may as well give up at first as at last."

In view of the depreciation of the currency, the slow collection of taxes, and the total absence of government credit, Paine realized that the only resource "was private credit, and the voluntary aid of individuals." He forthwith drew out the salary due to him as Clerk, wrote a letter to Blair M'Clenaghan, a wealthy merchant, proposing a voluntary subscription among his friends, and enclosed $500 (half of his entire funds) as his own contribution. M'Clenaghan communicated Paine's scheme to Robert Morris and others. They not only subscribed immediately to this appeal, 8 June, intended as a donation to be given in bounties to promote the recruiting service, but nine days later opened a permanent security-subscription which eventually developed into the Bank of North America and which supplied the army throughout the rest of the war. Paine at the same time wrote to Reed presenting other recruiting and provisioning schemes.

Paine attempted to bolster morale by describing these developments in *Crisis* No. 9 (10 June). He reported the loss of Charleston as a disguised blessing which would rouse the Americans from their "state of dangerous relaxation." He argued that Charleston, important as it was as a port, was still a secondary object in a continental war. Neither conquest of towns nor capture of garrisons, he reassured his readers, could reduce a country as extensive as America. Paine reported as an encouraging sign the organization of the subscription committee, proof that the cause of America stood "on the broad foundation of property and popularity." Once again Paine saw a solidarity of interest joining the wealthy class and the people.

During the summer of 1780 Paine had little to occupy his time. Most of the fighting was far away in the Carolinas, and the Pennsylvania Assembly was not in session. On 4 July Paine was honored at the commencement exercises of the University of Pennsylvania, where he and eight others, including seven clergymen, received the degree of M.A.

Impatient with inactivity and eager to use his abilities in a more spectacular fashion than had been recently possible, Paine proposed to Reed, 9 September, that Congress send him on a secret mission to England, where he would use his pen to foster sentiments of peace and recognition of American independence. He proposed to adopt the "cover of an Englishman who had made the tour of America *incognito*." In this way he could spread his ideas through the channel of the press, which he had always "considered the tongue of the world, and that which governs the sentiments of mankind more than anything else." To defray expenses, Paine suggested that Reed drop a delegate to Congress at the next election and apply the pay thus saved to the one-man expedition.

Partly as a blind to conceal his absence from public affairs, Paine revived his perennial project of writing the history of the Revolution and submitted his resignation as Clerk of the Assembly. Nathaniel Greene, however, to whom Paine later mentioned the project, expressed grave apprehension, and Paine himself realized that he might be taken by the British in retaliation for Major André, captured by the Americans and executed as a spy. He, therefore, reluctantly abandoned his scheme.

In October he published a "Crisis Extraordinary" on the unpopular subject of taxation—attempting to persuade the American taxpayer that it was to his interest to pay higher assessments. His reasoning was based on consideration of what the taxpayer's lot would be in the event of a British victory. England's purpose in the war, he charged, was to establish the same taxes in America as were paid in England, "eleven times heavier" than in America for the current year.

During this time Paine had made a number of attempts to regain amicable relations with the French embassy. La Luzerne, who had replaced Gérard, wrote to Vergennes, 16 December 1780, that Paine as a consequence of the Deane affair found himself "continually at loose ends." La Luzerne had hitherto kept Paine at a distance, but in view of the latter's circumspect conduct in recent months, wondered whether he should not make use of Paine's talents by sponsoring either his periodical articles or his history of the Revolution. The latter, he believed, "written while the war was still in progress and composed under our eyes and according to our directions, would perpetuate among the Americans the memory of that which they had endured, would dispose them in the future to be on guard against their former master, and would forestall in part the inconvenience which could result from the peace."

At this time Paine had still written nothing which could be classified as formal history. All his publications had been contemporary reporting. In the last week of the year, however, he published a work of historical scholarship based on painstaking research into rare manuscripts and printed sources. This was an examination of the claims of Virginia to the vacant western territory, which Paine published under the title *Public Good*. The work systematically scrutinizes charters and other sixteenth century English documents, which Paine in Philadelphia would have had no occasion or opportunity to consult at first hand. This curious circumstance has never been questioned or the obvious difference between this work of pure history and Paine's other pieces dealing with contemporary events commented on. The explanation is that Paine did none of the historical research himself. His materials came to him from other hands, and his own part in the work was limited exclusively to composition.

Paine had first mentioned the subject of the vacant "back lands" in *Common Sense*, where he had advocated selling them as a means of sinking the debt. Similar arguments had been used in Congress, but the state of Virginia claimed exclusive right to the largest share and set up a land office to sell them. Paine, struck with the magnitude of the wrong thus done to the other states, wished to enter the lists as their champion, but he could not do so because he lacked the necessary documentation to support his position. Moreover, realizing the vital need of national solidarity, he felt reluctant to start a controversy with any state in the union. In addition, he was on terms of intimacy and friendship with many Virginians. This reluctance had even led him to decline a proposal from members of the commission for settling the boundary line between Pennsylvania and Virginia. He declared that he would not interfere between two states.

As early as the summer of 1779, Major Trent and other gentlemen of the Indiana Company had represented to Paine the injuries they were likely to suffer by the conduct of Virginia in wresting from them a tract of land which had been ceded to them by the Indians. They hoped to interest Paine in writing on their behalf, but he replied tersely and decisively to the company,

"I never had nor ever would have any thing to do in private affairs." Late in 1780 Colonel George Morgan and others of the Indiana Company came to him with a number of historical documents which they said would be useful to the public regardless of their bearing on the company's status. Here were the proofs Paine had long wished for, papers which showed that the Virginia claims had no foundation in either right or reason. In a second interview Paine told the company representatives that he could use these papers for the public interest but that he would "on no account mix the matter with any thing relative to the private affairs of the company." He wrote his pamphlet, therefore, as though there had been no such body in existence as the Indiana Company. As soon as the pamphlet was published, Paine returned the documents to the company, which unanimously ordered a deed to be made out to him for a voter's share, which amounted to twelve thousand acres of land. At the time this was of so little importance to him that he neglected to apply for the deed. When he did so two years later, he brought upon himself the charge of being a hireling of the Indiana Company. Paine may also have accepted cash as well as land, for he wrote to John Laurens, 4 October 1781, "I expect Col. Morgan in town on Saturday, who has some money of mine in his hands."

As might be expected, the citizens of Virginia were highly incensed by Paine's pamphlet and later held it against him when it became question of reimbursing him for his services in support of the Revolution. La Luzerne, however, praised the solidity of its arguments and sent Vergennes a copy, remarking significantly, that some of its principles were the same as those which the Court of Madrid could invoke if it wished to enter into the discussion.

Paine at this time was about to set up a newspaper of his own, having arranged to purchase twenty reams of paper. But his "Crisis Extraordinary" and a letter to Vergennes had persuaded several members of Congress that it was possible to raise more money for carrying on the war and that part of it could be procured from France. Colonel John Laurens, son of the former President of Congress, was thereupon appointed Envoy Extraordinary, and he asked Paine to go with him as secretary. He told Paine that "he was not enough acquainted with political affairs, nor with the resources of the country, to undertake the mission; 'but,' said he, 'if you will go with me, I will accept it.'" John Witherspoon and other Congressmen opposed official rank for Paine, however, and the latter in order to avoid contention agreed to go merely as a companion, paying his own expenses. Major William Jackson was appointed Laurens's secretary. The English newspapers reported that because of Laurens's deficiencies in experience and abilities, Congress had put him under Paine's direction.

When he left, Paine was hardly at the peak of his popularity. Franklin's daughter, Sarah Bache, wrote to her father, 14 January 1781, "there never was a man less beloved in a place than Payne is in this, having at different times disputed with everybody. The most rational thing he could have done would have been to have died the instant he had finished his Common Sense, for he never again will have it in his power to leave the World with so much credit." Sarah Bache had previously exchanged words with Paine over the Deane affair, and since that time, she reported, he had "never even moved his hat to me." We must remember that Franklin's daughter had personal reasons to take Deane's side. Before the scandal had broken out in America, Arthur Lee had leveled charges jointly against Franklin and Deane in France. To the Franklins, therefore, the Lees and all their supporters were anathema.

Paine and Laurens sailed on the frigate *Alliance*, 11 February 1781. Because of the risk from British vessels, the captain, John Barry, had difficulty in rounding up a ship's company, and many British prisoners had to be pressed into service. Before sailing the crew had engaged in a brawl on Long Wharf with the crews of two French frigates. During the crossing troubles continued. The ship came so close to an iceberg that "the general cry was that she had struck, and was either a ground or on a rock." The sea "appeared a tumultuous assemblage of floating rocks . . . against which there was no defense." After an entire night surrounded by ice, the passengers once more felt water round the sides of the ship. Later in the voyage they pursued a large ship which seemed to be under the command of a smaller one. The latter turned out to be a Scottish cutter, which, "contrary to every principle of justice, honor, or ability," had captured the larger vessel, a Venetian merchantman completely free of contraband. The Scots had put the Venetian crew in irons and were convoying the vessel to Glasgow. The captain and officers of the *Alliance*, with the

warm approval of Paine and Laurens, decided "that the captiva-
tion by the cutter was contrary to the rights of neutral nations
and could be beheld in no other light than an act of Piracy,"
and they restored the merchantman to its original crew. This circumstance led Paine to speculate on the concept of the freedom
of the seas, a principle which two decades later he was to propose
for universal adoption in a pamphlet *Compact Maritime*.

These external events made the voyage exciting, and Paine created some violence of his own. According to a contemporary
manuscript biography of Captain John Barry, Paine during the
voyage had a duel with a French officer.

The *Alliance* landed at Lorient on 9 March, where the com-
mandant of the port gave Paine high compliments on the great
success and spirit of his publications. Paine found himself no
stranger in France, where people knew him almost as generally as
he was known in America. On the way from Lorient to Nantes,
Paine rode in the company of Jonathan Williams, commercial agent
for America and Benjamin Franklin's grandnephew. Writing to
Franklin about the encounter, 18 April, Williams confided that
Paine had taken up the cause of the Lees against Deane and that
Paine regretted Franklin's attachment to Deane. "We agree exceedingly well together, and are growing intimate," Williams wrote.
"I confess I like him as a companion because he is pleasant as well
as a sensible man, and I heartily wish that Party had not so good
an assistant," a reference to Paine's anti-Deane stand.

A citizen of Philadelphia, Elkanah Watson, who happened to
be at Nantes, published in his memoirs a colorful account of Paine's
arrival. "He was coarse and uncouth in his manners, loathsome in
his appearance, and a disgusting egotist, rejoicing most in talking
of himself, and reading the effusions of his own mind. . . . On his
arrival being announced, the Mayor, and some of the most distinguished citizens of Nantes, called upon him to render their
homage of respect. I often officiated as interpreter although hum-
bled and mortified at his filthy appearance, and awkward and un-
seemly address. Besides, as he had been roasted alive on his arrival
at L'Orient, for the **** and well basted with brimstone, he was
absolutely offensive, and perfumed the whole apartment." The
reader can hardly escape the conclusion from these asterisks that
Paine was suffering from venereal disease, but the manuscript ver-

sion of Watson's journal shows that such a conclusion is false. Here Watson declares that Paine had been "roasted alive on his arrival at l'Orient for the *scotch fiddle*," which is nothing but the itch! Because of his offensive odor, Paine "was soon rid of his respectable visitors, who left the room with marks of astonishment and disgust." Watson took the liberty, on Paine's asking for the loan of a clean shirt, "of speaking to him frankly of his dirty appearance and brimstone odor, and prevailed upon him to stew for an hour, in a hot bath." Paine would hear nothing of this until Watson promised him a file of late English papers to read in the bath. Watson instructed the valet in French, which Paine did not understand, gradually to increase the heat of the water until Monsieur should be "*bien bouilli.*" Paine "became so much absorbed in his reading that he was nearly par-boiled before leaving the bath."

Very little can be discovered about Paine's activities during this brief visit to France apart from a few references by members of Benjamin Franklin's entourage in Paris.

Laurens apparently dispatched the business of his embassy with address and alacrity. To gain the attention of Louis XVI he defied protocol and addressed him with youthful ingenuousness at a social function. It is probable, however, that without Franklin's softening influence, Laurens's direct methods would have offended the French Court. With Franklin's aid, he obtained six million livres as a present and ten millions as a loan. Although Paine, a warm admirer of Franklin, attributed the entire transaction to the efforts of Laurens alone, contemporary records show that Franklin arranged the transfer of substantial sums both before and after the arrival of Laurens.

Paine had practically no social life in Paris. During his entire stay he was nowhere received but in Franklin's house and Laurens's hotel although he made the acquaintance of a number of Americans.

After Laurens's mission was completed, Paine considered remaining in Europe, feeling that he could render more service to America by justifying her cause and explaining her affairs in Europe than by returning to the west. Laurens was strongly attached to his companion, however, and carried his importunities for Paine to return with him to such a height that the latter acquiesced. They sailed from Brest on the French frigate *Resolve*, 1 June, and arrived at Boston, 25 August, bringing with them two and a half million livres in silver, and convoying a ship and a brig laden with supplies. It took sixteen ox teams to transport the money to the National Bank of Philadelphia.

Paine had paid the entire expense of his trip out of his own pocket and was penniless on his return. When he parted company with Laurens, who remained at Providence, Rhode Island, the latter divided his funds with Paine, making a purse of about six guineas for each. Out of it Paine had to pay his expenses and those of a servant Laurens left with him and two horses for three hundred more miles. At Bordentown he was obliged to borrow a dollar to cross the ferry.

Paine now found himself financially worse off than ever. He had given up his clerkship and had spent all his savings. Also he had been frustrated in his publication plans in both America and Europe. During his absence, his enemies had circulated rumors that he had abandoned the republic and returned to England. Even though his friends castigated the shameful authors of these rumors, Paine's morale fell to a low ebb.

Just at this moment, 18 September 1871, Robert Morris, now superintendent of finance for the Congress, sent for him and "proposed that for the Service of the Country he should write and publish such Pieces respecting the propriety, Necessity and Utility of Taxation as might be likely to promote the Public Service of America, as the Support of the War does and ultimately must rest on the Taxes to be raised in the United States." This opportune recognition of Paine's talents probably revived his drooping spirits. Two days later he wrote to Morris suggesting that one quarter of the year's rents in Philadelphia be applied "to defray the expense of a body of Men sufficient to prevent the Enemy from destroying it" —the money to be collected by empowering tenants to pay directly into the treasury rather than to their landlords. Morris mentioned Paine's drastic tax scheme the next day at a conference of city fathers, but the measure was never adopted.

When Morris had solicited Paine's literary services, he apparently had not said anything about compensation. Paine wrote to Washington, therefore, to inform him of his impecunious condition (30 November). Since the circumstances of the country were now "rising into prosperity," he wrote, he must either share in improved conditions or return to Europe and live by his literary fame in France or Holland. He also made renewed overtures toward La Luzerne, who considered hiring him to write once more against Deane, whose pro-British letters from abroad were then being published.

On 24 January 1782 a deputation of army officers asked Paine to draw up for them a petition to Washington respecting their pay. Paine tried to convince them that this was an inopportune time to press for payments of any kind. The condition of the Treasury was inadequate, but improving, and any "demands just now might rather injure than promote their interest." Much as he wished to be of service to his former comrades in arms, Paine asked to be excused. He immediately sent Morris full particulars of this interview, and Morris once more asked him to call. According to Morris's diary (26 January 1782), Paine

observed that his Services to the Public had rather been neglected. I told him I could wish his pen to be wielded in aid of such measures as I might be able to Convince him were clearly Calculated for the Services of the United States; that I had no views or plans but what were meant for the Public Good, and that I should ask no man's assistance on any other ground; that it was true I had nothing in my power at present to offer as a Compensation for his Services, but that Something might turn up, and that I should have him in my mind.

Paine on 7 February showed to Morris a memorial of the army officers to be presented to their various states. Morris proposed some changes "tending to make it rather more Continental," which Paine approved and promised to adopt.

Since Washington had already twice expressed to Morris the wish that some provision could be made for Paine, Morris conceived the plan of engaging him "to write in the public newspapers in support of the measures of Congress and their ministers." Gouverneur Morris was "clearly of the same opinion." After sounding out Paine and finding him well disposed, Robert Morris obtained the co-operation of Robert Livingston, Secretary of Foreign Affairs, who was to furnish information from his department for Paine's writing.

On 10 February 1782, Morris, Livingston and Washington signed an agreement to allow Paine $800 a year, payable quarterly. For this, he was to urge in the newspapers that the legislatures of the several states allot sufficient taxes to the national government and that they extend the powers of Congress. Also he was to prepare the minds of the people for these developments and to comment on military transactions. The agreement was to be kept absolutely secret since "a salary publicly and avowedly given for the above purpose would injure the effect of Mr. Paine's publication, and subject him to injurious personal reflections."

Even today one who takes a sinister view of human character might conclude that Paine had used the army officers as a threat to cause trouble and that Morris had bought him off. Still a consideration of the military and financial conditions of the times will lead to the conclusion that all parties to the agreement acted in good faith. Morris specifically stated in his record of the transaction:

We wish to bring into the field an army equal to the object for which we are at war. We wish to feed, clothe, move, and pay that army as they ought to be done, but we wish also to effect these on such terms as may be least burdensome to the people, at the same time that the operations shall be every way effective.

Paine was not completely satisfied with the financial terms of his compact, but wrote to Morris, 20 February, asking either that he be compensated for his trip to France or that his salary might begin from the time of his returning to America. He had no difficulty in accepting Morris's proposal, he said, because he realized that it was made not only out of friendship, but also out of justice to him.

Pursuant to his agreement Paine wrote *Crisis* No. 10, March 1782. Although setting out with lively ridicule of a speech of George III, he devoted his serious attention to the nature of the American union and the means of continuing the war. After repeating his political philosophy that the war was a "war of the people in their own behalf," not the war of Congress, the assemblies or any government whatsoever, he stressed that self-interest required each section of the country to bear a just and proportionate share of the expenses. He exposed the error of blending "the affairs of each state, especially in money matters, with those of the United States." The expenses of individual states for carrying on domestic government were one thing, he argued; the expenses of the United States for carrying on the war were another. In this view he portrayed taxes as insurance money, that which is paid out to guarantee safety; in strict policy, the best money which could be laid out.

Despite his arrangement with Morris and Livingston, Paine continued to press both Washington and Morris for official recognition of his services. A piece in the *Freeman's Journal*, 6 March, commented on the "ungrateful treatment" he had received and marveled that he had not "appealed to the justice and generosity of America in favour of his injured character and lessened income." Possibly Paine himself had the item inserted. He admitted inserting a similar notice in the *Pennsylvania Journal*, 27 March, announcing the gift of twelve thousand acres of land from the Indiana Company as well as "very generous offers of friendship" from the gentlemen of South Carolina "for his public services." The latter announcement instead of bringing about further financial assistance, however, provoked the charge that Paine had written *Public Good* as a tool of the Indiana Company to gain public land for its use.

Paine denied the charge by explaining the circumstances of his writing the pamphlet. He had asked the newspapers to announce the gift of the Indiana Company that the company might be honored for doing that which "those who were infinitely more obliged and indebted to me have neglected to do. From me the states have received the unremitted service of seven years, and to them I have not been the expense of a private soldier." In justice to the state of Pennsylvania, Paine acknowledged a gesture of the Speaker of the House, F. A. Muhlenberg. When it appeared that the office of Register of Wills would become vacant, Muhlenberg had proposed that Paine apply, but Paine had declined since the duties of the office would have kept him from his public writing. He concluded with the comprehensive but by no means literally exact statement: "I never sought place, office, nor reward, since I have been in America."

Paine wrote to Washington and Robert Morris, 17 March 1782, inviting them to spend part of an evening at his apartment eating "a few oysters or a crust of bread and cheese" and discussing public policy. The ideas which Paine wished to broach, he later embodied in a letter in the *Pennsylvania Gazette*, 3 April. Continuing in the spirit of his *Crisis* No. 10, Paine here attempted to arouse willingness in his readers to pay increased taxes and to convince them that the nation desperately needed system and method in its finances. This letter, which has never been republished, is remarkable for the vigor of its style and the optimism of its tone. In reviewing the progress and development of domestic circumstances, Paine found the national prosperity as extraordinary as the Revolution itself. "We began with paper, and we end with gold and silver. We set out with parties, and we are approaching to unity. The strength, the property, and even the fashion of the country, are confederated in her support. Like robust and healthy youth, she hath shook off the agues of the winter, and steps forward with constitutional bloom and vigour. By suffering distresses, she hath learned both to bear and to prevent them; and the experience of every day, whether drawn from good fortune or from bad, whether from wisdom or mistake, hath added something to her cause, and much to her judgment." Strangely enough, he seemed to contradict the fundamental principle of *Common Sense* in arguing that "Government and the people do not in America constitute distinct bodies. They are one, and their interest the same. Members of Congress, members of Assembly, or Council, or by any other name they may be called, are only a selected part of the people. They are the representatives of majesty, but not majesty itself. That dignity exists inherently in the universal multitude, and, though it may be delegated, cannot be alienated. Their estates and property are subject to the same taxation with those they represent, and there is nothing they can do, that will not equally affect themselves as well as others." Actually this is only an apparent contradiction. Paine still meant that government and society are separate entities, but in America—and in America alone —the government is drawn directly from the ranks of all the people.

It appears that Paine wrote this appeal as well as all his other public statements at this time with the approval of the French Ministry. Barbé de Marbois, chargé d'affaires during the month of April 1782, reported to Vergennes that Paine had published nothing since his return from France without previously consulting La Luzerne. Barbé de Marbois had sounded Paine out on the progress of his history of the Revolution, trying to get a tentative date for the publication of the first volume, but Paine's answers had been ambiguous and evasive. Marbois concluded that Paine had so little liking for continued and uniform labor that there was little hope of his ever completing the task. He highly praised Paine's article on taxation, however, because of the importance of persuading the people to tax themselves. This would give creditors of the nation greater confidence in being paid and attach them even more firmly to the Revolution. He reported that Paine's views on taxation had great effect in Pennsylvania and New England, but other states, particularly New Jersey and Virginia, were intractable.

It would seem from a report of La Luzerne to Vergennes, 14 May, that the French paid Paine for his *Crisis* No. 11, published 11 May, which repudiated the British hope that America might be induced to make peace apart from her allies France and Spain. "The only manoeuvre which I have allowed myself," wrote La Luzerne, "has been to engage Paine to publish an article . . . which has been all the more favorably received because the writer abandoned his pen to the torrent of public opinion. He has merely given form to the reasoning of the multitude and presented them with firmer foundations by confiding certain particulars hitherto undisclosed. . . . I put off for a long time making use of the liberty you accorded me in regard to the favors to be accorded this writer, but it seemed to me appropriate to nourish his patriotism, which can become more useful from day to day."

It was Livingston who next persuaded Paine to take up his pen. He asked Paine to intervene in the case of Captain Asgill, one of the most moving episodes of the Revolution. Captain Huddy of the Jersey militia had been taken prisoner by the British and hanged without warrant or justification. General Clinton then demanded that the British officer in charge be delivered up as a murderer and that in case of refusal a British officer already in American hands should suffer in his place. The demand was refused, and Captain Asgill of the Guards was selected by casting lots, "a martyr to the general wickedness of the cause he engaged in." Livingston, worried lest public opinion abroad be turned against America, asked Paine to state the distressing affair in its true light. This Paine did in a "Supernumerary Crisis" (published 1 June) addressed to Sir Guy Carleton, placing upon him full responsibility for the plight of Asgill. "Give up the murderer, and save your officer" was the essence of his plea. Some time later, 7 September, Paine wrote privately to Washington urging that he spare Asgill's life. When Marie Antoinette, through Vergennes, wrote to the same purpose, Asgill was released.

During most of the spring and summer of 1782, Paine was working on his projected history of the Revolution. In November of the previous year he had borrowed from Robert Morris an internationally-famous work, *A Philosophical . . . History of the . . . Indies* (English translation, 1776) by the abbé Raynal, the last volume of which carried the title, *The Revolution of America* (1781). No doubt Paine originally considered Raynal's history as merely one of a number of reference works, but he soon conceived the plan of writing a refutation, to defend America from some of the abbé's errors and to acquire a European literary reputation for himself. It was an easy matter to apply the general historical materials in his possession to a particular consideration of Raynal's philosophical study.

Paine was aroused first of all by Raynal's assertion that there existed no moral foundation for the Revolution, that the whole dispute concerned taxation by the mother country. Paine indignantly replied that the colonies had rebelled against the most unjust law that had ever existed, the Declaratory Act, which asserted the right of Parliament "to bind America in all cases whatsoever." He accused the British Ministry of deliberately provoking the conflict in order to conquer America completely and affirmed, directly contrary to Raynal, that the American Revolution was the first in the history of the world to be founded on a reform of principles. After justifying the financial system of the United States with the confident assertion that its paper money would henceforth be stable, Paine proceeded to examine Raynal's theory that the United States had rejected British peace propositions in 1778 because of the French alliance. In this section, which he knew would delight Vergennes and the French Ministry, he absolutely denied Raynal's hypothesis. According to Paine, the treaty of alliance had absolutely no bearing on the rejection of peace offers, for news of the alliance had not reached Congress until after the refusal. "The rejection, therefore, must, and ought to be attributed to the fixed, unvaried sentiments of America respecting the enemy she is at war with, and her determination to support her independence to the last public effort."

This subtle distinction had a profound diplomatic significance. Had Raynal's theory been generally received, it would have made France appear as singly responsible for American victory. This opinion Vergennes would not have wished to be accepted for at least two reasons: The French would be able to criticize him for treating the United States as the equal of France and to reproach him for not demanding greater concessions; the English, on the other hand, would show more zeal in pursuing the war against France if they considered France exclusively responsible for the loss of her American colonies. Paine's assertion that they would have continued the struggle even without French aid annulled this view. By presenting the United States as the ally rather than the beneficiary of France, Paine supported the reputation of the United States in Europe and indirectly vindicated the foreign policy of Vergennes.

Paine's examination of Raynal's philosophical reflections on the alliance between France and the United States had essentially the same effect. In this section, devoted to "the well enlightened field of philosophical reflection," Paine delivered himself without reserve to his growing spirit of idealism, to his concept of human progress and the victory of truth. According to Raynal, the motives of France—a monarchy giving aid to a republic—were neither pure nor disinterested, and a concern for human happiness had nothing to do with the alliance. Paine reprobated this cynical reflection. Developing a theory from the *Crisis* that the cycle of civilization is not yet complete, he saw in the development of commerce, science and letters "a greater fitness in mankind to extend and complete the civilization of nations with each other at this day, than there was to begin it with the unconnected individuals at first." The alliance, he affirmed, was "not formed for the mere purpose of a day, but on just and generous grounds, and with equal and mutual advantages; and the easy, affectionate manner in which the parties have since communicated has made it an alliance not of courts only, but of countries." Paine did not state explicitly, but he implied that the alliance with France was a step toward the realization of a universal society, the idealistic conception with which he concluded his work.

Paine had his refutation printed at his own expense under the title, *Letter to the abbé Raynal, on the Affairs of North America:*

in which the Mistakes in the abbé's Account of the Revolution of America are Corrected and Cleared up.

Since his design was to secure a European reputation, he made a present of one hundred copies to be sent to France. His hopes were realized. The *Letter* was almost immediately translated in four different French versions and enthusiastically reviewed. La Luzerne sent a copy to Vergennes, 27 August, with the comment: "I have deferred until today using the liberty you have given me of offering him a gratuity. The work enclosed has for object the refutation of the daring principles contained in the work published under the name of the abbé Raynal, to demonstrate the falsity of his assertions in regard to the causes and motives of the Alliance; I have bestowed 50 guineas upon Monsieur Payne and have exhorted him to use his pen on objects of the same nature. He continues to gather material for the history of the revolution, but his natural indolence does not permit me to believe that he will ever reach the conclusion of his task, which is moreover beyond his talents." From this communication we see that French aid had indeed become a personal matter with Paine.

During the last three months of 1783, La Luzerne made payments to Paine totaling 1,530 livres (about $300). This was probably Paine's recompense for writing his "Supernumerary Crisis" (9 December 1783), an attack on a British pamphlet designed to allure Americans to buy British goods and at the same time to persuade Parliament to prohibit Americans from trading with the West Indies. La Luzerne had directed Paine's attention to the British pamphlet because it sought to turn American commerce away from France to England. He had then engaged Paine to counteract the false impressions created by the British writer and furnished him with materials for so doing. The French diplomat reported to Vergennes, 8 November, that the American newspapers still breathed hate and passion, but he promised that he would see to it that Paine's piece would be marked for its moderation and decency. And these are exactly the qualities which stand out. Paine urged that the American states band together in a strong union for commercial reasons, if for no other, and that America adopt retaliatory measures if Britain should maintain exclusive trade practices. He concluded with a burst of patriotism: "When we view a flag, which to the eye is beautiful, and to contemplate its rise and origin inspires a sensation of sublime delight, our national honor must unite with our interest to prevent injury to the one, or insult to the other."

He sent a copy of the *Letter* to the abbé Raynal in the fall of the year to the Earl of Shelburne, to whom he also addressed his *Crisis* No. 12. Shelburne had made a speech, somewhat conciliatory, but nevertheless arguing that "the independence of America would end in the ruin of England." Paine assured him in this *Crisis* that the independence of America had already been accomplished and that all England could do was to recognize it and conclude a peace as soon as possible. In expressing this opinion he set forth a narrow principle concerning war guilt, that "the guilt of a government is the crime of a whole country," a principle not only repudiated by liberal modern thought, but contradicted by his own tenet in *Common Sense* that society and governments are quite separate.

A few months later, pursuant to his agreement with Morris and Livingston, Paine returned to the question of internal taxation. Congress had proposed a five per cent duty on imported goods in order to meet interest and principal on foreign and domestic loans. Under the Articles of Confederation, the unanimous consent of the states was necessary for this as well as every other measure.

When the Assembly of Rhode Island adamantly refused to adopt the proposed duty, Paine not only wrote six letters defending the proposal which were printed in the *Providence Gazette* (21, 28 December 1782; 4, 11, 18 January, 1 February 1783), but with the warm encouragement of Robert Morris went in person to Rhode Island, paying his own expenses. On his return from France, Paine had been cordially received in Providence, and he now hoped that his personal influence would support his printed appeal. Feeling that the less the controversy was aired, the less the reputation of America would suffer, he tried to confine the debate to the Rhode Island papers. He began his argument with the self-evident observation that in order for Congress to borrow money it must make arrangements for repayment—and that the five per cent duty was the most expedient means of doing so. He pointed out that every American had a twofold citizenship—state and national. By failing to support one, he would endanger the other. It was necessary to talk less about independence, more about union. Tactfully, Paine observed that Rhode Island must pay an equal share of the common expenses in order to deserve an equal share of the public lands and other advantages of federation.

Paine's arguments had practically no effect except to diminish his popularity. Although they were published under the pseudonym "A Friend to Rhode-Island and the Union," certain personal allusions revealed his identity, and he was accused of being in the pay of commercial interests. Paine replied that "the merchant and the farmer are persons alike to me." His letters, he maintained, had been designed to make the merchant bear his just share of taxation along with the farmer and landowner. He represented no one class in society but sought "the general good, the happiness of the whole." His correspondence reveals, nevertheless, that he was careful to keep the patricians Robert Morris and Livingston informed of his letters in advance of publication.

His journey to Rhode Island involved also a delicate problem touching states' rights. The adversaries of strong congressional powers considered Paine as an agent of Congress meddling in local affairs, and when it became known—as we shall see later—that Paine was being considered for the post of historiographer, these advocates of local autonomy viewed him as a paid tool of the Congress. Three years later, the freemen of Smithfield formally charged that "Congress . . . employed several gentlemen, one of which was Mr. Paine, a great writer in favor of liberty, to attend our Assembly, to enforce" the five per cent impost. To counteract such impressions, James Madison and other statesmen vigorously affirmed that Paine's trip was a spontaneous measure of his own and in no sense a mission carried out at the behest of Congress.

On his return from Rhode Island, Paine wrote out a memorial to Livingston advocating, as a means of overcoming the stultifying effects of dissident states, the giving of legislative authority to Congress over all the states. He was, in his own words, the original proposer of "a general government over the Union."

Paine published his last *Crisis*, No. 13, on 19 April 1783, when "the times that tried men's souls" were finally at an end. In it Paine gave full reign to his spirit of optimism, his idealism and his happy complacency. Looking back over the stormy war years, Paine took pride that no other country could boast so fair an origin. "Her setting out in life, like the rising of a fair morning, was unclouded and promising. Her cause was good. Her principles just and liberal. Her temper serene and firm. Her conduct regulated by the nicest steps, and everything about her wore the mark of honor." Reflecting the reasoning of *Public Good* and his Rhode Island letters, Paine considered the union of the states as the great hinge on which the whole machine turned. On this, "our great national character depends."

It was the cause of America which had made Paine an author and incidentally contributed to his vanity. He believed that he had "added something to the reputation of literature, by freely and disinterestedly employing it in the great cause of mankind, and showing that there may be genius without prostitution." As though assuming that the end of the war meant the end of his role of historian, he took formal leave of the Revolution. Showing also that he still contemplated the possibility of pursuing his literary career in Europe, he concluded that whatever country he might hereafter be in, he would always feel an honest pride in the part he had taken and acted in America.

VII

A Bonus, a Bank, and a Bridge

D espite the persistence of his notion of returning to Europe, Paine was to remain in America for three more years. During that period his attention was to be devoted almost exclusively to three major affairs: the compensation due to him for his revolutionary services, the charter of the Bank of North America, and the construction of an iron bridge of his own invention.

When Paine's secret agreement with Robert Morris and Livingston came to an end, it was necessary for Paine to secure permanent subsistence. At the advice of Morris he drew up a letter to Congress, October 1783, narrating his services; a delicate task, he wrote to Washington, because of "the apprehensions of saying too little, or too much." After reviewing his principal contributions, he stressed his freedom from both party spirit and state preference. So national had he been, he wrote, "that the State I have lived in scarcely knows me as a citizen in anything but the Tax-book." Paine wanted the job of historiographer, but, because of the uncertainties attached to dependency on political bodies, he did not like the idea of appointment on a yearly salary. Instead he asked that Congress reward him fairly for his past service. If this were done on a scale to make him financially independent, he suggested, he might subsequently undertake the history of the Revolution on a purely voluntary basis exercising the utmost freedom from control. A committee of Congress appointed to consider Paine's request agreed that a "just and impartial account of the Revolution" should be compiled by an official historiographer and recommended that Paine be appointed to the office in view of his past contributions "without having sought, received or stipulated for any honors, advantages, or emoluments for himself." Unfortunately for Paine, the Congress took no action on the recommendation.

Paine spent most of the autumn of 1783 in Bordentown, New Jersey, where he had bought a house and five acres of land near the Delaware River, Paine had chosen this site to be near his friend Colonel Kirkbride. Congress, then sitting at Princeton, had provided as headquarters for Washington a mansion in nearby Rocky Hill. When Washington learned that Paine was living at Bordentown, he sent him a warm invitation to visit him. Not knowing whether Paine had taken up his new residence "for the sake of retirement or economy" or both, he suggested that Paine's visit might serve to remind Congress of his past services. Paine accepted the invitation in November, and while visiting talked science as well as politics with the nation's leading citizen.

The country people of the district had maintained that the creek at the bottom of the hill could be "set on fire," and the two friends investigated the phenomenon. Washington sat at one end of a scow and Paine at the other, each brandishing a lighted roll of cartridge paper held two or three inches over the water. When three or four soldiers began to disturb the bottom of the river with poles, Paine saw "the fire take from General Washington's light and descend from thence to the surface of the water." This was "demonstrative evidence that what was called setting the river on fire was setting on fire the inflammable air that arose out of the mud." Many years later when he was trying to ascertain the cause of yellow fever, Paine remembered this episode and described it in a newspaper article.

Although Paine now owned property in New Jersey, he still had not fixed a permanent residence in any state. South Carolina, where the Laurens family would have welcomed him, he considered too remote, and he had little inclination for Pennsylvania, both because of its ingratitude and because it "was the seat neither of science nor society." Pennsylvania, he felt, was drawing to herself laurels and honors she did not deserve. Perhaps because he was not yet honored with membership in the American Philosophical Society— it was to come 22 January 1785—Paine held a quite unfavorable view of that body. With his usual insistence on fact over tradition, he pointed out that "though there has not been a single experiment or improvement made by the Society for several years before the war nor since, yet the name of the thing has drawn to her the notice of the European Philosophical Societies and served to make Philadelphia appear in the world as the only seat of science in America, whereas it is as little, if not the least so of any in the Union, and owes all its reputation in that line to Dr. Franklin and Mr. Rittenhouse."

Paine would have preferred a residence in New York to any place he had yet visited in America, and that state turned out to be the first to show its gratitude. In April 1784 he was offered his choice of two farms, and on 16 June the Assembly of New York presented him with the one of his choice, the confiscated estate of a Tory at New Rochelle, a gift which Paine considered to be worth at least a thousand guineas. When he went to take possession, he gave a village fete. A young girl who was there recalled in later life that "he had something to say to everybody; . . . he sat in the shade and assisted in the labor of the feast, by cutting or breaking sugar to be used in some agreeable liquids."

At this time Washington, "unsollicited by, and unknown to Mr. Paine" was writing to Madison, Richard Henry Lee, and other prominent members of the Virginia Assembly, urging them to follow the example of New York. And Jefferson wrote to Madison to the same purpose. In June 1784 a bill was introduced to grant Paine land worth four thousand pounds, but it failed to carry on the third reading. John Marshall, whom Paine later came to detest, apparently led the fight for Paine. An alternative measure to sell the land and apply two thousand pounds of the money to purchase a farm for Paine was lost by a single voice. Madison in reporting these miscarriages to Washington expressed fear that "the world will give us as little credit for our policy as for gratitude in this particular." Richard Henry Lee expressed the theory that the plan had miscarried because of the antagonism aroused by Paine's opposition in *Public Good* to the Virginia claim.

Although he had resigned himself to having the states show their appreciation individually instead of jointly, Paine continued his agitation for national recompense. He wrote to Congress in August 1785, and again in September, requesting the reimbursement of his private expenses, which he estimated at six thousand dollars. On the report of a committee considering the first communication, Congress resolved, 26 August, that "Mr. Paine is entitled to a liberal gratification from the United States." Although Paine was in theory petitioning merely for the payment of his salary as Secretary of the Committee for Foreign Affairs and other expenses, part of which was in arrears, the Congress resolved, 3 October, that he be paid three thousand dollars in consideration of the preceding resolution which stipulated a "gratification." Gerry, chairman of the committee, explained privately to Paine that "the committee had consulted upon the subject, and they intended to bring in a handsome report, but . . . they thought it best not to take any notice of . . . Deane's affair or your salary. They will indemnify you, . . . without it. The case is, there are some motions on the *Journals of Congress* for censuring you with respect to Deane's affair, which cannot now be recalled, because they have been printed."

In the meantime Washington had verbally communicated his wish to John Dickinson, President of Pennsylvania, that that state would follow the lead of New York. On 6 December 1784, the Council sent a message to the General Assembly urging the appointment of a committee to consider a suitable acknowledgment of Paine's contribution. When the committee was appointed later in the month, Paine obligingly agreed to have the question of his services deferred. On 17 March 1785 the committee finally resolved that a bill be drawn setting aside five hundred pounds in Paine's favor as a "temporary recompense." The Assembly paid this amount and referred the matter of additional compensation to Congress, assuring its compliance in any further measures that body would recommend. As we have seen, Congress eventually provided three thousand dollars, and Paine became a relatively wealthy man. For this he owed little thanks to Pennsylvania, and he later asserted that its grant "was not equal to the money" he had relinquished to the state, exclusive of the service.

Paine attributed the niggardly response of the Pennsylvania Assembly to his having opposed the attitude of its principal members toward the Bank of North America. During the Revolution the latter institution had been given a charter by both the Continental Congress and the state of Pennsylvania. At the close of the war, because of a general shortage of specie, the farmers and mechanics agitated for the issuance of a plentiful supply of paper money. When the directors and stockholders of the Bank issued a petition against this paper money, the Pennsylvania Assembly, reflecting popular sentiment, authorized the issue of bills of credit to the value of one hundred and fifty thousand pounds and called for a petition to repeal the charter of the Bank. Newspaper articles and pamphlets for and against the Bank appeared in large numbers, and because of Paine's proletarian origins and sentiments, public opinion concluded him to be the author of some of those against it. Actually, however, Paine was a staunch defender of the Bank since it was the institution which had grown out of his scheme in 1780 for voluntary donations to support government credit. In 1785 he had deposited over eight hundred pounds of his own money. Unfortunately the Bank was being considered in the Pennsylvania Assembly at the same time as the matter of his own recompense, and his scruples obliged him to forego the company of his friends in the House. But despite this point of delicacy he made repeated attempts to convert the most violent opponents of the Bank.

In a private letter to Thomas Fitzsimmons, one of the founders of the institution, 19 April 1785, Paine described the move to repeal its charter as "an ill-digested, precipitate, impolitic, faithless, piece of business, in which party and prejudice is put for patriotism." Since a number of publications against the Bank continued to be ascribed to him, Paine published his letter to Fitzsimmons in the *Pennsylvania Gazette*, 21 December 1785.

Two months later Paine published a long *Dissertation on Government; the Affairs of the Bank; and Paper Money*, and subsequently in the newspapers nine letters supporting and amplifying his position. In Paine's day as well as ours, a banking institution was popularly considered as a vested interest, and the opponents to it considered themselves as champions of the rights of the people against the power of privilege. Paine's position rested on the paradox that the Bank actually stood for popular rights and liberties, whereas those who attacked it in the Assembly represented arbitrary power and the denial of natural rights. Paine's chief argument was that a legislature is a continuous responsible body, even though its members may change, and that the members of one session are bound by the action of previous sessions. To Paine, the opposition to the Bank looked like government by personal prejudice, and he saw in it a danger to "the rights and property of every man." In his *Dissertation* Paine made a distinction between law-making and negotiation. The latter comprehends all kinds of public business which the Assembly transacts with individuals or particular groups for special needs of the state. These acts, such as borrowing money or purchasing goods, are contracts, and like all contracts are binding for the duration of the agreement. "No law made afterwards can apply to the case, either directly, or by construction or implication; for such a law would be a retrospective law, or a law made after the fact." A law proper, however, unlike these contracts, binds every individual of the commonwealth. Since laws cover every citizen, "they may be altered, amended and repealed, or others substituted in their places, as experience shall direct, for the better effecting the purpose for which they were intended." But even contracts, Paine believed, cannot last indefinitely. "As we are not to live forever ourselves, and other generations are to follow us, we have neither the power nor the right to govern them, or to say how they shall govern themselves." This sentence foreshadows Paine's argument in *The Rights of Man* against Burke's theory of prescription. Paine added that since thirty years is the average duration of a generation, thirty years should also be the terminal point for all laws and acts. "Such as were proper to be continued, would be enacted again, and those which were not, would go into oblivion." The granting of a charter to the Bank, Paine regarded as being in the first category, a contract between the state and a particular group of individuals, and hence an agreement that could not be lightly set aside. He did not specifically apply his principle of thirty years' duration to the charter of the Bank, but strongly suggested that the application should be made.

As a result of the *Dissertation*, enemies of the Bank accused Paine of being "an unprincipled author whose pen is let out for hire," and some modern scholars have interpreted his position as drifting toward conservatism. Although Paine was now writing against radical friends who had stood with him in the Morris-Holker controversy, his fundamental political philosophy had not changed. A writer, "Atticus," nevertheless, excoriated him in the *Freeman's Journal*, 3 May 1786, as "a writer, who, having formerly vindicated the principles of freedom, abandons them to abet the cause of a faction; who exerts the little talent which Heaven has allotted him, for the acquisition of his daily bread, to vilify measures which it is his duty to respect, and who, having reaped a recompense more than adequate to his deserts, prostitutes his pen to the ruin of his country."

Paine replied from Bordentown, 18 May [*Freeman's Journal* 31 May], using the expression "intoxicating spirit of party." This gave another opponent an opening to insinuate that Paine frequently wrote under the influence of liquor. He made no direct accusation, but suggested that "the political gladiator, panting with the heat of a laborious controversy, demands the refreshment of a real beverage, and the generous auxiliary of a *spirit* not strictly aerial. Hence, as it was said of the Orations of Demosthenes that they smelt of the lamp, it may justly be said of some modern Essays that they smell of the *cask.*"

Paine ignored this insinuation, but wrote his subsequent newspaper letters to answer the serious objections of his critics, and to expand his arguments in favor of the Bank. The two most important have never been reprinted in editions of Paine's works. In one, *Pennsylvania Gazette*, 20 September 1786, he repeats from an earlier letter his opinion concerning a single legislature—that its simplicity of structure during the Revolution was a blessing, but later a curse. The action of the Assembly in revoking the Bank's charter (13 September 1785) seemed to him proof that "a single legislature, on account of the superabundance of its power, and the uncontrouled rapidity of its execution, becomes as dangerous to the principles of liberty as that of a despotic monarchy"; that it was "capable of being made a compleat aristocracy."

Paine's next letter in the *Pennsylvania Gazette* (8 November 1786) was a diatribe against paper money, which he described as "both the bubble and the iniquity of the day." He compared the issuing of bills of credit to "anticipating or forestalling the revenue of future years and throwing the burden of redemption on future assemblies." Even worse, he added, it banishes hard money from circulation and diminishes the value of revenue. The legislators who revoked the Bank charter had undermined all confidence in the Assembly. They "aimed at the pidgeon and shot the crow—they fired at the bank and hit their own paper."

Eventually the controversy was resolved in favor of the Bank, and for a short time Paine had no pressing public issue to excite him. He continued, however, to pursue political theory in a private discussion group founded in February 1787, The Society for Political Inquiries, of which Benjamin Franklin was the president. Paine was one of its forty-two members along with Robert Morris, Gouverneur Morris, James Wilson and Benjamin Rush. Another member, the historian William Rawle, tells us that there "was no formality of discussion" during the weekly meetings at Franklin's house. "Dr. Rush, who had great powers of discussion commonly took the lead. Gouverneur Morris was intelligent, sarcastic and abrupt. Dr. Franklin though very attentive, said but little after the subject was broached. Paine never opened his mouth; but he furnished one of the few essays which the members of the society were expected to produce. It was a well written dissertation on the inexpediency of incorporating towns." According to Charles Biddle, the meetings of the society were not well attended and the members were disturbed by the incessant talking of one of their number.

As a result of his newly-acquired wealth, Paine for the first time in his life had the leisure and the means to pursue his scientific interests. Late in 1785 he hired a carpenter and mechanic, John Hall, who had just emigrated from Leicester, England, to Philadelphia. For two years the two men worked together tirelessly. Paine, somewhat indulgent to himself on such matters as late rising, turned out to be a hard taskmaster for Hall—although the latter always remained a loyal friend. On the last day of the year, Paine sent Franklin a smokeless candle of his own invention. This candle had a hole in it parallel to its length, and the smoke was supposed to descend to the base rather than to mingle with the flame. On New Year's Day Paine dined with Franklin, and after tea the two scientists tried out the candles by blowing a gentle current through them, which they felt greatly improved the light.

In March 1786, another scientist, John Fitch, visited Bordentown. Fitch had been experimenting with steam navigation and knew that Paine had discussed the subject with William Henry of Lancaster in 1778. John Hall, who called all inventions "saints," referred to Fitch as a brother saint-maker, who came with a model of a machine to drive boats against the stream. Fitch offered both Paine and Hall a partnership, but both were too busy with their own experiments. Paine, however, pointed out some improvements in Fitch's steamboat and bought one of his maps of the Northwest for five shillings.

While gazing at ice-packs in the Schuylkill River, so heavy that they would have crushed the piers of any bridge, Paine conceived the idea of manufacturing a bridge composed of a single arch combining a number of separate sections, based on the principle of a spider's web. Paine at first intended his bridge to span the Harlem River near the estate of his friend General Morris. It was to be constructed of wooden beams and would extend three hundred feet across the river. Later he conceived of a single-arch iron bridge across the Schuylkill, and still later he planned to erect iron bridges across the Thames and the Seine. Paine affectionately called his bridge a child of "common sense" and devised its arch of "thirteen ribs, in commemoration of the thirteen United States." He enjoyed making symbolic connections between his various activities, and later in his career described one of his projects in diplomacy as a "political bridge." Paine took the idea of his bridge "from a spider's web of which it resembles a Section." He supposed that "when Nature enabled this insect to make a web, she taught it the best method of putting it together." Another idea he took from nature was "that of increasing the strength of Matter by causing it to act over a larger Space than it would occupy in a solid state, as is evidenced in the bones of Animals, Tails of Birds, Reeds, Canes &c. which were they solid with the same quantity of Matter, would have the same weight with a much less degree of Strength."

"Great scenes inspire great Ideas," Paine wrote to Sir Joseph Banks. "The natural Mightiness of America expands the Mind and it partakes of the greatness it contemplates. Even the war with all its evils had some advantages. It energized invention and lessened the Catalogue of Impossibilities. At the Conclusion of it every Man returned to his home and set himself to repair the ravages it had occasioned, and *to think of war no more.* As one among thousands who had borne a part in that memorable Revolution I returned with them to the enjoyment of quiet life, and that I might not be Idle, undertook to construct an Arch for this River."

Despite the statements of previous Paine biographers, Paine did not "invent" either the iron bridge or the principle of a single arch for bridge construction. A French architect, Vincent de Montpetit, had published in May 1783 a proposal to construct an iron bridge of a single arch from 120 to 600 feet in length. He had executed a model in iron in 1779 and described it in a memoir read at the Royal Academy of Sciences. During the following winter he placed the model on exhibition, and Paine may even have seen it during his first trip to France in 1781. The French bridge, like Paine's, was portable, that is, made of individual parts which could be assembled, dismounted and reassembled. The only novelty or discovery in Paine's bridge, therefore, was in the arrangement of the segments of the arch on the principle of a spider's web.

Paine at first planned a bridge of several arches, and by 12 December 1785 Hall had put together a total of nine arches in a working model of wood. In May 1786, Paine began work on a model of iron, which he hoped to have completed in two weeks. In June he sent Franklin a model of wood and another of cast-iron bars and invited the Pennsylvania Council to examine the construction. In November the Agricultural Society petitioned the House for exclusive right to erect over the Schuylkill a rival bridge to be constructed on three piers. Fearing that this competition might frustrate his own plans, Paine accelerated his own efforts and by December had produced another model of wrought iron consisting of a single arch. This was taken by sled to Franklin's house. The latter had once said to Paine, "books are written to please, houses built for great men, churches for priests, but no bridge for the people."

On the day after Christmas, Paine demonstrated his model to Franklin and Rittenhouse by allowing three men to stand on it. Rittenhouse believed that it would be sturdy enough for the Schuylkill, but feared that its construction would be too expensive. On New Year's Day 1787, the bridge was exhibited at the State House and inspected by the Assembly and civil personages. Hall observed that "their sentiments and opinions of it were as different as their features. The philosopher said it would add new light to the great utility. And the tailor (for it is an absolute truth) remarked it cut a pretty figure."

At one time Paine counted on Robert Morris to finance his bridge, but the latter's losses in various speculations made that expectation futile. Paine then hoped that the Assembly would charter a subscription company to raise $33,330 for the construction of the bridge, but months passed and no action was taken. Remembering the reluctance of the House to grant due compensation for his revolutionary activities, Paine abandoned hope in Pennsylvania and resolved to try his luck in France. Even though in

March the Pennsylvania Assembly appointed a second committee
to investigate the bridge, Paine had little faith in the outcome.
He wrote to Franklin, asking the latter for letters of introduction
to Vergennes and other influential members of the French Court
and to the commissioners of the Department of Public Works.
Franklin, who considered Paine his "adopted political son," obligingly recommended him to the Count d'Estaing, the Duke de la
Rochefoucauld, Jean-Baptiste le Roy and others. According to
Paine, it was on Franklin's express advice that he thought of submitting his model to the Academy of Sciences at Paris. Filled with
hope for his future as an inventor, Paine embarked for France,
26 April 1787.

Paine arrived one month later at le Hâvre, where he was forced
to deposit the model of his bridge with the customs officials. They
promised to dispatch it after him to Paris, however, as soon as
they should receive authority to do so. Paine immediately set
off for the capital in the company of a French gentleman whom
he had met on the boat. En route Paine took a day to visit the
palaces and other historical monuments of Rouen, "the place from
whence the kings of England date their origin." He was greatly
impressed by the order, richness, and plenty of the Norman coun-
tryside. He found "the people . . . very stout, the women exceedingly fair, and the horses of a vast size and very fat." In Paris, the
Count de Moustier invited him to dinner, 24 July 1787, with
Thomas Jefferson his fellow guest. He was entertained also by
Le Roy, who took him to visit eminent scientists and to see scientific curiosities.

On another occasion he dined with Jefferson and met another
Virginian, Lewis Littlepage, then acting as agent for the King
of Poland at Paris. Littlepage gossiped about the Venezuelan soldier-
hero, Francisco Miranda, whom Paine had met in New York
about 1783 and had considered "a man of talents and enterprise."
Littlepage told Paine of Miranda's success in getting himself introduced to the Empress Catherine of Russia and obtaining from
her a grant of four thousand pounds as a kind of retaining fee.
Paine was to encounter Miranda again during a subsequent residence
in France.

Paine formally presented the model of his iron bridge to the
Academy of Sciences, 21 July 1787. His friend Le Roy, along

with Jean Charles de Borda and the abbé Charles Bossut, served as a committee to report on its worth. Le Roy or some other member of the Academy apparently told Paine in confidence the nature of their deliberation, for Paine was able to report their views to George Clymer, 15 August 1787. A single arch of four or five hundred feet was such an unprecedented innovation and would attract so much attention that the committee had to be extremely cautious in the expression of its final judgment. The members found it more difficult to give reasons for their favorable opinion than to present the opinion itself. They agreed that the model was strong, that a bridge constructed from it would be strong also, but they were not agreed on the causes to which they should assign its strength. In a report of 29 August 1787, the committee endorsed Paine's model without reservation. They concluded that it was ingeniously conceived, that its construction was simple, solid and sturdy and that it deserved to be erected. They particularly observed that it provided a new example of an application of iron, for which until that time sufficient uses had not been discovered.

The day after the issuance of this report, Paine left for London to visit his father and mother. At least two of his friends remaining in Paris, Lafayette and Jefferson, then American Minister, tried to persuade the French government to erect across the Seine a bridge based on Paine's model. The enterprising Beaumarchais had in the meantime applied for a patent or privilege for erecting a rival bridge opposite the Tuileries. Paine expressed the fear—only too well founded—that despite all the pains he had taken and the money he had spent, some counterworking project would set itself up and the hope of great gain would set in motion tremendous schemes, but which would result in no bridge at all.

Paine again visited Paris in December 1787, but stayed only a few weeks. Returning to England, he sent Jefferson in February 1788 a memorial on a means of financing the bridge in France, a memorial which he asked Jefferson and Lafayette to read and then to have translated and presented to the Ministry if they agreed on its propriety. Apparently Paine made another journey to Paris later in the spring to further interest in his bridge. The only evidence on this point is a letter from Ethic de Corny, Syndic of the City of Paris and formerly *"commissaire des guerres"* during the American campaign, who had been presented to Paine by Lafayette. On

8 April 1788, De Corny wrote to the engineer Perronet, royal architect and member of the Academy, on behalf of Lafayette. The latter had desired to arrange an interview with Perronet on the next day in order to present Paine. In his letter, De Corny described Paine as a candidate "to erect an iron bridge of his own invention across the Seine between the King's Gardens and the Arsenal for the same price as a wooden bridge." For the construction, Paine envisaged modern methods, remarking to Jefferson in September 1788 that "a Bridge over such a River as the Seine, might be put in three Months time or less, as all the arches would be begun on at once, and the work would admit of as many hands being employed at the same time as you please."

During one of Paine's visits to Paris early in 1788, he and Jefferson discussed the arguments of James Wilson against incorporating a bill of rights in the American Constitution which Wilson had presented in the Pennsylvania convention for ratification. After returning to his own lodgings, Paine sat down and composed a lengthy memorandum developing some of the theories which later went into *The Rights of Man,* particularly a distinction between civil rights and rights of "personal competency" such as thinking and expressing opinions. Here he expressed one of the fundamental concepts of *The Rights of Man* (one which exercised Jefferson as well in a famous letter of 6 September 1789) that no generation has the right to bind a later one.

In the course of the summer of 1788, Jefferson tried to push Paine's bridge project at the French Court, but realized that Paine would be unable to take a step forward without an estimate of the cost, and even then he had strong doubts that anything would be done. Paine's proposal, he wrote 3 July, was "only taken up as the handmaid to another object, and will be executed only in the case it shall be found to ensure that." As Jefferson predicted, his efforts and those of Lafayette and De Corny proved fruitless. Paine, therefore, decided that he should henceforth concentrate his activities in the British Isles. On the advice of his friends, he obtained patents for England, Scotland and Ireland in order to assure for himself direction and management of the project. Having received the approbation of scientific experts, he then decided that it was time for him to consult practical ironmen who must be the final executors of the work.

He made arrangements with the most eminent ironworks in England, that of the four Walker brothers near Sheffield. Two of them visited him in London in September and saw his model. They decided that the bridge could be executed in wrought or cast iron, and agreed to erect an experimental arch as soon as Paine would come to their works in Rotherham. Paine arrived late in October. He had originally planned an arch of 250 feet, but discovered that this was too large to be constructed inside, and the bad weather prohibited outdoor work. He compromised, therefore, on an arch of 90 feet. He stayed in Rotherham until the first half was completed and then returned to London for the opening of Parliament. During his absence the rib was dismantled "and stowed away in a corner of the workshop . . . where it occupied so small a compass as to be hid among the shavings." Paine wrote to Thomas Walker from London, 16 January 1789, complaining of the weather, which had "put a stop to everything even to the Tides. Politics has been at a stand," he grumbled, "and Bridge building has partook of the general stagnation." Later he wrote that he planned to return to America as soon as he should have seen the outcome of the bridge, but promised to give the Walkers priority when he should dispose of his patents.

Paine returned to Rotherham on 19 April, and soon after this the experimental rib was "erected between a wall of a furnace belonging to the ironworks and the gable end of a brick building, which served as butments. The weight of iron in the rib was three tons," and it was loaded with twice its weight in pig iron. One of his friends who had seen it wrote to Paine praising its beauty and elegance. The rib was a segment of a circle of 410 feet diameter with "90 feet span, and 5 feet of height from the chord line to the center of the arch."

In June Paine proposed to the Walkers that they manufacture a complete bridge, erect it in London across the Thames, and then put it up for sale. A toll at a half penny for each pedestrian, he considered, would render the bridge a very advantageous financial project. By July, Paine and the Walkers had agreed on a plan and terms for constructing the bridge. The single arch was to be a 110-feet span with at least five ribs. The Walkers were to furnish all the materials, fit and frame them for erecting, and ship them to London. After that Paine was to assume all expenses of erection.

They intended first to exhibit the bridge and then put it up for sale. After paying all expenses, they were to divide the proceeds equally, one half going to the Walkers, the other half to Paine. Writing in September 1789 to Jefferson on the progress of the affair, Paine expressed satisfaction in his business acumen, a change from his earlier attitude in America: "Though I have a slender opinion of myself for executive business," he wrote, "I think, upon the whole that I have managed this matter tolerably well. With no money to spare for such an undertaking I am the sole patentee here, and connected with one of the first and best established houses in the nation."

By May of 1790, the bridge had been completed and was being transported by water from Yorkshire to London. It was twenty-four feet in width and as "portable as common bars of iron." Since it could be "put up and taken down at pleasure," Paine considered that it was "rendering bridges a portable manufacture." He even considered it probable that he would dismount it and send it to Paris.

A former merchant of Philadelphia, Peter Whiteside, then in London, had some financial interest in the bridge. His name appears as sole witness on the specifications which Paine submitted to obtain a patent, and Paine received some of his mail in Whiteside's care. According to Chalmers, who is the sole source for the story, Paine was indebted to Whiteside for 620 pounds, which he had borrowed for the bridge. Whiteside becoming bankrupt, his creditors served a judgment against Paine and had him arrested 29 October 1789 at his hotel, the White Bear in Piccadilly.

Records of Fleet Prison show that Whiteside was committed 1 May 1789 and that he remained there at least until 24 November to satisfy damages against a certain Joseph Caton of £833, s16, but there is absolutely no reference to Paine. The story of Paine's imprisonment has no other warrant but Chalmers's not entirely unblemished veracity.

The bridge was erected in August 1790 at Lessom Green (near Paddington) "in a plain field, where no advantage could be taken of butments without the expense of building them; . . . it served only as a specimen of the practicability of a manufactory of iron bridges." On the first working day, the foreman, an American named Bull, fell from the scaffold and tore a flap of seven or eight inches of flesh from his leg. As a result Paine himself had to supervise the entire operation every day from morning until night. Although Paine kept the area enclosed with the gate shut, a curious old gentleman one day gained admittance, spoke volubly about Rotherham to the workmen, and went away highly pleased, after giving them half a crown. Paine wrote to Walker, 8 August, "similar cases are happening every day, and the only way to render admission convenient will be by tickets and then people will not be consulting with themselves what they are to give." On 11 September, Gouverneur Morris inspected the bridge. He felt that the structure was not so handsome as Paine thought it was and wondered whether it would be as strong as Paine claimed. He admitted though that it had a very light appearance. At this favorable stage of the work, 25 September, Paine exhibited a mild degree of self-satisfaction: "I am always discovering some new faculty in myself either good or bad—and I find I can look after workmen much better than I thought I could."

After a year, the bridge was taken down without any injury—and could have been re-erected anywhere else. Paine felt that it would "produce a pretty general revolution in Bridge Architecture."

He attributed his abandoning of bridge operations to the publication in November 1790 of Burke's attack on the French Revolution and his own subsequent defense of representative government against Burke. Certainly Paine's bridge had not been the financial success he hoped—and there was little else that he could have done to safeguard his investment. Bridge-building is hardly a matter of private enterprise—and unfortunately for his hopes, Paine had undertaken to erect one at his own risk. When the prosecution of *The Rights of Man* made it necessary for Paine to flee the country, his bridge was already a financial failure.

During Paine's subsequent residence in France, a bridge suggested by his model was erected over the Wear near Sunderland in the County of Durham. The foreman on the project was William Yates, who had been in charge of the construction of Paine's bridge at Rotherham, although not its erection at Paddington. Paine had humorously dubbed him "President of the Board of Works." The Sunderland bridge was likewise cast at the Walkers' foundry. One of Paine's friends in high place, Sir Robert Smyth, wrote to Milbanke, an entrepreneur of the Sunderland bridge to claim a reimbursement for Paine. Milbanke replied that however desirous he may have been to see Paine's ingenious labors rewarded, the method by which the Sunderland bridge was being financed provided no means of compensation. An engineer, giving a retrospective view of the Sunderland bridge in the nineteenth century, reported: "We should probably make a fair division of the honour connected with this unique bridge" by conceding to its builder all that belongs to a "careful elaboration and improvement upon the designs of another, to the boldness of taking upon himself the great responsibility of applying this idea at once on so magnificent a scale, . . . but we must not deny to Paine the credit of conceiving the construction of iron bridges of far larger span than had been made before his time, or of the important examples both as models and large constructions which he caused to be made and publicly exhibited."

Thus closed Paine's career as a bridge architect. In 1803, as a sort of epilogue to his "pontifical works," to use his own phrase, he wrote a memoir on the history of iron bridges in which he offered his knowledge and experience to the Congress of the United States.

VIII

A Political Bridge

Although the primary object of Paine's voyage to France in 1787 had been the promotion of his bridge, he was unable to resist the temptation to continue in the role of statesman which he had from time to time been able to adopt in America. For an account of his political life during his second sojourn in France, we must depend almost exclusively on his own report in the Preface to the first part of *The Rights of Man.* Here he presents the following very interesting account of back-door diplomacy—his manner of proposing himself as emissary to negotiate between England and France.

When I came to France, in the spring of 1787, the Archbishop of Toulouse was then Minister, and at that time highly esteemed. I became much acquainted with the private secretary of that Minister, a man of an enlarged benevolent heart; and found that his sentiments and my own perfectly agreed with respect to the madness of war, and the wretched impolicy of two nations, like England and France, continually worrying each other, to no other end than that of a mutual increase of burdens and taxes. That I might be assured I had not misunderstood him, nor he me, I put the substance of our opinions into writing, and sent it to him; subjoining a request, that if I should see among the people of England any disposition to cultivate a better understanding between the two nations than had hitherto prevailed, how far I might be authorized to say that the same disposition prevailed on the part of France?

He answered me by letter in the most unreserved manner, and that not for himself only, but for the Minister, with whose knowledge the letter was declared to be written.

Solely on the basis of this account nearly every biographer of Paine has boldly stated that Paine entered into personal relations

118

with the Cardinal de Brienne, Archbishop of Toulouse. This is
obviously inexact. Paine's relations were with the latter's private
secretary. One cannot state with precision whether this was Souf-
flet de Mercy, first secretary of the Cardinal, or a subordinate.
At any rate, a long letter of eight pages addressed by Paine in August
1787 to some member of the French administration still exists in
France. It is either the one Paine wrote to the Cardinal's secretary or
another on the identical subject. This extremely important letter
has never been published nor has it been known to previous biographers. For this reason and also because it tells us precisely the
nature of Paine's efforts to promote peaceable relations between
France and England, it warrants a rather extended summary.

Paine based his proposals on the assumption that the passions or
prejudices of nations one against another are not of eternal duration and that the ministries of both France and England personally
desired that their national economy be adjusted to peace rather
than to the devouring vulcan of war. There remained, he continued,
"only the vulgar passions and prejudices of the commonality to
be removed in order to make way for a more friendly understanding between the two countries." These passions had been more
deeply rooted in England than in France, Paine felt, but no time
offered greater opportunity than that moment to eliminate them.

Paine considered that because the English people had been taught
to cherish prejudices against the French they lived in ignorance
of the true character of that nation. The ignorance and prejudices
of the French in regard to England were less serious, and for this
reason the two countries did not treat on equal terms. In other
words, France had an enemy in the vulgar prejudices of the English, which her negotiations with the Court could not reach. The
English people had been taught to consider France as a quarrel-
some nation, striving for universal monarchy. These prejudices
had been developed by the scandalous style of newspapers and
books of travel. "Except Sterne," Paine observed, "there is scarcely
a traveling English author, but who, on his return home, has
cherished and flattered those errors for the purpose of accomo-
dating his work to the vulgar palates of his readers." Under the
influence of these idle conceits, the English people were easily
incited to war. Paine felt encouraged, however, by the circumstances of the time.

First of all, the Hanoverian dynasty was at last firmly enough established for the reigning monarch, George III, to realize that the security of his reign no longer rested on creating rancor and prejudice against the French, who had supported the Stuarts. Pitt, the Prime Minister, would prefer to govern during an epoch of peace since he could not hope to rival his illustrious father as a War Minister. His ambition told him that as "a Peace Minister he may be great but as a War Minister he will be little." Also the outcome of the last war had proved to the English that they could be defeated, and this consideration had served to chasten their temper. Finally, the vast accumulation of debt and the taxes they had piled up had brought them to a much more reasonable way of thinking. The treaty of commerce then in effect also had a natural tendency to promote peace.

But Paine felt that there was much more to be done in England. His own effort would be to publish a pamphlet based on the "principle of philanthropy," a pamphlet in which he would attempt to reconcile the misunderstandings between the French and the English peoples. Before departing for England, Paine wished to be well assured—and he felt that it was within the power of his correspondent to do it—that there was "no disposition on the part of the French Ministry to break terms with England, if England gives no cause of a rupture." The Cardinal's secretary answered him "by letter in the most unreserved manner," and Paine delivered his letter to Edmund Burke when he returned to England. He made his way into Burke's inner sanctum thanks to a letter from Henry Laurens, which described him as an ingenious person, hoping to introduce his mechanical contrivances in England.

In *The Rights of Man*, Paine charged that Burke ignored the pacific message he brought, choosing to aggravate the animosities between England and France rather than to heal them, but at the time Paine presented his various letters to Burke, Paine saw nothing to criticize in Burke's attitude and was very pleased to accept his hospitality. Burke received Paine at his house and introduced him to several men of rank.

Even before delivering his letters to Burke, however, Paine had carried out his promise to the French secretary and brought out his pamphlet on Anglo-French political relations based on the principle of philanthropy, a pamphlet entitled, *Prospects on the*

Rubicon, or an Investigation into the Causes and Consequences of the Politics to be Agitated at the Next Meeting of Parliament. Although dated London, August 20, 1787, the pamphlet must have been written in France since Paine did not leave Paris until August 30. Indeed the pamphlet had probably already been composed when Paine wrote his letter to Brienne's secretary.

The title, *Prospects on the Rubicon,* alludes to the choice of Caesar and suggests the similar alternatives confronting England, which seemed to be on the verge of war with France. While there was still time to consider, Paine exhorted the British Ministry to weigh the sure evils of war against its doubtful advantages. He attempted to turn public opinion against war for two reasons: to spare the English people an increased burden of taxes; and to cement good relations between England and France. "Above all," he proclaimed, "I defend the cause of humanity."

The English Ministry had been flirting with the Stadtholder of Holland and seemed prepared to propose a joint alliance against France. Paine argued that such an alliance would be the fruit of political negotiations only and that a more solid foundation in national interest existed for cordiality between England and France. Pitt he described as a "war Minister in peace, and a peace Minister in war. Brave where there is no danger, and prudent where there is." War would mean the ruin of both nations, he predicted, but France with her superior wealth and population was better prepared for war than England. France had a much greater per capita wealth; England a greater per capita debt.

Paine's economics are now outmoded. Virtually a mercantilist, he considered gold and silver as the only form of capital. Paine's fundamental principle was that each nation, including England, should maintain adequate defense but not seek to dominate the military strength of Europe. In discussing the internal situation of France, he had nothing but good to say. He subscribed to the doctrine of the *bon roi*—the doctrine which kept the French Revolution from occurring long before it did. According to the theory of the *bon roi*, the state was a union of the common people and the monarch, and the nobles were to be submerged for the glory of the whole. Paine, therefore, interpreted events in France, where the provincial parliaments were beginning to pave the way for the Revolution, as "the majesty of the sovereign" uniting with "the majesty of the nation." The pamphlet supports the interpretation that Paine's political views grew out of his economic ones. It is a precursor of *The Rights of Man*, revealing the same spirit of opposition to the British government, but stressing foreign rather than domestic policies and using economic rather than political arguments. For this reason it was not widely read since most contemporary readers considered economics a gloomy and dull science. For this reason also, Paine was not prosecuted by the authorities. They had no reason to fear dangerous effects. It is significant to note that even before the French Revolution Paine was supporting the French government against the English—that is, when both nations were monarchies.

After leaving France in August 1787, Paine went directly to Thetford to visit his aging parents, but found only his mother, his father having died within the preceding five months. Paine settled a pension of nine shillings a week on his mother—equivalent to almost half his former income as gauger in the customs service, a sum presumably adequate for the support of an aged person. Paine stayed only three or four weeks in his birthplace, however, being anxious to return to London to promote his bridge and his amateur diplomacy. He wrote to the Marquis of Lansdowne in September 1787, putting him in mind of his signature "Common Sense" and describing himself as "a man who considers the world as his home, and the good of it in all places as his object." This is Paine's first recorded use of this phrase, which he repeated in *The Rights of Man* and which has ever since been used to describe him. Echoing the principles of *Prospects on the Rubicon*, he pointed out to Lansdowne the advantages of pursuing a policy of peace toward France in view of the friendly disposition of the French people.

In the summer of 1788, Paine made a tour of the northern iron foundries with Burke, during which he visited the Walkers. He also spent a week at Burke's estate and at the residence of the Duke of Portland in Buckinghamshire. Here he talked international politics, persevering in his attempt to solidify friendly relations between England and France. In a letter to an American friend at about the same time, he revealed his satisfaction in his "pretty close intimacy with the heads of the opposition" party, the Whigs, including Burke, Fox and the Duke of Portland.

The United States still not having sent an official minister to England, Paine hoped that a fall of the Pitt Ministry and a coming into power of his friends of the opposition would put himself in a position of transacting American affairs. He also wrote to Jefferson 15 January 1789 that he was in some intimacy with Burke, and that he would be introduced to the new Ministry after its formation. In the next month he wrote that "an interview for that purpose was agreed upon" to take place immediately on the formation of a new government, but as long as Pitt remained in power, Paine felt that Congress would be wasting money in appointing a minister at London. Necessary business, he felt, could be transacted through Jefferson in Paris. We shall see that Paine's amicable relations with the Whig moderates lasted only a short time, that is, until he returned from another trip to Paris in 1791 during which he had publicly urged the formation of a republican government in France.

Nearly all evidence seems to show that Paine was highly impressionable—that his writings reflect the views and sentiments of the people with whom he was most recently in contact. When he was friendly with the French royalist Ministry, he echoed the doctrine of *le bon roi* and the alliance between the King and people; when he dined with Burke and the moderates, he applied the same theories to England; when he revisited Paris during the Revolution and associated with young hot-heads he expressed views more radical than those of the Assembly, and when he returned to England, he broke all ties with his moderate friends and became the symbol of political radicalism for England.

Early in 1789, Paine's attention was equally divided between French and English politics. In January because of the illness of George III, Pitt had brought forward a proposal to discontinue the creation of new peers. Paine considered this to be an unconstitutional measure—illegal in regard to the so-called British Constitution, which Paine as a republican regarded as a mere hodge-podge. He explained to Thomas Walker, 16 January, that the limitation of the creation of new peers affected "the present house of Peers by augmenting its Powers—and . . . the house of Commons and the nation by establishing an Aristocrasy over themselves." Still persuaded that in England as well as in France the royal power should protect the common people against the power of the nobility, Paine explained that the Constitution assumes that the monarch is that part of government which is superior to and detached from all local interests, parts and parties in the nation and that it exercises its power to preserve an equipoise among those parts. "By dissolving the House of Commons, and referring to the sense of the nation by new elections, . . . it prevents an Aristocrasy establishing itself in that house—and by melliorating the House of Peers by new creations it prevents the same evil taking place there." Applying the doctrine of the *bon roi*, which he had previously adopted in France, Paine argued that in England "the monarchy is nearer related to the people than the Peers are." And echoing the poets Goldsmith and Churchill, Paine insisted that of all forms of government aristocracy is the worst. Paine's statement of these theories is important because it shows that his political thought developed gradually—that he had not always held the radical doctrines of *The Rights of Man*, which attacks both monarchy and aristocracy.

A month later he expressed the same political philosophy in another letter to Walker, 26 February 1789,—this time attacking the theory of Pitt that the Prince of Wales, then Regent because of the insanity of George III, held his executive power through the choice of Parliament. Paine argued that it passed to him simply through hereditary right. He held out for this subtle distinction —which he repeated in *The Rights of Man*—because it supported his contention that the rights of commoners are more closely identified with the monarch than with Parliament—that "the Right . . . of the Prince is a Right standing on the Right of the whole nation."

At the outset of the French Revolution, Paine still accepted the principle of monarchy for both France and England. His information concerning the assembling of the French States General, which of course led to the Revolution, came to him in a letter from Thomas Jefferson. Paine, in replying 26 February 1789, affirmed his theory of an internal alliance between the French King and the people —and remarked that such an alliance, because of the new strength it would bring to France, was most feared by the English. In a later letter, 18 September 1789, he remarked that the English people had begun to realize that France is a freer country than England. The English had not realized that they were living amid remnants of the feudal system until the Revolution in France brought these vestiges before their eyes. Previously they had been terrified by

arbitrary power and popery from abroad and had thought themselves extraordinarily free people, but the bugbear had lost its
force and they had begun to examine the aristocracy of their own
country. Paine, nevertheless, considered the ignorance of the English people unfathomable in regard to important matters of state
and finance. They had confidence in the credit and financial resources of the nation whereas Paine considered them extremely
precarious. If a war should ever break out against England, he
advised Jefferson in April 1789, the Bank of England "is the spot
where it ought to be prosecuted."

During the winter of 1789-1790, Paine returned to Paris to
visit his friends and see for himself the progress of the Revolution.
He wrote to Washington, 16 October 1789, announcing his imminent journey and suggesting that he hoped to take an active
political part: "a share in two revolutions is living to some purpose." It is not known exactly when Paine arrived in Paris, but
on 27 November 1789 he visited Gouverneur Morris there.

Paine maintained his interest in economic theory and continued
to favor French institutions. On 5 January 1790 he discussed with
Gouverneur Morris a treatise in the vein of *Prospects on the Rubicon*, a new work designed to show that the French national bank,
the Caisse d'Escompte, was more worthy of credit than the Bank
of England. Morris considered it an idle attempt not only because
the thesis was false, but also because, if true, the general discredit
it would produce would adversely affect the institution Paine was
trying to promote. Besides, Morris wrote in his diary: "the People
here are in general divided into those who know a great Deal and
those who know Nothing, consequently they are not to be affected
by those half Way Arguments which form the Excellence of
Payne's Writings. His Conceptions and Expressions are splendid
and novel but not always clear and just."

Through the Lafayette circle, Paine became acquainted with
a Belgian baroness, Cornélie de Vasse, author of two works of
somewhat frivolous literature, *The Confessions of a Woman of Gallantry*, 1782, and *The Art of Reforming Men and making them
Constant*, 1783. She and Paine, then in their early fifties, were
born in the same year. A letter in English from the Baroness to
Paine, 24 February 1790, indicates that she would have been pleased

to reach some degree of intimacy with her correspondent, but had actually not thus advanced:

I expect from your Friendship, you will be so kind to accompany me to morrow afternoon at the marqs. La Fayette's, I have to talk with him about a business of moment, & importance, as it relates [to] the welfare of the nation in general. I am my dear Sir your most affectionate Servant,

LA BARONNE DE VASSE

I will call at your hotel to morrow afternoon at five o'clock. an answer, if you please.

Paine remained in close contact with the Lafayette circle, and before his return to London in April the Marquis entrusted to him, as a present to be forwarded to Washington, the key to the outer gate of the Bastille, symbol of the oppression exercised by the *ancien régime*. Paine promised his French friends to return to Paris when the Constitution should be finished in order to march in the commemorative procession, carrying the American flag. In sending the key to Washington in June after his return to London, Paine described it as "an early trophy of the spoils of despotism, and the first ripe fruits of American principles transplanted into Europe." His heart had leaped with joy when Lafayette announced his intention of bestowing the key upon Washington, for Paine was firmly convinced that "the principles of America opened the Bastille."

At this time, Jefferson having returned to America in the summer of 1789, the only American with diplomatic status then in France was Gouverneur Morris. Although not an accredited minister, Morris carried a letter from Washington authorizing him to negotiate with the British Ministry. This letter gave him a certain prestige in France, which he was not inclined to share with Paine. Morris wrote in his diary, 26 January 1790, Lafayette "tells me that he wishes to have a Meeting of Mr. Short, Mr. Payne and myself to consider their judiciary. . . . I tell him that Payne can do no good for that altho he has an excellent Pen to write he has but an indifferent Head to think." Lafayette, however, seems to have had complete confidence in Paine and gave him for publication details of his own political opinions and activities. In a letter to Washington, 12 January 1790, Lafayette remarked, "*Common sense* is writing for you a brochure in which you will see a portion of my adventures. The result will be, I hope, happy for my country and for humanity." This is an extremely important reference to the embryonic state of *The Rights of Man*, which treats Lafayette's activities in the Constituent Assembly. It shows that Paine began his treatise on the French Revolution before he had any knowledge of Burke's opposition to it—and that he later revised his work by casting it into the form of an extended attack upon Burke.

During his sojourn in Paris, Paine made the acquaintance of a young Scotsman, Thomas Christie, a former medical student, who planned to follow his father's profession of banking. As Paine put it, he was spending some time on the Continent as a man of observation before undertaking "Atlas-like, the world on his shoulders." Actually Christie had gone to Paris as an agent of a British firm, Turnbull and Forbes, to collect 2,800 pounds sterling for grain and flour purchased by the City of Paris in September 1789. Paine found him extremely congenial company and admired his wide knowledge and extensive acquaintance with ancient and modern literary characters. Feeling that Christie would have much in common with Benjamin Rush, Paine introduced his young friend by letter so that they might have a "corresponding acquaintance." Including in the letter his optimistic appraisal of the Revolution, Paine reported that it was proceeding in good order—"little inconveniences, the necessary consequence of pulling down and building up, may arise, but even those are much less than ought to have been expected." Later, Paine and Christie witnessed together some of the most exciting moments of the French Revolution.

Paine continued to correspond also with his Whig friends in England, particularly Edmund Burke. According to the latter's eighteenth-century biographer, George Croly, Paine eagerly urged Burke "to introduce Revolution into England, by its established name of 'Reform!' Burke threw back the temptation, or the insult, at once. 'Do you *really* imagine, Mr. Paine,' was his reply, 'that the constitution of this kingdom requires such innovations, or *could exist with them*, or that any *reflecting man would seriously engage in them?* You are aware that I have, all my life, opposed such schemes of reform, because *I know them not to be Reform!*'" Croly alleges that Paine continued the correspondence, nevertheless, indeed that he wrote three days before the storming of the Bastille that the French reformers had already determined on the over-throw of the monarchy. Another of Burke's contemporaries, Robert Bisset, wrote that as early as 1788:

Paine prophesied that the same species of liberty would be extended to other countries; and, led away by his wishes, fancied all Europe would unite in overturning monarchy. Whether of himself, or from the suggestion of his French friends, Paine expressed his wishes that the British Opposition should coincide in the republican views, and *use parliamentary reform as the pretext*. Burke answered to him, "Do you mean to propose that I, who have all my life fought for the constitution, should devote the wretched remains of my days to conspire its destruction? Do not you know that I have always opposed the things called reform; to be sure, because I did not think them reform?" Paine, seeing Burke totally averse to his projects, forebore repetition. . . . Paine went to France early in 1789, and wrote several letters from Paris to Burke, explaining to him the schemes of the popular leaders. In one of these, dated July 11th, he copied a note received from a distinguished American gentleman, at whose house the republican chiefs held their most confidential meetings. "The leaders (said the note) of the assembly surpass in patriotism; they are resolved to set fire to the four corners of France, rather than not reduce their principles to practice, to the last iota. Do not fear the army, we have gained them." Here we see Mr. Burke learned from Paine, not only that they were determined to overthrow the existing orders, but that they had provided the most effectual means by debauching the army from their duty.

Some of the particulars in the accounts of Croly and Bisset are incorrect, particularly the statement that Paine wrote several letters from Paris in the spring of 1789 and another on 11 July, three days before the storming of the Bastille. There is no corroborating evidence that Paine was in France at all in 1789 until the late autumn, and he was certainly in England during July, for on the twentieth he wrote a letter to Jefferson from London. Actually it was from Jefferson that Paine derived his knowledge of the early events of the Revolution. Paine apparently combined this information with his own theories about the intellectual changes taking place in the French nation and passed on his impressions to Burke.

During the American Revolution, Paine had ample training in behind-the-scenes propaganda. He unquestionably enjoyed intrigue, and now he burned to attain some sort of official status as an emissary of the United States government. Significant is his comment to Jefferson in June 1787: "if you go to America this year I hope you will advise Congress not to send any Minister to this country. It would be all money thrown away." In other words, since Paine was already on the scene, there was no need to appoint any one else. In France he had begun in 1787 to use his taste and talent for political campaigning to promote himself as an unofficial diplomatic representative—and he soon sought to extend his influence to England. He entered into a confidential political correspondence with Jefferson in which he reported the views of Burke and other Whig leaders such as Fox, the Duke of Portland and Earl Fitzwilliam, and drew his own conclusions about the political future of England. Jefferson in return reported French developments. Jefferson valued the connection because he considered the Whigs as destined to control English policy. Burke on his side was anxious to understand and predict French behavior. Paine, of course, gained in a personal way, for the Whig leaders entertained him in luxury and treated him as a man of influence. Burke welcomed him and treated him with respect because of his reputation and his eminent connections. In the summer of 1788 Burke wrote to John Wilkes, "I am just going to dine with the Duke of Portland, in company with the great American Paine." The three-way intellectual exchange operated to everyone's satisfaction. Jefferson reported to Paine the progress of the French Revolution, and Paine passed on the reports with his own hopeful recommendations.

When Burke's biographers asserted that Paine kept Burke informed of French politics, their chief error was in chronology. We cannot know how much Paine communicated orally to Burke during the early months of 1789, but it is possible to show that the inflammatory epistle he allegedly wrote three days prior to the taking of the Bastille actually was not communicated until 17 January 1790. The original letter, which has recently come to light, reveals that the "distinguished American gentleman" to whom Bisset alluded was Thomas Jefferson. He had sent Paine a note about the loyalty of the French army to the Revolution on 11 July 1789 when Paine was in London. But Paine did not send Burke a copy of this note until January of the next year, when Paine had returned to Paris. Bisset misdated the letter by giving the date of the quotation rather than the date of Paine's writing.

This highly significant letter embodied Paine's customary optimism. He tried, as he later reported in *The Rights of Man*, to convince Burke "how prosperously matters were going on" in France. With absolutely no foresight of the events of 1792 and 1793, he glibly affirmed: "If we distinguish the Revolution from the Constitution, we may say, that the first is compleat, and the second is in a fair prospect of being so." Paine noted that the word "aristocrat" was currently being used in a sense similar to the word "Tory" in America. "It in general means an Enemy to the Revolution." He had been particularly impressed by seeing a group of schoolboys under arms, each with a real rifle: "The Boys, like those in America, emulate the Men."

To convince Burke of the success of the Revolution, Paine cited the refusal of De Broglie's troops to attack the people, the return of the King from Versailles to Paris after the taking of the Bastille, and the deputation of market women who congratulated the National Assembly on the New Year 1790. He compared the prosperous condition of the French Caisse d'Escompte with the alleged precariousness of the Bank of England, presenting the views of his proposed treatise on the subject which he had discussed that same week with Gouverneur Morris. Most significant of all, Paine expressed his opinion that "the Revolution in France is certainly a Forerunner to other Revolutions in Europe." This was for Paine wishful-thinking—for Burke warning of an imminent disaster. Paine's letter may indeed have had much to do with the violence of Burke's attack on the Revolution, in Parliament in the following month (9 February 1790).

Burke intended his speech as the opening of a crusade against the danger from France. He had his speech printed and within the week advertised a "public letter" in which he would justify his opposition to the Revolution. Paine, in Paris, was undoubtedly taken by surprise when Burke launched his attack. As soon as he saw Burke's advertisement, he announced to his friends in France and England that he would answer Burke as soon as his letter appeared. Since he had already begun writing his defense of the Revolution, Paine merely used Burke's speech to give his work a forensic character and a more direct application to England. As he himself wrote in 1800: "Mr. Burke's attack on the French Revolution served me as a background to bring forward other subjects upon, with more advantage than if the background was not there. This is the motive that induced me to answer him, otherwise I should have gone on without taking any notice of him."

Because of Paine's statement that he ceased to regard Burke as a "friend to mankind" after Burke made his violent speech against the French Revolution and because Burke had previously advocated conciliation with the American colonies, it has been generally assumed that Burke's political opinions suddenly turned from liberal to conservative. The truth is that Burke's opinions were always conservative. He had defended the American colonists partly because he was the paid agent of the colony of New York, certainly not because he ascribed to the principles of Paine's *Common Sense*. At no time did he accept the doctrine of the natural rights of man. In his speech on American taxation he had said in reference to the theory: "I do not enter into these metaphysical distinctions; I hate the very sound of them." He also took the conservative position that religion must be the strong support of the state. As early as 1773 he was warning the Commons against the increase of religious infidelity in France. No doubt Paine was flattered by Burke's personal attentions, but he must have been very naïf if he ever believed that Burke shared his democratic proclivities. At the beginning of their association, moreover, as we have already seen, Paine believed that reform would come to France through the monarch's good intentions. As the Revolution became more radical, so did his thoughts. On the subject of France, it was actually Paine's views rather than Burke's which underwent a change.

As soon as Paine returned to London in April 1790, he visited the opposition bookseller-publisher Debrett to inquire about Burke's announced pamphlet. Debrett told him that "he believed Mr. Burke was much at a loss how to go on; that he had revised some of the sheets 6, 7, 8, and one 9 times." Paine then visited other opposition leaders, Fox and Lord Stanhope, both of whom supported the French Revolution and opposed Burke's attack. A few days later, Debrett told Paine that Burke had stopped work on his pamphlet. Meeting one day a friend of Burke's on the street, Paine said, "I am exceedingly sorry to see a friend of ours so exceedingly wrong."

"Time," said Burke's friend, "will show if he is."

"He is," said Paine, "already wrong with respect to time past."

Even after Burke announced that he was writing a denunciation of the Revolution, Paine remained on good terms with him socially. They met several times later in the year and agreed not to mention French affairs. "This agreement is very fair," remarked Paine to a friend during the summer of 1790, "because he knows that I intend to reply to his Book."

Paine continued in London to serve as amateur news-gathering agency, relaying his information directly to the United States. On 2 June 1790, he tried to discover whether Spain was about to declare war so that the intelligence could be carried by a young friend John Rutledge, Jr., who was waiting to sail from Falmouth. On the morning of that day Paine accosted Burke on the way to Warren Hastings' trial, then interrogated the bookseller Debrett at his store, but learned nothing. Subsequently he visited both the French and the Spanish embassies, but there picked up only rumors. He returned to Debrett's in the afternoon and evening, finally satisfied himself that there would be no war, and then dashed off a letter for Washington and Jefferson.

While waiting for the appearance of Burke's pamphlet, Paine continued to follow with approving, but anxious glances the progress of the French Revolution. A riot had taken place at the end of May in the Faubourg Saint-Antoine. A rich stationer, accused of lowering his workers' wages, had been forced to flee his home, which was then stormed and pillaged. The disturbance stopped at this point, even though the authorities had great difficulty in dispelling the mob. William Short, then United States chargé d'affaires at Paris, had expressed fear that this mob violence was a bad sign for the future. Paine, more optimistic, felt that it served primarily to demonstrate the popularity of Lafayette, who had been called upon to calm the rioters. Paine was inclined to believe that the mob had been incited by money furnished by the English Court, the latter impelled not only by a "courtly and aristocratical hatred against the principles of the French Revolution" but also by a desire to hinder France from making necessary naval preparations for her own security or for an attack against England, should the latter go to war with Spain.

During the spring of 1790, Paine had written a half dozen letters to Lafayette without receiving an answer. Finally, he asked Short to serve as his "Minister Plenipotentiary" to reproach Lafayette for his neglect and to discuss with him a paper on French affairs which

Paine had written and wished to have translated and published in Paris as the work of a native Frenchman. Since he spoke of its selling for three or four sous, this is probably not the same paper which Lafayette alluded to in his letter to Washington of 12 January 1790. Paine's intention is significant: As early as June 1790 he hoped to play a personal role in guiding the progress of the French Revolution by his pen.

When Burke's *Reflections on the Revolution in France* was finally published in November, Paine's eagerness to attack it made him lose interest in all else.

IX

The Rights of Man

The first part of *The Rights of Man* was printed by J. Johnson, a supporter of radical causes, and announced for publication on 22 February 1791. As early as January of the preceding year Paine had told Lafayette that he intended to dedicate his work to Washington, and he probably contrived to have it published on the president's birthday. Paine's bibliographer, Colonel Richard Gimbel, has discovered evidence to show that pressure was exerted on Johnson to abandon the edition on the announced day of publication. The few copies bearing the Johnson imprint which now exist are apparently private copies given away on or before this date. A newspaper favorable to Paine announced two days later that "there is not now a copy to be had." Paine was not in London at the time, but had returned by the end of the month. On 7 March a further announcement was made in the press that his answer to Burke would once more make its appearance toward the end of the week. The sheets printed by Johnson were taken over by another printer, J. S. Jordan, who issued them under his own imprint on 16 March. Conway maintains that Paine left once more for Paris before the publication of this edition, leaving the supervisory details to William Godwin, Thomas Holcroft, and Thomas Brand Hollis. Conway also asserts that Paine sent the short Preface which appeared in the Jordan edition from Paris. The title "Preface to the English Edition" bears out this theory, suggesting he was at the same time preparing a French edition.

We know that Holcroft wrote a lyrical note to Godwin, unfortunately without date, but obviously sent shortly after publication of the Jordan edition.

I have got it—If this do not cure my cough it is a damned perverse mule of a cough—The pamphlet—From the row—But mum—We don't sell it—Oh, no—Ears and Eggs—Verbatim except the addition of a short preface, which as you have not seen, I send you my copy—Not a single castration (Laud be unto God and J. S. Jordan!) can I discover—Hey for the New Jerusalem! The millennium! And peace and eternal beatitude be unto the soul of Thomas Paine.

This may mean that Godwin and Holcroft in collaboration with Hollis had seen the Jordan edition through the press, but that the "ears and eyes" of government agents had caused them to exercise extreme caution in its distribution. Also the plethora of grammatical errors in the Johnson-Jordan edition—their absence in the edition printed by Jordan alone—may indicate that a group of zealous liberals such as Godwin, Holcroft and Hollis corrected Paine's grammar and saw to the printing of the second edition.

The trouble with this theory is that Paine's temperament would not have disposed him to accept revisions of his works from any source. Also it is not supported by the very complete and circumstantial journal which Godwin kept of his literary activities. He makes no reference to belonging to a committee to oversee *The Rights of Man* nor does he indicate meetings with Hollis and Holcroft. He does not mention Paine until 22 February 1791, when he writes, "Paine's pamphlet appears." Five days later he notes simply, "Call on Paine." On 14 May appears an interesting entry:

Scott a believer in spiritual intercourses lends Paine £40 to aid the publication of his pamphlet suspended for want of money (Lewis) H. Tooke states to the Const. Soc. Paine's offer of £300 (B. Hollis).

"Scott" is probably a reference to Paine's old patron in the excise, George Lewis Scott, who introduced him to Franklin.

On 4 November Godwin dined at the London Tavern with Paine, Pétion, Horne Tooke, Priestley, Kippis, Rees, B. Hollis, Lister and Morgan. We shall see that this was at a famous meeting of the Revolution Society. On 7 November Godwin wrote to Paine and had a reply four days later. On 13 November he dined at Johnson's with Paine and Mary Wollstonecraft, where they talked of monarchy, Horne Tooke, Johnson, Voltaire and religion. Later in that same month Godwin discoursed with other friends about Paine's iron bridge. In the next year, he began reading Part II of *The Rights of*

Man on 16 February, publication date, and on 2 March met Tooke and Paine. On 19 August he entered in his journal: "Corrections of Common Sense." This may mean that he was seeing an edition of Paine's first work through the press (perhaps a new edition, the ninth, published by Jordan), but there is nothing to indicate that he was ever involved with *The Rights of Man*. Thomas Brand Hollis, furthermore, categorically denied that he himself had seen *The Rights of Man* in manuscript. But whether published by Paine alone or by Paine with the assistance of a committee of sympathetic radicals, *The Rights of Man* stirred up a violent tempest in the British climate of political opinion.

One scholar has called the "great controversy in which Burke and Paine were the principal antagonists . . . perhaps the most crucial ideological debate ever carried on in English." In it Burke presented the case for government by tradition, Paine for government by reason. Burke maintained that a privileged class—the aristocracy—should rule because the generations during which it had exercised its powers had given it ability and experience. Paine argued for democracy on the grounds that the privileges of aristocracy could not be inherited—that all men had equal rights to govern themselves. Some modern critics have viewed the debate as a discussion of empiricism versus idealism, regarding Burke as the spokesman of practical, tested methods and Paine as the advocate of visionary and unrealistic ideals. Actually this is misrepresenting the issues. Although in a sense Burke's work is an apotheosis of the British system of "blundering through," and Paine's a vindication of government by plan, the two adversaries were not really debating experience versus theory, but two different systems of government— that based on precedent and that based on natural rights—both of which are essentially theoretical.

Burke began the attack in his *Reflections* by vigorously denying the alleged similarity between the French Revolution and the English Revolution of 1688, a relationship proclaimed by the French leaders and by such English sympathizers as Richard Price, a Unitarian minister and advocate of the American cause, who had declared that the English King "is almost the *only* lawful king in the world, because the *only* one who owes his crown to *the choice of the people*." Burke emphatically denied that the English King owed his crown to the choice of the people. The principle that the mon-

archy rests on the will of the people, Burke declared to be seditious
and unconstitutional, basing his argument on the declaration of right
which settled the succession of the Crown at the time William and
Mary ascended the throne. Since in this declaration, not one word
was said about the right of the people to choose their own governors,
Burke argued that the principle of popular choice could not be
maintained at any time.

According to Burke, the principles of 1688 followed tradition
and the language of tradition. To avoid all appearance of election
and "to exclude for ever the . . . doctrine of 'a right to choose our
own governors' " the parliamentary leaders repeated a pledge from
the time of Elizabeth to "submit themselves, their heirs and posteri-
ties for ever." And if the English ever possessed the right of
revolution, they renounced it forever in 1688.

Burke founded his argument on the doctrine of hereditary right
and prescription—the recognition in civil law that rights become
established through a long exercise of their corresponding powers.
Burke insisted that the traditional rights of Englishmen could be
preserved only through a hereditary Crown; one could not be
guaranteed without the other. He was, therefore, disturbed to "see
the National Assembly openly reprobate the doctrine of prescription," which, Burke declared, one of the greatest of the French
lawyers had described with truth as "a part of the law of nature."
We may observe parenthetically that by citing this phrase, Burke
was inconsistently borrowing from the opposing doctrine of abstract
rights.

Burke poured out his most violent abuse against what he called
the "clumsy subtlety of . . . political metaphysics," by which he
meant theories of abstract rights and government on *a priori* principles. He contrasted examples of antiquity, precedents, charters
and acts of Parliament with the despised theory of the rights of
man. The French monarchy could have been reformed, he argued,
without tearing down the whole structure for the sake of an abstract
metaphysical subtlety. By this wholesale destruction, the nation
had sacrificed its experience from the past. According to Burke,
the French should have proceeded on their old constitution (tradition), imposing reforms, rather than starting out anew. The members of the Third Estate, he charged, had neither authority nor

practical experience. Most of them represented the lowest order of "mechanical" lawyers.

The rights of Englishmen, Burke insisted, were based on heredity, acquired over a long period of service and acceptance, rather than on abstract rights guaranteed to all men regardless of birth or circumstances. Liberty in the abstract is good and a blessing, Burke declared, but in its practical applications frequently pernicious. Is it proper, he asked, "to felicitate a madman, who has escaped from the protecting restraint and wholesome darkness of his cell, on his restoration to the enjoyment of light and liberty?"

The strongest sections of Burke's tirade consist of particular indictments of the practice of the revolutionists. These are the most moving and convincing sections since it is incontestable that there were terrible abuses in the carrying out of the Revolution. The reader is likely to forget that abuses in practice in no way discredit the principles of a movement. Skillfully applying his rhetoric to stir the emotions of pity and terror, Burke denounced the inhuman treatment of the royal family.

The sufferings of Marie Antoinette inspired Burke's most famous passage, one formerly known to every schoolboy: "I thought ten thousand swords must have leaped from their scabbards to avenge even a look that threatened her with insult. But the age of chivalry is gone. That of sophisters, economists, and calculators, has succeeded; and the glory of Europe is extinguished for ever."

Burke's rhetoric triumphed in this passage, but he was less fortunate in another prophesying the pernicious results of a rift in relations between scholars and their former patrons, the nobility and the priesthood. He predicted: "Along with its natural protectors and guardians, learning will be cast into the mire, and trodden down under the hoofs of a swinish multitude." Burke's opponents seized on the unlucky phrase "swinish multitude," accusing him of so designating the common man. Later Burke explained that he had intended to limit the phrase to the movement in French politics which brought literary men to the guillotine and that he "never dreamt of our poor little English *piggen riggen* who go about squeaking and grunting quite innocently." Not even a graceless apology, but implicit admission that for him the common man did constitute the swinish multitude.

Paine in answering Burke considered his *Reflections* merely in the light of a "dramatic performance" because of the liberties taken with fact. In discussing the relation of the French Revolution to that of England in 1688, Paine agreed that no similarity existed, but found points of difference other than Burke's to distinguish the two upheavals. Burke had called the English legal, the French illegal; Paine termed the English disturbance merely a change in governments not a revolution at all. The French rising alone was a revolution. This distinction he based on his fundamental principle from *Common Sense* that people are not to be confounded with governments.

Paine next ridiculed Burke's paradox that the people would take up arms to prove that they have no rights. The Parliament in 1688 had the right to change the form of government, he asserted, but not to bind and control posterity. This would be a gratuitous assumption of authority which it did not possess. No group of men may bind others "to the end of time." Each generation is free to act for itself. Recurring to the argument of *Common Sense*, in which he had asserted the inglorious parallel between the doctrine of hereditary monarchy and original sin, Paine accused Burke of setting up monarchy as a sort of political Adam. In reply to Burke's theories of prescription or "precedents drawn from authority," Paine asserted that if laws continue in force for several generations, it is because each generation accepts them anew, not because the laws are inviolable. Those who argue by prescription, Paine charged, do not go back the whole way into the past, but stop at the point advantageous to them. If we go back beyond any privilege, we will find an opposite principle, and if we go back to the "time when man came from the hand of his Maker" we find man only. His rights originated there.

This was Paine's vindication of the doctrine of natural rights. He argued that all civil rights, on which Burke based his system of hereditary privilege, are based on natural rights. These he defined as rights of the mind and rights to act for one's own happiness which do not conflict with the rights of others. When man enters into civil society, he throws some of his natural rights into the common stock. Each civil right is gained by the exchange of a natural right.

According to Paine, there are three historical bases of government: superstition (rule by priesthood), power (rule by conquest), and common rights of man (rule by reason). Only the last has risen out of society or the social compact. Aristocracy, he charged, arose out of conquest, and a hereditary aristocracy is as ludicrous as a hereditary poet-laureateship. Here Paine followed Benjamin Franklin who had earlier ridiculed a hereditary professorship of mathematics. Government is not a compact between the governors and the governed, Paine argued, but a compact entered into by individuals with each other to produce a government. Hence Burke's charge of "metaphysics" leveled against government by plan is fallacious. A constitution framed for a new government is not an intangible myth, he insisted; a constitution has a real, not an ideal existence. Burke's confusion on this score, Paine charged, was further evidence that he had investigated nothing to its source. Governments either arise out of the people or are imposed upon them. The English government arose out of conquest, and the English had no constitution—a favorite doctrine with Paine.

Paine taunted Burke for failing to go into a comparison between the English and French constitutions. Burke could not do it, Paine asserted, because a British Constitution does not exist. Paine proceeded on his own path, however, to compare the British and French governments, consistently showing the superiority of the French.

In reply to Burke's indictment of particular events of the Revolution, Paine asserted that there actually had been less bloodshed in France than in certain upheavals in other countries. In France there were no personal animosities—no drive for revenge such as that shown by the English against the Scots in 1745. Paine agreed with Burke's characterization of Louis XVI as moderate, but pointed out that the rebellion was not against the King, but against despotic principles. That the Revolution occurred under a mild reign instead of a harsh one was not in its reproach, but in its favor. It was not excited by personal hatred, but by principle.

Burke's sentimental concern over the demise of chivalry and the neglect of the clergy gave rise to Paine's charge that he pitied only the nobles—that he was unfeeling or indifferent toward the victims of the Bastille. "Not one glance of compassion, not one commiserating reflection, that I can find throughout his book, has he bestowed on those who lingered out the most wretched of lives, a life without hope, in the most miserable of prisons. . . . He is not affected by the reality of distress touching his heart, but by the showy resemblage of it striking his imagination." And matching Burke phrase for memorable phrase, Paine jeered, "he pities the plumage, but forgets the dying bird."

It is almost impossible to avoid taking sides in a discussion of Paine against Burke. People are inevitably partisans of one or the other. A modern historian, for example, has declared that the debate "has been decided in favor of Burke as clearly as the debate over the relation between the motions of sun and earth has been decided in favor of Copernicus." According to the Burkities, anyone who affirms with Paine, the possibility of a system of government established on principles of justice and reason is an irrational optimist. Yet one may argue that Burke's so-called sound and practical system is in itself based on a metaphysical subtlety far more abstract than Paine's natural rights.

Burke's version of the theory of prescription is a form of abstract reasoning highly remote from practical life. Certainly it is now obsolete to argue that the continued acceptance accorded to the exercise of a privilege exalts the privilege to a right based on moral sanction which must be passed on to succeeding generations. Indeed Burke himself had earlier in his career ridiculed the method of vindicating privileges by prescription or precedent. In 1775 Wedderburne, the Solicitor General, in defending an unconstitutional proceeding, the employing of German troops without the consent of Parliament, delivered a speech filled with examples from history. Burke crushed him with the comment: "Let us strip off this learned foliage entirely from his argument; let us unswathe this Egyptian corpse, and bereave it of its salt, gum and mummy, and see what sort of a dry skeleton it is underneath—nothing but a precedent!" This is in essence a rejection by anticipation of his whole elaborate defense of privilege based on prescription.

The best that may be said for Burke is that he conceived of society as an organism or a community with its own laws of growth. Yet in the *Reflections* he had only one authority—precedent—the dry bones of the past. Paine appealed to justice and equality. Although these are abstractions, they are the principles upon which all law is presumably established and hence superior to the law.

Perhaps the greatest tribute to Paine's work was the extraordinary number of copies which circulated and the concomitant alarms of the British government, which led to the attempted suppression of the work itself and the prosecution of its author, printer and those concerned in its distribution. Paine was writing on the side of history, for his point of view has indisputably prevailed in the western world. In this sense he has triumphed over Burke.

From the point of view of style, however, the superiority probably rests with Burke. His measured eloquence and classical thundering, on one side, his subdued irony and epigrammatic scorn, on the other, enrich and enliven his thoughts. Burke can be reread with great pleasure—Paine with somewhat less. Burke's emotional fervor casts a warm glow over his printed words even 150 years after their composition. Paine as usual excels in ridicule, vigorous reasoning and self-possession, but these are qualities which, although they bring conviction, do not stir the feelings.

The purist Horace Walpole objected that Paine's style was so coarse that he seemed to be as intent upon degrading the language as the government. As an example of Paine's delicate rhetoric, calculated for English fishwives, Walpole cited: "We do not want a king, or lords of the bedchamber, or lords of the kitchen, or lords of the necessary house."

Sir Samuel Romilly, eminent legal reformer, found *The Rights of Man* written in a "wild but forcible style, inaccurate in point of grammar," flat in the presumably witty passages and ridiculous in its metaphors. He considered it, nevertheless, "full of spirit and energy, and likely to produce a very great effect." Six weeks later he remarked how greatly the book of Burke had lost its prestige as a result of Paine's work; "its warmest admirers at its first appearance begin to be ashamed of their admiration." Another observer, the Earl of Charlemont, considered *The Rights of Man* "a work of great genius," but one which should be "read with some degree of caution." He observed that Paine "does, indeed, tear away the bandage from the public eye, but, in tearing it off, there may be some danger of injuring the organ." La Luzerne, then French Minister at London (17 May 1791), regarded Burke's *Reflections* as acrimonious and digressive, but nevertheless eloquent and filled with noble sentiments on the attachment due to the King and the advantages of a limited monarchy. He found Paine's refutation rather weak in principle, but alluring to the common people and written with great vehemence. He reported that the republican clubs had reprinted twenty-five thousand copies to be sold at nominal prices and even to be given away in the most remote sections of England and Ireland. This mass distribution, he affirmed, had already had a great effect and would continue.

In the United States, too, the influence of *The Rights of Man* was tremendous. It succeeded almost single-handed in checking a growing anti-French sentiment and turning public opinion in favor of France. John Adams's *Discourses on Davila*, 1791, a virulent diatribe against the French Revolution, had virtually crystallized American opinion until the publication of *The Rights of Man*. Louis Otto, French Consul in Philadelphia, reported 23 July 1791 that largely as a result of Paine's work the newspapers had blossomed out in essays, tracts and epigrams against Adams, and the French Revolution had regained its prestige. A British agent, George Hammond, reported four months later that Paine's pamphlet, although it had not added to his popularity, had "produced a very open diversity of sentiment" between Jefferson and Adams.

This came about because John Beckley, Clerk of the House of Representatives, lent to Jefferson the only copy of Paine's pamphlet then in America with the request that after reading it Jefferson send it to a Mr. J. B. Smith, whose brother wished to bring out an American edition. Jefferson not only sent on the pamphlet but wrote an accompanying letter expressing his satisfaction at finding that "it will be re-printed here; and that something is at length to be publicly said against the political heresies which have sprung up among us." The wily publisher S. H. Smith printed this recommendation over Jefferson's title of Secretary of State in his edition of *The Rights of Man*, 1791, and everyone took it as a denunciation of Adams's *Discourses on Davila*, as indeed it was. Jefferson and many others thought Adams to be favorable to hereditary monarchy and aristocracy. The edition created a sensation: here was the Secretary of State hurling Paine against the Vice President. The British government also felt affronted: the Bible of its arch enemy was being dedicated to the President of the United States and endorsed by the Secretary of State. Henceforth in the United States, support of France was identified with the Republicans; opposition to France, with the Federalists.

When Jefferson attempted to placate Adams by explaining that he had not written his endorsement of *The Rights of Man* for publication, many Republicans regretted his lack of spirit. Instead of merely hinting disagreement with Adams's aristocratic principles, stormed *The American Annual Register for 1796*, Jefferson "ought to have taken the bull by the horns. He should have pointed out *Rights of Man* as an antidote" to the political arsenic of Adams. "There was no use in fighting eight years for liberty, if she must lick the spittle of a Vice President."

Madison came immediately to Jefferson's defense (12 May 1791). He found British sensibility concerning the indignity to the Constitution truly ridiculous. "If offence could be justly taken in that quarter, what would France have a right to say to Burke's pamphlet and the Countenance given to it & its author? . . . What, in fact, might not the U.S. say, whose revolution & democratic Governments come in for a large charge of the scurrility lavished on those of France?"

At the same time that the Republican chiefs were defending Paine's principles in the United States, they were trying to find a place for him in the Washington administration. Madison, hearing that Jefferson was making efforts in that direction gave his enthusiastic support (13 July 1791). "Besides the advantage to him, which he deserves, an appointment for him at this moment would do public good in various ways." Jefferson and Edmund Randolph had been trying to persuade Washington to appoint Paine postmaster. "It seemed to be a fair opportunity for a declaration of certain sentiments," wrote Randolph to Madison, 21 July 1791. "But all that I have heard, has been, that it would be too pointed, to keep a vacancy unfilled, until his return from the other side of the water." Perhaps it would have been unreasonable to keep the job open until Paine had time to return from France, but it is too bad that he did not at least have an opportunity to decline the post by explaining that he preferred to stay in Europe, having dedicated himself to the French Revolution.

A Republican Manifesto for France

In the midst of the turmoil caused by the publication of his book, Paine mysteriously returned to France. We do not know exactly when Paine left for Paris, but it must have been between 7 March and 7 April 1791, at which time William Short reported his arrival to Morris.

During this sojourn in Paris, Paine shared lodgings with a Mr. Hodges, whom Gouverneur Morris described as his "fellow Traveler." Shortly after their arrival Morris visited their "wretched Apartments," but found at home only Hodges, who spoke of Paine as "being a little mad." Perhaps he was referring to a public appeal which Paine had made for the formation of a republic in France before anyone else had even hinted at the idea. This appeal came out of Paine's association with the aristocratic Condorcet, philosopher of the Revolution; abbé Emmanuel Sieyès, astute political theorist who later became one of the members of the Directory; and Achille du Chastelet, a youthful colonel in the French army, who had previously served in America, where he had absorbed rabid republican sentiments.

Paine's acquaintance with Condorcet dated from his second visit to Paris in the winter of 1789-1790. They had become ardent admirers of each other's works, Condorcet going so far as to say that all the friends of liberty, truth and reason venerated Paine for the independence of his character, the disinterestedness of his conduct, and the profound reason and energy in his works.

In 1791 Paine, with Condorcet and Du Chastelet, jointly formed a club composed of only five members named the Republican Society. The names of the other two members are not known, but they were probably either Brissot de Warville, editor of *le Patriote françois*, organ of the moderate constitutional faction; Nicolas de Bonneville, co-founder of another club, the Cercle Social, a political-philanthropic group with which Paine was already associated; or François Xavier Lanthenas, a rather inept politician, who later translated several of Paine's works. According to Paine, this club opposed Louis XVI "not so much on account of his personal offenses, as in order to overthrow the monarchy, and to erect on its ruins the republican system and an equal representation."

On 20 June 1791, the King and his family had abandoned Paris to join the royalist garrison in Metz. Just before midnight at a village in the east, Varennes, the royal party had been apprehended and forced to turn back. When news of the royal flight broke in Paris, hordes of people assembled in the streets to denounce the monarch's treason, and the tocsin sounded public danger. In the midst of the mob demonstrations, Paine visited the chambers of his young Scots friend, Thomas Christie, who lodged in the historic Palais Royal, scene of many of the most violent outbreaks of the Revolution. On this occasion Paine remarked with his usual coolness, "You see the absurdity of monarchical governments; here will be a whole nation disturbed by the folly of one man."

Paine, Christie, and another Englishman, John H. Stone, then sallying forth to see what was doing at the Tuileries, found the royal apartments filled by people who had burst into the palace. This was a "mob of principle" concerned over the national crisis and not intent on drunkenness and plunder. Returning to the Palais Royal, Paine and his friends found various citizens reading aloud a proclamation of the Assembly that nothing should interfere with the completion of the Constitution.

According to Chalmers, on this same occasion, an officer proclaimed the order of the National Assembly that everyone in the crowd must be "silent and covered. In an instant all hats were on." Paine in the excitement had lost his red, white and blue cockade, emblem of liberty and equality, and consequently remained bareheaded. The mob, noticing his condition, assumed that he was unfriendly to the cause and began to cry out "*Aristocrat! Aristocrat! à la lanterne! à la lanterne!*" Hang him to the lamp-post! In great haste Paine put on his hat and eventually succeeded in explaining his true sentiments to the crowd.

Inspired by the foolish behavior of Louis XVI, Paine composed his incendiary manifesto, advocating the proclaiming of a republic and gave it to his young friend Du Chastelet for translation. The latter called in Étienne Dumont for aid, but Dumont protested against its radical notions and pointed out the drawbacks in raising a republican standard without the concurrence of the Assembly. He asked Du Chastelet whether he had consulted with the leaders, particularly Sieyès and Lafayette, and learned that he and Paine had acted entirely on their own. Du Chastelet translated the document himself, made a few trifling alterations in the text, and signed it with his own name, the law requiring the signature of a citizen on each printed paper. On 1 July Paine and Du Chastelet covered the walls of Paris with their manifesto. It created a great furor and was immediately denounced in the Assembly. As Étienne Dumont remarked, "It was an American and a young madcap of the French nobility who had put themselves in the vanguard to change the face of Europe." This is no exaggeration. Paine was literally the first to call publicly for the creation of a republic in France as he had previously been the first in America. The deed permeated his entire personality. He was still "inflated to the Eyes and big with a Litter of Revolution" when he encountered Gouverneur Morris three days after putting up the placard.

The King's inglorious flight had given Paine the occasion to charge in his manifesto that since the monarch had abdicated, the mutual obligations which may have existed between him and the people were henceforth dissolved. The history of France, Paine declared, had been chiefly concerned with the misfortunes caused by the vices of kings. But now that France had attained the age of reason she would see the absurdity of retaining an office which required neither virtue, wisdom nor talent and which might devolve upon a madman, an imbecile or a tyrant.

The next day, 2 July, Paine's manifesto was published in full in Brissot's *Patriote françois* together with the comments of various members of the National Assembly. Two of them accused its author of being a criminal and a madman. On the same day, the Republican Society published its own periodical, *le Républicain ou le défenseur du gouvernement représentatif*, for which Paine wrote the leading article. He outlined the principles of the journal and attacked the notion found in Montesquieu that the republican system is adapted only to small nations. Somewhat vague concerning the method which the French should use to abolish the evils of hereditary succession, he argued primarily that the Revolution had until then been too timid, but held out hope for reform since the Constitution had not yet been completed. "Only when the French Constitution conforms to the *Declaration of Rights*," Paine affirmed, "can France be justly entitled to be called a *civic empire;* because then only will its government be the empire of laws based upon the grand republican principles of Elective Representation and the Rights of Man."

By an unusual stroke of either craft or good fortune, Paine engineered a journalistic exchange in the course of which Sieyès threw the weight of his enormous prestige behind the principle of establishing the Constitution on the Declaration of Rights. Sieyès, known as the defender of the Third Estate, had gained extensive renown with a pamphlet published in 1789, *Qu'est-ce que le tiers état?* He was elected to the States General and later to the Convention, where he attempted to give practical form to his theories. On 6 July 1791 Sieyès wrote a letter to the principal French newspaper, *le Moniteur,* in which he defended his preference for monarchy over a republic. Paine replied in a letter which was printed 16 July, in both the *Républicain* and the *Moniteur* and followed in the latter by a rejoinder from Sieyès. The text of Paine's letter (dated 8 July) is identical in both periodicals apart from a few minor textual variations. Condorcet saw to its publication in the *Républicain* and he probably concerted with Sieyès to have it published in the *Moniteur* as well. The opposition between Sieyès and Paine was only superficial, and they covered each other with compliments. Indeed several contemporaries maintained that Sieyès and Condorcet prearranged that Paine should have the victory in the debate.

Joseph Lakanal, fellow member with Condorcet of the Committee of Public Instruction, revealed in 1796 that Condorcet had told him one day that he, Paine and Sieyès had jointly occupied themselves with preparing the French people to accept a republic. They had agreed that in order to succeed in their attack on the throne they must proceed with moderation. It was arranged that Sieyès should first touch on the question of royalty and defend it half-heartedly. Condorcet and Paine were then to reply with superior arguments. This carefully elaborated campaign led Lakanal to consider "Condorcet, Thomas Paine and Sieyès as the first founders of the republic in France."

While Paine was still in Paris, a curious observer in England sent him four questions concerning the Constitution of France. Paine wrote out replies to his "officious questioner" and turned them over to Condorcet for translating and printing. The latter published them in the next year in *la Chronique du mois*, a publication of the Cercle Social, a circumstance which has given rise to the erroneous assumption that Condorcet himself was the proposer of the questions. A paragraph in the London *Morning Chronicle*, 12 July 1791, however, reveals that the queries came from England. Each question was phrased so that an affirmative answer would indicate a deficiency in the French Constitution. Condorcet in an ironic note observed that the questioner hoped for such a response to each query whereas the austere republican Paine had the bad grace to adhere to his principles and reply in the negative.

He gave, nevertheless, extremely moderate answers. The first question concerned the balance between legislative and executive powers, the second the alleged weakness of the executive powers, the third the unicameral organization, and the fourth the means of expanding and improving the Constitution. Only the third, that concerning unicameralism, had any important relevance to Paine's previously published works. Originally Paine had followed Franklin in favoring a unicameral system. We have seen, however, that in September 1786 he found more evil than good in a single legislature. In his answer concerning the French system Paine recognized the disadvantages of both the unicameral and the bicameral forms and proposed a compromise. He advocated a legislature divided into two equal sections. Each section would in turn discuss some question while the other section listened. "Then, after each section had heard the arguments of the other, the debate would be closed, and the subject finally submitted to the decision of the entire legislature." This plan, Paine felt, would obviate the inconveniences of a single chamber and still not entail the evils inherent in two.

The subject of unicameralism was crucial in France. Largely because of the influence and prestige of Franklin, a number of Frenchmen, including Condorcet and La Rochefoucauld, were advocating a single chamber for the new government. We have seen that Paine had had nothing to do with the unicameralism of the Pennsylvania constitution, but many observers, including John Adams and Cheetham, maintained that Paine had been a prime mover. Because the reign of tyranny set in soon after France had adopted a single chamber, Adams and Cheetham attributed all evils of the Terror directly to Paine's influence. Cheetham asked the rhetorical question: "May not Paine's constitution of Pennsylvania have been the cause of the tyranny of Robespierre?" We have seen, however, that in 1791 Paine proposed a quite different system for France, and he incorporated essentially the same plan in the second part of *The Rights of Man.*

It is impossible to decide absolutely whether Paine's fundamental moral and political opinions were basically practical and pragmatic or whether they were entirely theoretical and idealistic. Because of his opposition to Burke, Paine is generally known in history as the defender of reason, of the application of theory and idealism to government and everyday conduct. It is possible that his contacts with French *philosophes,* especially Condorcet and Bonneville, fostered this interest in abstract ideas. His earlier writings on the American Revolution were inspired by particular events and are relatively less marked by abstract ideas or metaphysical reasoning than those on the French Revolution.

Paine's ideological tendencies were certainly displayed in his "Answers to Four Questions" whether or not due to the influence of Condorcet and Bonneville. Notice particularly his maxim: "In every land throughout the universe the tendency of the interest of the greatest number is in the direction of good rather than of evil, and the inevitable result must be to elevate the science of government to a height of perfection of which we have now no conception." Here is a profession of faith in the perfectibility of man which Condorcet, perfectibilian par excellence, could hardly have surpassed. Henceforth Paine was to devote his entire energies and talents toward applying the principle of natural rights to government. And in so doing he was consistently to sacrifice his personal welfare.

XI

"The Revolution of the World"

On the same day Paine wrote his letter to Sieyès, 8 July 1791, he left Paris for London in the company of Étienne Dumont and Lord Daer, a young Scotsman, who had imbibed libertarian and republican principles in France and dreamed of inoculating his own country with revolutionary doctrines. Dumont considered Paine a caricature of the vainest type of Frenchman. "He believed that his book on *The Rights of Man* could take the place of all the books of the world, and he said to us quite sincerely that if it were in his power to demolish all the libraries in existence he would do it without hesitation so as to destroy all the errors of which they were the depository—and with *The Rights of Man* begin a new chain of ideas and principles. He knew by heart all his own writings and knew nothing else."

Paine arrived in London on 11 July in time to celebrate, three days later, the second anniversary of the fall of the Bastille, the new national holiday of France. An assemblage of one thousand gentlemen met at the Crown and Anchor tavern under the auspices of the Revolution Society to commemorate the event. Paine was expected to attend, but his physicians dissuaded him, finding him too fatigued from the ardors of his journey. By a curious irony, Burke was present at the same tavern, but in a private room with the Council of the Royal Academy. According to the he-gossip Horace Walpole, "the villain Paine" had returned from France especially for the gathering, but "finding that his pamphlet had not set a straw on fire, and the 14th of July was as little in fashion as the ancient Gunpowder Plot, he dined at another tavern with a few quaking conspirators."

151

The large and important Revolution Society was one of a number of political clubs organized in both France and England to foster constitutional reform. The societies in England grew up out of the Glorious Revolution of 1688. Soon after this event, leading Whigs began holding annual meetings on the fourth of November to commemorate the deposing of James II. In the 1770's developed a radical political organization called the Honest Whigs, which sponsored a secret Masonic-like group called the Constitutional Whigs, Grand Lodge of England.

Most influential of all such English clubs was the Society for Constitutional Information, which had existed since 1780, but developed renewed vigor after the outbreak of the French Revolution. Its aims were moderate constitutional reform. The distinguished legalist Horne Tooke was the most prominent member, and Paine himself held honorary status. He attended its meetings whenever he could, on 22 July 1791 for the first time. On 1 April 1791, the society passed resolutions strongly recommending Paine's *The Rights of Man* and published them in various newspapers. It supervised the printing of a cheap edition of the work and later distributed over eight thousand copies of Paine's letter to Dundas. Independent societies for constitutional information grew up in industrial centers such as Manchester and Sheffield. On 14 March 1792, the members of the Sheffield group declared that they had "derived more true knowledge from the two works of Mr. Thomas Paine, intituled 'Rights of Man . . .' than from any other author on the subject."

Closely allied with the Society for Constitutional Information was the London Corresponding Society, most radical of all the clubs, established in January 1792 by a shoemaker, Thomas Hardy. Composed primarily of working men, the society contended for universal suffrage and annual parliaments, taking *The Rights of Man* as its gospel. Paine, although a good friend of Hardy, seems not to have been a member.

The most moderate of these societies was an association of Whig gentry known as Friends of the People, which by and large supported the liberal but cautious principles of Fox. Organized in 1792, this society in the following month repudiated Paine's "great plans of public benefit" on the ground that he spoke the indefinite language of delusion leading to dangerous and uncontrolled innovation.

On 4 November 1791 Paine attended a dinner of the Revolution Society at the London Tavern. During the banquet, which lasted five hours, 250 guests celebrated the anniversary of the deposing of James II. Paine's former bridge-building associate, Thomas Walker, was in the chair. Among the toasts were "Mr. Paine, with thanks for his Defense of the Rights of Man." Paine in response proposed "The Revolution of the World," a phrase which long after remained in the minds of the guests. Sixteen years later Thomas Hardy, for example, was still stirred by Paine's sublime concept. Paine was not a member of the Revolution Society, but one of its official publications explained that he belonged to other clubs with identical principles.

The resemblance of the English reform societies to the Jacobins in France and the practice of sending complimentary addresses back and forth from one country to the other led the English government to consider the organizations as dangerously subversive. The English societies, moreover, worked in close co-operation with each other, giving the appearance of a common front. With the exception of the Friends of the People, they uniformly commended Paine and his writings.

In the spring of 1792, the Constitutional Society of Manchester prepared an address of congratulation to be delivered to the Jacobins in Paris, confiding it to John Watt, who was then in Paris for business, and Thomas Cooper, who was there for pleasure. Burke, on hearing of this address, made a speech, 30 April, denouncing "men who scrupled not to enter into an alliance with a set in France of the worst traitors and regicides that had ever been heard of, the club of the Jacobins." He charged that "agents had been sent from this country, to enter into a federation with that iniquitous club, . . . that those worthies of Manchester undertook . . . to represent all England." Cooper angrily accused Burke of taking advantage of the ignorance of the people and seeking to perpetuate it. "I think the time is not far distant," he retorted, "when the People . . . will regard it as we do now, an honour conferred on Mr. Watt and myself, that public report has connected our names on this occasion with that of *Thomas Paine*."

On 11 May 1792 the Constitutional Society of London also

prepared an address to the Jacobins, which Watt and Cooper presented on the 27th. Paine may have been its author since a manuscript of the address in his handwriting was discovered in 1898. The address repeated Paine's theory that tyrannical governments had destroyed the natural friendship of the French and English peoples.

Paine, on 18 May 1792, communicated to the Constitutional Society requests from every part of the country that a cheap edition of *The Rights of Man* be brought out. Since he had been informed that the Ministry intended to bring a prosecution against him, he felt that the whole nation had a right to become acquainted with the works which were becoming the subject of prosecution. The society on the same day thanked Paine and resolved to "contribute its utmost Aid towards supporting the Rights of the Nation, and the Freedom of the Press, and him who has so essentially and successfully contributed to both." The Constitutional Society transmitted Paine's letter to all associated groups, including the London Corresponding Society, which forthwith, 15 June, opened a subscription for Paine's defense.

On the fourth of August a gathering was scheduled for the Crown and Anchor to commemorate the abolishment of feudalism in France, but "certain unnamed and skulking persons"—government agents—prevailed on the master of the tavern to refuse admittance to the group. Paine thereupon drew up an address to take the place of the proposed meeting. In it he congratulated the French people upon their revolution and rejoiced in the prospect of the consequent immediate reduction of taxes in England. He reasoned that if, as all English administrations had maintained, the restless ambition of the Court of France required an annual expenditure of seventeen millions for military defense, the end of the Court of France should immediately mean the end of the enormous burden of taxation in England. He ironically expressed astonishment "that any part, or any members of our own government, should reprobate the extinction of that very power in France, or wish to see it restored, to whose influence they formerly attributed (while they appeared to lament) the enormous increase of our own burdens and taxes." This address Paine showed to Horne Tooke and other gentlemen, who, fully approving it, held a meeting to make it public and subscribed fifty guineas for advertising. The address was signed by Horne Tooke as chairman and published under the title, *Address and Declaration at a Select Meeting of the Friends of Universal Peace and Liberty, Held at the Thatched House Tavern, St. James' Street, August 20, 1791*. As Paine had allowed Du Chastelet to sign his republican manifesto in France, so he allowed Horne Tooke to sign his address in London, feeling perhaps that Tooke's legal reputation would carry greater weight than his own pamphleteering one.

Despite a strong thread of vanity in his personality and an obvious sentiment of self-satisfaction concerning the prestige and influence of his own literary works, Paine probably undertook his political writing for the good it would accomplish, not for personal glory and fame. He even believed that he would have preferred a life of retirement, withdrawn from political turmoil and agitation. In a letter to Washington concerning *The Rights of Man*, written shortly before the Thatched House Address, he remarked,

After the establishment of the American Revolution, it did not appear to me that any object could arise great enough to engage me a second time. I began to feel myself happy in being quiet; but I now experience that principle is not confined to time or place, and that the ardor of Seventy-six is capable of renewing itself. I have another work on hand which I intend shall be my last, for I long much to return to America. It is not natural that fame should wish for a rival, but the case is otherwise with me, for I do most sincerely wish there was some person in this country that could usefully and successfully attract the public attention, and leave me with a satisfied mind to the enjoyment of quiet life: but it is painful to see errors and abuses and sit down a senseless spectator.

XII

Continuation of The Rights of Man

During the years 1791-1792 there was scarcely a single issue of any London newspaper which failed to mention Paine in one way or another—for the most part unfavorably. Many journals devoted whole columns to him, printing doggerel verse, gossip, invective, controversy and editorial comment. Paine's burst of publicity, however, lasted only briefly. Before the publication of *The Rights of Man* he had rarely been mentioned in the London press, and after his removal to France interest in his affairs waned. Even the subsequent publication of *The Age of Reason* brought him only sporadic attention in British newspapers.

Although the government marked Paine as a dangerous incendiary immediately after the appearance of the first part of *The Rights of Man*, he was by no means the only radical in England at the time, nor was he the only author harried by the authorities. Meetings of sympathizers of the French Revolution were regularly broken up, and a famous anti-Revolution demonstration in Birmingham on 14 July 1791, led to rioting for two days during which the home of Joseph Priestley was pillaged and burned. Not until November 1791 did Paine sense that he and *The Rights of Man* were being singled out. "By what I can find," he wrote to William Short in Paris, "the Government Gentry begin to threaten. They have already tried all the under-plots of abuse and scurrility without effect; and have managed those in general so badly as to make the work and the author the more famous; several answers also have been written against it which did not excite reading enough to pay the expence of printing."

In the same month he wrote to his former scientific assistant in

Philadelphia, John Hall, describing his recent writings as his "political Bridge." Forced to admit that the tide of sentiment was still running the wrong way, he claimed, nevertheless, that a change was beginning to take place. "I have so far got the ear of John Bull that he will read what I write—which is more than ever was done before to the same extent. *Rights of Man* has had the greatest run of anything ever published in this country, at least of late years—almost sixteen thousand has gone off—and in Ireland above forty thousand—beside the above numbers one thousand printed cheap are now gone to Scotland by desire of some of the [friends] there."

Radical as it may have seemed to the administration, however, the first part of *The Rights of Man* did not openly advocate revolution in England, and it is doubtful that a prosecution of the work would have been upheld in court. It was the second part, vilifying the British Constitution, which became the target of prosecution.

Paine began working on this part in France between April and July 1791 and had completed a considerable portion by September when he had returned to London. According to Cobbett, while Paine was making arrangements for publication he concealed himself in Fetter Lane and no one knew where he was "except Mr. Horne Tooke . . . and Mr. Chapman," the printer. This statement is confirmed by the fact that the newspapers carried no record of any of his personal activities subsequent to his toast on the fourth of November to the Revolution of the World.

Paine's friend Thomas Christie had introduced him to Thomas Chapman, the printer, who agreed to publish a new edition of Part I as well as the first edition of Part II. By the middle of January 1792 Chapman had printed over one hundred pages and had promised to complete the work within a fortnight, that is, before the opening of Parliament on the last day of the month. Suddenly Chapman returned Paine's manuscript and refused any inducement to go on with the work. Paine was forced to find another printer, and the work failed to appear by the opening of Parliament.

Two different explanations exist to account for these circumstances: Chapman's and Paine's. Paine in an Appendix to *The Rights of Man* makes no direct charges against Chapman, but suggests by the manner in which he narrates the events of printing that Chapman was coerced by the Pitt Ministry to suppress the work. Paine emphasizes three suspicious circumstances: first, Chapman, when he began to print the work, had offered Paine a thousand pounds for the copyright, which Paine refused on the ground that he "would never put it in the power of any printer or publisher to suppress or alter a work of mine, by making him master of the copy, or give to him the right of selling it to any minister"; second, after the printing had been nearly completed, Chapman abruptly refused to continue the work "on any consideration"; third, a scheme in the text to reduce specific taxes had been so closely duplicated by Pitt in a parliamentary speech that the conclusion was almost inescapable "that either the author had taken the hint from Mr. Pitt, or Mr. Pitt from the author." Paine does not directly assert that Pitt had seen his work, but remarks plainly enough that "the manner in which the work was returned, and the particular time at which this was done, and that after the offers he [Chapman] had made, are suspicious circumstances."

Chapman gave his version of the affair at the subsequent trial of Paine for seditious libel, a trial at which the accused was not present! At the very least, we must discount the evidence of Chapman as that of an interested party. According to his testimony, Paine called on him, 16 January, after dining with Johnson, the publisher, at St. Paul's Churchyard. Paine was "rather intoxicated by liquor," a condition which Chapman considered, according to his knowledge, somewhat unusual. Paine introduced the subject of religion, bringing on a virulent debate with the Chapmans, who were pious dissenters. Mrs. Chapman made a remark near ten o'clock, particularly offending Paine. The latter, rising up in great passion, "said he had not been so personally affronted in the whole course of his life before." He declared that "he had a very bad opinion of dissenters in general"; that he "believed them all to be a pack of hypocrites," that he intended to deal very cautiously with them, and that in the morning before Chapman should proceed any further in his work, he wished to have a settlement with him. Chapman allegedly was pleased with this turn of events since it gave him a pretext for giving up the work, which he had already decided not to continue, fearing that part of it had an extremely dangerous tendency. Accordingly, on the next morning, he returned to Paine all of his copy. The latter then called upon him, profuse in apologies, attributing his bad conduct to the influence of liquor, and asked that Chapman proceed with the work. The latter, however, would not on any account take it up again. Chapman declared, moreover, that he had previously made three separate offers to Paine to buy the copy during different stages of the printing. The first was a hundred guineas, the second five hundred, and the last a thousand. Paine refused all offers, answering that since he intended to publish a cheap edition of his work, he wished to keep all rights in his own hands.

This testimony is extremely interesting since it is the first time in the life of Paine that he was openly and publicly accused of the abuse of intoxicating liquors. Even Chalmers had not thought of this charge, which was frequently leveled against Paine after his return to America in 1802 and even more extensively after his death. If Chapman's evidence is true, it is worth noting that he added that the condition was "rather unusual" to his knowledge.

Both Jordan and Johnson, Paine's previous publishers, were involved in the sale of the second part of *The Rights of Man*. On 7 February, Paine sent Chapman a request that all the remaining sheets be delivered to Jordan, and on 21 April he wrote to Jordan asking him to settle finances with Johnson. Apparently Paine expected that the authorities would make trouble for his publishers, for on publication date, 16 February 1792, he sent Jordan a letter, naming himself as the sole author and publisher and instructing Jordan to communicate with him in care of Johnson in the event of any difficulty, and to send also for Horne Tooke. The edition printed by Jordan was sold also by Johnson, and Paine at least twice drew drafts on Jordon of 150 pounds to be paid to Johnson.

In these proceedings Horne Tooke seems to have played an equivocal and not very admirable role. Because of Tooke's legal prestige and prominence in the Society for Constitutional Information, Paine apparently relied on him to serve as trouble-breaker. Yet when Tooke himself was put on the stand in 1794, he attempted to minimize his sympathies with Paine and the reform movement.

It is noteworthy that the society had approved the relatively innocuous first part of *The Rights of Man* and not the sequel, which was far more incendiary. At Paine's trial the Attorney General admitted that he had not found reason to prosecute Part I since its circulation was limited to judicious readers, but Part II was "ushered into the world in all shapes and sizes, thrust into the hands of subjects of every description, even children's sweetmeats being wrapped in it."

Paine's own explanation was that since the original edition was expensively printed to be bound in a single volume with Burke's *Reflections*, "the high price precluded the generality of people from purchasing." He would have himself preferred to print a cheap edition at the outset, but had been advised that the more expedient method would be to let the work come out first in the usual style of printing. But many cheap editions of both parts followed. In May he undertook an edition "for the benefit and information of the poor at the price of thirty shillings per hundred." In a letter to the Constitutional Society, 4 July 1792, Paine explained that the work could not have been produced at such a low price were it not for the tremendous number printed. The book had already produced over a thousand pounds profit, and Paine requested the honor of donating the money for the use of the society. By devoting the profits of *The Rights of Man* to public good as he had previously dedicated those of *Common Sense*, he felt that he had "done by the people of England the same as . . . by those of America."

The section entitled "On Constitutions" in the second part of *The Rights of Man* was primarily responsible for the prosecution. Here Paine elaborated his former charge that the British have merely a government, not a Constitution. He argued that "from the want of understanding the difference between a constitution and a government, Dr. Johnson, and all writers of his description, have always bewildered themselves." The alleged British Constitution, Paine interpreted as merely a series of attempts to abate tyranny and make it less intolerable. This was Paine's analysis of such documents as the Magna Charta and the Bill of Rights. The latter, he maintained, was merely a bargain "which the parts of government made with each other to divide powers, profits and privileges." Not only was the British Constitution illusory, according to Paine, but its policy of preaching up precedents meant blind obedience to principles and opinions the reverse, in general, of what they ought to be. The upholders of antiquity, he charged, to answer some purposes spoke of the past as times of darkness and ignorance; to answer others, as the light of the world.

Not neglecting economic arguments, Paine asserted that in England and other monarchical governments, millions of pounds were paid annually out of public taxes for the support of the King "while thousands who are forced to contribute thereto, are pining with want, and struggling with misery. Government does not consist in a contrast between prisons and palaces, between poverty and pomp; it is not instituted to rob the needy of his mite, and increase the wretchedness of the wretched." As an example of the best development of the science of government, Paine described the origin and functioning of the American Constitution, but suggested as an improvement his scheme of dividing the legislature into two groups for debate—the plan he had first discussed in his answer to four questions.

The second part of *The Rights of Man* had the same phenomenal success as the first. By the end of the year it was estimated that the sale of the two parts combined extended to two hundred thousand copies. The Shakespeare scholar, Edmund Malone, reported in December 1792 that for several weeks "not less than four thousand per week of Paine's despicable and nonsensical pamphlet have been issued forth, for almost nothing, and dispersed all over the kingdom. At Manchester and Sheffield the innovators bribe the poor by drink to hear it read."

Almost immediately after the publication of the work, Paine became subject to a series of legal vexations. While attending the anniversary dinner of the Society for Constitutional Information, 13 April 1792, at the London Tavern, he was arrested by a bailiff at the suit of a certain Mark Gregory and others for an indebtedness of two hundred pounds. Apparently the arrest was made at the commencement of the festivities before Paine had begun to dine. He was carried hatless in a coach to the King's Head sponging house, where he arrived about six o'clock. About an hour later the booksellers Joseph Johnson and George Wilkie provided bail. The *Morning Chronicle*, only London newspaper friendly to Paine, tried to cover up the incident by reporting merely, "after Mr. PAINE withdrew, his health was given," but the other newspapers filled in with gusto the savory details of the reasons for Paine's abrupt departure.

Paine attended another meeting of the Constitutional Society seven days later, and then left London to stay with his aunt in Bromley, Kent. Three weeks later he learned that the government was about to institute proceedings against his publisher, Jordan, and he immediately returned to town. He discovered that the same day, 14 May, Jordan had been served with a summons to appear at the Court of King's Bench on the following Monday. Paine asked Jordan to meet him at Horne Tooke's, where they arranged that Jordan should be defended by an attorney named Bonney, Paine paying expenses. But Jordan, lacking confidence in Paine's arrangements, engaged another attorney. Tooke became angry at Jordan's timidity and spoke to him sharply, telling him to go about his business and leave the defense to Paine. Jordan, however, took the easiest way out by pleading guilty, which meant merely admitting that he was indeed publisher of the work in question.

On 21 May the government began its prosecution against Paine by leaving a summons for trial on June 8 at his lodgings, and on the same day it issued a proclamation against seditious writings. This proclamation, although making no specific mention of either Paine or *The Rights of Man*, was intended to restrict sale of the work and to induce an adverse verdict from the jury which would try the author.

The immediate effect of the proclamation was vastly to increase the circulation of the book. Even the Home Secretary, Henry Dundas, admitted that it gave Paine's writings a degree of consequence they would not otherwise have possessed.

On 25 May a debate over the proclamation began in the House of Commons. Fox disapproved, charging that it was insidious and ambiguous. It implied a desire to discover the author and publisher of *The Rights of Man* despite the obvious fact that these were well known. If it were really intended to apply to Paine, Fox argued, this purpose should have been directly and unequivocally stated. The main object of the framers, was to throw out vague aspersions and engender unnecessary alarms. They hoped to divide the Whig party by creating suspicions and distrust and by turning the moderates against the extremists. Fox feared that the proclamation could be used against such organizations as Friends of the People, which, sympathetic to Fox, had formally repudiated Paine.

Secretary Dundas in rebuttal justified the fact that prosecution of *The Rights of Man* had not been instituted until fourteen months after publication. He pointed out that the danger came from the principles adopted from the book by the reform societies "and sedulously inculcated throughout the kingdom in a variety of shapes." The passages incorporating these principles were uniformly drawn from the second part, which had appeared only three months previous to the prosecution. Dundas had in his hand the resolution of the Constitutional Society of Sheffield, and he hoped he was not to be told "that there was no ground for alarm and apprehension, nor any sufficient cause for the Proclamation, when great bodies of men in large manufacturing towns, adopted and circulated doctrines so pernicious in their tendency, and so subversive of the Constitution and Government of the country." Dundas explained that the initial prosecution was directed against the printer rather than the author since proof of authorship must first be established. The mere presence of the name *Thomas Paine* on the title page would not be admitted as proof in a court of judicature.

Paine thereupon addressed an open letter to Dundas, 6 June 1792, pointing out that he had done exactly that which he had been accused of not doing. In place of the English system of "hereditary nonsense" he had established the purely representative system as exemplified in America. In that country, he jibed, "there is not that class of poor and wretched people that are so numerously dispersed all over England, who are to be told by a proclamation, that they are happy." He repeated his arguments from his letter to the French Ministry that an alliance should be formed between England and France—an alliance which would eliminate all military expenditures. Wiping out both the civil list and the army, Paine maintained, would bring prosperity to the English economy and happiness to the English people. He had written *The Rights of Man*, he explained, to promote this measure.

In June, Paine noticed in the newspapers an advertisement of a proposed meeting to be held at Epsom to consider the proclamation, which Onslow Cranley, signer of the advertisement, described as "His Majesty's paternal, and well-timed attendance to the public welfare." Paine addressed to Cranley a letter which he asked to be read at the meeting. In this letter, after summarizing the principles of *The Rights of Man*, he charged that the purpose of the meeting was to influence in advance a jury about to be convened in Middlesex to consider *The Rights of Man*, "In short, that it is dictating a verdict by proclamation." The letter was handed to Cranley at the meeting, and when the latter saw that it was signed by Paine, he described Paine before the meeting as "the common enemy of us all." A similar meeting was scheduled for Lewes in July, and Paine, following his practice, wrote to the presiding officer, requesting that a statement be read at the meeting. In it he summarized the circumstances of his composing *The Rights of Man* and explained why the second part had excited an alarm among the placemen and pensioners greater than that aroused by the first part—this was his demonstration that the abolishing of the pension list would reduce taxes by six millions and still allow ample revenue for aiding the poor and aged.

The very existence of the proclamation against seditious writings—a proclamation framed specifically to combat *The Rights of Man*—together with the various meetings and addresses to supplement it must have warned Paine that the government would soon take steps to restrict his freedom of speech, if not of action. Paine felt more than ever convinced, he wrote in his letter to Dundas, that the thousand pounds which had been offered Chapman for the copyright to *The Rights of Man* had been offered in order to silence him. In his letter to Cranley he pointed out that no less than forty pamphlets had been written to refute *The Rights of Man*, and that for almost eighteen months the Court newspapers had daily poured forth abuse against him. "And now that every attempt to refute, and every abuse has failed, the invention of calling the work a libel has been hit upon."

During May and June because of the reprisals against *The Rights of Man*, various journals reported prematurely and inaccurately the flight of Paine to France, alleging that he sought to escape bailiffs, constables and jailors. On 11 June the *Morning Chronicle* remarked that Paine, respecting whose flight so many false reports had been circulating, was at that moment "very quietly sitting to Mr. ROMNEY, the painter, for his portrait in defiance of the Attorney-General and the Proclamation."

Paine's trial had been scheduled for 8 June, but it was postponed until December. On the anniversary of the French Revolution, 14 July, Paine dined with an Irish society and had to miss a more imposing gathering at the Shakespeare Tavern presided over by Horne Tooke.

From June to September, Paine lodged with his friends the Rickmans in London. During that time a large and a small edition of

The Rights of Man were being printed for Rickman, and Paine himself read the proof. According to Rickman, Paine enjoyed a peaceable routine of philosophical leisure and sprightly conversation. He passed his time writing, answering his correspondence, visiting his acquaintances, strolling in the public walks, and entertaining his intimate friends. Paine's correspondence must have been extensive, for he said in one of his letters written late in 1791 that if he were to answer all the communications he received, he should require half a dozen clerks.

During February and March 1792, Paine called frequently on Gouverneur Morris despite their former animosity and their perpetual disagreement. On 16 February, Morris read Part II of *The Rights of Man* and told Paine he ran a great risk of being punished. Paine seemed cocksure of bringing about a revolution in Great Britain, but Morris thought he would be promoted to the pillory. Later in the month, when Paine seemed to Morris to become every hour more drunk with self-conceit, they quarreled over French affairs. Morris held that the divided state of affairs in France worked against all reform schemes everywhere, but Paine declared that the riots and outrages in France were nothing at all. Morris broke off the debate by accusing Paine of not believing his own declarations.

Goaded by the proclamation and the series of trumped-up addresses issued by government-sponsored meetings, Paine in the summer of 1792 wrote a long *Letter Addressed to the Addressers on the Late Proclamation*. The work was published in the fall after Paine had returned to France to take a seat in the National Convention. Impatient with the temporizing of the Whig moderates, Paine abandoned hope for reform within the British political organization as then constituted and openly called for revolution and abolishment of the monarchy.

There may have been some question concerning the seditious nature of *The Rights of Man*. There was none concerning the *Address*. It was an open appeal for swift and immediate revolution. Paine characterized the reform of Parliament by applying to the benevolence of Parliament itself as a "worn-out, hackneyed subject." The phrase "temperate and moderate reform" as used by the Foxites and the Society of Friends of the People, formerly Paine's friends and associates, Paine now interpreted as meaning "a continuation of the abuses as long as possible. If we cannot hold all let us hold some."

Instead of appealing to Parliament, Paine proposed the election of a national convention to establish a new Constitution—an election in which every man of twenty-one years or over should be entitled to take part. Here again we see Paine's opposition to authority and tradition, his preference of abstract principles. *"On the pure ground of principle,"* he argued, "antiquity and precedent cease to be authority, and hoary-headed error loses its effect. The reasonableness and propriety of things must be examined abstractedly from custom and usage; and, in this point of view, the right which grows into practice today is as much a right, and as old in principle and theory, as if it had the customary sanction of a thousand ages." In direct contrast to Burke, who considered a constitution to be the evolution of practical experiments in government, Paine defined a constitution as "a thing antecedent to a government, . . . the act of a people creating a government and giving it powers, and defining the limits and exercise of the powers so given."

In the election of an English national convention, Paine wanted no property qualifications of any kind. He proposed that this convention review the whole mass of laws of the nation to retain the useful ones and drop the rest—and that subsequently at the expiration of every period of twenty-one years a similar review take place. Because of this last provision, one cannot say that Paine by advocating the revision of common law and the drawing up of a theoretical constitution was putting theory above practice. He very clearly proposed a balance of the two.

When he wrote this pamphlet in the summer of 1792, Paine must have realized that the addressers, i. e. the Ministry would inevitably proceed from prosecuting the work, *The Rights of Man*, to prosecuting its author, but it is hard to believe that he was influenced by a sense of impending danger when he decided to leave England for France on 12 September 1792. His trial was not scheduled to take place until December.

Paine did not steal away on impulse on the spur of the moment, but left deliberately to take his place in the French Assembly, accompanied by Achille Audibert of Calais, who had been delegated to go to London to escort him, and by John Frost, a liberal English attorney.

Their departure was no secret, for the Ministry sent a post-chaise to keep them under surveillance all the way. At Dover they were detained and searched. An Englishman, J. Mason, who crossed with Paine on the packet from Dover to Calais has left an account of the insulting event:

. . . the officers of the Customs came and insisted on searching them, which, after some objections on their part, was submitted to, as force was threatened in case of refusal. The officer said they had an information which Mr. Audibert wanted them to produce, but they did not. They were kept an hour and 5 minutes in the room, with the door locked a great part of the time. Mr. Frost (I heard him) said he wanted to go to the necessary, and they refused to let him go. They examined their papers very strictly, and opened some of their letters, the most suspected no doubt, and took the directions of the others, even asked what money they had. Mr. Paine told that in the packet he had about 25 guineas; I believe they made him count them. I think, but am not positive as to this. Mr. Audibert said he tore a letter that their curiosity might not be satisfied in reading it, notwithstanding it was of no consequence according to his account.

Mr. Audibert complains violently of the ill-treatment they received, and being kept in prison an hour and 5 minutes, after his having been so serviceable to numbers of English at Calais; threatens he will publish it in all the English papers; if they will not put it in, he says he will have bills posted up at his expense in London to publish it to the nation. This group of 3 set off to-morrow, I believe, for Paris, therefore the National Assembly will be informed of it in the course of a few days. This company went on board the packet immediately on being liberated. The packet was followed till out of the pier, which might be a quarter of an hour, by numbers of people to stare at Tom Paine as they called him. He was hissed a great deal, and many ridiculous speeches made relative to his trade (he has been a stay-maker at Dover). The crowd increased very much: the wind being slack the packet was obliged to be towed out: I believe had we remained much longer they would have pelted him with stones from the beach. Personally he is a very mean looking man. It is in my opinion a disgrace to them, rather than a merit, that a better representative cannot be found at home without having recourse to a foreigner like him. He is the very picture of journeyman tailor who has been drunk and playing at nine-pins for the 3 first days of the week, and is returning to his work on Thursday. We arrived at Calais, and as soon as he was known to be on the shore, the people flocked to see him, and it was talked of saluting him with the guards as he passed the Place d'Armes. It rained hard, and I left him.

Paine must have felt a weight on his heart, knowing that he was being virtually driven from his native land. Henceforth he was to struggle for his equalitarian ideals exclusively in France and the United States. His situation during the Channel crossing symbolized the uneven ambivalence of his whole career—harassed and reprobated by the government of one country; heralded and eulogized by the government of another.

Where Liberty Is Not

According to a tradition repeated by many biographers of Paine, Franklin at one time remarked in his hearing: "Where liberty is, there is my country." Paine replied, "Where liberty is not, there is mine." Although the story must be written off as apocryphal, Paine's dedication to the principle of liberty unquestionably characterized his sojourn in France between 1792 and 1802.

He had acquired a moderate fame in France during the American Revolution when his *Common Sense* was translated in *Affaires de l'Angleterre et de l'Amérique,* 1776, a periodical of American propaganda, and later Franklin paved the way for his favorable personal reception in 1787 by giving him letters of introduction to his liberal friends. In 1791 when *Common Sense* was translated anew in two rival editions and its republican doctrines were being associated with events in France, Paine's vogue spread throughout the country. After two separate translations of *The Rights of Man* appeared in March and April 1792, the *Moniteur* described its author as "the most determined champion of republican principles."

Among Paine's heralds in France was the Prussian-born Baron Jean Baptiste (Anacharsis) de Clootz, one of the few personalities in the French Revolution whose career was more amazing than Paine's own. Himself a journalist and vain of his colorful prose, Clootz marveled at the fear which Paine's writings had inspired in the British government. "Imagine," he wrote in the *Patriote fran-çois,* 14 April 1792, "that an engineer like Thomas Paine paralyzes the entire English fleet; a single journalist wields as much power as Brest, Toulon and Rochefort [French naval bases]. Opinion, you see, is more than ever queen of the world." Two months later

169

Brissot de Warville commented in the *Patriote*, 14 June, on the English prosecution of Paine and the debate in Parliament over the proclamation. The aristocracy had showed itself completely without shame, he reported, and even Fox and Lansdowne had failed to render Paine the tribute he merited. Brissot attributed their snobbish attitude to the fact that Paine had once been a schoolmaster—they were catering to the prejudices of the aristocracy at the very moment they were attacking it.

At this time, Robespierre, already a power in the Assembly and soon to become a virtual dictator, considered Paine "one of the most eloquent defenders of the rights of humanity." He cited *The Rights of Man* in his political journal, *le Défenseur de la Constitution*, June 1792, however, primarily as a means of attacking Lafayette. Paine in his book had rather ostentatiously described his friendship with the French General and had reported some details concerning the National Assembly which he had received on Lafayette's authority. Robespierre, denying Paine's contention that Lafayette was one of the founders of French liberty, took it upon himself for the public good and for Paine's information to correct two of his facts. Paine had stated that Lafayette was elected Vice President of the Constituent Assembly because the early days of the Revolution demanded a firmer and more vigorous leadership to struggle against the power of the Court than that afforded by the Archbishop of Vienne who held the office of President. Paine had also affirmed that Lafayette had hastened to propose his declaration of rights in order that should the Assembly be dissolved, the declaration would remain as a monument of what had been intended for the public good. Robespierre denied that the Assembly held any great respect for Lafayette. He maintained that a vice president had been elected merely to relieve the stress and strain on the president, who was of an advanced age and was obliged to preside night and day over continuous sessions of the Assembly. Robespierre flatly declared, moreover, that not a single member at that time lacked the courage to withstand the menaces of the Court. As for Lafayette's declaration of rights, Robespierre implied that it was so pallid and ambiguous that the heroical motives which Paine attributed to it were simply ridiculous.

Despite the somewhat unfavorable overtones of Robespierre's comments, foreshadowing his eventual denunciation of Paine, the latter's reputation continued to grow in France. The impetuous Guadet, a prominent Girondin, on 23 August 1792 sponsored a decree in the Convention conferring French citizenship upon Paine along with Priestley, David Williams, Anacharsis Clootz, Pestalozzi, Washington and others.

This decree of citizenship helped bring Paine to the attention of the French electorate although it was not then necessary to be a French citizen in order to serve in the Convention. Paine's name was first brought forth, 2 September, in the electoral assembly of Pas de Calais as a strategic device to attain the election of a local dark horse. Keeping the name of this native son a secret, an orator launched forth into praise of Paine, intending later to make a comparison with his candidate. Another orator took up the thread, however, and suggested electing Paine himself: among his reasons: "it was a means of interesting the English people in the Revolution and to unite irrevocably the two peoples," a goal which had been dear to Paine ever since his letter to Brienne's secretary. This reasoning aroused violent opposition. It was argued that the majority of the electors had no idea of the principles of Paine, and that his election might have quite the contrary effect of that which was expected. During the actual balloting, Paine was the fifth candidate to be chosen, Robespierre and three others being named before him. These four were elected unanimously, but Paine had a rival, who was not eliminated until the third ballot. As soon as Paine was elected, Achille Audibert, one of the electors, volunteered to go to London to inform Paine personally. He arrived in London on the seventh or eighth of September, and, as we have seen, left with Paine on the twelfth.

The National Convention received notice of Paine's election by Pas de Calais on 9 September. Three other departments also announced their selection of Paine: Oise, 5 September; Aisne, 12 September; and Puy de Dôme, 17 September. Because of the personal visit of Audibert, Paine accepted the nomination of Pas de Calais rather than that of the other departments.

When Paine arrived in Calais, 13 September, the soldiers at the Place d'Armes were drawn up to receive him. The officer in charge embraced him and presented the national cockade. "A very pretty woman, who stood by, desired she might have the honour of putting it in his hat, expressing her hopes that he would continue his exertions in favour of Liberty, Equality, and France." After this ceremony, Paine walked to an inn on the Rue de l'Égalité, where he was to lodge. En route he was "attended by men, women, and children, crowding around him, and calling out '*Vive* THOMAS PAINE!' He was then conducted to the Town-Hall, and there presented to the Municipality, who, with the greatest affection, embraced their new Representative. The Mayor then addressed him in a short speech, which was interpreted to him, by Mr. AUDIBERT, to which PAINE (laying his hand on his heart) replied, saying, his life should be devoted to their service."

Apparently Paine left for Paris on 16 September, enjoying a leisurely journey. He arrived in Paris on the nineteenth, and on the following day made his initial appearance in the Convention during a dramatic night session. His entrance, according to John Frost, the liberal lawyer who was present, excited great curiosity among both men and women and occasioned no small interruption. First to embrace him in the French manner with a kiss on both cheeks was the president of the Society of Friends of Equality at Montpellier, Pierre-Joseph Cambon, a patriot who, after the flight of the King, had written a violent anti-monarchical address parallel to Paine's *Republican Manifesto*. Paine "entered his name on the roll of parliament, and went through the forms of office with a great deal of nonchalance." According to Frost, he was in very good spirits because of the flattering reception he had everywhere encountered, but was "rather fatigued with the kissing."

Paine began immediately to take an active part in the deliberations of the Convention. Under the leadership of Danton, drastic reforms of the judicial system were being discussed, among them the proposal that any citizen from any class in society could be elected judge whether or not he had any acquaintance with the form of law. Indeed the motion seemed particularly aimed to discriminate against lawyers. Paine, at the session of 22 September, realizing the absurdity of electing judges ignorant of the law, immediately expressed his concern to one of his colleagues, Goupilleau. The latter moved that consideration of the proposition be adjourned so that every member could participate, not only those with a talent for impromptu delivery. Paine, who was unable to speak French at all, had pointed out that if reform were undertaken piecemeal it would be impossible to retain any consistency in the judicial system and that under the present state of affairs it was essential for justice to be administered by men possessing a knowledge of the laws. Danton, worried perhaps by Paine's prestige and the attention created by his recent arrival, decided not to push the matter. He stated, therefore, that his proposal was perfectly compatible with Paine's meaning, that he did not believe that the judicial order should be changed at that moment, and that he thought merely that the area of choice should be extended.

Danton's proposal, on the surface, does seem to be an absurdity, but when seen in perspective of the development of the Revolution it is quite comprehensible. The judicial structure was the last vestige of the *ancien régime*. The privileges of the royalist administration and the aristocracy had been completely wiped out, but the judicial authority remained. Hence when profiteers and aristocratic exploiters of the people were brought to trial, they were systematically exonerated in the courts. The people wanted to rectify this situation—and the proposal to create an entirely new type of judge was intended to do it. When Paine opposed this reform, he was taking a very conservative position—one much more reactionary than he probably realized. Paine undoubtedly had no conception of the reasons behind the measure he opposed. Had he understood the background, he would probably have remained silent—despite his zeal for self-expression. It is hard to say how much effect this initial public declaration had on his popularity. Probably such leaders as Danton and Robespierre began instantly to wonder whether this Englishman was really, at heart, so sympathetic to the new order as he pretended to be in his writings. Even an English observer, writing in the *Morning Chronicle*, 4 October, commented that Paine's "speech in favour of the lawyers was not fortunate." This critic was astonished to find that Paine had prejudices in favor of a privileged class hanging about him and was even ready to believe that there had been some mistake in the translation of his remarks. If Paine really entertained the prejudices in favor of government officials which this writer detected, they may have stemmed from his own career as an official in the excise service.

The Convention at this moment was dominated by two factions, the Jacobins and the Girondins, almost but not exactly, equivalent to radicals and conservatives. In both groups cliques and strong personalities stood out. At first the Jacobins were the party of dissent and opposition while the Girondins dominated the Convention. Later the Jacobins took over almost complete control.

The term Girondin, during the period of the Convention, was used to designate the delegates from the city of Bordeaux and those of a similar temperament. These men were intellectuals of strong humanitarian motives, but of middle class antecedents. Like Paine they believed in the power of human reason to rule man as an individual and in society, but like Burke they also believed in the stability of property. They reflected the point of view of the provinces rather than that of Paris. For this reason they were accused of being exponents of a loose political system pejoratively described as federalism.

The Jacobins stemmed from a political club and debating society founded when the Assembly first met at Versailles in 1789 under the name of the Breton Club. After the club moved to Paris it took the name Friends of the Constitution in 1791, and later, because it met in a building on the rue Saint-Honoré formerly occupied by Dominican monks, it adopted the nickname of these monks, the Jacobins, so-called because their first convent had been on the rue Saint-Jacques. The strength of the society lay in Paris —although branches of the club existed in other cities—and it reflected an urban point of view. Their leaders were middle class in origin, but they came to identify themselves with the interests of the common people, and they were more likely to be swayed by motives of political expediency than abstract reasoning. They prided themselves on supporting a firm and vigorous central government.

During the earliest meetings of the Convention, the delegates sat where they pleased, but they gradually drifted into an arrangement according to political sympathies. Jacobins and Girondins placed themselves respectively on the left and right of the President's chair, and the most advanced thinkers moved into a group of high seats at the back of the hall. From this circumstance the radical bloc was known as *La Montagne* (The Mountain). Although the majority of the Mountain were also Jacobins, there were some, such as Grégoire and Thibaudeau, who had no connection with the society. Hence the violent and extremist position symbolized by Marat and Robespierre should be considered Jacobin rather than Montagnard. Paradoxically the Girondins were anti-clerical, the Montagnards either pious or tolerant of the Church. "The weapons of the Girondins," wrote Thomas Carlyle, were "Political Philosophy, Respectability, and Eloquence. The weapons of the Mountain . . . those of mere Nature; Audacity and Impetuosity which may become Ferocity, as of men complete in their determination, in their conviction."

The personal nucleus of the Girondins was Mme. Roland, whose salon served as political clearinghouse for the party leaders, including Vergniaud, Gensonné, Buzot and Brissot. Paine and Condorcet were not considered party members, but they found the Girondin milieu congenial to their own principles, and in the Convention they co-operated with the Girondin leaders. Among the Jacobins, the most influential was undoubtedly Robespierre. Others included Marat, Danton and Barère, the latter a close friend of Paine's.

On 11 October 1792 Paine was appointed to a committee to frame a new constitution, a group which dissidents charged was under the domination of Jérôme Pétion, who had once been a boon companion of Robespierre, but after being elected mayor of Paris, in November 1791, had listened to the eulogies and blandishments of the Girondists and severed his ties with Robespierre. In addition to Paine and Pétion, the committee members included Sieyès, Brissot, Vergniaud, Gensonné, Barère, Danton and Condorcet, the latter having been commissioned to prepare a first draft for preliminary discussion. According to Durand de Maillane, a member of the Convention who later wrote its history, Robespierre and his henchman Couthon, irked that they were not included in the committee, combined to nullify its work. They proposed to the Convention, therefore, that no discussion of the Constitution take place until after the debate on the trial of Louis XVI.

Although tradition has it that Condorcet did most of the work for this Constitution, and Paine's admirers claim the declaration of rights which preceded it for Paine, it is more logical to assume that all members of the committee took a hand. Indeed Brissot even sought advice outside of the Convention itself, sending to England to secure the assistance of Franklin's friend David Williams. Paine himself wrote for the committee an English manuscript of at least forty-five pages setting forth articles to be substituted for the provisions in the monarchical Constitution of 1791. The only evidence of the composition of this manuscript is a reference by Paine in a letter found among the papers of Danton in the French National Archives. Paine told Danton that by means of the new Constitution, France should become the orator of Europe. "She must speak for other nations who cannot yet speak for themselves. She must put thoughts into their minds and arguments into their mouths, by shewing the reasons that has induced her to abolish the old system of Monarchical Government, and to establish the representative. The late constitution sacrified too much to ceremony and to the impolitic apprehension of giving umbrage to foreign courts: whereas there is more to be hoped for, by enlightening foreign nations than there is to be feared from foreign courts."

Mme. Roland, an intimate of several of the constitution makers, considered Paine's talents inadequate for the cold discussion of a committee or the continued labor of a legislature. She admired Paine for his daring thoughts, his original style, and his audacious manner of pronouncing strong truths in the midst of people whom they would offend, but she believed him more suited to throw out sparks—to inspire a club or excite a tavern—than to discuss the fundamentals of government. Actually most of Paine's works were the product of solitary concentration rather than of inspiration in exciting company. He was essentially a writer, not a talker. Mme. Roland knew nothing of his economic essays during the American Revolution or of his literary collaboration with American legislators and French diplomats. Perhaps she had not even read *The Rights of Man*. She apparently considered Paine as a somewhat less eccentric counterpart of his Prussian colleague in the Convention, Anacharsis Clootz.

The latter, who had been awarded French citizenship in the same manner as Paine, by decree, called himself The Orator of the Human Race and dedicated himself to the ideal of a universal republic. He argued that China, New York and Arabia should become districts of France. Although Clootz had talked with Paine about his grandiose notions and actually claimed him as a disciple, Brissot, who had been present at their colloquy, declared in the *Patriote français* (24 November) that Paine did not take the eccentric Prussian seriously. Paine believed that "the Rhine, the Alps, the Pyrenees, and the ocean are the natural limits of the French Republic."

While working in the committee on the Constitution, Paine continued to attend the meetings of the Convention. One of the first tasks assigned by his fellow deputies was that of presenting the congratulations of Consul General of Calais to the Convention. Unable to speak French, Paine cast his remarks in the form of a letter, 27 October, and asked the President of the Convention, M. E. Guadet, to read it in his behalf. Referring to the institution of royalty, Paine marveled at the folly of their ancestors who had put them under the necessity of abolishing a phantom. The members greeted his witticism with applause.

During the same month, an influential Irishman, Lord Edward Fitzgerald, came to Paris expressly to enlist Paine's aid in fomenting a revolution in Ireland. He wrote to his mother, 30 October: "I lodge with my friend Paine,—we breakfast, dine, and sup together. The more I see of his interior, the more I like and respect him. I cannot express how kind he is to me; there is a simplicity of manner, a goodness of heart, and a strength of mind in him, that I never knew a man before possess."

Fitzgerald told Paine that there were then in Ireland four thousand volunteers who assembled every now and then for one-day periods to prepare the battle for freedom. If it were possible to give these volunteers the means to subsist as a group for only three months, Fitzgerald assured Paine, a successful revolution in Ireland would be inevitable. Paine did all he could to promote French participation. In December he sent Pierre le Brun, Minister of Foreign Affairs and friend of Brissot, a clipping from a Belfast newspaper containing details of radical sentiments expressed by the Society of United Irishmen, one of the clubs to which Paine belonged. He himself drew up a statement on Irish affairs which he proposed to discuss with Le Brun in the presence of Du Chastelet, who was to serve as interpreter. In this memorial, now in the French Ministry of War, Paine proposed that instead of sending a fleet to Ireland, the French government should merely aid the native revolutionaries. Basing himself on Fitzgerald, he cited the volunteer troops regularly assembling for drill and added that there were only about one fourth as many British troops in

Ireland, for the most part recruited in the country and easy to be won over. All that remained for France to do in order to foment the insurrection was to advance 200,000 pounds sterling, which would be reimbursed if the uprising succeeded. In February 1793, Fitzgerald reported to the chiefs of the United Irishmen in Dublin that "Paine had nearly a design to come over here." But the Irish thought "that at present he would do more harm than good."

In the same month, as a result of Paine's representations, Le Brun approved the engaging of an Irish-American officer, Colonel Eleazer Oswald, whom Paine had known since the beginning of the American Revolution, to travel incognito in Ireland and sound out the dispositions of the people. He left at the end of the month and returned on 8 June with a very discouraging report. The "volunteers" had been completely disarmed and intimidated, and the whole land was in a deplorable state of economic chaos. Although the people were moody and discontented, there was little hope that they would rise to obtain justice.

During his first months in the Convention, Paine developed an intimate friendship with the American poet, Joel Barlow, whose career had much in common with Paine's. Both had been active in the American Revolution, both afterwards participated in the English constitutional reform movement, and both lived in Paris during the French Revolution and carried on various negotiations with its leaders. On 7 November 1792 Paine formally offered homage to the Convention in Barlow's name by presenting the latter's printed work, *A Letter to the National Convention . . . on the Defects in the Constitution of 1791.* Since Paine was serving on the Constitutional Committee, he was an appropriate bearer of his friend's offering. Paine's colleague, Bishop Grégoire, proposed that honorable mention of the work be made in the minutes and that Barlow's name be added to the list of foreigners given the rights of French citizenship.

In company with many Englishmen and Americans, Paine at this time lived at White's Hotel, 7 Passage des Petits-Pères, an establishment which later changed its name to the Hôtel de Philadelphie. On 18 November an elaborate civic festival took place at White's under the auspices of the Friends of the Rights of Man. Although intended to be purely British, the festival was attended by citizens of various nationalities, by deputies of the

Convention, including Paine, and by officers of the armies stationed in Paris. The rooms, "decorated with civic and military trophies," were filled to capacity, according to the *Annual Register*, 1792, and the bands of the first regiment of cavalry, and of the German legion assisted at the ceremony. In addition to toasting victories of the French armies, the celebrants drank to "Thomas Paine, the new mode of advertising good books by proclamation and the court of King's Bench." This meeting became notorious throughout the British Isles because Lord Edward Fitzgerald and Sir Robert Smyth, an English banker with offices in Paris, renounced their titles. Smyth proposed the toast: "The speedy abolition of all hereditary titles and feudal distinctions."

Meanwhile the chief business of the Convention concerned the fate of Louis XVI. On 7 November, Jean Baptistte Mailhe, outlined the questions relative to his trial, and on 13 November the formal debate began.

The deposed monarch was suspected of treasonable attempts to regain his throne, particularly of communicating with foreign powers, of appealing to his brothers for aid, and of attempting to flee the realm. Discovery of incriminating papers in a secret safe in the walls of the Tuileries Palace led to great indignation against the King's duplicity and alarm at the menace of foreign invasion. Before the discovery of these papers the mild-mannered King had held a good chance of preserving his head; afterwards public opinion seemed determined to exact it as a penalty for his foolishness.

Paine, who felt gratitude for the part Louis XVI had played in the struggle for American independence and who considered him objectionable only as a monarch, not as a person, realized that the treatment accorded to Louis XVI would have a crucial influence on the progress of the Revolution. If Louis XVI were dealt with in an inhumane manner, the rest of the world would condemn the French people and their new government; if, on the other hand, the anti-revolutionary behavior of the deposed monarch were ignored, the honor of republican principles would suffer an affront.

Paine, unable to address the Convention in the French language, had his reasons for putting the King on trial read aloud in translation (21 November). He explained that he had chosen this means of communication because "circumstances demonstrated to what degree it was necessary for France that Louis XVI continue to enjoy good health," perhaps fearing that hard treatment or accidental injury might incapacitate Louis and thus enlist world sympathy on his behalf before he could be legally tried. He may also have felt that the monarch's physical presence was needed at the trial in order to bring out evidence of his dealings with other nations. Paine in his letter argued that Louis should be tried not in a spirit of vengeance but in accord with sound policy—to expose the existence of an international conspiracy to defeat the Revolution.

"Louis XVI considered as an individual," Paine argued, "is an object beneath the notice of the Republic; but when he is looked upon as a part of that band of conspirators, as an accused man whose trial may lead all nations in the world to know and detest the disastrous system of monarchy, and the plots and intrigues of their own courts, he ought to be tried." It is to the interest of France, Paine continued, that all nations be as free as herself so that she no longer be forced to keep up an army and navy. The trial of Louis by showing the heinousness of the European nations conspiring against France would operate as a stimulus to world revolution.

On 6 December took place a debate concerning the manner in which the proposed trial should be conducted. The young Secretary of the Convention, Saint-Just, read Paine's views:

It is not only Louis XVI that we are going to judge; it is the monarchy. We have knowledge of the treaties of confederation made at Padua, at Pilnitz; it is a general conspiracy of kings against peoples, and the more Louis will appear innocent, the more it will be evident that kings have the art of deceiving. It is on the basis of these proofs of conspiracy that it is necessary to judge Louis XVI.

Thus I propose that his interrogation be conducted as follows. The president will say to him:

Louis Capet, on the 14th of July 1790 you pledged to the nation to respect your oath, and you are accused of having violated it.

You are accused of having conspired with Leopold, with Francis, and some other kings against the sovereignty of the French people.

You are accused of furnishing these despots money for the purpose of subjugating the French nation.

You are accused of having favored the emigrés and the conspirators.

You are accused of having sent to the frontier armies too weak so that they were cut into pieces by the enemy.

You are accused of having, on the 10th of August, assembled forces at the Tuileries in order to slaughter the citizens who had assembled to ask you to put the nation and our frontiers in a state of defense.

Paine evidently communicated his opinion on the trial of Louis XVI to his English-speaking acquaintances, for Gouverneur Morris recorded in his diary 28 December that Paine had told him in confidence that he intended to move in the Convention to send the King and his family to America. A spy for the British government, George Monro, residing in the English colony at White's Hotel, in a letter of 31 December wrote that Paine advocated the banishment of the royal family from France and that he was composing a formal statement of his opinion. To Paine, and to almost every Frenchman, banishment was a charitable and humane proposal, but to Monro it was an abomination, and he concluded that he should not be surprised if Paine some day received the fate he deserved, presumably disgrace and capital punishment.

XIV

The Rights of Man on Trial

While Paine was working to help create a new government for the French people and to save its deposed King from death, the royal government of England was seeking vainly to intimidate Paine and to annihilate his literary works.

To set the stage for Paine's approaching trial the government attempted to stir up popular feeling against him by inciting outbreaks and demonstrations. On 11 December a mob assembled outside Thomas Walker's house in Manchester, broke windows, and dipersed only after Walker fired at them with a musket. The next morning another mob assembled. When Walker went out to address them, he was received with the cry, "Jacobin, damn the Jacobins, damn Tom Paine, down with the Rump." Throughout November and December, Paine was burned in effigy in literally scores of communities throughout the kingdom. Aristocrats maintained that the Painites bribed the common people with money and liquor to cry up Paine and *The Rights of Man*, whereas the radicals accused the government of using the same means to create demonstrations against him. The wealthy rector of a village in Suffolk, according to the *Morning Chronicle*, 8 March 1793, offered a number of poor people two guineas to burn Paine in effigy. They accepted and speedily performed the business. "An intelligent gentleman" in order to show "how little can be learnt, or depended upon with respect to the sentiments of the common people on politics," hereupon "offered the same people two guineas more to burn the jolly rector in effigy," to which offer they responded with the same alacrity as to the first, burning their ecclesiastical dummy before the parson's own door. Similarly in Hertfordshire, where the effigy of the Unitarian Priestley was burnt, one of the mob asked another—"Pray who is this Dr. Priestley that there is such a fuss about?" "Nay," says the other, "I know not; but I believe he is some Bishop."

On one occasion Paine was burned in effigy accompanied by the chanting of ribald stanzas set to the tune of "To Anacreon in Heaven," the music later adopted in America to "The Star-Spangled Banner." A broadside commemorating the event furnished both words and music: *The Knave's Necklace; or Every Rogue a Halter . . . Sung at a loyal Association . . . previous to burning Tom Paine in Effigy.* Another broadside, entitled *Paine, Sin and the Devil,* presented Paine as the incarnation of an unholy trinity, *Tres Juncti in Uno.* The tract, purveying "Intercepted Correspondence from Satan to Citizen Paine," revealed the intimate relations between Satan and his beloved disciple Thomas. It is interesting to observe that the English associated Paine with the devil solely because of his political beliefs. This attack had nothing to do with Paine's radical religious views in *The Age of Reason,* which had not yet been published.

Paine's friends issued broadsides of their own, attempting to circumvent the royalists. One bore the lurid title, *The Last dying speech and confession of Tom Paine, who was executed at Birmingham, February 12, 1793, for certain high crimes and misdemeanors.* It seemed to be an attack on Paine, and even Conway took it as such, but actually it was a defense of *The Rights of Man* by means of irony. Paine was declared an enemy of the poor people because of his proposal to reduce taxes, eliminate poverty, educate the illiterate, extirpate war and "promote universal peace, civilization and commerce." His crimes were "so flagrant that all the *Governments* in the world, except American and France, . . . thought it necessary to prohibit his libellous Works, *lest the people should read them!"*

In November 1792 Paine received news that the British government's legal action against *The Rights of Man* was gathering momentum, and he wrote a bitter and caustic letter to the Attorney General, Sir Archibald Macdonald, who was in charge of the prosecution. Since Paine did not know Macdonald as a man, he wrote without personal animosity, primarily to explain why he had left England without remaining to contest the injustice of the prosecution: he had deemed his duties in the Convention to be far more important or he would "have stayed to have contested the injustice of that prosecution." The open manner of his leaving proved his intention. The fact that the prosecution was carried forward despite the absence of the accused demonstrated, according to Paine, that its object was not Thomas Paine, the individual, but "the right of the people of England to investigate systems and principles of government." Paine warned the English government that the reprisals which had taken place in France against political oppression (already bloody and horrible even though the Reign of Terror had not yet begun) might have their counterparts in an English revolution. This threat made inevitable the guilty verdict in Paine's approaching trial—although even without this added provocation the decision was almost certain to have gone against him.

English liberals such as Horne Tooke organized a fund for Paine's defense, and Thomas Erskine, Attorney General for the Prince of Wales, one of the most eminent legal minds of the time, was engaged as chief counsel. He was told in plain terms by the royal government that he must not defend Paine, and he actually lost his office for doing so. Erskine was assisted by the solicitor Bonney, the same whom Paine had previously engaged to defend Jordan. Liberal opinion regarded the trial, which took place 18 December, as a test case to measure freedom of press in England, to determine how far the government could go in proscribing writers and publishers. Most contributors to the defense fund were supporting liberty of the press rather than Paine as an individual. Even Paine gave this explanation of his own participation. Although considering himself as a foreigner and not the object of the prosecution or affected by the outcome in any way, he subscribed his money to support the English people against the infringment of their rights by the prosecution. At the trial, the Attorney General read Paine's letter accusing the government of fraud and corruption, deriding the capacity of Mr.Guelph (Paine's name for George III) and his profligate sons, and accusing the prosecution of packing the jury. In the midst of his reading, the Attorney General interjected, "If I succeed in this prosecution he shall never return to this country otherwise than *in vinculis, for I will outlaw him.*"

In the face of Paine's wholesale admission of a desire to overthrow the entire English system of government together with his particular insult for the jury, there was little Thomas Erskine could say. He struggled valiantly, however, to vindicate a tradition of free thought and free speech and to show that intellectual conformity cannot be imposed by force. Erskine had apparently considered the case as a *cause célèbre* and had hoped through it to make his eminent reputation still greater. He had confided to his associates that he would make a speech to "astonish the world, and make him to be remembered when Pitt and Fox and Burke, etc. were all forgotten." After "speaking for four hours, and fainting in the usual form"—fainting was then a common histrionic device of lawyers—he concluded with the principle: "Constraint is the natural parent of resistance, and a pregnant proof that reason is not on the side of those who use it." Even before the Attorney General could begin his reply, however, the foreman of the jury rose to declare that no reply was necessary. The verdict was announced—guilty—and Paine was henceforth an outlaw and *The Rights of Man* contraband. Erskine consoled himself with the thought that he had won a moral victory. When he left the court, he was cheered by a crowd of people, some of whom took the place of his horses and drew his carriage in tribute through the streets of London to his home. Paine and his liberal supporters, however, were dissatisfied with Erskine's conduct of the trial. They accused him of embellishing commonplaces for his own glory, but failing to defend *The Rights of Man*.

After the legal decision against Paine, the government widened its conception of treasonable writings and tightened its restrictive measures. Most notably it initiated a series of prosecutions against printers and booksellers who handled *The Rights of Man*.

Although Paine was inured to the blusterings of the British government and affected to be indifferent to his prosecution, he was upset at the thought that the common people would turn against him. Gouverneur Morris noticed at a dinner given for several Americans (20 December 1792) that Paine looked downcast at the news that he had been burnt in effigy. It may be also that he reproached himself subconsciously for having left England instead of remaining to face his accusers. Indeed Paine's closest associates in France, members of the Cercle Social, condemned him precisely for this in their publication, *Bulletin des amis de la vérité* (21 January 1793). Although they had earlier quoted with approval passages from Paine's *Address to the Addressers,* the editors now regretted his lack of intrepidity. Had he shown the courage to dedicate himself to the liberty of England instead of vainly remaining at Paris to defend Louis XVI, they wrote, he would have been in London to plead his own cause in person.

Paine kept a close eye on political developments in England, and no doubt assisted his Girondin friend Brissot when the latter made a highly significant report in the Convention, 12 January 1793, on the policies of the British government. Brissot attributed the outstanding measures of the Pitt administration, foreign and domestic, to fear of repercussion from Paine's writings. In essence he argued that England had broken off peace negotiations with France, not because Louis XVI was on trial, but because Paine had published *The Rights of Man.* Brissot based his interpretation of British affairs on Paine's doctrine of the separation of society and government—the people wanted peace, the Ministry, war. But despite the aggressiveness of the Ministry, Brissot insisted, the British nation was poorly prepared for war and was not a serious threat to France. His purpose was to unmask the phantom of power on which the Pitt Ministry traded—the legend of British military strength. During the autumn Pitt had fervently expressed a desire to avoid war and had attempted to secure the good will of the French Minister. Then suddenly, Brissot reminded the Convention, this pacific spirit disappeared: "The King of England by two proclamations of the first of December, ordered the calling up of the militia, convoked Parliament for the 14th of December when it was not due to meet until January, ordered the troops to march toward London, fortified the Tower, armed it with canon, and deployed a formidable array of weapons." And against what were all these preparations destined? Not against a foreign enemy, but against the book *The Rights of Man.*

The minister announced that this work had perverted all men's minds that it had formed a revolutionary sect which proposed to overthrow the English government and replace it by a National Convention; that this sect had its secret committees, its clubs, its correspondencies; that it had intimate ties with the Jacobins of Paris; that it sent out apostles to excite revolt throughout England; that a conspiracy to overturn the throne was in readiness, etc., etc. He praised the English constitution to the skies and to prove its goodness, he caused to be arrested author and printers who did not think as he did; he had them prosecuted in the courts, torn apart by his newspapers or by addresses ordered by the court and sent by special courier throughout all parts of the kingdom. Finally, as though his artillery, his agents, and his courts were not enough to overwhelm these unfortunate revolutionaries, the English minister raised on every hand clubs founded by his pensioners to preach the excellence of the English Constitution and to declaim against reformers and the French Revolution. . . . He made a rapid and numerous coalition of all the creatures of the court, men in place, nobles, rich landowners, capitalists and all men who live by abuses. . . . In this climate of opinion, it was sufficient for the minister to sound the tocsin against anarchy and cry that the constitution was in danger; for at this phrase, *the constitution in danger,* the man in place fears for his perquisites, the noble for his titles, the priest for his superstition, the landowner for his land, the worker for his bread; in this way the conspiracy against all revolution became by necessity universal.

XV

A King on Trial

During the month of January 1793 the fundamental political problem of the Convention and the entire French nation was the trial of Louis XVI. Everyone except the royalists agreed that he was guilty of treason. The problem turned on what should be the tribunal which was to judge him. The Montagnards wanted the Convention to decide, and the Girondins wanted the decision to be referred directly to the people. This was an anomalous situation since the Montagnards, the more radical party, were here advocating minority rule or the dictum of authority; whereas the Girondins, accused by their enemies of aristocratic sentiments, were advocating an appeal to the people. On the subsequent issue of the punishment of Louis, the Montagnards and many Girondins ruthlessly and inflexibly insisted upon death. Paine, like his friend Condorcet, had the genius of pleasing no one. He voted against the Girondins on the issue of referring the decision to the people and against the Montagnards on the question of capital punishment.

On 26 December 1792 Buzot proposed that plebescites be held in the departments to allow the people to express their will. Debate on this proposition and on other issues raised by the trial of Louis continued until 7 January, when the cloture was invoked. At this time, Paine, who had still not expressed an opinion on the punishment of Louis, moved that the views of all delegates who had not yet spoken on the subject be printed. His motion was carried, and subsequently 109 opinions were printed and distributed, of which Paine's was the eighty-eighth. This speech was not read before the Convention on 7 January when Paine prepared

it, but on 19 January. In his opinion Paine stressed both his ab-
horrence of monarchy and his "compassion for the unfortunate,
whether friend or enemy." Paine depicted Louis XVI as a victim
of circumstances rather than a personal villain. Responsibility for
the evils which he had committed, Paine felt, lay more with the
Constituent Assembly than with Louis himself, for after what Paine
considered his abdication in the flight from Paris in June 1791,
the Assembly had insisted on bringing him back. After reviewing
his own attempts to bring about a republican government at that
time by means of his and Du Chastelet's manifesto, Paine declared
that he was "far more ready to condemn the Constituent Assembly
than the unfortunate prisoner Louis Capet." Then, pointing to the
experience of the English with the Stuarts, Paine recommended
exile rather than death as the most expedient means of getting rid
of undesirable dynasties. He suggested that Louis Capet be detained in prison until the end of the war and then banished to the
United States.

On 15 January 1792 the deputies began voting on three questions
concerning the King. First: Was Louis Capet guilty of conspiring
against the state? Paine voted *yes* with the overwhelming majority
of the Convention. Second: Should the judgment of the Convention be submitted to the people for ratification? Paine voted *no*
with the Jacobins, once more the majority opinion. On the next
day, the third and crucial question: What punishment had Louis
merited? Some discussion arose over what percentage of votes
should be required for the death penalty. Several delegates argued
for a two-thirds majority. Danton arose and fiercely halted the
discussion: "What are you about? You have decided the fate of
the nation by a simple majority. You required no more to declare
the Republic, or to declare war; . . . and now you need a greater
majority to judge an individual. Some maintain that the judgment
was not definitive. . . . And I, I ask you whether the blood of
battles which flows today for this man does not flow definitively."
A simple majority was decided upon. When Paine's turn came, he
repeated his sentiments from his printed opinion: detention until
the end of the war and perpetual banishment thereafter.

After the votes were counted, Vergniaud, President of the Convention, declared in lugubrious tones that the assembly had voted
the supreme penalty. One of the delegates in casting his vote for

death had added that should the Convention pass the capital sentence, it should consider whether it might not be in the public interest to defer its execution. Twenty-five others adopted this expedient of recommending a reprieve. The King's defense counsel called for an appeal, and it was decided that another vote be taken on this issue. On 18 January discussion began. The advocates of instant death spoke in the name of humanity. "No reprieve," said Tallien; "humanity requires it; we must shorten his agony. It is barbarous to leave him in doubt as to his fate." Couthon and Robespierre spoke in the same vein. The next day everyone who had not been heard clamored for a chance to speak.

When Paine was finally recognized, he mounted to the rostrum and stood mute as a post while the Secretary, Bancal, his close friend, read his opinion. Bancal had scarcely uttered Paine's initial words, an expression of genuine sorrow over the previous day's sentence, when he was interrupted by Marat's protest, "I deny the right of Thomas Paine to vote on such a subject; as he is a Quaker; hence his religious views run counter to the infliction of capital punishment." Disorder broke out, allayed by shouts of "free speech," which at last enabled Bancal to go on with the reading.

Paine, after alluding to his struggles for freedom in America, looked into the future to predict with keen insight the manner in which royalists would exploit the judgment against Louis. His execution would "assume the aspect of having been performed from a spirit of revenge rather than from a spirit of justice." Paine had expected the Convention to vote in favor of the penalty which the people would have voted, imprisonment during the war and exile afterward, and he hoped that the Convention would reconsider its sentence. Would France wish to run the risk of losing its only ally and grateful friend, the United States, which regarded Louis as its benefactor? At this moment both Thuriot and Marat interrupted to denounce the translation, to assert that these were not Paine's opinions. Garran-Coulon then affirmed the correctness of the translation—and Paine himself, standing at Bancal's side, attested that these sentiments were his own. Bancal continued reading. Paine begged his fellow deputies to delay the execution, to deprive the English despot, George III, the pleasure of seeing Louis sent to the scaffold—the man who had helped his dear brothers of America cast off their chains.

Again Marat protested, repeating the accusation that Paine had voted against the death penalty because he was a Quaker. Paine replied that he had been influenced only by reasons of public policy and morality. He then insisted on the reading of his printed opinion, which was carried out despite the protests of the extreme left. Finally Bancal read an appended clarification in which Paine reconciled his two votes—that against submitting the decision to the people and that against the penalty of death. This statement does not appear in editions of Paine's works. He argued that "the Convention as the political organ of the nation decreed the abolition, or in other words, the *political* death, of royalty; and our constituents have by their approbation ratified and confirmed this decree. It is then the duty of the Convention to carry out a complete execution of this decree without uselessly troubling the primary assemblies. The banishment of Louis Capet and his family after the war is the *political* complement of the first decree, and we are sufficiently authorized to inflict this kind of punishment."

It was a speech of Barère which sealed Louis's fate. After sentiments on the inhumanity of keeping a man in an indefinite state of reprieve, he turned to the broad philanthropic aims of the Revolution and reminded the Convention of the reforms it could institute once the unpleasant business of the unfortunate Louis were disposed of. Stop wasting time, he urged. The Convention listened spellbound and proceeded to vote Louis's life away. On the final issue of a reprieve, a minority of 310, including Paine, voted in favor; 380 voted against.

There is little doubt that Paine worked harder than any other member of the Convention to save the life of Louis XVI. Even Bertrand de Moleville, an ardent royalist and implacable enemy of republicanism who took refuge in England during the trial, gave Paine the highest tribute for his speech in the monarch's favor. He considered it "to the eternal shame of the Assembly that Thomas Paine, misguided by the fanaticism of the most ardent demagogery, was the most wise, the most humane, the most courageous, in a word, the least culpable of all his colleagues." Even the principal Girondins voted for the death penalty with the exception of Rabaut Saint-Étienne, who voted solitary confinement, and Condorcet, who advocated the most rigorous punishment short of death.

Paine must have realized that he was making bitter enemies by his determined defense of the King. The outbursts of Marat and Thuriot undoubtedly gave him a premonition of the days ahead should the Jacobins win out over their foes. Before long the Girondins and their friends were being systematically proscribed and purged. Paine was suspected both for his own words and for his associations. At a meeting of the Jacobin Society, 11 March, a member read a letter declaring that Paine's discourse on the fate of the King was the work of Condorcet and Brissot, who were together the brain and sinew of the Girondin movement. The Jacobins may have believed this accusation, but it is scarcely credible for the main reason that the actual votes given by the three men were completely different. Paine spoke out for banishment; Condorcet, for the most severe penalty short of death; and Brissot, for death. No wonder though that Robespierre and others came to view Paine with suspicion. In paraphrasing Paine's opinions in a printed letter to his constituents, Robespierre gave a factually accurate and superficially objective account of the speech, but nevertheless showed his displeasure. After quoting Paine's affirmation of a personal desire for Louis's reprieve, Robespierre reported: "The part of the assembly where the warmest patriots were seated began to murmur in protest."

This was in a sense the most dramatic crisis in Paine's life. With his dogged single purpose and faith in human benevolence, he was attempting to withstand the forces of dissent and protest which had been building up for generations. To the majority of the Convention, the King was a symbol of a past era—and the King had to be destroyed with the era. Paine was in a sense more realistic than the Jacobins. He realized that the King was a symbol also to the rulers of hostile nations, who would bitterly resent the King's execution. Were Louis regarded merely as a man—and treated with leniency, as Paine proposed, France might have been spared some of the animosity of foreign powers. As usual Paine pleased nobody. The Girondins ignored his appeal for mercy, the Jacobins condemned him as a sentimental tool of the Girondins, and the English reviled him as a regicide merely because of his presence in the Convention. Yet this was Paine's moment of sublimity. He was playing a major role in one of the most significant scenes of the century. Although he was not applauded, he at least held the center of the stage and his words stirred the hearts of multitudes.

XVI

A Firebrand on Trial

Although the trial of Louis XVI signaled the downfall of the Girondins and Paine with them, they remained nominally in control of the Convention for several weeks. Paine continued to attend the sessions and was even given an additional responsibility. On 1 February, Fabre d'Églantine, a minor poet and dramatist, and several other members proposed that a manifesto be drawn up to acquaint the peoples of the world with the justice of the cause of the French people and of their inalterable will to perish rather than to allow their rights to be destroyed. The proposal was ratified and Paine and three others were commissioned to frame the address. The other three were Condorcet, Paine's earlier collaborator; Fabre d'Églantine, author of the project and a henchman of Danton; and Barère, friendly to both Paine and Robespierre and archenemy of Marat. According to Barère, Paine had little to do with the actual writing because of his inadequate knowledge of French. "The despotism of composition was abandoned to the philanthropic genius of Condorcet." No trace of the address has survived unless a fragment published in Condorcet's works under the title "*La République française aux hommes libres*" may be a vestige.

Paine had previously been appointed to the committee to draw up a new constitution. On 15 February 1793 Condorcet gave a long speech introducing a "Plan of a Declaration of the Natural, Political and Civil Rights of Men," comprising thirty-three articles. It is impossible to determine how much of this declaration is the work of Paine, of Condorcet, or of any of the other collaborators. The committee was later padded with five Jacobins, and a new draft—

largely the work of Hérault de Séchelles—was drawn up in great haste and adopted, 24 June.

The issue which led to the downfall of the Girondins and the ascendancy of the Jacobins was the attempted impeachment of Marat for inciting a dictatorial coup. Paine, an innocent bystander who had virtually no dealings with Marat, was dragged into the proceedings as a political red herring. The stratagem succeeded. Attention was directed from Marat's large-scale activities to a ludicrous personal incident involving Paine, and Marat was not only acquitted but boosted to a height of tremendous prestige. Paine unwittingly hastened the fall of his friends, the Girondins, and brought about his own eventual imprisonment.

On 5 April Marat issued an address to the departments warning against a counter-revolution in the Convention. He invited the people to pillage the shops of merchants guilty of malversation and hang the proprietors at the door; he argued that the incompetence of the Convention would force the nation to abolish democracy in favor of a strong single leader; and he accused the Convention of harboring a nest of traitors in its midst. On 12 April, Guadet read to the Convention Marat's incendiary address and demanded his impeachment. On the next day the Convention decreed that Marat should be tried on charges of instigating pillage and murder, of plotting to overthrow the sovereignty of the people, and of contriving the debasement and dissolution of the Convention. Paine was not in attendance on this day and therefore did not cast a vote against Marat.

Paine's friendship with the Girondist leaders in itself put him in the opposite camp from Marat, but his personal involvement with the radical journalist grew out of the purely accidental circumstance of his taking new living quarters. Early in 1793 Paine had moved from White's to another hotel near the rue de Richelieu and shortly after moved again to a suburban mansion at 63 rue du Faubourg Saint-Denis, variously reported by legend to have been the residence of Ninon de Lenclos, beauteous patroness of the arts, and Mme de Pompadour, mistress of Louis XV. Here Paine shared an apartment with a neurotic young English doctor, William Johnson, and another Englishman William Choppin.

The apartment consisted of three rooms; "the first for wood, water etc., with an old fashioned closet chest, high enough to hang up clothes in; the next was the bedroom; and beyond it the sitting room, which looked into the garden through a glass door; and on the outside there was a small landing place railed in, and a flight of narrow stairs almost hidden by the vines that grew over it." Here could be seen ducks, turkeys and geese, which, for amusement, Paine "used to feed out of the parlor window on the ground floor. There were some hutches for rabbits, and a sty with two pigs. Beyond was a garden of more than an acre of ground, well laid out, and stocked with excellent fruit trees."

William Johnson, shortly after Marat's inflammatory outburst of 5 April, developed the notion that Marat intended measures against Paine's life. Seized by a fit of melancholy, he decided to commit suicide. He made out a will dividing his property between Choppin and Paine and also drew up a statement of his emotional reaction to the menace of Marat: "I came to France in order to enjoy Liberty, but it has been assassinated by Marat. Anarchy is even more cruel than despotism. I cannot endure the doleful spectacle of the triumph of imbecility and inhumanity over talent and virtue." He then stabbed himself twice with a knife, called to Choppin from the top of the stairs, thrust his declaration into Choppin's hand, and announced that he had killed himself. When Paine also climbed the stairs, Johnson gave him his watch as a token of farewell.

Although Johnson's wounds proved to be only superficial, Paine decided to use the situation as a stroke against Marat. He showed Brissot Johnson's declaration and Brissot published it in his *Patriote françois*, 17 April, together with the explanation: "A sad event has just informed the anarchists of the baneful results of their frightful doctrine. An Englishman, whose name I withhold, abjured his country because he detested royalty; he came to France, hoping to find liberty; but he sees only its mask on the hideous visage of anarchy. Tormented by this spectacle, he decided to kill himself. Before dying, he wrote with his trembling hands these words which we have read on a paper now in the hands of an eminent foreigner." The words which followed were those accusing Marat of assassinating liberty.

The grotesque incident reflected credit on no one concerned. Even Paine's friend Sampson Perry felt that there were suspicious circumstances. In a letter to a certain Mme Moreau, he observed that "it is a mysterious affair & ought to be cleared up. Some people regard the whole as a farce others as a trajedy. at all events the occurence is liable to do an Injury to the good Cause in which you & myself take so much Interest & so much praise."

Mme Moreau immediately wrote to the public authorities giving a full account of the affair and urging that it be investigated immediately and advised that Sampson Perry be called to the stand on the first day so that his testimony would force the others to speak without reserve.

Mme Moreau's letter reached the authorities just at the moment that the case against Marat was being prepared. The anti-Marat forces decided to use Johnson's mental breakdown as an example of the pernicious influence of Marat's writings so that the episode became an issue in *l'affair Marat*.

The trial lasted less than seven hours, over two-thirds of which was devoted to Johnson's attempted suicide, an incident having absolutely no bearing on the political crimes of which Marat was accused. As Mme Moreau had advised, Sampson Perry was called as the first witness. He testified that he had been extremely sorry to see the article in the *Patriote françois* because it would tend to make people in England believe that Marat, whom he considered a useful man, was setting all France in a turmoil. He testified also that Johnson's faculties had begun to decline. It was Perry's opinion that when Johnson read that threats had been uttered against the deputies who had voted for the appeal to the people in the trial of Louis XVI, his affection for Paine had led him to seek to destroy himself in order not to be a witness to the demise of his friend. Perry assured the court moreover that he had heard discourses at Paine's home tending to establish the belief that Marat had maintained that all foreigners should be massacred, particularly the English.

When Paine was called as a witness, he declared that he had known Marat only since the coming together of the Convention, and that he had spoken to him only once. That had been in the halls of the Convention. At this time Marat had maintained that the English people were free and happy and Paine had replied that they were groaning under a double despotism. Paine remarked that he did not personally consider the article in the *Patriote françois* as having relation to the intended prosecution of Marat, but he affirmed that

Johnson had given himself two thrusts of his knife because he had learned that Marat was going to denounce him. At this point Marat objected that it was not because he was going to denounce the young man that Johnson had stabbed himself, but because he intended to denounce Thomas Paine.

When Johnson, still in a weakened condition, was called to testify, he was asked whether his reading of Marat had decided him to take his own life. Johnson replied that the decision came from reading in the journal of A. J. Gorsas that Marat had said that all those who had voted for the appeal to the people in the trial of Louis XVI should be massacred. Although Paine was not among the delegates who had voted for the appeal to the people, Johnson apparently thought that he was. He testified further that his friendship for Paine had made him want to destroy himself, but he denied that he had made a will in Paine's favor.

This attention to the tragi-comedy of Johnson's pathetic behavior obscured the real issue of Marat's trial—the allegedly treasonable and incendiary passages in his writings. Although Marat was questioned on one or two of his statements, the major point was not whether they were treasonable but whether they had incited Johnson's melodramatic action. The jury apparently decided that if only unstable minds such as Johnson's were influenced by Marat's fulminations, his words could not be considered dangerous to the welfare of the state.

Marat was acquitted amidst applause. Two municipal officers escorted him arm in arm through the streets followed by a large band of admirers proclaiming him Father of the People. He was triumphantly led to the hall of the Convention, where Danton prevented the president from closing the session. From the rostrum Marat delivered a speech, partly modest, partly exultant, while Danton beamed with approval. This complete vindication of Marat was in good measure due to Paine's zeal to denounce him in the press. Had Paine kept Johnson's plight a secret, the result of the trial might have been quite different.

Paine later confided to A. C. Thibaudeau, one of the moderates in the Convention who survived until the reign of Louis Napoleon, that Marat had one day said to him in English in the hall of the Convention, "Is it really possible that you believe in republicanism? You are too enlightened to be the dupe of such a fantastic dream."

This may have been the conversation to which Paine alluded on the witness stand. As soon as Marat was indicted, Paine wrote a letter to the Jacobin Society reporting this encounter and sent a copy to the *Moniteur,* but it was never published. Paine later believed that this circumstance had some influence on his own proscription.

Paine appeared as a witness in another trial in May—that of his Latin-American acquaintance General Francisco Miranda—but this time the proceedings caused no public sensation. Miranda had been serving in the French army with the rank of general under the command of General Dumouriez. In February 1793 Dumouriez and Miranda undertook the invasion of Holland, but were forced to retreat to Belgium. There in a battle with Austrian troops under Archduke Charles they suffered a crushing defeat. Miranda's soldiers, in particular, ran from the field of battle in ignominious flight. Dumouriez, in reporting to the Ministry of War, ascribed the defeat in large measure to Miranda's withdrawal. Miranda in retaliation denounced Dumouriez as a traitor and accused him of having proposed a march on Paris to restore a constitutional monarchy. Orders were issued 24 March 1793 for Miranda's arrest, and he was imprisoned in the Conciergerie.

At his trial between 12 and 16 May, Miranda called on his liberal friends, including Paine and Joel Barlow, to testify in his behalf. Paine declared that he had known Miranda for ten years, first in America, then in England, and finally in France, and that Miranda had everywhere appeared as a defender of human liberty. In London Paine had felt that Miranda's language and political principles were identical with those he had maintained in America. When Paine had published *The Rights of Man,* Miranda strongly supported Paine's arguments against Burke and in so doing made many enemies among the English aristocracy. Paine had been delighted to learn that Miranda had accepted a command in the French army. He felt that if the principles of the Revolution were to prevail in other countries, Miranda would be extremely useful in the task of delivering Spanish America and rendering the riches and commerce of this vast territory free and open to the rest of the world.

Paine had once encountered Miranda in Paris by accident after his arrest, but had not had time enough for a lengthy conversation. Still he had observed that Miranda did not have the air of a guilty man—indeed he seemed to be exactly the same as on former occasions. "It is impossible," Paine concluded, "for one man to know another man's heart as he knows his own; but from all that I know of General Miranda I cannot believe that he wanted to betray the confidence which the republic had placed in him, especially because the destiny of the French Revolution was intimately linked with the favored object of his heart, the deliverance of Spanish America— an object for which he has been pursued and persecuted by the Spanish Court during the greatest part of his life." The trial ended with the unanimous opinion of the jury that Miranda was not a traitor. Paine's defense of Miranda meant still another step toward his own eventual imprisonment, for the trial represented a vital phase of the Girondin-Montagnard conflict. The Girondins supported Miranda as the Montagnards had defended Marat. When the latter faction came into power, they had still another reason for considering Paine *non grata*.

Paine continued to spend his leisure moments at White's Hotel, rendezvous of Englishmen in Paris. On one occasion he got into a serious altercation with an officer in His Majesty's service, Captain Grimstone, a staunch supporter of the English Constitution and enemy of the French Revolution. Sherwin, who described the incident in detail, located it in a coffee house in the Palais Royal, but the more reliable Paris police records place it at White's. As Paine and the captain were giving full expression to their diverse political views, the latter called Paine a traitor to his country. Paine responded with unruffled good humor, which so infuriated Grimstone that he struck Paine a violent blow, nearly knocking him off his chair. According to Sherwin, Grimstone was immediately taken into custody since striking a deputy to the Convention was considered an insult to the nation at large and was punishable by death. Paine immediately appealed to Barère, President of the Committee of Public Safety, for Grimstone's release, which was granted after much difficulty. The terse police report, written some time after the event, says nothing about Grimstone's arrest. During one of the orgies at White's, it stated, "there arose a dispute which developed into a brawl between Thomas Paine and another Englishman of the same clique, who hit Thomas Paine in the face and who after escaping and going into hiding later became reconciled with the said Thomas Paine."

Another incident of the kind, concerning one of the brothers of

Mary Wollstonecraft, is related by a Quaker physician, Dr. John Walker. Young Wollstonecraft "had written home, expressing the hope that the British navy, in which he had been, would never debase its flag." When the letter got into the hands of the French police and Walker asked Paine to intervene, he observed, "My interference, at this moment, would be premature. Let them alone awhile, till their fury be somewhat dissipated in the violence of their proceedings, and then I shall not find any difficulty in obtaining his liberation."

Rickman tells us that Paine customarily arose about seven at the rue Faubourg Saint-Denis and took breakfast with his English friends and a retired French officer of extremely aristocratic proclivities, whose scientific interests nevertheless brought him into harmonious relations with Paine. "With these select friends he would talk of his boyish days, play at chess, whist, picquet, or cribbage, and enliven the moments by many interesting anecdotes. . . . He often lamented that there existed no good history of America, and that the letters written by Columbus, the early navigators, and others, to the Spanish court, were inaccessible, and that many valuable documents, collected by Philip II, and deposited with the national archives at Simania, had not yet been promulgated."

The endemic suspicions created by the defection of General Dumouriez coupled with the charges and counter-charges passing at the Convention—some of them literally incitements to massacre—rendered Paine fearful that the new French Republic would end in a disgraceful ruin. He abandoned hope that liberty could be extended to all Europe—not because of the "intrigues of aristocracy and priestcraft" but because of the tumultuous misconduct of French internal affairs. Despite his disillusionment he wrote to Danton, 6 May, suggesting measures to avert the downfall of France. Each day, he observed, the danger of a final rupture between Paris and the country districts was becoming more acute. As a solution he suggested that France follow the American plan of fixing the capital at a place removed from the metropolitan center. He also gave a brief account of American experience with price fixing and inflation. Paine was most disturbed by the neglect of moral principles in France, which injured the character of the Revolution and discouraged the progress of liberty all over the world.

Referring to the aftermath of the Marat trial, he composed a moral sermon on the prevailing "spirit of denunciation." "If every individual is to indulge his private malignancy or his private ambition, to denounce at random and without any kind of proof, all confidence will be undermined and all authority be destroyed. Calumny is a species of treachery that ought to be punished as well as any other kind of treachery. It is a private vice productive of public evils; because it is possible to irritate men into disaffection by continual calumny who never intended to be disaffected." The vicious denunciation of the twenty-two Girondins by the sections of Paris, he concluded, fell to the ground because "calumny becomes harmless and defeats itself when it attempts to act upon too large a scale." Most of Paine's acquaintances in the Convention were on that list— and he affirmed that there existed no "better men nor better patriots" than they.

Having given up faith in world revolution, Paine determined to return home to America as soon as the Constitution should be adopted. In April he had received the somber news that the house and barn on his farm at New Rochelle had burned down, and he wrote to Jefferson that he would "not bring money enough to build another."

On May 31, when Paine appeared at the gates of the Tuileries, he was stopped by Hanriot, commander of the guards. Paine showed his card of deputy, but Hanriot replied roughly that he could use it to make curling papers. Danton, who was just coming out of the hall of the Convention, came up and warned Paine in English not to think of going in, for as a friend of Brissot's, he might be included in the list of proscriptions. When Paine remarked that Vergniaud was right in saying that the French Revolution was like Saturn, it devoured its own children, Danton caustically replied, "Revolutions cannot be made with rose water."

Three days later, on 2 June, a momentous date in the Revolution, Barère proposed to the twenty-two suspected Girondins that they voluntarily resign their powers, but they indignantly refused. Meanwhile detachments of the Paris National Guard had surrounded the Convention and made its members literally prisoners. Responding to pressure from the mob outside and the extremists inside, the Convention voted to suspend and imprison the accused Girondins. This was the final blow. Within the year most of them were dead.

Back in Pas de Calais, local politicians rejoiced in the proscribing of the Gironde. They even persuaded the people of six districts to vote an address to the Convention, 18 June, declaring their indignation at the conduct of Paine and his like-minded colleagues, who, the address affirmed, had totally lost the confidence of their constituents.

During the summer of 1793, Paine used to find relief from his political anxieties by walking alone after dark in the garden of his apartment in the rue du Faubourg Saint-Denis. He cursed "with hearty good will the authors of that terrible system that had turned the character of the Revolution." He later explained, "I went but little to the Convention, and then only to make my appearance; because I found it impossible to join in their tremendous decrees, and useless and dangerous to oppose them. My having voted and spoken extensively, more so than any other member, against the execution of the King, had already fixed a mark upon me: neither dared any of my associates in the Convention to translate and speak in French for me anything I might have dared to have written."

Nevertheless, despite the proscription of his closest friends and unmistakable signs that he would probably share their fate, Paine did remain in the Convention and even continued political activity beyond its confines. He wrote several letters in behalf of his friend Colonel Oswald and later in the summer attempted to use his influence with the foreign office in behalf of some American sea captains then detained at Bordeaux. As a result of the war which had broken out between England and France, the British had seized American ships carrying cargo to France. The French in reprisal carried out an identical policy toward American vessels destined for England. The captains of the American vessels being held at Bordeaux at first appealed to Gouverneur Morris, the American Minister, but he simply told them that "they had thrown themselves into the lion's mouth, and it was for them to get out of it as best they could." After they left his chambers, however, Morris changed his mind and wrote to the French Minister, 20 August, predicting that the embargo would "severely aggrieve the parties interested, and put an end to the commerce between France and the United States." The captains turned to Paine, who advised them to take their case to the Convention. Accordingly they wrote a petition, 22 August: "We . . . do not come to you to demand the rigorous execution of the treaties of alliance which unite us to you. We confine ourselves to asking for the present, to carry provisions to your colonies." The captains also drew up a petition to Sylvanus Bourne, American Consul, asking him to intercede with the provincial assemblies, and Paine drew the attention of his friend Barère to their plight.

Barère, a highly efficient administrator, had an uncanny dexterity in evading compromising involvements, which is no doubt why he could remain on good terms with Paine while the latter was under a cloud at the Convention. One day in August Paine had run into Barère on the boulevards. Barère had asked him something in French which Paine could not understand, and they had gone together to the Foreign Ministry to get the services of an interpreter. Barère first asked Paine some polite questions about the plan of the Constitution which Paine had presented to the committee on which both had served. Paine promised to send it to him the next day. Barère then asked about the advisibility of sending commissioners to the United States to seek an alliance in the war against England. Paine promised to write out his opinion in detail and have it translated at the Foreign Office. In a document of twenty pages, he described the advantages of sending commissioners to America and said that he expected to return himself at the end of the year. He added that he would do everything he could in the interests of France, but that he would not consider it appropriate to serve personally as one of the commissioners—since his countrymen would prefer to see him return home in his former character of an American citizen.

In a subsequent letter to Barère, 5 September, Paine repeated his enthusiastic endorsement of the plan to send commissioners to America. He described Jefferson, then Secretary of State, as an ardent defender of the interests of France, but Gouverneur Morris as badly disposed. The latter was unpopular in America, Paine confided, and heartily disliked by the Americans in France, including the sea captains at Bordeaux. Paine was confident that they would write to him rather than to Morris about requesting a convoy from the Convention to keep their vessels from falling into British hands. At this time Paine anticipated returning to America on one of the vessels due to leave Bordeaux in October 1793, a resolution which, if carried out, would have spared him months of sickness and despair in prison.

Barère, or some other official in the Ministry of Foreign Affairs, wrote out a memorandum, 13 September, proposing Paine as one of the commissioners to be sent from the Convention to America. This writer considered Paine an ideal emissary to stir the common people, but unfortunately lacking in the poise and distinction necessary to carry on diplomatic negotiations. According to the memorandum: "Paine could be useful as guide and interpreter, but not as principal agent. Although he has a considerable following in America, there are also enemies who could harm the mission. It is especially through the medium of the newspapers that Paine arouses the minds of men. The people are greatly drawn to him, and it is to the people that Paine must address himself. To sway the government, we must employ other agents. To succeed with Americans, one must combine much dignity, a perfect self-possession and, if possible, a knowledge of the English language."

Paine worked very closely with Barère in an effort to get American aid for France, a reversal of the situation in 1776. In his *Mémoirs* Barère gave Paine the credit for vital shipments of grain and rice which came from the United States in 1794. Paine "indicated methods, facilitated correspondence and worked long hours in the bureau of foreign affairs in order to bring about this massive purchase of provisions, so much the more necessary that without this aid our armies and the departments would have been menaced with a terrible famine." Despite Barère's friendship for Paine and his eventual recognition of Paine's services to France, it was Barère who delivered the speech leading to Paine's imprisonment. Barère later apologized to Paine "by saying he felt himself in danger and was obliged to do it."

XVII

In Luxembourg Prison

We now come to a consideration of Paine's arrest and imprisonment and the part played in it by Robespierre and Morris. We have seen the series of events by which Paine came to be distrusted by the Convention: 1) the trial of Louis XVI, bringing Paine in direct opposition to the sentiment of the majority through his heroic efforts to save the life of the deposed monarch; 2) the trial and vindication of Marat, revealing Paine's rather sordid conspiracy with Brissot to disparage the popular idol in the press; and 3) the fall of the Girondins, completely discrediting Paine's most intimate friends and collaborators in the Convention, particularly Condorcet and Brissot. As Sampson Perry pointed out, "When Brissot fell, Paine was in danger." According to Perry, Robespierre despised Paine because of their inimical philosophies. Paine had more faith in the pen than in the guillotine. "Robespierre said, that method might do with such a country as America, but could avail nothing in one highly corrupted like France. To disagree in opinion with a mind so heated, was to incur all the resentment it contained." After Robespierre's own death on the guillotine, a memorandum was found among his papers reading, "Demand that Thomas Paine be decreed of accusation for the interests of America as well as of France."

On 3 October 1793 André Amar, furiously denounced, in the name of the Committee of General Safety, the seventy-three representatives who had voted in June against expulsion of the Girondins, accusing them of conspiring against the French people. His most virulent strokes were leveled against the "faction of Brissot," in which he included Paine. Brissot was particularly condemned for considering France as a powerful nation when advocating war with the rest of Europe, but as a weak nation in arguing that Louis XVI should not be executed in order to keep the good opinion of other nations. "At the same time, the Englishman, Thomas Paine, called by the faction to the honor of representing the French people, dishonored himself in supporting the opinion of Brissot and in assuring us on his own account of the displeasure of our natural allies, the United States of America, which he did not blush to depict as filled with veneration and gratitude for the tyrant of the French people." To describe Paine as an Englishman rather than an American was a natural device for an enemy wishing to convict Brissot of treason. The pointed reference to the United States may well have been based on Robespierre's opinion that the arrest of Paine would be "for the interests of America as well as of France."

Oddly enough, it was Robespierre who defended the seventy-three accused, arguing that the number was too large and that some of the suspected delegates had voted according to their conscience. "The Convention must not multiply the guilty." Paine was momentarily saved. Within a month, however, the accusations had been renewed against twenty-one of the imprisoned Girondins and they had been found guilty and executed.

Despite the violent assault of Amar and the fate of the Girondins, Paine still did not attempt to flee the country. One can only wonder why in September he had laid plans to return to America in the next month, but when October arrived and the danger had become much more acute, he made no effort to leave. During this time, he later wrote, "I saw many of my most intimate friends destroyed, others daily carried to prison, and I had reason to believe, and had also intimations given me that the same danger was approaching myself." Foreign military reverses as well as domestic political factionalism conspired to render Paine's position untenable in the Convention. As soon as the security of the nation was menaced by attack from without, the cosmopolitan character of the Revolution was succeeded by ultra-nationalism.

In November Paine's name again came to the attention of the Convention in the interrogation of one of its members, Pierre Manuel, a former schoolmaster who had voted with Paine at the trial of Louis XVI and resigned immediately after. Before his accusers he declared that he had placed himself at the side of Thomas Paine in proposing the King's deportation to America because of the moral and political advantages which this solution would bring to the people. Manuel was beheaded after a perfunctory hearing.

On 25 December, Robespierre read in the Convention an important report "On the Principles of Revolutionary Government," in which he was expected by the Committee of Public Safety to denounce the presence of foreigners in the Convention. But he failed to mention either Clootz or Paine, the only foreigners who were members. Barère took the floor to repair Robespierre's omission. "The Committee of Public Safety," he said, "had charged its representative to acquaint the French people how the decree admitting foreigners to the national representation is harmful to their interests." This was the same man who three months previously had sought Paine's advice on a vital diplomatic question.

Barère was succeeded on the floor by Bourdon de l'Oise. "I am going to cite another fact," he said, "to support what Barère has already said. The patriotism of Thomas Paine has been highly praised. Well, since the Brissotins have disappeared from the floor of the Convention, he has not set foot in the Assembly, and I know that he intrigues with a former agent of the Ministry of Foreign Affairs," a reference to either Genêt or Louis Otto, with both of whom Paine had been on friendly terms. The Assembly thereupon decreed "that no foreigner could be admitted to represent the French people."

This decree, innocuous in itself, was the preliminary to Paine's arrest and imprisonment. His fellow lodgers, Johnson and Choppin, had already fled the country as an aftermath to the trial of Marat, but Paine remained in his apartments, daily expecting to be apprehended. "Two days after they were gone," he wrote, "I heard a rapping at the gate, and looking out of the window of the bed room I saw the landlord going with the candle to the gate, which he opened, and a guard with muskets and fixed bayonets entered. I went to bed again, and made up my mind for prison, for I was then the only lodger. It was a guard to take up [Johnson and Choppin], but I thank God, they were out of their reach. The guard came about a month after in the night, and took away the landlord Georgeit; and the scene in the house finished with the arrestation of myself."

On 27 December the Committee of General Safety ordered the arrest and incarceration of Paine and Anacharsis Clootz as well as the examination of their papers. On that night Paine went to his former residence, the Hôtel de Philadelphie, in the Passage des Petits-Pères, where he encountered a company of Americans. Since his lodgings were about a mile and a half away, he took a bed for the night at the hotel. Between three and four of the next day, 28 December, he was awakened by a knock at his door. Outside he found the proprietor, two officers of the committee and five policemen, who said that they had come to arrest him and examine his papers. Paine dressed and asked the guards to escort him to the room of Achille Audibert, the friend who had notified him in London of his election to the Convention. By means of Audibert as interpreter, Paine explained that an important literary work of his was then being printed and that part of his manuscript was to be found at the Hôtel Grande Bretagne on the Rue Jacob, the dwelling of his friend Joel Barlow and another American, Colonel Blackden.

Since their lodgings were located close to the press where Paine's book—*The Age of Reason*—was being printed, Paine had asked Barlow to pick up the proofs as they came from the printers. Barlow had in his possession the first thirty-one pages of manuscript and Paine had left the remainder, pages 32 to 76, in his apartment. Barlow had received only one proof sheet, which he had corrected and returned to the printer. Paine wanted to be taken to Barlow so that there would be an American citizen to witness the examination of his papers. He also wanted to give Barlow the rest of his manuscript to make sure that the publication of *The Age of Reason* would not be interrupted by his imprisonment. The commissioners later declared in their official report that Paine's affirmation that his papers were to be found in Barlow's possession was nothing but a subterfuge to obtain the presence of his countryman during their examination. By the time the commissioners had come to this conclusion it was eight o'clock in the morning and they were worn out with fatigue. They took refreshment and rested until eleven o'clock before proceeding to Paine's apartment, where he showed the officers the manuscript of *The Age of Reason*. The interpreter remarked, "This is an interesting work which should do much good." Paine showed him also another manuscript written for the Committee of Public Safety, entitled "Observations on the Commerce between the United States and France," a work which has since disappeared. The commissioners examined Paine's papers until four in the afternoon, but found nothing suspicious. After drawing up a report, which all signed, they conducted Paine to the Luxembourg prison, first allowing him to turn over to Barlow the manuscript of *The Age of Reason*.

Three weeks after Paine's arrest a group of sixteen Americans residing in France presented a petition to the Convention calling for his release. They were headed by the same William Jackson who had accompanied Paine and Laurens to the French Court in 1781. Other personal friends were Joel Barlow and Peter Whiteside. One of the group, Thomas W. Griffith, had himself just been released from prison on the previous day, where he had been held for over two months on a charge of being a British agent. It is noteworthy that Paine's friends by-passed Gouverneur Morris, probably realizing his hostility to Paine, and the petition lacks his signature, perhaps one of the reasons that it had no effect in obtaining Paine's release.

Assuming that the only reason for Paine's detention was the circumstance of his being both a foreigner and a member of the Convention, the petitioners stressed the fact that he had been invited to France by the French people. Restraining his liberty, they warned, would be playing into the hands of the despots of Great Britain, who had prosecuted Paine in their own land. As proof of his complete innocence and the purity of his moral and political principles, they pointed to the scrupulous examination which his papers had received. They claimed him as a fellow countryman, asked permission to return him to his own country, and offered themselves as guarantors of his conduct while he remained in France.

A formal reply was given by Vadier, then President of the Convention as well as President of the Committee of General-Surety, the officer who had signed the order for Paine's arrest. After commonplace remarks on the solidarity between France and the United States, he complimented the petitioners on their generous wish to have Paine returned to their midst. Then he justified Paine's arrest without making any concessions or promises.

"Thomas Paine was born in England; this was unquestionably sufficient to have him come under the security measures prescribed by the revolutionary laws. One may add, citizens, that if Thomas Paine has been the apostle of liberty, if he has collaborated forcefully in the American Revolution, his mind has not perceived the nature of the Revolution which has regenerated France; he has conceived the system only in the light of the delusions with which the false friends of our revolution have surrounded it. You, like us, should have deplored an error hardly consistent with the principles which one admires in the highly estimable works of this republican author." This high-sounding ambiguity seems to have no other meaning except that Paine belonged to the wrong faction. Griffith in describing the presentation of the petition reported significantly: "Not a few members hissed during the reading of parts of our memorial, in which Paine's attachment to republican principles was asserted." Griffith pointed out also that Robespierre was head of the committee to which the petition was referred. No wonder then that it had no effect.

The legality of Paine's arrest depended primarily on his citizenship. If he were a subject of France or of England (the latter then at war with France), the French government would have had exclusive jurisdiction over his activities in France, at least according to the rules then being applied. But if he were a citizen of the United States, that government would have been concerned in any action taken against him. As we know, Paine was born in England and became a citizen of the United States by participating in the American Revolution and an honorary citizen of France by decree of the National Assembly. From the point of view of the United States, he was American; from the point of view of France he could be considered French—although he was actually arrested under the terms of the act prohibiting foreigners from serving in the Convention. Paine maintained that he was no more French than were Washington, Pestalozzi, Priestley, David Williams, or any of the other eminent men similarly accorded honorary citizenship by the Convention. The difference was, however, that none of these other citizens had accepted a seat in the National Convention and the privileges which accompanied it. It is hard to see why Paine's status should have been any different from that of the Prussian Anacharsis Clootz, also a delegate to the Convention, who was arrested at the same time as Paine and died on the guillotine.

Despite the personal animosities between himself and Morris, Paine was forced to turn to the American Minister as the only official who could speak in his behalf in the name of the United States. We have already seen the deep-rooted antipathy between Paine and Morris which had come to the fore when they took opposite sides in the Deane affair and attacked each other personally in debating the principle of war profits. Although they were reconciled in 1782, when Paine was engaged to write articles defending the Congress, Morris undoubtedly considered Paine as a useful employee rather than a friend or colleague. Later in his records of Paine's visits in London and Paris, we notice a tone of supercilious scorn. He describes Paine as "a little mad," "inflated to the Eyes," and "drunk with Self Conceit." While Morris was serving as official Minister to England and semi-official Minister to France, he probably resented Paine's efforts to share or pre-empt his functions. But even though he may have been secretly delighted over Paine's fate, he carried out his duty by writing (14 February 1794—26 Pluviôse) to Chemin Deforgues, Minister of Foreign Affairs.

Thomas Paine has just applied to me to claim him as a Citizen of the United States. These (I believe) are the facts which relate to him. He was born in England. Becoming subsequently a citizen of the United States, he there acquired a great celebrity through his revolutionary writings. In consequence he was adopted as a French citizen, and then elected a Member of the Convention. His conduct since that period is out of my jurisdiction. I am ignorant of the reason for his present detention in the Luxembourg prison, but I beg you, (if there are reasons unknown to me which prevent his liberation) please be so good as to inform me of them, so that I may communicate them to the government of the United States.

Five days later Deforgues replied:

In your letter of the 26th of last month you reclaim the liberty of Thomas Paine as an American citizen. Born in England, this ex-deputy has become successively American citizen and French citizen. In accepting the latter title and in occupying a seat in the Legislative Corps, he has submitted himself to the laws of the Republic and has in effect renounced the protection which the law of nations and the treaties concluded with the United States would have been able to assure him.

I am not aware of the reasons for his detention, but I presume that they are well founded. I am nevertheless going to submit to the Council of Public Safety the request which you have addressed to me, and I shall promptly acquaint you with its decision.

Conway argued that this correspondence reveals collusion between Morris and Deforgues, that Morris had made it clear to Deforgues that he preferred Paine to remain in jail, but that he wanted proof to show to his superiors in Washington that he was doing all that was necessary for Paine and that Deforgues had obligingly furnished him with the desired document. No collateral proof exists to support this theory. The correspondence itself shows that Morris stated the true facts concerning Paine's citizenship, that Deforgues assumed that Morris was attempting to claim Paine, and that Deforgues quite naturally took the position that since Paine was a member of the Convention he came under French law. Conway omitted to report moreover that someone in the Foreign Ministry had inscribed on Morris's letter: "Acknowledge reception and tell him that the minister will take steps."

Morris sent Paine a copy of Deforgues's reply, but Paine was not satisfied. He wrote to Morris, 24 February: "I have made an essay in answer to the Minister's letter, which I wish you to make ground of a reply to him. They have nothing against me—except that they do not choose I should be in a state of freedom to write my mind freely upon things I have seen. Though you and I are not on terms of the best harmony, I apply to you as the Minister of America, and you may add to that service whatever you think my integrity deserves. At any rate I expect you to make Congress acquainted with my situation, and to send to them copies of the letters that have passed on the subject. A reply to the Minister's letter is absolutely necessary, were it only to continue the reclamation. Otherwise your silence will be a sort of consent to his observation."

Morris kept Jefferson, Secretary of State, informed, writing 21 January:

Lest I should forget it, I must mention that Thomas Paine is in prison, where he amuses himself with publishing a pamphlet against Jesus Christ. I do not recollect whether I mentioned to you that he would have been executed along with the rest of the Brissotins if the advance party had not viewed him with contempt. I incline to think that if he is quiet in prison he may have the good luck to be forgotten, whereas, should he be brought much into notice, the long suspended axe might fall on him. I believe he thinks that I ought to claim him as an American citizen; but considering his birth, his naturalization in this country, and the place he filled, I doubt much the right, and I am sure that the claim would be, for the present at least, inexpedient and ineffectual.

Morris gave a further report, 6 March:

Mr. Paine wrote me a note desiring I would claim him as an American, which I accordingly did, though contrary to my judgment, for reasons mentioned in my last. The Minister's letter to me of the 1st Ventose, of which I enclose a copy, contains the answer to my reclamation. I sent a copy to Mr. Paine, who prepared a long answer, and sent it to me by an Englishman, whom I did not know. I told him, as Mr. Paine's friend, that my present opinion was similar to that of the Minister, but I might, perhaps, see occasion to change it, and in that case, if Mr. Paine wished it, I would go on with the claim, but that it would be well for him to consider the result; that, if the Government meant to release him, they had already a sufficient ground; but if not, I could only push them to bring on his trial for the crimes imputed to him; seeing that whether he be considered as a Frenchman, or as an American, he must be amenable to the tribunals of France for his conduct while he was a Frenchman, and he may see in the fate of the Brissotins, that to which he is exposed. I have heard no more of the affair since; but it is not impossible that he may force on a decision, which, as far as I can judge, would be fatal to him: for in the best of times he has a larger share of every other sense than common sense, and lately the intemperate use of ardent spirits has, I am told, considerably impaired the small stock he originally possessed.

Probably had he wished, Morris could have pressed more forcefully his claim that Paine was an American citizen. We must not forget, on the other hand, the hissing which took place when Paine's countrymen presented their petitions to the Convention—and the absolute uselessness of their claiming him as a citizen of the United States. Morris was probably quite right in assuming that Paine's best hope of survival lay in his remaining silent. As a matter of fact, Paine also held this view, for he made absolutely no personal application to the Convention for his release until he heard of the execution of Robespierre. In his own words: "I was determined not to write a line during the time of his detestable influence." He also believed that it suited the purposes of Morris and the Committee of Public Safety that he should continue in confinement. "The former wished to prevent my return to America, that I should not expose his misconduct; and the latter, lest I should publish to the world the history of its wickedness. While that Minister and the Committee continued I had no expectation of liberty. I speak here of the Committee of which Robespierre was member."

Luxembourg prison, formerly a palace, had at first the atmosphere, if not the comforts, of a luxury hotel. Originally it was reserved for the Girondin deputies accused of federalism, but after they had been executed, it was used for the incarceration of male and female English citizens. The keeper of the prison, a septuagenarian named Benoit, displayed a genuine humanitarian sensibility. Paine termed him "a man of good heart," who showed "every friendship in his power, as did also all his family, while he continued in that station." When Benoit received new inmates for whom there were no beds, he seemed to suffer more than the prisoners themselves in being obliged to conduct them to completely unfurnished rooms. He tried to compensate for the lack of comfort by social amenities, introducing new arrivals to the coteries which he felt would be most compatible. Here the English ladies apparently learned French arts of love. Sometimes they were visited by dandies from the municipal guard. The accomplished gallantry of the prisoners one day led a police administrator to remark, "Do you know the reputation you have among the public? That the Luxembourg is the principal brothel of Paris; that you are a group of prostitutes and we are the ones who serve you as panders." This publicity made the administration separate the two sexes. Despite this precaution a young man from the outside one day bribed his way into the prison and in broad daylight enjoyed the favors of his mistress. The inmates lived in small communal groups, doing their own cooking and cleaning. They paid for their own board, fortunately kept down to a modest sum. When a prisoner was too poor to pay his share, the kind Benoit arranged for a more opulent inmate to assume his expenses.

Paine had a room on the ground floor "level with the earth in the garden and floored with brick." After six months he suffered an attack of fever that was almost fatal. He complained that his room was so wet after every rain that he could not guard against

taking colds that continually retarded his recovery. Toward the
end of his confinement, he found fuel difficult and candles impossible to obtain. He was deprived of "more than half the common
necessaries of life." This austerity apparently had nothing to do
with the financial resources of the prisoners, for Paine had ample
funds. Sampson Perry recounts that Paine, hearing that an order
had been given to dispossess the prisoners of knives, forks, other
sharp instruments and money, took off the lock from his door and
hid several gold coins and a large bank note inside. After recover-
ing from his fever which lasted five weeks, he found his money
intact, but missed about three hundred of his comrades who had
been sent to the guillotine. Although the prisoners were allowed
to keep no sharp instruments of their own, barbers were admitted
to shave them.

At first Paine was able to keep up his literary work. One month
after his imprisonment he composed a dedication of *The Age of
Reason* to his fellow citizens of the United States.

I put the following work under your protection. It contains my
opinion upon religion. You will do me the justice to remember, that I
have always strenuously supported the right of every man to his own
opinion, however different that opinion might be to mine. He who
denies to another this right, makes a slave of himself to his present opinion, because he precludes himself the right of changing it.

The most formidable weapon against errors of every kind is reason.
I have never used any other, and I trust I never shall.

Paine maintained that he wrote *The Age of Reason* as a partial
means of combating the prevailing spirit of irreligion in France.
Since the Convention had totally abolished "everything appertain-
ing to compulsive systems of religion," Paine feared that the nation would lose sight of morality, humanity and true theology in
the wreckage of superstition and false theology. In prison he debated the subject with Anacharsis Clootz, an advocate of absolute
atheism. A friend of Helen Maria Williams who visited the prison
found Paine in daily controversy with Clootz, who ridiculed him
for "still indulging so many religious and political prejudices."
Here Paine encountered other fallen heroes of the Convention,
the idealistic Hérault de Séchelles and the enigmatic Danton. When
Danton encountered Paine on being admitted to the prison, he

greeted him in English, and added, "What you have done for the happiness and liberty of your country, I have in vain tried to do for mine. I have been less fortunate but not more guilty. . . . They are taking me to the scaffold; well, my friends, I shall go gaily."

Toward the middle of March 1794, a French prisoner, Denis Jullien, became Paine's cell-mate. Seven months later he was accused of having been a spy for Robespierre, and Paine was asked to testify concerning his behavior. Paine did so freely, but made clear that his knowledge of Jullien extended only until the middle of June, when the outbreak of his fever required his removal to a larger room. Paine considered Jullien to be a "man of strict honour, probity and humanity." Together they had agreed in detesting Robespierre because of his "sanguinary malignancy" and the hypocrisy of his harangue on the Supreme Being. In order not to be overheard by anyone else, they had written out their opinions in English and burned them as soon as read.

While Paine was suffering from fever, there had been wholesale denunciations of prisoners and consequent executions, but Paine was completely unconscious of what was going on around him. When he later heard that Jullien had given evidence in the cases of some of the suspected prisoners, Paine concluded that he had either been forced to do so or had done it "from motives of rendering service to the accused." Paine's statement portrayed the prison atmosphere: "That the accused were not guilty of any counter revolutionary conduct is what I also believe; but the case was that they and all the detained saw themselves shut up like sheep in a pen to be sacrificed in their turn, as they daily saw that others of their Camarades had been and every expression of discontent, which the misery of such a situation extorted from them, was converted into conspiration by the Spies of Robespierre, who were distributed in the Prisons."

In May 1794 Paine prepared a new edition of *The Rights of Man* stripped of its national and personal references and designed for "the Use and Benefit of all Mankind" rather than merely the English and the French. He wrote a fresh Preface and apparently found a means of sending his manuscript to London, where it was printed by Daniel Isaac Eaton.

During his illness Paine shared a room with three Belgians, Jo-

seph Vanhuele, later Mayor of Bruges, Charles Bastinit and Michael
Rubyns. They devoted to him "unceasing and anxious attention
. . . by night and by day." Paine was attended also by the prison
physician, Dr. Markoshi, and by two fellow inmates, a physician
(Dr. Graham) and a surgeon (Mr. Bond), who were part of the
suite of a British officer, General O'Hara. This was the same officer
who at the surrender of Cornwallis in 1781 had made a point of
tendering his superior's sword to Rochambeau rather than to Washington. At the risk of causing them embarrassment with the British
government, Paine in the second part of *The Age of Reason* publicly thanked them for their care.

Paine remained in a state of semiconsciousness for several weeks.
The first thing he learned after his recovery was that Robespierre
had been executed, 28 July. Eight years later Paine explained the
miraculous manner in which he had himself escaped the guillotine.

One hundred and sixty-eight persons were taken out of the Luxembourg in one night, and a hundred and sixty of them guillotined next
day, of which I now know I was to have been one; and the manner I
escaped that fate is curious, and has all the appearance of accident.

The room in which I was lodged was on the ground floor, and one of
a long range of rooms under a gallery, and the door of it opened outward and flat against the wall; so that when it was open the inside of
the door appeared outward, and the contrary when it was shut. I had
three comrades, fellow prisoners with me, Joseph Vanhuele, of Bruges,
since president of the municipality of that town, Michael Rubyns, and
Charles Bastini of Louvain.

When persons by scores and by hundreds were to be taken out of the
prison for the guillotine it was always done in the night, and those who
performed that office had a private mark or signal, by which they knew
what rooms to go to, and what number to take. We, as I have stated,
were four, and the door of our room was marked, unobserved by us,
with that number in chalk; but it happened, if happening is a proper
word, that the mark was put on when the door was open, and flat against
the wall, and thereby came on the inside when we shut it at night, and
the destroying angel passed by it. A few days after this, Robespierre
fell, and Mr. Monroe arrived and reclaimed me, and invited me to his
house.

Few doubts have ever been cast upon this romantic tale, which
Paine told for the first time in November 1802, shortly after his
return to the United States. But it should be pointed out that the

story depends entirely on hearsay and cannot possibly be authenticated. In October 1795 in the Preface to the second part of *The Age of Reason*, Paine specifically disclaimed any knowledge of the cause of his escape but attributed it to his fever. "I have some reason to believe, because I cannot discover any other, that this illness preserved me in existence." After quoting Robespierre's memorandum against him, he continued: "From what cause it was that the intention was not put in execution I know not, and cannot inform myself, and therefore I ascribe it to impossibility, on account of that illness."

While Paine was languishing in prison, a friend, François Lanthenas, supervised the publication of his translation of *The Age of Reason*, and on 7 August 1794, he presented a printed copy to Merlin de Thionville along with an appeal to the Committee of Public Safety to re-examine the grounds of Paine's detention. This was a rather bold move on the part of Lanthenas since he himself had once figured on a list of proscribed members of the Convention from which he had been removed only by a whim of Marat's. Another of Paine's faithful friends, Achille Audibert, wrote to Thuriot, member of the Committee of Public Safety, to the same purpose (20 August). Paine himself had shortly before appealed to the Convention and the Committee of Public Safety (6 August). He explained that despite his eight months' imprisonment this was the first time he had addressed the Convention because Robespierre, his inveterate enemy, had rendered any attempt on his part to obtain justice "not only useless but even dangerous." To acquaint the Convention with the true state of affairs he pointed out that the only cause of his arrest was being "a foreigner," a foreigner invited to France by its national assembly at the hour of her greatest danger. He was, moreover, "a citizen of the United States of America, an ally of France, and not a subject of any country in Europe, and consequently not within the intentions of any of the decrees concerning foreigners."

Ten days later Paine learned that James Monroe, a new minister, had arrived from America to supplant Morris, and Paine hastened to acquaint him with his plight, enclosing a copy of his letter to the Convention. Within the week Paine sent two more appeals to Monroe—but received no direct reply. In September one of his friends reported that Monroe had no orders from the

Congress concerning Paine and that he was not considered an American citizen. Monroe would do all in his power for Paine, but the best he could hope would be liberation out of compliment to America or the opportunity to stand trial. Paine was so completely taken aback by the notion that he was not considered an American citizen that he wrote a forty-three-page memorial asserting the contrary. He pointed out that it was somewhat extraordinary that the idea of his not being an American citizen should have arisen precisely at the time that he was imprisoned in France for not being a Frenchman.

In the meantime he had addressed another petition to the Committee of General Surety, which his friend Vanhuele, who had been released, delivered. Vanhuele later reported to Paine that his letter had put Bourdon de l'Oise into a raging passion. On 18 September Monroe wrote Paine a reassuring letter unequivocally declaring that he personally considered Paine an American and as such entitled to his services as Minister. This letter is important as the only official declaration on the much-debated point of Paine's citizenship. "By being with us through the revolution," Monroe declared, "you are of our country, as absolutely as if you had been born there; and you are no more of England, than every native of America is." Paine was considered by his fellow Americans "not only as having rendered important services in our own revolution, but as being, upon a more extensive scale, the friend of human rights, and a distinguished and able advocate, in favour of the public liberty."

Paine in reply, 4 October, thanked Monroe for his friendly and affectionate letter. Showing signs of the recovery of his health and vanity, he attributed his imprisonment to his "literary and philosophical reputation." He was "the victim of the principles and . . . the talents, that procured . . . the esteem of America." He could not understand, however, why he was still being held, since the system of terror had been overthrown and the new government should have no apprehension that he would blacken the names of its members to the world.

Nine days later Paine showed increased signs of impatience. He had been in prison almost ten months—two months after Monroe's arrival. The latter circumstance, he complained, might give rise to the suspicion that his imprisonment was justified or that he had lost his reputation in America. He still appreciated Monroe's efforts as a friend, but urged him to act more in his official character and consider the affront to American prestige. "As a Minister you have to look beyond me to the honor and reputation of your Government." Paine believed that Monroe had been imposed upon in accepting the view that he would be released in the course of time without direct interference. Again Paine insisted that Monroe claim him as an American and not rely on the promises of men whom he did not know. "I have always been taught to believe that the liberty of a citizen was the first object of all free governments, and that it ought not to give preference to, or be blended with, any other."

A month later Paine wrote once more to Monroe, this time enclosing an address as a model for Monroe to submit to the Committee of General Surety. Paine was never noted for his tact, but this intransigent address shows that at this point in his career he had completely lost sight of the meaning of the word. The language which Paine suggested to Monroe came perilously close to accusing the committee of seeking to alienate American citizens from France and thus endangering the alliance between the United States and France. In other words, Paine confidently believed that American public opinion would turn against France as long as he was detained in prison. So that his personal merits should not be overlooked he proposed the following:

Of the patriotism of Thomas Paine I can speak fully, if we agree to give to patriotism a fixed idea consistent with that of a republic. It would then signify a strict adherence to moral justice, to the equality of civil and political rights, to the system of representative government, and an opposition to all hereditary claims to govern. Admitting patriotism to these principles, I know of no man who has gone beyond Thomas Paine in promulgating and defending them, and that for almost twenty years past.

Fortunately Monroe in appealing to the Committee of General Surety, 1 November, did not adopt the address which Paine had proposed, but wrote a very diplomatic letter of his own. Carefully avoiding all points of doubt or controversy, Monroe politely but firmly asked that the French government bring Paine to trial if he were guilty of any criminal offense or release him if he were not.

The letter shows that Monroe was possessed of exactly the necessary qualities of tact and sober efficiency which the situation required. Monroe of his own volition paid high tribute to Paine's character and achievement—indeed he used terms much more complimentary than those proposed by Paine himself. There is no reason for believing that Monroe's flattering estimate of Paine was anything but sincere. Praise was hardly needed to enforce the simple request that Paine be released if he were not guilty of a crime.

Monroe dispatched his letter to the President of the Committee of General Surety, who promised to communicate its contents immediately to the Committee of Public Safety. The conference between the two committees took place that night or the next day, for on 4 November Monroe received the order for Paine's release, which he immediately had carried into effect.

XVIII

Return to the Convention

Monroe, who was loyal, generous and considerate, took Paine to his own home and invited him to remain as long as sickness or financial need would require. To Madison over a year later Monroe wrote that Paine would continue to be his guest "till his death or departure for America, however remote either the one or the other event may be."

Apparently Paine's physical condition was at first not bad enough to keep him within doors. Only two days after his release he met on the street a friend, Hamilton Rowan, a leader in the struggle for Irish independence, who had just escaped from prison in his homeland, where he had been held for political activities. Paine returned to Monroe's residence to inform him of the encounter and to let him know that "he should not dine with him that day." Monroe asked to meet Rowan and Paine obliged. Twelve years later in the New York *Public Advertiser* Paine published an account of the interview. Monroe received the Irish patriot with "great cordiality and respect. Mr. Rowan then took his leave and when they were descending the stairs to go their country walk, Mr. Monro called Mr. Paine back and said to him, 'As Mr. Rowan has met with a great many difficulties it is most probable he may be in difficulty with respect to money; please to tell [him] from me that I will supply him.' " In this published account of Monroe's "nobleness of heart," Paine gives no date for the episode, but by means of Monroe's correspondence it may be determined and verified. On 7 November 1794 Rowan wrote to Monroe: "The very friendly offer which Mr. Paine yesterday made me in your name demands my most sincere thanks. It highly flatters my feelings." Rowan added that he knew of no one else from whom he would rather accept financial aid, but asserted he was no longer in need since a remittance had just arrived from London.

Many years later when Rowan heard of Monroe's election to the Presidency, he wrote to one of his friends: "He was *most kind* to me in Paris. His conduct in preserving Tom Paine from the course of life he was too much attached to, gave to me, an almost indelible impression of his *principle*." One may wonder whether Rowan was referring to drinking, which had an adverse influence upon Paine's career in other periods. Yet the only course of life which Monroe seems to have been concerned about was Paine's propensity for political controversy in print, and Monroe's remonstrances on this subject seem to have been notably fruitless.

On 8 December 1794, A. C. Thibaudeau, a moderate member of the Convention, formally requested the assembly to restore Paine to his seat. "I appeal in favor of one of the most zealous defenders of liberty, of a man who has honored his century by the energy with which he has defended the rights of man, who has gloriously distinguished himself by the role he has played in the American Revolution. I have never heard a single reproach uttered against Thomas Paine. Naturalized as a French citizen by the Legislative Assembly, he was named representative of the people. His expulsion from the Convention was merely the fruit of intrigue, the pretext being a decree which excluded foreigners from representing the nation. There were only two in the Convention. One is dead [Anacharsis Clootz]. But Thomas Paine, who effectively contributed to establish liberty in a nation allied to the republic, still exists. He lives in distress. I urge that he be recalled to the Convention." Thibaudeau's motion was immediately adopted unanimously.

Paine wrote to thank Thibaudeau nine days after his motion, attributing his delay in replying to the inconveniences attached to translating from one language to another. He announced his intention to accept the invitation of the Convention: "I want the whole universe to know that although I have been a victim of injustice, I do not attribute my sufferings to those who were not concerned, and I am far from inclined to seek reprisals even against those who were directly responsible." But since he expected to return to America in the spring, he wished to be assured that returning to the Convention would not jeopardize his plans. By means of an interpreter Thibaudeau assured him that his post of delegate would not interfere with this desire and that he could even have a leave of absence if he did not wish to resign.

Paine was probably grateful for being restored to his seat, but he had undoubtedly lost confidence in the capacity of the French nation to become the molder of a new humanitarian society. Some years later he rather cynically characterized French volatility: "They first voted me out of the convention for being a foreigner, then imprisoned me on the ground of being a foreigner, then voted me in again by annulling the vote that declared me a foreigner."

As Paine sat on the benches of the Convention, the romanticist Charles Nodier pictured him as a somewhat pathetic old man—although he was actually in his fifty-eighth year. Nodier described this "aging Anglo-American" as a "professed revolutionary, naïf, fanatic, monomaniac, full of candor, who had succeeded by his unrealistic theories in making of legal liberty an institution against nature and of deism an impiety; an honest and unaffected person, nevertheless, who displayed in the most ill-fated day of our annals all the courage of virtue." Nodier remembered particularly the paradoxes in Paine's character; "a man of virtue, bold in doctrine, cautious in practice; likely to deliver himself instantaneously to revolutions, but incapable of accepting their dangerous consequences; good by nature and sophist by conviction."

The Convention's Committee of Public Instruction had been delegated to study means of aiding scholars and artists. One of its members, the poet, M. J. Chénier, reported to the Convention on 3 January 1795 a scheme of awarding pensions to citizens who had performed eminent literary services. Paine was first on the list, and Chénier exhorted the Convention to make amends for maltreating him.

A caprice of tyrants banished him as a foreigner from the floor of the National Assembly. You have revoked that inhospitable decree, and we no longer see in Thomas Paine a man of genius without fortune but a cherished colleague of all the friends of humanity, a cosmopolite persecuted equally by Pitt and by Robespierre. This has been a notable epoch in the life of this philosopher, who used the weapons of *common sense* against the sword of tyranny, the *sacredness of the rights of man* against the Machiavellism of English politics, and who by his two immortal works has deserved well of the human race and consecrated liberty in two worlds.

Noble sentiments even though Paine never received a sou of the proposed pension.

The Convention also decreed the execution of a treaty of friendship and commerce between France and the United States. Monroe, aware of these developments, felt that something could be done for the good of both Paine and the United States. He wrote to the Committee of Public Safety, therefore, proposing that Paine be appointed an official envoy to carry the Convention's decree to America. Monroe argued that Paine was better fitted than anyone else to serve as confidential agent between the two republics because of his long residence in France and his close acquaintance with the numerous vicissitudes of its government. Unfortunately the committee replied that Paine's position in the Convention would preclude his accepting such a commission. This decision, according to Paine's interpretation, was based on the fact that an application to the Convention for a passport would have made his mission public and nullified its confidential nature.

Paine remained in Paris, therefore, to carry on his work of improving Franco-American relations. He also kept an eye on the other countries of Europe. Pleased with the efforts of the people of Holland to accomplish a reform in their government, he composed for their benefit a tract on the essentials of political organization. As his work neared completion, the French Assembly issued a report concerning a new national constitution which was to be submitted for ratification. Paine naturally scrutinized it with great interest. Finding some of the articles of the proposed Constitution and some of the points in the report "repugnant to reason and incompatible with the true principles of liberty," he readapted his treatise to fit the problems in France and had it printed for submission to the Convention under the title "Dissertation on the First Principles of Government."

While waiting for the translation to be completed, Paine spoke to Thibaudeau about the principles of his work and sent him a long letter (6 June 1795) urging him to persuade his colleagues to revive the equalitarian spirit of the Revolution. When equality of rights is recognized as a sacred and indispensable principle, he remarked, one may excuse a failure to put the principle into practice as an accidental accompaniment of the turmoil of revolution. Such a deviation could be adjusted as soon as a constitution guaranteeing the principle should be established. On this ground Paine had been able to condone his own imprisonment. But he considered a constitutional denial of the equality of rights a repudiation of the Revolution itself. Paine was referring to a section in the proposed Constitution embodying a property qualification for citizenship. This he attacked as a perfidious plan which would lead to civil war or counter-revolution. The members of the Convention had been elected according to the principle of equal rights, and if the Convention adopted a new basis of inequality, Paine maintained, it would cease to be a legal and representative authority. Furthermore the Convention had no right or authority to abridge the equality of rights, which exist in nature and are not a concession of one man to another or of one class to another. "Every individual possesses his rights in themselves or from nature, and anyone who proposes to deprive another of his rights is proposing to commit robbery."

Even from the narrow perspective of political expediency, Paine wrote to Thibaudeau, it would be a fatal error to interfere with the equality of rights. Any abridgment of this principle would sap the strength of the French armies which until then had valiantly resisted the incursions of foreign invaders. French fighting strength lay in the tenacious loyalty of the common soldier to the principles he was defending. Could the politicians expect, Paine asked, that "conscripted soldiers who had marched against the enemy only in consequence of the principle of *equality of rights* would continue to bear arms for the principle of *distinction of rights* for which they would suffer the privation while others reaped the advantages?"

In his printed "Dissertation" Paine followed the reasoning of *The Rights of Man* to demolish the hereditary system, but gave a novel twist to his argument by treating the "science of government" as comprehensible to "the meanest capacity" even though it had been traditionally enveloped in mystery "for the purpose of enslaving, plundering and imposing upon mankind." In thus treating politics as a subject which the weakest mind could master, Paine in effect followed the same reasoning which the deists had applied to religion and the classical literary critics had applied to esthetic appreciation: in politics, religion and art, fundamental truth is readily perceptible to all men when stripped of the excrescences of superstition, prejudice and authority.

On 7 July Paine once more stood at the tribune of the Convention while the translation of a speech of his was being read. His purpose: to present the substance of his tract on government and in so doing to expose the contradictions between the principles of 1789 and the proposed Constitution embodying property qualifications for the franchise. Referring to his prosecution in England and his imprisonment in France, he repeated his fundamental distinction between society and government. He had not been "persecuted by the *people* either of England or France. The proceedings in both countries were the effects of the despotism existing in their respective governments." In applying the principles of his tract, Paine spoke out against two provisions of the proposed Constitution which conflicted with the "grand object of the Revolution" and the sentiments of the individuals who accomplished it. One of these articles limited citizenship to those who paid direct taxes and the other, attempting to palliate the first, conferred citizenship on every French soldier who had served in the cause of liberty. Paine showed the injustice of disenfranchising all those who paid indirect taxes and pointed out that even the soldiers were not actually very favorably treated since their families and descendants would be excluded from the rights of citizens unless they also paid direct taxes. He finished by warning his fellow legislators: "if you dispense with principles, and substitute expedients, you will extinguish that enthusiasm and energy which have hitherto been the life and soul of the Revolution; and you will substitute in its place nothing but a cold indifference and self-interest, which will again degenerate into intrigue, cunning and effeminacy."

Nothing but "cold indifference" greeted Paine's fervent plea. Only two other members of the Convention had ever advocated universal suffrage, Paine's friend and translator, Lanthenas, and an obscure idealist, Julien Souhait. The Convention murmured uncomfortably, and no one rose to support Paine, hardly a surprising circumstance since none of the American state constitutions at the time conferred any broader suffrage than that of the projected Constitution. It was ordered, however, at the end of the session that Paine's speech be printed and presented for further consideration.

The new Constitution of 1795 established a bicameral legislative corps divided into a Council of Five Hundred, each member aged at least thirty, which initiated laws; and a Council of Elders (the Ancients), 250 in number, each at least forty years of age, which either approved or rejected the laws proposed by the lower House. The administrative body was to be a Directory of five members appointed by the Ancients from a list submitted by the Council.

With the adoption of the new Constitution, the Convention went out of existence—and with it Paine's position as deputy, the only elected office he ever held in either England, America or France. Hereafter Paine was to be simply a private citizen. Although it was impossible for him to give up his political preoccupations entirely, he was henceforth obliged to confine himself to newspaper writing and idealistic intrigue with acquaintances in high place. For the rest of his life he was also to be plagued with the notoriety he acquired by publishing *The Age of Reason*—henceforth in certain quarters he was to be patronized, ridiculed and spat upon as deist, infidel and atheist.

XIX

The Age of Reason

"He who should offer to prove the being of a God, would deserve to be turned out of company for insulting his maker." Thus wrote Paine in 1778. He considered the existence of God as a point so clear and evident in itself that it suffers by any attempt to prove it. In *The Rights of Man*, although condemning ecclesiastical hierarchies and establishments, Paine declared: "Every religion is good that teaches man to be good; and I know of none that instructs him to be bad."

Yet there is no doubt that a large part of his *Age of Reason* is a savage attack on Christianity, including the practices of its adherents. These two contrary attitudes cannot be completely reconciled. The most that can be said for Paine's consistency is that he at all times defended religious belief as socially beneficial and individually satisfying. Before *The Age of Reason*, Paine's defense embraced religion in general, including Christianity; after *The Age of Reason*, he rejected Christianity in favor of deism, or the Religion of Nature.

Although most people view *The Age of Reason* as a formal attack on religion, Paine maintained that he wrote it specifically to keep the French people from "running headlong into atheism." In a famous letter to Samuel Adams, 1 January 1803, Paine affirmed: "I had the work translated and published in their own language to stop them in that career, and fix them to the first article (as I have before said) of every man's creed who has any creed at all, *I believe in God.*"

Paradoxically, Paine's French associations may account for both Paine's alarm over atheism and his sudden animosity toward Christianity. We will remember that one of his closest friends had been Condorcet, one of the pioneers in scrutinizing the history of religion from a positivist viewpoint. From Condorcet and his associates Paine may have acquired the habit of analyzing the miracles and mysteries of Christianity. A previously dormant heterodoxy may then have grown into strident iconoclasm. Condorcet could at the same time have served Paine as a warning. Condorcet was a philosophical foe of all religion, a skeptic, recognizing in the universe the existence of matter alone. This extreme materialism was antithetical to Paine's ingrained belief in the existence of a creator or first cause in the universe. Paine was a profound deist, unequivocally opposed to atheism. He may well have begun *The Age of Reason* as an antidote to the materialistic spirit of Condorcet. It is true, as some of Paine's critics objected, that only a minor part of the work is directed against atheism, but warning the French nation against godlessness may still have been his original purpose. In Part I he established the superiority of the religion of nature over all forms of revelation. Only in Part II did he launch out against the scriptural foundation of Christianity, and he probably felt impelled to do this because the first part had been subject to slashing attacks from Christian theologians.

Bibliographical evidence seems to indicate that the first edition of *The Age of Reason* was a translation in French by Paine's colleague in the Convention, François Lanthenas. Whether it was published in 1793, as Paine said in *Prosecution of The Age of Reason*, or early in 1794, still has not been determined. In an Appendix to the first part of *The Age of Reason* and in a Preface to the second part, Paine says that on 28 December 1793, when he was taken to prison, the entire first part was still in manuscript except for one page of proof in the possession of Joel Barlow. It is doubtful that virtually the entire book could have been translated and published in the three remaining days of the year. Yet Paine may have been speaking only of an edition in English since Lanthenas later affirmed that he had translated the work before November 1793 and had it printed at about the same time. If both his and Paine's statements are correct, Lanthenas must have translated the work from Paine's manuscript copy in 1793, had it printed in French, and then returned the manuscript to Paine before he was taken to prison.

To carry out his purpose of defeating atheism, Paine began *The*

Age of Reason with his own creed. He believed in one God, in the equality of man, and in doing justice as a religious duty, and he hoped for happiness beyond this life. But he did not accept the creed of any established church. "My own mind is my own church." He did not condemn those who believe otherwise, but insisted that each man's happiness requires that he be mentally faithful to himself. "Infidelity does not consist in believing or disbelieving; it consists in professing to believe what he does not believe."

In the eighteenth century, a system such as Paine's was commonly called natural religion—presumably based entirely on the observation of nature and reasoning from it. Christianity was a species of revealed religion—based on supernatural communication from God to man. Paine argued that there is no occasion for revealed religion: the creation itself proves the existence of an almighty power. Paine even denied that the Scriptures are a revelation at all: a revelation must come directly from God whereas Scriptures come at second hand and are taken upon trust. Consequently, the human language itself, no matter in what form, cannot be the Word of God. Christianity is a species of atheism, worship of a man rather than God; it contains considerable manism and not much deism. The real Word of God, Paine insisted, is the creation we behold. True theology, therefore, consists of mathematics and astronomy, the study of the works and wisdom of God.

Arguing that Christianity is a compound of fables, Paine like other deists before him sought to establish a parallel between Greek mythology and Christian traditions. The Virgin Mary he compared to Venus; the Trinity and saints to the Pantheon; the fall of Satan to Jupiter's victory over the giants, and the espousal of the Virgin by the Holy Ghost to the story of Jupiter and Leda. Paine warned his readers against being imposed upon by the three modes of superstition in Christianity: mystery, miracle and prophecy. He offered in their stead reason and scientific observation. "The creation we behold is the real and ever-existing Word of God, in which we cannot be deceived. It proclaims His power, it demonstrates His wisdom, it manifests His goodness and beneficence."

When Paine emerged from prison and went to Monroe's house for convalescence there were already a number of published replies to Part I of *The Age of Reason*. He probably began writing Part II almost immediately, now armed with a Bible to confute his antagonists. He maintained that he had not been able to consult a Bible when writing Part I.

The second part was published originally in Paris late in 1795 in both a French translation and in English. Unfortunately for Paine an unscrupulous Englishman who set the type for the edition in English made a manuscript copy filled with errors and sent it to England, where it was printed and sold by a publisher, H. D. Symonds. When Paine saw an advertisement of this edition, he immediately exposed it as fraudulent. He sent to his own publisher, Daniel Isaac Eaton, a printed copy with instructions to make a cheap edition of it.

Since all the writers who had attacked the first part of *The Age of Reason* used the Bible as an authority, Paine designed Part II as a proof that the Bible is not the Word of God. He supplemented the scientific argument, the essence of Part I, with moral and textual arguments. In the moral argument, he asserted that many of the actions of the Israelites, said to be carried out by the express command of God, are horrible crimes, shocking to humanity, and contrary to moral justice. "We read in the books ascribed to Moses, Joshua, etc. that they (the Israelites) came by stealth upon whole nations of people, who, as history itself shows, had given them no offense; *that they put all those nations to the sword; that they spared neither age nor infancy; that they utterly destroyed men, women and children; that they left not a soul to breath.*"

By means of the textual argument, Paine sought to prove that various books of the Bible could not have been written by the men accepted by tradition as their authors and that other books were written at historical periods far removed from the time assigned to them by tradition. The books of the Pentateuch, for example, were written several hundred years after the time of their supposed author, Moses. Paine characterized these books as attempted histories of the life of Moses written by ignorant men. He discredited all of the books of the prophets by pointing out that none of them except Isaiah are named in the Books of Kings and Chronicles, which cover the periods when the prophets themselves were supposed to have lived. The Book of Isaiah, Paine considered prose run mad—bombastic rant without meaning. The Book of Job, Paine admired, but cited the opinion of Spinoza that it is not a Hebrew book at all. The astronomical allusions in the book, Paine felt, are

Greek, not Hebrew. Ecclesiastes, Paine described as the "solitary reflections of a worn-out debauchee . . . who, looking back on scenes he can no longer enjoy, cries out, 'all is vanity.'" Ruth, he called a foolish story "about a strolling country-girl, creeping slyly to bed with her cousin Boaz."

Turning to the New Testament, Paine pointed out miscellaneous discrepancies, disagreements and contradictions in the Gospels. As one example, he cited the genealogies of Christ in Matthew and Luke, which have only two names in common—one has forty-three generations, the other only twenty-eight. The Epistles of Paul, Paine termed an attempt to prove doctrine by argument, specifically the doctrine of the resurrection of the same body as an evidence of immortality. Paine asserted that the argument proves the contrary—that the same body, if resurrected, would die again. For his part, he would prefer to have a better body. He required "a more elevated idea than is contained in the gloomy doctrine of the resurrection." For Paine, consciousness, not body, was the essence of continued existence.

The influence of Christianity, Paine charged, has been consistently pernicious, for it has been propagated by the fire, the sword, and the faggot. The fragments of morality which the New Testament contains, Paine considered as the natural dictates of conscience and no part of revelation. He accepted the doctrine of not retaliating injuries, but rejected that of loving one's enemies, considering it vague and feigned morality—a hypocritical doctrine, which, if practiced, would offer premiums for crime. Paine did not advocate returning evil for evil, but argued that it is not incumbent on man to reward a bad action with a good one. This would overturn all practical justice. Paine's study of the Scriptures had revealed that the absurdities, contradictions and falsehoods they contained were more numerous and striking than he had imagined when he wrote Part I of *The Age of Reason* without the benefit of a Bible.

The opinions I have advanced in that work are the effect of the most clear and long-established conviction that the Bible and the Testament are impositions upon the world, that the fall of man, the account of Jesus Christ being the Son of God, and of his dying to appease the wrath of God, and of salvation by that strange means are all fabulous inventions, dishonorable to the wisdom and power of the Almighty; that the only true religion is Deism, by which I then meant, and mean now, the belief of one God, and an imitation of His moral character, or the practice of what are called moral virtues—and that it was upon this only (so far as religion is concerned) that I rested all my hopes of happiness hereafter. So I say now—and so help me God.

In a sense there was nothing new in Paine's attacks on Christianity. Such deists and skeptics as Pierre Bayle, Shaftesbury, Voltaire, Bolingbroke and Diderot had previously developed most aspects of the scientific, moral and textual arguments. But they had attacked only partially and by innuendo. Paine was the first author to make the direct statement that the Bible is not the Word of God in clear, forthright language which the common man would understand and enjoy reading.

During Paine's lifetime appeared more than thirty answers to *The Age of Reason*, of which the most serious and distinguished was *An Apology for the Bible*, 1796, by Richard Watson, Bishop of Llandaff. Most theologians and authorities on Christian apologetics accept Watson's answer as the standard work. But as Conway has pointed out, Watson's defense was actually a capitulation. He first of all praised Paine's astronomical rhapsodies, setting forth evidence of the existence of God. He virtually admitted the textual argument although he held out for more accuracy in the Scriptures than Paine granted, and attempted to explain certain discrepancies. Only in regard to the moral argument did Watson put up a determined fight. Here he revived the reasoning which Bishop Joseph Butler had used in his *Analogy of Religion, Natural and Revealed* (1736) to confute the deists. Butler had contended that all the objections raised against a Christian God for allowing evil in the universe apply with equal force to the God of the deists. Actually this reasoning does not apply to Paine at all, for he had not condemned God for allowing evil to exist in the world. That he had not undertaken a consideration of the problem of evil may be counted as a weakness in his work—but it cannot be said against him, as Watson implied, that he had cried out against a system which allows infants to be "swallowed up by an earthquake, drowned by an inundation, consumed by fire, starved by a famine, or destroyed by a pestilence." He had condemned a God who specifically commanded his followers to massacre innocent children and carry out other "cruel and murderous" orders. This condemnation applies to the God of the Scriptures and not to the God of the deists. Paine undoubtedly felt that Watson had a weak case. Sampson Perry wittily observed that probably the only notice which "the stern reformer" Paine would take would be to ask "if there be in the Bible an apology for a bishop." Paine almost immediately began writing a reply to Watson, which he mentioned in his will as still existing in manuscript, but it has been published only in a garbled version.

Watson's *Apology*, filled with quotations from Paine, circulated among all orders of society in England at the behest of pious Christians. Those who read Watson came into direct contact with Paine, and as a result many accepted his principles. *The Age of Reason* itself circulated in England in large measure because of the London Corresponding Society, which persuaded the publisher Thomas Williams to bring out a cheap edition. A tract on *The Rise and Dissolution of the Infidel Societies*, 1800, declared that the Society "was the sole medium which, for the first time, made infidelity as familiar as possible with the lower orders."

In 1797 the Crown brought action against Thomas Williams for printing *The Age of Reason* on the grounds that it was a blasphemous work. The prosecutor was the same Thomas Erskine who in 1792 had defended Paine against the Crown attacks on *The Rights of Man*. Paine affected not to be surprised by Erskine's inconsistency "for it is difficult to know when a lawyer is to be believed." Paine took notice of the proceedings, nevertheless, by publishing *A Letter to Mr. Erskine*, 1797, repeating his contention that the Bible is not the word of God. He argued that until this point was clearly established, his book could not in any sense be considered a blasphemy. To prove the human origin of the Bible, Paine gave as principal evidence the multiple contradictions in the two stories of the creation in Genesis. The single reflection that the Bible is filled with contradictions, ambiguities and immoralities, he asserted, is in itself proof that it could not be the Word of God.

What! does not the Creator of the Universe, the Fountain of all Wisdom, the origin of all Science, the Author of all Knowledge, the God of Order and of Harmony, know how to write? When we contemplate the vast economy of the creation, when we behold the unerring regu-

larity of the visible solar system, . . .—when we trace the power of a
creator, from a mite to an elephant, from an atom to an universe—can
we suppose that the mind that could conceive such a design, and the
power that executed it with incomparable perfection, cannot write without inconsistence, or that a book so written can be the work of such
a power?

Paine's faith in "the perfection of the Deity" would not permit
him to believe that a book so manifestly obscure, disorderly, and
contradictory could be His work. The fact that it had to be
protected by law proclaimed to the world, Paine charged, that
there is no evidence to prove the Bible the Word of God. Paine
was at his satirical best in deriding the town merchants and country
squires who made up the juries for cases such as the prosecution
of his book. They were manifestly incompetent to judge matters
of theology.

Talk with some London merchants about Scripture, and they will
understand you mean *scrip*, and tell you how much it is worth at the
Stock Exchange. Ask them about theology and they will say they know
of no such gentleman upon 'Change. Tell some country squires of the
sun and moon standing still, the one on the top of a hill, the other in a
valley, and they will swear it is a lie of one's own making.
Tell them that God Almighty ordered a man to make a cake and bake
it with a t—d and eat it, and they will say it is one of Dean Swift's black-
guard stories. Tell them it is in the Bible and they will lay a bowl of
punch it is not, and leave it to the parson of the parish to decide.

Paine contended that every man's religion should be a private
affair between himself and his creator and that no third party, such
as government or prosecutor, has the right to interfere. Religious
worship was a sacred duty, but it was not to be confounded with
Christianity. Paine professed the "*sincere* and *religious* belief that
the Bible is not the Word of God." This was not infidelity, as
Erskine called it, but the reverse. It was "a pure religious belief,
founded on the idea of the perfection of the Creator." To convince Erskine that there could be establishments for public worship
professing no faith in the Bible, Paine described a French religious
group called the Theophilanthropists with which he had some
connections, and concluded his pamphlet with a brief history of
its activities.

In 1797 Paine applied the essential ideas of his *Letter to . . . Thomas Erskine* to a situation in France. During the Revolution many Catholic privileges had been revoked, including the ringing of church bells. This practice was banned not only as a symbol of sacerdotal privilege but as objectionable noise-making, just as in modern times certain cities have placed restrictions on automobile horns. After the ferment against the priests had begun to subside, Camille Jordan, a pro-clerical legislator, introduced a petition calling for the restoration of bell-ringing and other concessions. Paine immediately published a letter *On Worship and Church Bells* (*Rédacteur*, 21 July), confuting Jordan with his principle that no religion has a right to special sanctions or privileges. From his letter to Erskine he repeated almost verbatim the maxim that "religion is a private affair between every man and his Maker . . . in which no third party has any right to interfere." Terming bells a public nuisance and priests at best idle pretenders, Paine argued that the state had more important concerns: the welfare of the poor and aged, the education of the young, and the propagation of morality unfettered by superstition.

XX

Friendship with Monroe

Several months after Paine's release from prison, the malady which he had there contracted, returned to plague him anew. Monroe wrote in September 1795 that the symptoms of his illness were so grave that there was danger that he would not survive more than a month or two at the most. According to William Cobbett, Paine lived for a time as a helpless invalid, suffering from a type of paralysis which took away the use of his hands. "Mrs. Monroe showed him all possible kindness and attention. She provided him with an excellent nurse, who had for him all the anxiety and assiduity of a sister. She neglected nothing to afford him ease and comfort, when he was totally unable to help himself. He was in the state of a helpless child who has its face and hands washed by its mother. The surgeon was the famous Dessault, who cured him of an abscess which he had in his side."

One of Paine's German admirers, C. F. Cramer, translator of part of *The Rights of Man* and commentator on several of Paine's writings, went to visit him in company with Barlow. In a letter to Klopstock, 26 November 1795, he reported his distress at Paine's suffering "incurably from the torture of an open wound in the side, which came from a decaying rib."

Despite the gravity of his illness, Paine's rugged constitution triumphed with a full recovery, and as his health improved he began to turn his attention once more to American politics.

In June 1794, John Jay had been sent to England to adjust differences that had arisen out of the peace treaty of 1783. In his negotiations Jay gave the British many valuable trading privileges, but the advantages he gained for the United States in return were not at the time apparent. Paine expressed his sentiments in a private letter to Samuel Adams, 6 March 1795. He condemned the treaty and reprobated Jay's method of operation. All Americans, he asserted, must react with shame and indignation to the note of Jay to Grenville. To declare "that the *United States has no other resource than in the justice and magnanimity of his Majesty*, is a satire upon the Declaration of Independence, and exhibits [such] a spirit of meanness on the part of America, that were it true, I should be ashamed of her. Such a declaration may suit the spaniel character of Aristocracy, but it cannot agree with the manly character of a Republican."

In January 1796, Monroe revealed alarm and embarrassment over Paine's renewed political activity. Writing to Rufus King, American Minister to Great Britain, Monroe expressed uneasiness over a piece against Jay's Treaty intended for publication in England which Paine had given to King when the latter was a visitor at Monroe's house. Obviously King as one of the enthusiastic supporters of the Jay Treaty would have been a most inappropriate carrier of the manuscript. And although Monroe shared Paine's opposition to the treaty, he still wished to suppress the letter because Paine was known to be a guest in his house. Monroe could hardly countenance attacks emanating from his own residence upon official actions of the American government. Monroe advised King, therefore, not only to send the letter back but also to request Johnson, Paine's bookseller, to publish nothing on the subject. "For altho Mr. Paine's political principles are sound, and his comments upon all political subjects may be so likewise, yet I do not think that this is a veritable theater for this publication in regard to our political transactions especially when it is considered that he lives in my house." Apparently King followed Monroe's advice since no work by Paine concerning Jay's Treaty is known to have been printed in England.

Monroe told Madison, 20 January 1796, that shortly after Paine's release he had spoken to his guest, asking him to write nothing for publication, either in America or Europe, on American affairs. He based his request not on the merit or demerit of American policy, but on the injury which such essays would do to Monroe himself. But Paine had "denied the principle, intimating that no one wo^d suppose his writings which were consistent, were influenced by anyone; that he was accustomed to write upon publick subjects & upon those of America in particular, to which he now wished to turn his attention, being abt. to depart thither & reside there for the future." Monroe insisted, nevertheless, that he was forced to guard his name and character against "any improper imputation or compromittment whatever." Paine finally agreed to desist, more from "an apparent spirit of accommodation" than from a conviction that Monroe's demand was reasonable or his argument sound.

Here the matter rested until Thomas Pinckney came to visit Monroe en route from Spain to London. Paine then entrusted Pinckney with another letter to be carried to Johnson for publication in England. Pinckney having asked Monroe's opinion, the latter strongly advised him against carrying anything he did not see and approve. Pinckney adopted this counsel and authorized Monroe to ask Paine what was in the letter. Paine admitted that it contained an extract of another he had written to Frederick Muhlenberg in Philadelphia upon English and American affairs which he intended should be published with his name. Monroe revived the argument he had previously used, and Paine this time "made little other reply than to observe, he was surprised." Monroe in relating these events to Madison entreated him to confer with Muhlenberg and to have the letter suppressed.

Madison replied, 7 April 1796, in reassuring terms. Muhlenberg had not received any letter from Paine and had given his promise to pay due regard to Monroe's request if he were to receive any. By this time a violent letter from Paine to Washington accusing the latter of treachery had been received in America. Reporting this, Madison assured Monroe that nothing had passed "that betrayed the least association of your attention to T. P. with the circumstance; nor am I apprehensive that any real suspicion can exist of your countenancing or even knowing the steps taken by T. P. under the impulse of his personal feelings or political principles."

Paine's suffering in a French prison did not cause him to lose his fundamental opposition to the British government, and during his convalescence he composed two economic works which were considered radical and sensational in their day although now outdated by changing conditions. One, *Agrarian Justice*, was a proposal for an inheritance tax; the other, *The Decline and Fall of the English System of Finance,* a prediction of the collapse of the Bank of England due to excessive inflation.

Paine wrote *Agrarian Justice* in the winter of 1795-1796 as his solution to the central problem of civilization—that it tended to make one part of society more affluent, the other part more wretched, than would have been the lot of either in a primitive state. To eliminate economic injustice of all kinds, not merely agrarian, Paine proposed a ten per cent tax on all inheritances of real and personal property, the resulting funds to be redistributed as old age pensions. A revolutionary concept in the eighteenth century, but in our day far short of schemes in actual operation.

In *The Decline and Fall of the English System of Finance,* Paine tried his hand at economic forecasting. Following a notion he had already introduced in the *Crisis,* Paine attacked the English government through its economic system. He set out to prove that within twenty years the nation's currency would fail. His reasoning was based on a ratio he had himself discovered revealing that the national debt mounted in continual progression after every war. He believed that this economic ratio was as infallible as Newton's ratio of gravitation, in other words, that political and economic laws exist in a state of nature parallel to the laws of physics and chemistry. It happened that the Bank of England suspended payments in the following year—and Paine characteristically felt that his own work had been a significant contributing factor.

Paine presented this pamphlet, 27 April 1796, to the French people, as was his custom, and to both the Council of Five Hundred and that of the Ancients, predicting that the Machiavellian government of England was drawing toward its end. Lanthenas, now a member of the Council of Five Hundred, had done the translation and contributed a Preface in which he remarked that timid French capitalists, having been shown the insolvency of the British government by means of Paine's pamphlet, should hereafter invest money in their own nation now become prosperous and stable.

A member of the upper House enthusiastically proclaimed that the work should be placed under the eyes of everyone concerned with financial matters. Hereupon the Council voted that it be officially printed and distributed. The Directory on the same day ordered one thousand copies for use in propaganda warfare. They considered Paine's work "the most combustible weapon which France could at this moment employ to overthrow and destroy the English government." They were confident that if it were circulated in financial centers where large quantities of British funds were held, these would be unloaded and England "immediately reduced to the nakedness and abandonment to which she must inevitably descend." A few weeks later the Directory arranged the printing of an edition in German, which the translator, Dorsch, had particularly keyed to influence the financiers of Holland, Switzerland, and Germany, "whose interests are essentially linked to those of the Bank of London." The Directory sent one hundred copies of this edition to the Ministry of Foreign Affairs to be distributed by French agents in foreign countries. Once more the British government was made aware of the single influence of Thomas Paine. Before the end of the year, thirteen English editions were published in London as well as five refutations. Translations appeared in all major languages of Europe, and two Germans published refutations in French.

One of the long-range effects of Paine's pamphlet was to convert the fiery English journalist William Cobbett from an implacable enemy to a fervent disciple. As soon as Cobbett read it in 1810, the charm began its work. Cobbett later declared in his *Papers Against Gold* (Letter XXV) that Paine's essay "in the space of twenty-five pages conveys more useful knowledge upon this subject, and discovers infinitely greater depth of thought and general powers of mind, than are to be found in all the pamphlets of the three score and two financiers, who in this country, have . . . favoured the world with their opinions on the money system." Cobbett began a systematic campaign to rehabilitate Paine's reputation, culminating in his spectacular seizure of Paine's remains and his transporting them to England.

During the entire period of his sojourn with Monroe, Paine's bitterness toward George Washington continued to ferment. He had first expressed his resentment at the latter's official and private neglect in February 1795. At this time he composed a tart letter protesting to Washington the silence of the American government in the face of his imprisonment, the neglect by Morris of the interests of America in France, and the "pusillanimous conduct of Mr. Jay in England." The letter revealed disappointment over

Washington's conduct, but not bitterness or absolute condemnation. Monroe, seeing the letter, asked Paine not to send it, and Paine complied with the request.

He continued to brood, however, over the nation's dishonor and his personal suffering, both of which he attributed to the Washington administration. In September 1795 he suffered the relapse in health which gave birth to rumors that he had died. Although the London *Chronicle* printed a refutation of these reports, a letter appeared in the Philadelphia *Aurora*, 14 January 1796, regretting his death from fever contracted in prison. Madison in his correspondence throughout January still repeated the reports of Paine's death. During his sickness Paine composed an intemperate letter, 20 September 1795, unequivocally accusing Washington of conniving at his imprisonment, a letter which he sent and which actually reached Washington. Paine left an avenue for reconciliation, admitting "I ought not to have suspected you of treachery," but "I shall continue to think you treacherous, till you give me cause to think otherwise." Four days later he wrote to Madison: "I ought not to have suspected Mr. Washington of treachery but he has acted towards me the part of a cold blooded traitor." Paine could think of only three possible motives for Washington's neglect: to keep Paine silent so that Washington and the Federalist faction might exclaim louder against the French Revolution; to restrain Paine's opposition in an attempt to dominate the American government; and to gratify the English government.

Since Paine received neither apology nor explanation from Washington, his suspicions turned into firm conviction, and he determined to expose the President's perfidy to the world. He left Monroe's house sometime between January and June of 1796 and spent most of the summer at Versailles, probably at the home of Fulwar Skipwith, American Consul. On 13 May, the Directory especially exempted Paine from a decree which obliged all former deputies to the Convention to move away from Paris. Monroe reported to Madison, 5 July, that "Paine having resolved to continue in Europe some time longer and knowing it was inconvenient for me to keep him longer in my family and wishing also to treat on our politics which he could not well do in my house, left me some time since. He thinks the President winks at his imprisonment and wished he might die in gaol, and bears him resentment for it; also he is preparing an attack upon him of the most virulent kind. Through a third person [Dr. Enoch Edwards] I have endeavoured to divert him from it without effect. It may be said I have instigated him but the above is the truth."

According to Edwards, Monroe later suspected Paine of injuring him with the Directory, having received reports that the Directory doubted his representations concerning the temper and dispositions of the United States. Monroe asked Jean François Reubell and his colleagues in the Directory whether Paine had contradicted any of his information, but Reubell evaded a direct answer.

Both Edwards and Monroe attempted to persuade Paine to abandon his scheme to denounce Washington, but literary pride as much as vindictiveness caused him to remain firm. He told Edwards that it was of no consequence whether Monroe's writings were suppressed or not, but what he wrote himself "was for posterity." Edwards sent Monroe a memorandum on Paine's activities, 21 July 1796, but advised him not to write to Paine on the subject. As things stood, he maintained, it would be but a matter of suspicion where and how Paine got his information, but if Monroe were to write him a letter, it would appear to be an acknowledgment of their close relations, which Paine might publish. In his letter to Madison, 5 July, Monroe had expressed the hope that Paine's information would appear to proceed from other sources and that his own name would not be involved. For the first time revealing the strain which Paine's writing had put him under, Monroe confided to Madison that he had been embarrassed from every quarter for talking to Paine and that he had not looked for such ingratitude as well as breach of confidence.

Paine prepared his exposé in the form of a long open letter to Washington, 30 July 1796, which he sent to Benjamin Franklin Bache in Philadelphia for publication. Bache, editor of the Republican *Aurora* and nephew of the famous Benjamin Franklin, shared Paine's bitter distrust of Washington and was the logical man to sponsor Paine's blast in America. In his letter Paine gave a detailed account of his imprisonment, holding Washington responsible for the fact that until Monroe's arrival he had not been considered as an American citizen. He explained that he was making public the causes of his personal resentment because Washington's private conduct matched the corruption and mismanagement of his administration. In political as well as in personal relations, Paine accused Washington of unprincipled selfishness. "It has some time been known by those who know him, that he has no friendships; that he is incapable of forming any; he can serve or desert a man, or a cause, with constitutional indifference; and it is this cold, hermaphrodite faculty that imposed itself upon the world and was credited for a while, by enemies as by friends, for prudence, moderation and impartiality." Washington's character, Paine summarized as "a sort of nondescribable, chameleon-colored thing called *prudence*. It is, in many cases, a substitute for principle, and is so nearly allied to hypocrisy that it easily slides into it."

Concluding with a re-estimation of Washington's role in the American Revolution, Paine flatly denied his generalship. He summarized Washington's strategy as "doing nothing" and asserted that the great American victories were those of other commanders. Washington's own campaigns were distinguished by nothing but prolonged languor. Characterizing the President as "treacherous in private friendship . . . and a hypocrite in public life," Paine warned him that "the world will be puzzled to decide whether you are an apostate or an impostor; whether you have abandoned good principles, or whether you ever had any."

Washington nowhere in his correspondence alludes to receiving Paine's personal letter from France, but he once described the printed version as an absolute falsehood. Nor did he ever offer any explanation of his failure to investigate Paine's imprisonment. It has been suggested that Washington deliberately ignored Paine in order to avoid creating obstacles to the developing alliance with England. More probably he did not even know about Paine's incarceration until Monroe submitted his report. Paine's animosity grew out of an exaggerated sense of his own importance. He thought that the whole administration from the President down should have been rocked by the catastrophe of his imprisonment. But in reality it may not have come to the attention of anyone in the administration except Randolph, Secretary of State, and he may have accepted Morris's appraisal of the situation and considered a complete silence as the most expedient means of dealing with Paine's plight.

Bache printed an excerpt from Paine's *Letter* in the *Aurora* on

17 October 1796, and on election day in the next month he printed
other excerpts as propaganda in favor of the republican doctrines
of Jefferson against the allegedly royalist sentiments of Adams. On
6 February of the next year he advertised the separate pamphlet
version. It caused a sensation, but instantly turned public opinion
against its author. It may have done more to damage Paine's reputation in America than any other circumstance of his life—even
the publication of *The Age of Reason*. Although Washington's
prestige had already begun to decline, the average American resented the bitterness of Paine's attack. After all, Washington was
the Father of His Country, and Paine was throwing mud because
of a purely personal quarrel. Typical of the attitude of the Federalists and of all but Paine's warmest adherents was the comment
of William Cobbett in the *Political Censor* (November 1796), "It
is clear that the old ruffian has been ordered to write it by the
Convention," and the French were now hoping that as a result of
"these sweepings from Tom's brain" that "General Washington's
head is kicking about the streets of Philadelphia." Several years
later an erstwhile admirer of Paine (*Aurora*, 20 November 1802)
revealed that he had read *The Age of Reason* more fervently than
the Bible, but he had become Paine's bitter enemy after reading
the letter to Washington. Some Federalists considered Washington more sacred than Christianity.

The Washington administration was aware that Paine was writing disgruntled letters while under Monroe's roof, and this circumstance probably had something to do with the recall of Monroe
without explanation in August 1796 and the sending of Charles
Cotesworth Pinckney as a replacement. The traditional view of
historians is that Monroe had been recalled at the instigation of
Pickering, Hamilton, Wolcott and other Federalists on the grounds
that he had not adequately defended his country's policies. The
fact that he failed to shelter Washington from Paine's blasts may
also have been involved.

Before returning to the United States, Monroe had other important relations with Paine in connection with the South American
adventurer Miranda, at whose trial Paine had served as a character
witness. Paine now warned Monroe against Miranda on the basis
of new information he had acquired concerning Miranda's prior
activities in England. Miranda had been negotiating with Pitt in

1790 concerning Nootka Sound, a territory on the northwest coast of America, now British Columbia. England had been on the verge of taking up arms against Spain to support her claims to Nootka Sound. Pitt shrewdly realized that an uprising among the Spanish colonies in America would promote the English cause, and he encouraged Miranda to draw up plans to incite an insurrection. To Miranda's disappointment, England and Spain settled the dispute peaceably in a convention in October 1790, and in the next year Pitt sent Miranda five hundred pounds for his services. Considering this a trifling sum, Miranda during the ensuing months negotiated for continuing financial compensation. When Paine learned about this episode in Miranda's past he denounced him to Monroe.

A few days after his trial in France, Miranda went to see Paine, and Paine later returned the visit. "He seemed desirous of satisfying me that he was independent," Paine wrote, "and that he had money in the hands of Turnbull and Forbes. . . . He entered into conversation with respect to Nootka Sound, and put into my hands several letters of Mr. Pitt's to him on that subject; amongst which was one which I believe he gave me by mistake, for when I had opened it, and was beginning to read it, he put forth his hand and said, 'O, that is not the letter I intended'; but as the letter was short I soon got through with it, and then returned it to him without making any remarks upon it. The dispute with Spain was then compromised; and Pitt compromised with Miranda for his services by giving him twelve hundred pounds sterling, for this was the contents of the letter. . . . Miranda was in Paris when Mr. Monroe arrived there as Minister; and as Miranda wanted to get acquainted with him, I cautioned Mr. Monroe against him, and told him of the affair of Nootka Sound, and the twelve hundred pounds."

Miranda was released from prison in May 1793 and later reimprisoned at two other periods. He was confined continuously from 9 July 1793 until January 1795. He was arrested again 27 November of the same year and remained either in prison or under surveillance until his final departure from France, 3 January 1798. Two undated documents among Miranda's papers show that Paine promised Miranda that Monroe would do his utmost to bring about Miranda's release from prison. It seems strange that Paine should intercede with Monroe in Miranda's behalf at the same time he was issuing cautions against Miranda's political behavior. Probably he allowed his human sympathy to master his patriotic indignation.

Sometime in the spring of 1797, Paine sent a memorandum to Monroe concerning some suspicious-looking documents he had seen at Miranda's home. Monroe, either accepting Paine's statement or wishing to test it, wrote to Miranda, inviting him to turn over the papers of importance to the American government which Miranda had allegedly told Paine he wished to deposit with him. Miranda refused to admit Monroe's messenger. Fearing that some move was on foot to compromise him in the United States, Miranda then wrote to his friend Alexander Hamilton to explain the situation. He used the body of his letter for general disparagement of Paine and Monroe and confined his discussion of Monroe's communication to the postscript. On the next day Miranda replied to Monroe, explaining that Paine had mistaken some old innocuous notes for current negotiations.

Monroe's prompt attention to Paine's tip shows that he had not lost confidence in Paine's judgment despite his previous embarrassment over Paine's rash publications.

XXI

Amateur Diplomat Once More

Paine viewed Monroe's recall as another example of the tyranny and injustice of the Washington administration. And when he learned of Charles Cotesworth Pinckney's arrival in Bordeaux, he wrote to the French Ministry of Foreign Affairs (31 November 1796), urging that Pinckney's credentials not be honored.

When Pinckney actually presented himself in Paris, the French government declined to receive him, not because of Paine's advice, but because of a declared policy to recognize no American plenipotentiary until redress of grievances brought on by Jay's Treaty.

After Monroe returned to the United States, he demanded that the administration reveal the motives for his recall. His letters to Timothy Pickering, Secretary of State, on the subject (6, 8 July 1797) were published in the Paris *Moniteur*. In them Monroe argued: "It is not conformable to the principles of an elective government, to blast the reputation of a citizen without exhibiting the motives thereof." The editors of the *Moniteur* sided with the administration against Monroe. "A government which is responsible," they affirmed, "must necessarily possess the right of recalling, removing or employing those who possess, or have lost their confidence."

Paine came immediately to Monroe's defense in the pages of a daily newspaper the *Bien informé* (27 September 1797), edited by Nicolas de Bonneville, who had been an associate of Paine and Condorcet during the early years of the Revolution. The editors of the *Moniteur* showed, Paine charged, that they knew "neither Monroe's integrity nor the intrigues of Pitt in this affair." Monroe's letters, he asserted, do not "deny the right of government to withdraw its confidence from any one of its delegates, representatives, or agents." Monroe had spoken out because in recalling him the Federalist administration had done more than recall an agent: it had accused Monroe of "lighting the torch of discord" in both France and England. "The refutation of this absurd and injust reproach is the chief object of his correspondence." Paine saw in the situation the double influence of the British Prime Minister, Pitt, and Washington's Federalist administration—joint framers of the infamous Jay Treaty. Monroe and the Republicans he viewed as the organs of internal American democracy and the solidarity of French-American revolutionary principles. "Imagine the triumph of Pitt," he concluded, "if Monroe and the other friends of freedom in America, should be unjustly attacked in France."

Although Monroe was recalled in the summer of 1796, he did not leave Paris until spring of the following year, when Paine also had the intention of returning to America. Late in March 1797 Paine went to Le Hâvre to await the departure of a suitable vessel for the United States. He waited around in Le Hâvre for three or four months, but finally decided against sailing on account of the risks of being seized at sea by an English cruiser. He later discovered that the vessel Monroe sailed in had been visited by a British frigate "that searched every part of it, and down to the hold, for Thomas Paine." He also found an additional motive to remain in France. The French government projected an invasion of England, and Paine was eager to participate.

While waiting for a suitable vessel in the spring of 1797, Paine wrote to his American friends about the deplorable state of French-American diplomatic relations, which he attributed to Washington's pro-British policies. According to French eyes, Jay had actually reneged on a French-American declaration of neutrality embodied in the treaty of alliance in 1778. Jay enraged the French by agreeing that the British might seize enemy property in neutral ships and that foodstuffs also could be confiscated if paid for. In February 1796 the Directory informed Monroe officially that it considered the alliance between France and the United States to be broken. In March, the French government gave Monroe a note setting forth its objections to the treaty—principally that the United States had completely acquiesced in the British interpretation of maritime law. It seemed to the French that the United States had "tacitly acknowledged the pretensions of England to extend the blockade to our colonies and even to France, by the force of a proclamation alone." According to Paine's shrewd analysis, as soon as Jay's Treaty appeared the French "began to suspect that Mr. Monroe was sent for the purpose of amusing them while Jay was to act a contrary part in England. They waited however to see if the President would ratify it; then, what notice Congress would take of it, and it was only till after the last chance was passed that they broke out. They then told Mr. Monroe they had rather have the government of America for an open enemy than a treacherous friend."

Paine had two suggestions for repairing the damage done by the Jay Treaty. One was for all the neutral powers to unite for the protection of their own rights, a proposal which he later amplified into a lengthy pamphlet entitled *Pacte maritime*. The other was for France to declare "that if England molested neutral ships coming to, or going from France, that France would take the cargoes of all neutral ships going to or coming from England." Paine made the latter proposal to Minister Charles Delacroix de Constant, and in July the Directory pronounced the decree which Paine had advocated, that the French would treat neutral vessels "in the same manner as they suffer the English to treat them." Next the Directory recalled Pierre August Adet, French Minister to the United States, and appointed no successor. When Charles Cotesworth Pinckney arrived in Paris to replace Monroe in December 1796, the Minister of Foreign Affairs as we have seen, declined to receive him or any other American plenipotentiary until French grievances had been adjusted. The French also began to seize American ships and cargoes.

In an effort to restore harmonious relations and to obtain compensation for confiscated ships, the Adams administration during the summer of 1797 appointed John Marshall, Elbridge Gerry, and Charles Cotesworth Pinckney as special envoys. Paine had in the meantime expanded his scheme for remedying the Jay Treaty by means of an association of neutral nations, and he proceeded to present it separately to the Directory and to the American commissioners. The essence of Paine's plan as embodied in his *Pacte maritime* was the substitution of *unarmed* neutrality for *armed* neutrality. He proposed that all neutral nations associate and declare publicly that if any belligerent power should molest any vessel belonging to any of the associated powers, the whole association would close its ports to the offending nation. Shortly before the arrival of the American commissioners, Paine wrote to Talleyrand (28 September 1797) a brief letter advising him how to deal with the situation.

Two days later Paine sent Talleyrand his plan and Talleyrand answered ten days later with an exceedingly polite expression of thanks and gratitude.

At about the same moment that Talleyrand was replying to Paine, the latter was making overtures to Marshall, who had then arrived in Paris. On 11 October, Edward Church, formerly American Consul at Lisbon, called on Gerry, but found only Marshall. He had come to deliver Paine's urgent representation that the present was a very unfavorable moment to press the French for any sort of settlement. Church added that a plan which he was not at liberty to discuss was at that moment before the Directory and that if the commissioners waited for it to receive proper consideration, it "would prove extremely advantageous to the United States." This mysterious plan was that of Thomas Paine. That night Paine sent Marshall a copy together with a letter explaining its relevancy to the crisis of the moment. Paine also enclosed page proofs of a letter he had written concerning an internal French crisis which had taken place on the 18 Fructidor (4 September). He considered these materials as necessary briefing for the commissioners concerning French attitudes and problems. Regarding purported American proposals that the United States cede to France the same advantages which England enjoyed under the Jay Treaty, Paine replied that France already took them as her right as a consequence of the treaty of commerce of 1778. In his opinion, "this sacrifice of Neutral Rights" was not "consistent with the good of Neutral Nations considered collectively and as forming a common interest." Paine's thought rose above the interests of both the United States and France to embrace the concept of international co-operation. In 1792 he had endorsed the revolution of the world; in 1797 he called for the co-operation of the world.

Paine further advised the commissioners not to press the matter of compensation for vessels and cargoes. Since America had "made a *merit* of disowning all gratitude to France for the aid received in the American Revolution," Paine felt that France would be strongly disinclined to make any settlement. Although the French government would be glad to heal the breach, Paine saw no means by which this could be accomplished short of a general measure such as his proposal of organized neutrality.

Marshall submitted a routine report of Paine's plan to the administration in Philadelphia. Showing no enthusiasm for Paine or his proposal, Marshall explained: "I think it material to forward this paper to you because from the continuance this man receives one has reason to suppose that it was not written without the knowledge and approbation of the [French] government." In his private journal, Marshall characterized Paine's letter as "an insult which ought to be received with that coldness which would forbid the repetition of it." This will sufficiently explain why Paine's plan was not adopted—and why Paine launched an attack against Marshall years later on his return to the United States. Talleyrand seems to have had a higher esteem for Paine as mediator than had some of the diplomats of his own country.

Students of American history are familiar with the abrupt end of the American mission. French intermediaries designated by the letters X Y and Z presented a thinly-disguised proposal that the' Directors be bribed, and the Americans indignantly refused. Paine, who apparently had ways of knowing what was taking place, criticized the commissioners for dealing with unauthorized persons (29 May 1798) and condemned the Directory for not making public the identity of X Y and Z.

In 1800 Paine published the French version of his pamphlet on international co-operation under the title *Pacte maritime* at Bonneville's press. In addition to the project for organized neutrality it contained three other articles on maritime affairs, one of which "On the Jacobinism of the English at Sea" he had earlier printed separately and distributed among high government officials. Extracts were printed in various newspapers, including the *Moniteur*. In October Paine sent Jefferson separate copies of the four articles, authorizing him to have them published in American newspapers and in pamphlet form. Jefferson carried out Paine's wishes, and on 11 February 1801 an English edition of the complete *Compact Maritime* appeared in Washington. Although published in separate editions in French and in English, this pamphlet has never been re-printed in collections of Paine's works. Only the nucleus of the pamphlet, the *Compact* itself, has been included, and this merely because Paine later adapted it with revisions in phraseology as part of his seventh "Letter to the Citizens of the United States."

XXII

Relations with the Directory

When Paine returned to Paris from Le Hâvre in the spring of 1797, he took up residence with his young friend of long standing, Nicolas de Bonneville at 4 rue du Théâtre Français. It was a "reception of hospitality" offered to Paine for a week or a fortnight, but which stretched out into a period of five years. Bonneville gave up his study and a bedroom to his guest. Paine's habits had not changed since the days of the American Revolution. He slept late, read the newspapers, and then chatted with his host about the topics of the day. He never went out after dinner without first taking a nap, and he never hired a coach for a pleasure journey, preferring to walk, thus combining exercise and economy.

Paine had been on intimate terms with Bonneville ever since April 1792 when the latter published a translation by Lanthenas of Part II of *The Rights of Man*. Bonneville consistently devoted his printing facilities to promoting the ideals of the Cercle Social, the revolutionary club which he and the abbé Fauchet had organized in 1790. The name was an obvious symbol, representing the reunion of all branches of humanity in a common center of love and friendship. Bonneville gave the same name to his press. The nucleus of the Cercle Social was a former Masonic lodge established at the Palais Royal. Its members believed that Freemasonry and the French Revolution had identical aims of regenerating the human race. Bonneville tried to turn the activities of the club toward Masonic ideals and Fauchet tried to channel them in Christian directions. By and large the club members were highly idealistic theorists who wished to make over the basic foundations of society.

A few months after Paine had taken up his abode with Bonneville, a *coup d'état* took place in France, making the complete triumph of military-conservative forces over the last vestiges of constitutional government. It was swept away on 4 September 1797 (18th Fructidor).

On this date the members of the Directory with the support of the army took over the basic administrative functions, proscribed all opposition, and established a veritable dictatorship. A proclamation ordered that anyone advocating a return to either royalty or the Constitution of 1793 would be shot on sight. With the assumption by the Directory of all executive powers, the military dictatorship of Napoleon was only a brief step away.

One might imagine that Paine would have immediately started agitating against the revival of autocracy on the 18th of Fructidor. Instead he publicly supported the new regime. Realizing from our vantage point that the seeds of the Napoleonic empire were sown by this *coup*, we may be surprised at Paine's stand. Paine, however, could see only the past. What he feared was the revival of monarchy, the return of the Bourbons. Also the events of the 18th of Fructidor had not been precipitated by the group which actually seized control, but by royalist and reactionary forces. A faction among the most-recently elected members of the Council of Five Hundred had conspired to overthrow the Directory and restore the monarchy. The Directory had then assumed all powers primarily to suppress this counter-revolutionary conspiracy. Paine pointed out these circumstances in a pamphlet issued by Bonneville early in October. Its title: *Letter of Thomas Paine to the People of France, and the French Armies, on the Event of the 18th Fructidor, and its Consequences.* Evidence of the significance which the new administration attached to this work—and of the highly-privileged status accorded its author—is seen in the fact that a French edition appeared several weeks later translated by Adet, former Minister to the United States. After praising the Constitution of 1795 as the best ever to be devised by human wisdom (its only defect being the narrowing of suffrage), Paine justified the coup which had nullified the Constitution. The dictatorship he depicted as an interim arrangement rendered necessary by counter-revolutionary plots. Indeed Paine found parallels in the American Revolution. "At one time Congress invested General Washington with dictatorial power. At another time the government of Pennsylvania suspended itself and declared martial law." Considering the provocation of the counter-revolutionary plot and the danger of invasion from enemy despots, Paine could not see "what else, or what better, could have been done" than had actually taken place. Turning to England, Paine found the source of her troubles—domestic and external—in the Hanoverian succession—the fact that the head of a German electorate should rule over the British nation. He forecast that there would be no lasting peace until France should some day "take up that subject and make the return of the elector to his electorate one of the conditions of peace" —one of Paine's notably unfulfilled prophecies. Because of the Hanoverian dynasty and the belligerence of the Pitt administration, Paine predicted virtual bankruptcy for England. Her financial condition was so desperate, Paine charged, that Pitt preferred to keep the nation in a state of war rather than to return to peace, when he would be forced to account to the nation for the ruinous effect of his policies. For this reason alone, Paine taunted, Pitt had broken up the recent peace negotiations at Lille. In conclusion, Paine suggested his plan of unarmed neutrality as a means of avoiding the enormous cost of establishing and maintaining a navy.

Paine sent copies of his work to the Directory, 11 November 1797, together with a letter advising them to make a public declaration attributing to England responsibility for the breaking up of the peace negotations at Lille. The Executive Director, François de Neufchâteau, answered, 13 November, that he prized Paine's work all the more because it was "offered to him by one of the old friends of liberty."

One of Paine's frequent visitors in 1797 was the English Quaker, Dr. John Walker, who highly admired *The Rights of Man* and had no antipathy toward *The Age of Reason*. One day Walker found himself at a dinner with Paine, James Napper Tandy, an Irish republican, and other British exiles. Tandy, taking a wine glass, made the fervent toast: "Gentlemen, may the tri-coloured flag [of France] float on the Tower of London, and on the Birmingham Tower of Dublin Castle." Paine, joining in the toast, noticed that Walker refrained. He called out gaily, "Walker is a Quaker with all its follies, I am a Quaker without them."

On 3 March 1797 Paine made the acquaintance of another of the extensive circle of Irish republicans in Paris, Theobald Wolfe Tone. The latter liked Paine very well even though finding him "vain beyond all belief." A bouncing egoist like Paine himself, Tone gave in his diary one of the most penetrating and unbiased views of Paine's personality anywhere to be found.

He converses extremely well; and I find him wittier in discourse than in his writings, where his humour is clumsy enough. He read me some passages from a reply to the Bishop of Llandaff, which he is preparing for the press, in which be belabors the prelate without mercy. He seems to plume himself more on his theology than his politics, in which I do not agree with him. I mentioned to him that I had known Burke in England, and spoke of the shattered state of his mind, in consequence of the death of his only son Richard. Paine immediately said that it was the Rights of Man which had broken his heart, and that the death of his son gave him occasion to develop the chagrin which had preyed upon him ever since the appearance of that work. I am sure the Rights of Man have tormented Burke exceedingly; but I have seen myself the working's of a father's grief on his spirit, and I could not be deceived. *Paine has no children!* . . . He drinks like a fish, a misfortune which I have known to befall other celebrated patriots. I am told, that the true time to see him to advantage is about ten at night, with a bottle of brandy and water before him, which I can very well conceive.

A more flattering view was given by a Cape Cod sea captain, R. R. Crocker, who met Paine at about the same time. Crocker described him as "a well-dressed and most gentlemanly man, of sound and orthodox republican principles, of a good heart, a strong intellect, and a fascinating address."

Paine's American friend Joel Barlow returned in September 1797 to Paris from Tunis, where he had been on a mission to redeem some American sailors. Paine introduced Barlow to Citizen Sottin, Minister of Police, in an attempt to expedite Barlow's movements under the new government. Paine at this time was anxious for the arrival of the American comissioners recently appointed by Congress so that his countrymen in Paris would have some official to represent them. Paine had been acting in the capacity of go-between for various acquaintances and was probably becoming weary of the task. A certain Ebenezer May, for example, wrote to Paine from Calais in November 1797, asking him to use his influence to secure an order from the Minister of Police to allow May's "little wife," who had no passport, to accompany him from Calais to Paris. For a period of over thirty days Paine alternately visited and wrote to the police until the required permission was granted. In August of the preceding year he had made similar efforts to procure permission for his banker friend, Sir Robert Smyth, to go to Hamburg, where he could draw on his English funds. In April 1798 he wrote on behalf of an Irish-American named Connolly who was arrested and eventually liberated only on the payment of a large sum of money. Referring to this and similar transactions, Paine charged that "the orders of the Directory" were being "made a trade of."

During his residence with Bonneville, Paine contributed regularly to the latter's newspaper, *le Bien informé*, one of the most influential organs of the period. We have already noticed his loyal defense of Monroe which appeared here.

On the day before the fateful 18 Fructidor, Paine contributed an exposé of the English aims at the peace negotiations then in progress at Lille. He charged that the English desire to retain possession of the Cape of Good Hope would guarantee the East India Company a monopoly of the trade to China and the Indies. Paine warned the French that this must not be allowed. He proposed instead that the Cape of Good Hope be maintained as a free port, open to all nations, and that all of them guarantee its neutrality. The expenses of maintaining the harbor should be borne by the users and assessed on a tonnage basis. The Dutch, Paine felt, could best be assigned the task of supervising and maintaining the port. The Cape, halfway between Europe and India, could then "be considered as a sort of hostelry, where voyagers after such a long journey, would stop for rest and refreshment."

It is quite probable that the French commissioners would have concluded a peace beneficial to England had it not been for the *coup* of the 18th Fructidor which overthrew the Anglophile royalist clique and restored a more determined leadership. Negotiations were broken off, and the English emissary, Malmsbury, returned to England. Paine reported with gusto in the *Bien informé* (28 September) the circumstances of his arrival in London. As soon as it was known that he had returned without accomplishing his mission, the stock exchange fell immediately almost fifty per cent.

It was in the pages of the *Bien informé* that Paine returned to his ambitious maritime project of a descent upon the British Isles, a subject which was to bring him into personal contact with Napoleon

and remain his major public occupation during the rest of his sojourn in France. On 14 December he published an article arguing
that it would be easier to land ten thousand men in England than to
send them to India. Because of the Dutch alliance, France had acquired an extensive coastline on the North Sea, admirably suited to
preparing an invasion. Paine proposed that the assault be executed
by means of gunboats which could be brought right up to the
English coast.

Paine proposed not only the means of invading England, but in
the subsequent issue of the *Bien informé* drew up a scheme for
obtaining ten million livres for constructing a minimum of a thousand gunboats. Comparing France favorably with England—where,
he pointed out, Pitt's naval budget for 1798 was fourteen times the
proposed sum for French gunboats—Paine felt that new taxes were
not necessary, that the sum could be raised by patriotic contributions. He himself subscribed a hundred livres. Citizen Villers, in a
motion of order to the Council of Five Hundred, had stated that
various citizens wished to contribute to the descent upon England.
Paine, admiring the patriotic spirit of these noble citizens and wishing to give something of his own, proposed a plan to allow every
citizen to share in the honor of annihilating a government which,
as Paine was fond of repeating, was the plague of the human race.

Preferring to underrate rather than to exaggerate the resources of
the nation, Paine estimated the population of France at twenty-
five million people. Assuming the number of male citizens over
twenty years of age to be five million, he established five categories,
each based on the ability to contribute. Half of the five million—
the industrious poor—could be counted on for nothing but their
good will. The other half Paine divided into ten groups in descending order of wealth. The average gift to be expected from the
richest group was twelve livres, and from the poorest group, twenty
sous. In this way two and one half million heads-of-families could
be counted on to contribute the necessary ten million livres. Paine
was careful to insist that the patriotic and voluntary character of the
scheme be preserved. Each person would have free choice to place
his name under whichever category he wished. If some citizen in
very moderate circumstances wished to subscribe under the first
class or some wealthy man wished to subscribe under the class of
twenty sous, each could have perfect liberty, "for it is the equality

of rights and not of fortunes which is the principle of equality."
Parenthetically, this is a highly significant principle in a consideration of Paine's economic views.

In the light of this background we are in a position to understand
a letter written by Paine to the Council of Five Hundred on 28
January, 1798, and published the following day in the *Bien informé*
with a reply expressing the gratitude of the Council. "Though it is
not convenient . . . ," Paine wrote, "in the present state of affairs, to
subscribe to the loan toward the descent upon England, my economy
permits me to make a small patriotic donation. I send a hundred
livres, and with it all the wishes of my heart for the success of the
descent, and a voluntary offer of any service I can render to promote it." He thus contributed nearly ten times as much as he requested from the average contributor in the richest group of citizens.

Attempting to keep alive the notion of a descent upon England,
Paine inserted in the *Bien informé* (15 January 1798) a passage
from Gibbon concerning an early Roman attack on Britain illustrat-
ing the principle that the superiority of naval forces could not
guarantee the British against foreign invasion. Two months later
the *Bien informé* reported the remarks of the astronomer Le Français de Lalande concerning the extraordinary brightness of the sun
at that time. During fifty years' observation of the heavens, Lalande had rarely before seen the sun without spots. Paine, on hearing
this report, wrote to his excellent friend Bonaparte, according to
the *Bien informé* (18 March) that "the sun without clouds rejoiced
at the descent upon England."

While Paine had been living at the country home of Fulwar
Skipwith, American Consul, in the summer of 1796, he drew up an
elaborate document, complete with a map of the North Sea, setting
forth "Observations on the Construction and Operation of Navies
with a Plan for an Invasion of England and the Final Overthrow of
the English Government." Apparently intending it for the use of
both the American and the French governments, Paine showed it
first to Monroe, then had it translated by Lanthenas. A copy of
this version was carried by Boissy d'Anglas to Carnot in 1797, when
the latter was president of the Directory, and an English version was
given to La Révellière-Lépeaux, who succeeded to the presidency.

According to Paine, the Directory adopted the plan, constructed
250 ships, and then abruptly changed its policy. The plan was re-

vised when Napoleon was appointed Commander-in-Chief of the Army of England. He agreed in a conference at his home that Paine should accompany the forces as a political advisor. Napoleon's expression at the time was "Only let us land." "The intention of the expedition was to give the people of England an opportunity of forming a government for themselves, and thereby bring about peace." As late as February 1806, Paine was still thinking that Napoleon might carry out a descent upon England, and he hoped that the Emperor would not forget "that he owes the project of a descent to an American citizen"—that he would be disposed to treat the United States favorably since he owed the project to Paine.

Although Paine's influence with the Directory shortly waned, he retained his prestige with the colony of Irish revolutionists who were waiting about in Paris for the much-discussed descent upon Ireland. In February 1798 he attended a patriotic rally at which he proposed the toast: "To the three guaranties of republics—that there be freedom of opinion! that there be equality of rights! and that the majority govern the rest as it governs itself." On the succeeding St. Patrick's Day, Paine attended the banquet of the Irish, sitting on the left of their chieftain, Napper-Tandy. In June he presented to the Directory a memorial signed by a group of Irish patriots then in France. Fearing that the tyranny of the British government would force their unfortunate compatriots to expose themselves to partial and premature insurrections, these Irish republicans asked the Directors to grant them merely one thousand men and five thousand guns to be used at the crucial moment. This nominal assistance, they felt, would be sufficient to assure the liberty of their country. Later in the year Paine wrote to the Directory concerning the fate of Irish officers commissioned in the French service who had fallen into the hands of the English and been hanged. Paine had a remedy to keep other Irish officers from running the same risk when the long-awaited invasion should take place. He drew his scheme from an episode in the American War for Independence. The British had taken General Lee prisoner and threatened to hang him. Congress, which had no British generals as prisoners, replied that six lieutenant colonels would be considered hostages for Lee's safety. The British thereupon retracted their threat and Lee was eventually exchanged. Paine recommended that Irish officers in His Majesty's Service held prisoner by the French be considered as hostages for the officers of Irish nationality serving in the French army. The Whig *Morning Chronicle* in London (18 November 1798) reprinted this letter from the *Bien informé* and added a very cool retraction of any sympathy it may have previously felt toward Paine.

Three years later Paine worked out a scheme for a direct attack upon Ireland from American shores, which he published in the *Citoyen français* 28 September 1801. Taking for granted the cooperation of the United States, he advocated this invasion as a form of retaliation against the piracy and insults of the British government.

Paine may have written this merely as a propaganda threat against the English. Even for Paine this project seems hopelessly unrealistic. He never mentioned it upon returning to America, although when it appeared in the *Citoyen français*, he pointed it out to the American Consul, Fulwar Skipwith.

A similar scheme had appeared in the *Bien informé* (12 September 1798), a detailed exposition of the manner in which a French fleet could descend upon all the ports of the United States and burn them one by one. This article was attributed to Paine by his enemies and widely circulated in England and the United States as "Tom Paine's Plan for Revolutionizing America."

Paine's prestige was declining in all directions. Not only were the idealistic principles which he shared with Bonneville too radical for the militaristic Directory, but he was, paradoxically, suspected of intriguing with British agents. The Paris police viewed him with constant suspicion as a source of information concerning all members of the British colony. On 13 March 1798, the Minister of General Police sent out an order to the Paris division instructing the apprehension of an Irish priest named Somerville or Sommers, accused of being an English spy. A letter addressed to Paine mentioning Sommers had fallen into police hands, and the Paris bureau was instructed to interrogate Paine concerning his knowledge of British agents.

Bonneville, who shared Paine's lack of discretion, was having similar difficulties. He had the imprudence to print in the *Bien informé* (17 September 1798) a satirical report of a visit which Sieyès, then one of the Directors, was making to the Court of Prussia. To disparage Sieyès' reputation as a constitution-maker,

Bonneville ridiculed his personal characteristic of taciturnity. "If there were organized at Berlin a club of mutes," Bonneville wrote, "Syeyès should be named the president, the dean of silent men." The Directory was not amused by this jesting at the expense of one of its illustrious members, and it prohibited the further publication of the *Bien informé*. Paine immediately wrote to the Executive Directory in an effort to use his supposed influence in Bonneville's behalf. Pointing out that he had lived with Bonneville since before the 18th Fructidor, Paine described the journalist as "an honest uncorrupted Man and as firm a Patriot as any that I know." "He is besides a very industrious man—a good husband—a good Father, and a good friend." Paine stressed that his intercession was an act entirely voluntary—and he hoped that the ban on the *Bien informé* would be lifted on account of the pains Bonneville had taken to establish his journal and because none but wholehearted patriots were subscribers. Bonneville was forgiven this offense and his printing privileges were restored, but later he was sent to prison for another article in the *Bien informé*, comparing Bonaparte to Cromwell.

Probably because of this unfriendly surveillance, Paine in the fall of 1799 went to stay with a friend in Dieppe and then spent the following winter in Bruges with his former prison mate, Vanhuele. England was then attacking French troops in Holland, and Paine spent a few days with his old acquaintance General Brune, formerly a journeyman printer employed by Bonneville, hoping to see "the last of John Bull." Unfortunately it was the French who were defeated. When Paine returned to Paris, the Consuls of the Republic through the Secretary of State sent down an order to the Minister of Police, 15 April 1800, directing that Paine be told "that the police are informed that he is behaving irregularly and that at the first complaint against him he will be sent back to America, his country." Paine had come under suspicion because certain political sentiments in the *Bien informé* had been considered subversive. It is clear that Paine's irresistible urge for political expression was continuing to complicate his life. Apparently the warning had some effect, for Paine practically abandoned his journalism until his final departure from France in 1802.

He could not resist, however, the urge to interject himself once more in what he considered American affairs. Despite the XYZ scandal, which nullified the mission of Pinckney, Marshall and Gerry, John Adams sent two other envoys extraordinary, Oliver Ellsworth, Chief Justice of the Supreme Court, and Patrick Henry, in an attempt to assure the French of American good will. When Adams's commissioners arrived, Skipwith and Joel Barlow, friends of Jefferson, called upon them, but were coldly received. Paine had no reason to expect a more cordial reception, but he persisted in his role of amateur diplomat by also seeking out Ellsworth. Beginning with about as untactful a note as could be imagined, Paine told the Minister Plenipotentiary that he had little chance of accomplishing anything at all. According to Paine, the Jay Treaty was at the root of all the trouble, and Adams had aggravated it by foolishly recalling Monroe, the only man who could be of any service. Quite naturally, Ellsworth "put on the dull gravity of a judge" and was silent during all of Paine's harangue.

Finding no encouragement from Adams-appointed diplomats, Paine devoted his attention once again to internal French affairs. As a stroke against Napoleon he had translated and printed in Paris Jefferson's speech at the opening of Congress, "by way of contrast," he confided to Henry Redhead Yorke, "with the government of the First Consul." The copy in the Bibliothèque Nationale is inscribed in Paine's hand, "From Thomas Paine to his good [friend] the Citizen Grégoire." He also wrote out for an unnamed government official (31 July 1800) a long discussion of internal public improvements such as canals, bridges and manufactures together with a scheme for financing them. The memoir in a sense brought together the essence of Paine's ideas from his prior writings on economics, bridge construction, and naval strategy. He insisted that English commercial supremacy had come about only because of the improvement of her manufactures, and that France possessed natural resources capable of greatly outdistancing English commercial development. He repeated his rhapsodic forecasts of the glories of iron bridge construction and, modestly omitting all reference to himself, described the successful completion of the bridge at Sunderland, England, which had been based on his model. Finally, he pointed out the economic value of communications through a network of canals and the strategic value of a waterway between Cherbourg and Brest which would enable fleets in the two ports to unite internally.

During the next year Paine apparently remained quiet, waiting for an appropriate sailing for New York. At any rate we have no trace of any literary activities during this period except his piece in the *Citoyen François* concerning the descent on Ireland. By September 1801 he was so disgruntled with the government of Napoleon and prospects of invading Great Britain that he confided to Skipwith, "I give up all hopes that any good will be done by France—that honor is reserved for America."

About this time, a young Englishman, Lewis Goldsmith, arrived in Paris and was taken in charge by Paine and Barlow. He described a dinner at the latter's house. Among the other guests were Paine, Robert Fulton, inventor of the steamboat, Volney, member of the Senate and author of a famous deistical work, and General Kosciusko. During the conversation Barlow described Napoleon as "the very butcher of Liberty, the greatest monster that Nature ever *spewed!*" He also charged the different revolutionary governments of France with plundering America. "If it had not been for us they would literally have starved, and what return have we received for our kindness?" Paine interrupted Barlow, "and very jocosely observed, that 'it served the Americans right, they should have suffered the rascals to starve, slaves should not be fed by the hands of free men.'"

Two days later Paine took Goldsmith to the home of Tallien to enable his English friend to judge the character of some of the French leaders. Paine sat next to Goldsmith at dinner as his cicerone and gave him "the nomenclature of the party." Among the guests were Mercier, a celebrated journalist, and Santerre, who had escorted Louis XVI to the scaffold. Paine described Mercier "as a very funny, witty, old man, who had just as sound notions of liberty as he had of astronomy" (he was a pronounced anti-Newtonian). Goldsmith replied that he had recently read Mercier's *Tableau de Paris* in which Tallien had been cruelly abused. He was therefore "astonished to see Mercier and Tallien visiting each other. Paine smiled, and said, that in the course of the Revolution persons dined together for the purpose of making each other talk, and then denounced the conversation to the Committee of General Safety."

A few days later, Goldsmith invited Paine, Tallien, Santerre, Merlin de Thionville and Holcroft to a breakfast *à la fourchette*.

During the conversation the French guests expressed the doctrine that the most legitimate right which exists is that of the strongest. "Mr. Holcroft attempted to say something against this doctrine, but Paine desired him to hold his tongue, as he might as well talk of honor to a gang of thieves as to contradict revolutionary Frenchmen in their notion of right and wrong." That same evening Goldsmith dined with Paine at Barlow's, other guests including Kosciusko, Lafayette, Volney and Fulton. Volney led off the political conversation with a violent tirade against English statesmen. "'It would puzzle me, if I were called upon, to say which of your two parties in England I despise most, your Pittites or your Foxites. The former wished to see a continuation of our troubles and miseries.'—'Which you commenced yourselves,' interrupted Paine. . . . 'As to your Foxites, [continued Volney] I believe them to be the rankest rascals on earth. How can men who call themselves friends of liberty, have been the friends and advocates of *Robespierre* and *Marat?*' . . . Here *Barlow* and *Paine* vindicated the characters of some of the Foxites, but agreed in the main point, that it was their line of conduct in Parliament, which prevented the British Cabinet from interfering more effectually in the affairs of France." In reporting this conversation, Goldsmith suggests that Paine wished England had overcome France, a supposition disproved by Paine's active propagandizing for the invasion of England in this same year. Yet he may have joined in the denunciation of Marat and Robespierre in such a way as to make Goldsmith believe he would have welcomed English interference. Although Goldsmith later became a royalist, he directed his animosity against the French Revolution, not against Paine, and he never disparaged either Paine's character or his writings. He seems to be about as reliable, therefore, as any other eyewitness of Paine's French sojourn.

Another young Englishman, Henry Redhead Yorke, who visited Paine in Paris just before Paine returned to America in 1802, has written a romantic circumstantial account of Paine's relations with the First Consul. Yorke tells of Napoleon's inviting Paine to dinner shortly after he had been appointed commander of the Army of England. Amid rapturous ecstasies, Napoleon declared that every city of the universe should erect a golden statue to Paine. Napoleon assured him that he always slept with a copy of *The Rights of Man* under his pillow. When a meeting of the Military Council of Paris was called to discuss the projected invasion, Paine was present by special invitation. The majority opinion held the measure to be dangerous and impracticable; chief opponent was General d'Arcon, an engineer who had gained his reputation as organizer of the siege of Gibralter. Maintaining that the English controlled the sea, he argued that the invasion was doomed to failure unless supported by an uprising among the British people. Napoleon replied, "That is the very point I mean—here is Citizen Paine, who will tell you that the whole English nation except the Royal Family and the Hanoverians, who have been created Peers of the Realm and absorb the landed property, are ardently burning for fraternisation."

Paine's reply, in this narrative, goes absolutely contrary to the opinion expressed in Paine's formal plan for the invasion of England which he had shown to Monroe and presented to the Directory. Pointing out his long absence from England and adding that he could judge only by what he knew of it during his former residence, he expressed the opinion that although the people were very disaffected, the army would cut the expedition to pieces provided that it had previously managed to elude the fleet. "The only way to England," Paine presumably said, "is to annihilate her commerce." When asked by Napoleon how long this would take, Paine answered that everything depended on a peace. From that moment, according to Yorke, Napoleon never again addressed a word to Paine. On his return from Egypt when he encountered Paine at a grand dinner for the generals of the republic, Napoleon stared him full in the face, while remarking in a loud voice to General Lasnes, "The English are all alike; in every country they are rascals." Subsequently, according to Yorke, Paine came to detest and despise Bonaparte, and to affirm that he was "the completest charlatan that ever existed."

Walter Savage Landor, who also saw Paine in 1802, confirmed Paine's hostility toward Napoleon. Paine considered him "wilful, headstrong, proud, morose, presumptuous. . . . There is not on record," Paine presumably declared, "one who has committed so many faults and crimes with so little temptation to commit them. . . . Tyrants in general shed blood upon plan or from passion: he seems to have shed it only because he could not be quiet." Landor described Paine's face on another occasion as "blotched and his hand unsteady with the wine he took. The host gave him a glass of brandy and he talked very well; an acute reasoner, in fact a monstrous clever man." Perhaps these English observers, Goldsmith, Landor and Yorke exaggerated Paine's hostility to Napoleon. In several references to the Emperor in his later writings, Paine showed absolutely no rancor; and he always vindicated the expediency of attempting to invade England.

When Yorke visited Paine in 1802, he felt that he had never seen "such a filthy apartment" in the whole course of his life. "The chimney hearth was an heap of dirt; there was not a speck of cleanliness to be seen." Three shelves were filled with pasteboard boxes used as filing cabinets. "In one corner of the room stood several huge bars of iron, curiously shaped, and two large trunks; opposite the fireplace, a board covered with pamphlets and journals, having more the appearance of a dresser in a scullery than a sideboard." Paine entered the room attired in a long flannel gown. Yorke was shocked by his appearance. Time had made dreadful ravages upon his frame. His countenance was melancholy because of his disappointment over the direction the French Revolution had taken. When Yorke expressed the hope that much might yet be done for the republic, Paine exclaimed, "Do you call this a Republic? . . . I know of no Republic in the world except America. . . ." In the course of their long conversation, Paine told Yorke that he intended to dispose of his American property, live on the interest, and amuse himself by writing memoirs of his life and correspondence. He valued his estate at about seven thousand pounds. Paine had also written to Jefferson that he had invented a new type of carriage wheel which he planned to take to the United States along with his bridge models and "make a business of them."

Paine showed Yorke a letter he had received from Jefferson, inviting him to return to the United States aboard a naval vessel. This letter was soon to become one of the most famous documents of the decade and excerpts were to be published in newspapers all over the United States as well as in London and Paris. As far back as 1 October 1800, Paine had confided to Jefferson his desire of taking passage on a government ship. "If any American frigate should come to France," he wrote, "and the direction of it fall to you, I will be glad you would give me the opportunity of returning." His reason for making the request was that he was still an outlaw in Great Britain, and if any British naval vessel should have captured a French or American vessel with Paine on board during the course of the Napoleonic wars, he would have been returned to England and probably hanged for treason.

Jefferson replied, 18 March 1801,

You expressed a wish to get a passage to this country in a public vessel. Mr. Dawson is charged with orders to the capt. of the Maryland to receive and accomodate you with a passage back, if you can be ready to depart at such short warning. Rob R. Livingston is appointed Min. Plen. to the republic of France, but will not leave this till we receive the ratification of the Convention by Mr. Dawson.

Dawson, a Congressman from Virginia, was serving merely as a messenger to transport a treaty to be signed in Paris. Only after the ratification of this treaty could Livingston, the new American Minister, sail to take up his duties. When Jefferson's enemies, the Federalists, learned that Jefferson had offered Paine passage on a government vessel, they immediately accused him of sending it to France for the express purpose of escorting Paine.

When Dawson arrived in Paris, he went to Paine's residence accompanied by General Kosciusko to pay his respects and to deliver Jefferson's letter. Paine, proud of Jefferson's token of esteem, connived at its being noted in the French press, and the item was reprinted in the Washington *National Intelligencer* (15 July 1801). Political dynamite lay concealed in the seemingly innocuous announcement that Dawson "delivered him a very affectionate letter from Mr. Jefferson, in which he invites him to return to America, and offers him a national vessel for his passage." This in effect implied that the invitation came unsolicited and that a naval vessel had been intended for Paine's sole use.

The Federalist press howled and screamed against Jefferson's friendship for Paine. Ever since the publication of *The Age of Reason* and the letter to Washington, the Federalists had labeled Paine an atheist and accused him of all the excesses, real and imaginary, of the Reign of Terror. Now they alleged that Jefferson shared every one of Paine's opinions and approved of every phase of his conduct. By hitching Paine to the President, the Federalists hoped to persuade the American people that the Republican administration sought to turn the United States into a mob-dominated anarchy of atheism and immorality.

The *National Intelligencer,* semi-official voice of the Jefferson administration, hereupon published (3 August) a combination vindication and apology. Paine had requested passage on a vessel sent to France on regular business; he had done so because he was fearful of being made prisoner by the British were he to sail on a private vessel; and he had made his request prior to Jefferson's election. "We imagined that it was possible for an individual of one set of religious principles to feel charity for the misfortunes of a fellow mortal of another set, or of no religious opinions whatever; we imagined that virtue was not exclusively confined to one kind of political sentiments; and we imagined that a country might feel grateful for the distinguished services of a man, rendered in a period of difficulty and danger, though such a man might afterwards avow opinions which some might think good, others might think bad."

Dr. William Eustis, a Republican member of the House of Representatives, sent this paragraph to Paine while he was still in Paris, adding the information that it had embarrassed some of the Republicans in Massachusetts, for it "appeared like a half denial of the letter or as if there was something in it not proper to be owned, or that needed an apology." Offended particularly by the reference to charity in the paragraph, Paine also felt that Jefferson was seeking to disclaim his friendship. He later told Jefferson that this scruple had led him not to accept the invitation, and Jefferson, always loyal, assured him that he had never sought to disavow his letter. Actually Paine's correspondence reveals that he delayed his passage for reasons quite independent of events in America. Instead of taking the *Maryland,* he had preferred to wait for the westward sailing of the later ship which was to bring Livingston. When this vessel arrived, it was ordered to the Mediterranean, instead of to the United States, and shortly after, when peace was declared Paine no longer needed the protection of a national vessel.

When Paine returned to Paris from Bruges in the spring of 1800, he had used up his liquid capital. He once again went to live with his friend Bonneville, paying no board, but in return offering Bonneville and his family a similar asylum in the United States. When Mme Bonneville and her three children eventually decided to take advantage of this invitation, Paine promised in addition to leave her the principal part of his property, a promise which he faithfully performed. As we have seen, both Paine and Bonneville, were in bad repute with Napoleon's police, and the *Bien informé* was shortly suppressed as a consequence of the article comparing Napoleon to Cromwell. Bonneville had never been rich, but this stroke almost wiped him out economically. Luckily two of Paine's English Admirers, Sir Francis Burdett and William Bosville, showed their appreciation of *The Rights of Man* by presenting Paine with five hundred louis d'or to enable him to even his accounts with Bonneville and to return to the United States.

Clio Rickman came from London to bid Paine farewell, and after a few days together in Paris the two friends set off for Le Hâvre. On 1 September Paine embarked for the United States. Rickman waved his parting wishes—and after the sails were lost to sight, remained on the beach to put his valediction into verse.

> Thus smooth be thy waves, and thus gentle the breeze,
>   As thou bearest my Paine far away;
> O! waft him to comfort and regions of ease,
> Each blessing of freedom and friendship to seize,
>   And bright be his setting sun's ray.

❧ XXIII ❧

Baltimore and Washington

As a result of the publicity given Jefferson's invitation, the American press knew well in advance of Paine's arrival that he was preparing to return home. A Federalist organ, the Baltimore *Republican; or The Anti-Democrat,* characteristically reported 18 October 1802, that since the masters of American vessels in Le Hâvre had been reluctant to accept Paine as a passenger on any terms, "our pious president thought it expedient to dispatch a frigate for the accomodation of this loathsome reptile."

On Saturday 1 November Paine, now sixty-five years old, disembarked at Baltimore. He was given a noisy and enthusiastic reception by a large crowd assembled on the pier. Not only the Jeffersonian Democrats, but leading Federalists as well, "were the foremost to visit him, and with smiling friendly expressions, make him welcome in the city" (*American Patriot,* 6 November). Paine displayed a model of his iron bridge, which particularly impressed the Baltimoreans. He had still not given up expectations of making his fortune as an engineer—for he was hopeful through Jefferson's influence of interesting Congress in buying his designs.

While Paine was still in the process of accustoming himself to the feel of dry land, and before he could make arrangements for proceeding to Washington, he was placed under arrest on the familiar charge of indebtedness. A certain Mr. O'Maly then in Baltimore maintained that out of charity he had formerly lent Paine fifty guineas, and he was bringing suit to regain it. The Federalist press reported that Paine had borrowed the money during his confinement in Luxembourg prison. Paine, through the *American Patriot,* 13 November, roundly denied that he was in the

273

least indebted to O'Maly on the score of charity or any other. Although avoiding direct statement, the newspaper gave the impression that O'Maly had previously brought legal action against Paine for the same amount in Paris, but had lost his case. When the transaction occurred, O'Maly had apparently been acting as commercial agent for a merchant named M'Coy, a particular friend of Paine's, who had given the letter of credit. O'Maly had advanced the money to Paine on the strength of this security. In Baltimore Paine offered to repay the sum in question to M'Coy, but would have nothing to do with O'Maly.

The episode served as a bitter reminder to Paine of the ingratitude of his chosen homeland. He had run afoul of the law in each one of the countries he had tried to serve with his equalitarian theories; first England, then France, and finally the land which had originally provided him the vision of social perfection, his beloved America.

Chagrined by his hostile reception at Baltimore, Paine on Sunday 9 November set off for Washington, confident that he would there find at least one cordial greeting, that of the President. The Federalists in the meantime were again making capital out of Jefferson's invitation by raking up the most sensational of Paine's religious pronouncements and associating them with Jefferson. They dinned in newspapers all over the land: The President had personally invited to Washington the world's most notorious deist and social leveler.

When Paine finally arrived in the capital, he was given the cold shoulder by all except ardent Republicans. L. A. Pichon, the French chargé d'affairs, attributed the general neglect of Paine to the effectiveness of the Federalist attacks. He reported to Talleyrand (21 December) that Paine received no invitations and saw no one except Jefferson, who defied public opinion in treating him like an old friend. Paine apparently was admitted "freely and frequently" to Jefferson's "house and table." This is the expression of William Plumer of New Hampshire, who arrived in Washington a few days after Paine to take his seat in the Senate. When Plumer called on Jefferson to pay his respects, he mistook the President for a servant because of his casual dress, "an old brown coat, red waistcoat, old corduroy small clothes much soiled, woolen hose, and slippers without heels." While Plumer was talking,

"Thomas Paine entered, seated himself by the side of the President, and conversed and behaved towards him with the familiarity of an intimate and an equal." From Plumer we learn also that "Bradley (as Vice President *pro tem*) is giving dinners; and in imitation of the President, admits that miscreant Paine to his table. Neither Jefferson nor Bradley invites Federalists to dine with Paine. In this they show their prudence."

Albert Gallatin, Secretary of the Treasury and now married to the Hannah Nicholson whom Paine had known in her teens sixteen years previously, also invited him to dinner as did another member of Jefferson's Cabinet, Major General Henry Dearborn, Secretary of War.

Four dinners at four of the most eminent boards in the nation. This was not bad, but it was still not a social season. For the rest of the time Paine was forced to content himself with the cuisine and company of Lovell's hotel. Here, according to Manasseh Cutler, he enjoyed no association with members of Congress. "He dines at the public table, and, as a show, is as profitable to Lovell as an *Ourang Outang*, for many strangers who come to the city feel a curiosity to see the creature."

Almost as soon as he had installed his several cases of bridge models and wheels, Paine began striking back at the Federalist faction in a series of letters "To the Citizens of the United States," most of which he published in the *National Intelligencer* and which were reprinted by sympathetic editors throughout the country. Paine distinguished these letters on major issues of national policy from "others of a less public character" which he was to continue to publish until his death. In his first two he accused the Federalists of considering "government as a profitable monopoly, and the people as hereditary property." During the early days of the republic, he declared, the term Federalist meant someone who recognized the absolute necessity of a common representative government for all the states. Once the politicians who had adopted the name had come into office, however, they attempted to destroy elective and representative principles. Under John Adams, their leader, they had tried to turn America into a hereditary monarchy. They had hoped to attain their end by means of a standing army and an enormous revenue—and to obtain these they had frightened the people with fantastic tales of internal treason and an imminent

French invasion, threats which Paine pooh-poohed as absurd. To silence the Federalist attacks on his religion, Paine in his third letter narrated the most spectacular events of his sojourn in France, showing that luck or Providence had consistently been on his side. His miraculous escape in the Luxembourg prison from the guillotine and from British frigates at sea was demonstration enough, he taunted, that Providence had accorded him special protection. Since Providence could not be accused of patronizing infidelity, Paine insisted, his religious views must be both pious and rational. Even his material affairs had prospered. His property had so greatly increased in value, he declared in his fourth letter, that he was independent in circumstances—and his economy made him rich. His health was good, and his state of mind bright and cheerful in contrast to the rage and malice of his mortified opponents.

Two days before publication date of Paine's third letter, the editor of the *Aurora*, William Duane, confided to Jefferson (27 November 1802), that it had given him considerable uneasiness because it reopened the subject of *The Age of Reason*. Duane had unsuccessfully tried to dissuade Paine from discussing religion by predicting that he would be deserted "by the only party that respects or does not hate him, that all his political writings will be rendered useless, and even his fame destroyed." Another leading Republican, Levi Lincoln, aware of the growing anti-Paine sentiment among his fellow party-members, hastened to assure Jefferson (6 December 1802) that he held a contrary opinion. The violent Federalists, he was sure, could neither say nor do anything more against Paine than they had already said or done. They dreaded his writings "as they would a scourge of scorpions." It would be poor policy therefore for the Republicans to join with the Federalists in denouncing, or in any sense deprecating, Paine. For the Republicans, Lincoln affirmed, Paine was a tried and trusted champion.

Indeed since John Adams, the leading Federalist, was a Unitarian, holding essentially the same theological views as Paine, it was somewhat inconsistent for the Federalists to denounce Paine's religion. Even before Paine's arrival in the United States, the *Aurora*, 7 August 1801, pointed out that many Federalists were of the same religion as Paine. "Any person who reads the *Gazette of the United States* and the *Washington Federalist* will soon be convinced that notwithstanding their clamour that they are as thorough-going deists, as the author of the *Age of Reason*." The Republican press widely accused the Federalists of using Paine's deism as a cover to discredit his political principles. "The pretence usually made is indeed his *Age of Reason*," affirmed the *Aurora*, 3 August 1801, but the true cause is his attack on royal privilege. "It is not Thomas Paine's want of *religion*, but his *want of faith* in kings and priests that has made him the object of Tory detestation." "Mr. Paine was, is, and ever will be hated by the tory federalists as a politician, his religious sentiments have been denounced for political purposes and nothing else" (11 Jan. 1803).

The Federalists continued to clamor so noisily against Jefferson's inviting Paine to return on a national ship that Paine, to expose their "malignant falsehoods," published the complete text of Jefferson's invitation in his sixth letter to the people of the United States, 23 April 1803. This tactic instead of silencing the Federalists gave them new material for abusing Jefferson.

Paine attempted also to keep a hand in national diplomacy, and on Christmas Day 1802, he broached to Jefferson the subject of the purchase and settlement of Louisiana. Although he had himself never traveled farther west than Lancaster, Pennsylvania, he had been consulted on the political future of the Louisiana territory as far back as 1793, when he was a member of the French Assembly.

In the fall of 1802, Spain, after agreeing to cede Louisiana to France, proclaimed a drastic limitation of American privileges in the port of New Orleans and on the Mississippi. Paine advocated compromise rather than beating the war drums. He felt that the United States should offer to buy Louisiana provided that a majority of its inhabitants consented to American rule. France needed money, he argued, and would realize that nothing could keep the Americans from forcibly seizing New Orleans if it were not peacefully ceded. Before sending these comments to Jefferson by letter, Paine talked over the scheme with a fellow guest at Lovell's Hotel, Dr. Michael Leib, Representative from Pennsylvania. The next day Jefferson told Paine orally that negotiations for the purchase were already under way. When Paine passed this information on to Leib, the latter replied that he had known of Jefferson's measures, but had concealed his knowledge in order that Jefferson might have the support of Paine's concurring opinion.

The Federalists, who had consistently held an anti-French position and thrived on fomenting fears of invasion, brought forth a resolution in the Senate, 14 February 1803, authorizing the seizure of New Orleans. They would have been delighted to see the United States involved in a war with Spain or France or both. Jefferson, whose administration depended upon harmonious foreign relationships, had to placate the clamorous Westerners who were agitating for immediate energetic action in Louisiana. The most sensible among them, however, realized perfectly well that American sea power was no match for that of either France or Spain. It would have been possible to take possession of New Orleans, but to maintain access to the sea lanes was quite another story.

Paine pointed out these facts in a public letter in the *Aurora* (14 May 1803) pleading for restraint, good government and civil manners in international affairs. The seizure of New Orleans, he argued, would merely lead to its being blockaded, and commerce would then be ruined instead of merely hampered. "To the measures of Administration, supported by the firmness and integrity of the majority in Congress, the United States owe, as far as human means are concerned, the preservation of peace, and of national honor."

When Monroe in the spring of 1803 set off once more for France, this time as Minister Extraordinary to negotiate for the purchase of Louisiana, he carried with him letters from Paine to be delivered to the latter's European friends as well as a lengthy memorandum in which Paine suggested methods for his coming to the best of terms with the French government. Paine pointed out that nobody in France knew much about Louisiana but that the man in the government who was best informed and who had it under his control was Nicholas Madgett, an Irish patriot employed in the Ministry of Foreign Affairs who was friendly to Paine and under obligations to him. Paine also urged that Spain, a monarchy, be a party to the treaty of purchase in order to make it binding in the event that France should later revert to a monarchical government and repudiate the acts of previous regimes.

Shortly after Monroe arranged the Louisiana purchase for fifteen million dollars, Paine sent a long letter (2 August 1803) to Senator John C. Breckenridge, one of the most ardent proponents of the acquisition of the territory, to offer advice on the manner by which the purchase should be ratified in the Senate. On the same day Paine wrote to Jefferson offering suggestions for governing the new territory. Since the present inhabitants had no knowledge of democratic processes, Paine proposed that Congress institute a provisory government during the tenure of which the inhabitants could practice electing local officials and prepare for eventual full participation in national government. He informed Jefferson that he had thousands of British friends in all ranks of life, many with wealth, whom he might influence to settle in the new country.

The next issue on which Paine felt competent to offer his knowledge of French affairs to the President and to the public was that of Santo Domingo. Ever since the proclaiming of the Negro Republic of Haiti on 1 January 1804, the French, who had formerly held the island as a colony, had set up a blockade in an attempt to regain sovereignty. Paine advised Jefferson, 1 January 1805, that the situation was bound to cause trouble for the United States. If American merchantmen were to force their way through the blockade, the French would be incensed, and if the United States respected the blockade, the aggrieved people of Haiti would turn pirates and threaten all American shipping in the area. Paine felt that the best solution would be for the United States to offer itself as a moderator between the two parties. If, by serving as mediator, the United States could arrange for the French to withdraw their forces and the Haitians to give in return a monopoly of their commerce for a period of years, both parties would be satisfied and the United States would gain the confidence and good will of all the people of the West Indies.

New Rochelle and New York

Paine had proceeded directly to Washington, on his return to America, probably because he hoped that Jefferson would offer him an advisory post in the government. But when he realized that this expectation would not be gratified, he tired of the bleak and inhospitable atmosphere of the federal city and set off for New York in February 1803. En route he stopped again in Baltimore to visit Dennis Driscol, editor of the *American Patriot*. Reaching Philadelphia on 21 February, he inspected the Museum of Charles Willson Peale in Independence Hall, a combination temple of science and deism, where a model of Paine's iron bridge was immediately put on display.

On 24 February Paine arrived at Bordentown to visit his old friend Colonel Kirkbride and to inspect his own property. Four days later the friends drove by chaise to Trenton, where Paine intended to take a stage for New York City. When Kirkbride tried to reserve a seat for him, the proprietor of the stage emphatically declared "he'd be damn'd if Tom Paine should go in *his* stage," giving as his reason that Paine was an infidel or deist. The proprietor of the other stage gave Kirkbride the same refusal for the identical reason. Paine then decided to go to New York by chaise. As the two friends were starting out, a large mob descended upon them accompanied by a drummer beating the rogue's march. As Paine and Kirkbride drove through the crowd, hoodlums tried to frighten their horse by drumming and hallooing, but the riders escaped. Both Paine and Kirkbride were well-known Republicans, having established the first Republican club in Bordentown, and the Federalists were using this means to discredit them.

Paine arrived in New York City two days later, 2 March (*American Citizen* 3 March), and was immediately welcomed by the leading Republicans, including James Cheetham, a radical journalist recently arrived from England. A committee was chosen (16 March) to offer Paine a public testimonial dinner, which was held at the City Hotel, 18 March, with a "numerous company" present.

Paine returned to his house in Bordentown for the summer months on account of an epidemic of yellow fever in New York. In the fall he went to Stonington, Connecticut, to visit an acquaintance from France, Captain Nathan Hayley. There he naturally fraternized with the local Republicans and became interested in Connecticut politics. The leading Federalist of the state was Oliver Ellsworth, who had once haughtily rebuffed Paine in France. In a letter to Elisha Babcock, editor of the Hartford *American Mercury*, 10 October 1803, Paine accused Ellsworth of being a monarchist, but admitted that the charge of plotting to overthrow the Constitution and establish a monarchy may not have been valid against the Federalists as a whole party.

A contingent of Republican "Seventy Six men" from New London under the guidance of Nicolli Fosdick, visited Paine in November and found him "sociable & civil in Conversation, untill he had made too free with ardent Spirits." This overindulgence brought out Paine's vanity and imprudence. He read aloud with great pride a letter which Jefferson had written him about Louisiana. Although hearing the President's words gave pleasure to the assembled Republicans, Fosdick considered Paine's public airing of the letter quite improper. Apparently Paine had previously read it several times in different companies, and Fosdick wrote to warn Jefferson (12 November) against Paine's imprudence.

On another occasion Fosdick observed to Paine that the circulation of *The Age of Reason* in America had hurt the Republican cause rather than benefited it. Paine categorically disagreed and disclosed that he was getting ready to publish a third part. Fosdick confided the fact to Jefferson and urged that steps be taken to prevent its publication. He admitted that at least half of the group which had visited Paine shared the latter's religious convictions, but felt nevertheless that further heterodox publications should be suppressed. It had been Fosdick's policy to excuse *The Age of Reason* by saying that it had been written particularly for France, a country inclining to atheism, but obviously if Paine published the same principles in America this excuse would no longer serve. Although Fosdick felt that Paine should not be treated with so much confidence as formerly, he still preserved a great tenderness toward the "old gentleman" and did not wish to hurt his feelings. He invited Paine to visit him in New London when Paine should return to New Rochelle.

The British Consul General in New York, Thomas Barclay, knew that Paine was visiting Captain Hayley in Stonington. Barclay had reports that Hayley was on the point of sailing in his ship, the *Brutus*, with a view to capture British merchant ships, and he believed that Paine might take passage with him for France. He passed on this suspicion to his superiors in London (3 October), advising that the British navy consider the *Brutus* a lawful prize and that Hayley and Paine be taken prisoner and committed for trial. "The former as an American Subject, having a French commission in 1797; the latter as a British Subject in the Service of France in the last War." Paine was actually considering such a voyage, having written to Jefferson (23 September) that if Napoleon's descent upon England should be successful he would be tempted "to make another passage cross the Atlantic to assist in forming a Constitution for England."

Instead of putting to sea once again, however, Paine took up residence at his estate in New Rochelle. During his stay in Europe, the large stone house on the property having been consumed by fire, Paine was obliged to expand a small cottage originally constructed in 1793, which is still standing as a memorial to Paine. During 1803 and 1804, while waiting for his own residence to be completed Paine lived alternately in New York and in New Rochelle with various inhabitants of the village.

The pious villagers looked upon Paine as an emissary of the devil in their midst, and used him as a bogy-man to frighten children. One of the village lads, who later became a politician in New York City, remembered a foray which he and some older boys made into Paine's orchard. Paine came out of the house, but instead of pouncing upon the marauders as their fears had led them to anticipate, assisted "the boys in getting apples, patting one on the head and caressing another, and directing them where to get the best."

Late in November 1803, Paine received word of the death in

Bordentown of Colonel Kirkbride. Paine regretted the moment of his passing, not only because he had not been at his old friend's side, but also because, had Kirkbride lived, he would, as a staunch Republican, have "rejoiced at the triumphant success of the last election," in which the Federalists were almost everywhere defeated.

During the winter Paine was once more in New York, where he accepted the hospitality of William Carver, another emigrant from England. Although possessing only the rudiments of education, Carver had intellectual pretensions and was respected in the community as a blacksmith and veterinarian. As a boy he had known Paine in Lewes and had occasionally saddled his horse. According to Gilbert Vale, Carver "had a comfortable home, was liberal, and kept a horse and chaise; but, above all, he was honest, independent, and openly avowed the opinions, political and theological, of Mr. Paine." For two years Paine associated on terms of unruffled harmony with this "esteemed friend" until they had an unfortunate misunderstanding over money matters. Carver's subsequent conduct revealed him to be less principled than Vale believed.

Paine's most intimate and loyal friend at this time was probably John Fellows (1759-1844), a former soldier of the American Revolution and graduate of Yale College. He had begun a career as bookseller and publisher in New York City around 1793, publishing an American edition of *The Age of Reason* in 1795 and securing the copyright for Paine. At the turn of the century, Fellows became an auctioneer and later supervisor of the city waterworks. In 1804 he and Paine were fellow lodgers at the home of a certain James Wilburn. As a dedicated deist and outspoken Jeffersonian, Fellows considered Paine as an oracle, although Paine occasionally adopted a patronizing attitude toward Fellows. While Paine lived in New Rochelle, Fellows served as his literary agent and performed other services.

Another close associate was Elihu Palmer (1764-1806), graduate of Dartmouth, former minister and, during Paine's residence in New York, leader of the deistical movement in that city. He had been stricken with blindness from yellow fever during an epidemic in Philadelphia. When he arrived in New York in 1794, a body of deists unanimously asked him to lecture, and from this association developed an organization known as the Deistical Society of New York, later called the Columbian Illuminati, a group closely linked to the political fortunes of De Witt Clinton. Palmer envisaged the construction of a church building to be called The Temple of Nature, a project to which Paine was sympathetic, but Palmer died before the idea gained any widespread support. In 1802 Palmer established a deistical journal, *The Prospect, or View of the Moral World*, to which Paine in 1804 contributed eighteen papers. Palmer married a woman, described by Fellows as possessing "good sense, and fine moral feelings, and . . . as strong an interest as her husband in promoting the cause of truth." After Palmer's death, his widow nursed Paine during one of his final illnesses.

During his first winter in New York, Paine suffered an attack of gout which so incapacitated him that he was unable to write, and after his recovery a fall on the ice kept him bedridden for another month. Political affairs were running so smoothly, however, the Republicans controlling fourteen states out of seventeen, that Paine found no American issue crucial enough to occupy his pen. He addressed a letter, therefore, "To the People of England on the Invasion of England," which was published in the *Aurora*, 6 March 1804. Reviving his former hope of fomenting a revolution in England, Paine discussed the probable results of a successful invasion of the country by Napoleon. He described in detail his gunboat scheme during the Directory, although not claiming it as his own, and revealed his agreement to accompany Napoleon on the expedition "to give the people of England an opportunity of forming a government for themselves," in other words to lead a revolution. Assuming that the French were still planning an invasion which would bring on a rebellion of the British people, Paine argued that their government was unprepared both in arms and spirit to resist. Since the English people might soon be offered the opportunity of building a new government, Paine advised them to follow the example of the American Revolution and to heed the warning offered by the French.

During the summer of 1804 Paine once more took up residence at his farm in New Rochelle, adjacent to the Connecticut border. He again began reading Connecticut newspapers, and was unable to resist intruding his own opinions concerning political issues. The state of Connecticut had not during the Revolution, like other states, drawn up its own constitution, but had merely readopted the original charter granted to the colony by Charles II. The Republicans were supporting a movement to form a new constitution, and Paine, whose political efforts in England, France and the United States had been devoted to the concept of the pre-eminence of principle over tradition, published two pieces advocating a constitutional convention in the Hartford *American Mercury*, which Paine's friend Barlow had founded in 1784 in collaboration with Elisha Babcock. The latter, who remained as publisher, printed (6 September 1804) an extract of a letter Paine had written to him arguing that the Republicans should not set out to "reform their legislature for the purpose of obtaining a constitution." The constitution, he affirmed, is a law to the legislature, defines and limits its powers, and must therefore be created directly by the people. In a much longer essay entitled "To the People of Connecticut, on the Subject of a Constitution" (2 August), Paine set forth the steps by which a constitutional convention should be organized and advocated that the adoption or rejection of the constitution be decided by simple yea and nay votes.

Undoubtedly the most sensational political event of 1804 was the death of the Federalist chief Alexander Hamilton in a duel with the Republican scapegrace Aaron Burr. The Federalists immediately afterwards filled the presses with extravagant eulogies of the fallen leader, presenting Hamilton as a martyr to a noble political cause. Paine, who as far as we know never had personal dealing with Hamilton, entered the lists to protest against Federalist fulsomeness. Although few other men would have dared defy the tradition of *de mortuis nihil nisi bonum*, Paine published two pieces in the *Aurora* strongly objecting to funeral orations on Hamilton. He said nothing directly against Hamilton personally, but a great deal against the device of using him as an *exemplum* of political virtue and wisdom. Hamilton's funeral eulogist had been Paine's foe Gouverneur Morris. Paine was therefore contending more against the orator than the deceased statesman, who he admitted was "a man of some private merit." In "Remarks on Gouverneur Morris's Funeral Oration on General Hamilton," 7 August, Paine used strong language about Morris's "incurable folly." "Experience is lost upon him. In business he is a babe, and in politicks a visionary; and the older he grows the more foolish he becomes." Paine pulled the Federalists to bits with even more energy and scorn than he had used to cry down George III during the Revolution. And during the next three years his pen was to grow even more rancorous and abusive.

Some time during 1803 Mme Bonneville and her three sons came to the United States, taking advantage of Paine's offer to provide them a refuge. Probably the authorities prevented Bonneville himself from leaving France, but he sent his family with the confidence that Paine would take full charge of them. After their arrival, Paine wrote to Bonneville, putting him at ease over the future of his children and exhorting him to join them in the new world. Bonneville was grateful, and publicly expressed his appreciation in an edition of his essays published after Paine's death.

When Paine's adopted family arrived in America, he placed at their disposal his farm at Bordentown, but Mme Bonneville, only half Paine's age and accustomed to the movement and glitter of Parisian boulevards, soon found the quiet of the sleepy village unendurable. Although completely without resources of her own, she adamantly insisted upon coming to New York, where Paine tried to set her up in business as a French teacher.

In 1804 the oldest boy returned to France, and Paine with the rest of the family took lodgings in the home of James Wilburn in Gold Street, leaving his farm in the care of a certain Christopher Derrick. Mme Bonneville was not of a thrifty disposition, and since Paine was committed to bearing all the expenses of the family, the two frequently came into conflict over money.

In December 1804 Paine sent his godson and namesake, Thomas Paine Bonneville, to be tutored in Stonington by a deistical friend, the Reverend John Foster. In the spring of the following year when Paine returned to his farm at New Rochelle, Mme Bonneville remained in New York with the understanding that she would later entrust both Thomas and his brother Benjamin to Paine for their education. Benjamin later became a distinguished officer in the United States army and the subject of a biography by Washington Irving. Mme Bonneville developed a reluctance to part with her sons and when Paine's friend John Fellows attempted to put some pressure on her, she talked of keeping Benjamin with her. Paine would not hear of it, determined to give the boys equal education and "not make chalk of one and cheese of the other." When he insisted that "they must both come or both stay away," Mme Bonneville gave in but decided to come along herself. Unfortunately, she found New Rochelle no more to her liking than Bordentown, and proved a perpetual encumbrance to Paine. "She would not do anything, not even make an apple-dumpling for her own children." Almost immediately Paine sent her back to New York to work as a governess, keeping both boys at New Rochelle. Benjamin, however, shortly rejoined his mother, but Thomas stayed on. When Paine returned to New York, he discharged Derrick, and left both Thomas and the farm in charge of a neighbor. Paine still closely supervised all details of his ward's welfare, on one occasion authorizing a new outfit of clothing. "He shall not want for anything if he be a good boy and learn no bad words."

Paine's farm, rectangular in shape and about a mile and a half in length, contained one hundred acres of meadow and an equal amount of both grazing and timber land. The location was pleasant and healthy, "commanding a prospect always green and agreeable as New Rochelle produces a great deal of grass and hay." In 1805 he sold one-fifth of the land for four thousand and twenty dollars, a respectable sum of money for those days, and used the proceeds to improve the house and grounds. He decorated two bedrooms for himself and the boys, choosing separate patterns of wallpaper for the two rooms. He possessed, however, practically no furniture: six chairs and a table, a straw-bed, a feather-bed, a bag of straw for Thomas, and cooking utensils. He lived upon "tea, milk, fruit pies, plain dumplings, and a piece of meat" when he could get it.

Although Derrick no longer lived on the farm, he continued to work there to pay off a debt of $48. Apparently disgruntled with this arrangement, he began drinking heavily on Christmas Eve of 1805, borrowed a gun, and fired at Paine while the latter was sitting in the living room of his farm. The story reached the newspapers—being picked up and reprinted as far abroad as the London *Morning Post* and the Paris *Moniteur*—and was interpreted as sensational evidence of the hostility with which Paine was regarded by his neighbors. He was not hit although the ball passed through the wall a few inches below the window.

On 7 June 1805 Paine published the eighth and last of his letters "To the Citizens of the United States," his first in two years and, he believed, his "most important." This was a firm and vigorous attack upon the Federalists couched in restrained and dignified language in contrast to the knock-about terms of his other forensic

pieces. It represented Paine's final retort to Federalist aspersions of
Jefferson for inviting him to sail in a public vessel. Assailing the
Federalists' record during the Adams administration, Paine charged
that they had plotted to enforce and perpetuate their control by
spreading reports of the danger of an invasion from France. These
reports they had used as a pretext for levying a tax of two million
dollars annually and raising a standing army of fifty thousand men.
Paine argued that the Federalists should be either condemned or
vindicated by the simple process of establishing whether or not the
danger of an invasion from France had actually existed. The three
Americans who had enjoyed the best opportunities of knowing the
intentions of the French at that time, Paine declared, were Fulwar
Skipwith, Joel Barlow and himself. And all three could give evidence to the absolute impossibility of an invasion. The Federalists'
purpose, Paine alleged, was a concealed counter-revolutionary plot.

In the next month Paine published in the *American Citizen* (23,
24 July), an attack on a Virginia Federalist, Thomas Turner, in
which he loosed a barrage of rough and ready invective. Turner
had written a public letter with no reference to Paine, but defaming
Jefferson, and Paine set to work "examining the component parts of
this putrid production." Paine's ostensible purpose was to "expose
the baseness of the federal faction," but he was actually defending
the honor of his friend, Jefferson. Because of the uncommon as-
perity of his style, outdoing even his blast against Gouverneur
Morris, he used a new pseudonym "A Spark from the Altar of '76"
instead of "Common Sense," but he imagined that some readers
would recognize some of his usual sentiments and expressions.

This was the period when several states were scrutinizing their
constitutions and, like Connecticut whose problems Paine had commented on in 1804, considering either revision or substitution. As
usual Paine formed and published his own opinions. The general
defect of all the old constitutions, Paine argued in the *American
Citizen* (26 June), was that they were modeled too closely after
the English system of government.

In specific reference to Pennsylvania, Paine published a long letter
of three parts in the *Aurora* (31 August; 4, 7 September), developing his objections to the veto power being held by the governor.
Next he launched into a defense of arbitration in civil cases to super-
sede courts of law. The state he argued, must bear the expense of

supporting courts of criminal law since a crime is an offense against the state, but cases of private property among individuals should be referred to the arbitration of impartial and judicious men of the neighborhood. The government should be concerned only in establishing rules of procedure. Making a new and extreme application of his concept of abstract principle over tradition, Paine argued that "every case ought to be determined on its own merits, without the farce of what are called precedents." In courts of arbitration justice and good judgment should preside. Beyond this Paine affirmed that the whole judicial system should be reformed, particularly that all French and Latin jargon and all reference to foreign adjudication should be abandoned. "Every case in America ought to be determined on its own merits, according to American laws." He repeated also from his earlier writings his views concerning bicameralism. The Senate he unequivocally opposed as an aristocratic body, an imitation of the English House of Lords, which Chesterfield had called "the Hospital of Incurables." He advocated a variant of the system which he had earlier presented in his "Answer to Four Questions" and in *The Rights of Man*, the dividing a single representative body into two chambers, each debating and voting upon measures separately and the final decision being determined by the total votes of both chambers.

Two years later Paine wrote at length on what he considered a fundamental weakness of the Federal Constitution, an ambiguity concerning tenure of judges. His comments were inspired by the conduct of Chief Justice John Marshall during the trial of Aaron Burr, but possibly stemmed in part from his resentment at Marshall's having spurned his plan for an association of neutral nations in 1797.

In a long discussion in the *Public Advertiser* (10 October 1807), Paine criticized the article in the Federal Constitution which declares that the "judges both of the supreme and inferior courts shall hold their offices during good behavior." Paine argued that "if the judges are to hold their offices during good behaviour there must be a power somewhere to judge of that good behaviour or of the breach of it, but of this the constitution is silent, and herein lies its defect." Paine attributed this deficiency to the fact that in the constitutional convention the judiciary department had been planned by lawyers, who as potential judges made their removal as difficult as possible.

From this general criticism of the Constitution, Paine proceeded to an indictment of the particular conduct of Chief Justice Marshall in the trial of Aaron Burr for treason. He charged that "the trial of Burr has been an enormous expence upon the United States" in great measure through "the contrivance of the Chief Justice. Burr has six council who take turns to interrupt the progress of the trial by repeated motions to arrest the evidence."

Immediately after Burr's discharge, Paine wrote out a proposed amendment to the Federal Constitution, which he addressed to Dr. Samuel L. Mitchill, Republican Senator from New York, but the latter never brought it before the Senate. Paine proposed to "alter the words as they now stand in the article, 'the judges both of the Supreme and inferior courts, shall hold their offices during good behavior,' to add *but for reasonable cause, which shall not be sufficient grounds for impeachment, the president may remove any of them, on the address of a majority of the houses of Congress*." As a reason for the amendment Paine said nothing about the Burr trial, but merely observed that the people have no share in the appointment of judges nor control over them afterwards. Not only may they become domineering or dangerous, but they "lay open to the intrigues of a foreign enemy, or any corrupt party in the states associated with that enemy." (*Public Advertiser*, 22 January 1810)

Cheetham caustically observed in the *American Citizen*, on the following day, "It seems that because Burr could not be hanged as the law now stands, the law was to be altered so as to hang somebody else."

XXV

Jarvis and Carpenter

Paine's correspondence about the practical problems of his farm shows that he had no knowledge of agriculture. He had a theoretical devotion to farming as the noblest of professions, having once written to Henry Laurens a statement of physiocratic principles much like Franklin's, naming farmers and cultivators as "the first useful class of citizens." But he would never have undertaken a country life had his farm not been given to him by New York State. In New Rochelle, Paine depended entirely upon hired help or tenants and was able to keep things running only by selling off parcels of land. In 1806 he left the farm and, after lodging for a short time in a tavern at New Rochelle, returned definitively to New York City.

Since his agricultural activities brought him no money, Paine revived his almost perennial project of publishing an edition of his works. He also wrote to Jefferson (30 Sept 1805) about the motion which had been defeated in the Virginia legislature in 1784 to award him a tract of land. Since only Pennsylvania and New York had ever made any acknowledgment of his services during the Revolution, he proposed to Jefferson that Congress take up the subject for all of the states. Jefferson failing to reply, Paine's feelings were hurt, and he addressed the following curt note (14 November):

Thomas Paine's compliments to Mr. Jefferson desires to be informed if he received a letter from him beginning as follows "I write you this letter entirely on my own account, and I begin it without ceremony." The letter then speaks of a motion made in the Virginia legislature for making an acknowledgment to Thomas Paine for his services during the revolution.

Jefferson, distressed over his friend's sensibility, replied (22 November) that since nothing could have been done for Paine until the meetings of the national Congress and of the Virginia legislature, he had deferred writing until he could furnish some concrete information. He explained that he could personally accomplish very little in either legislative group; in the Virginia legislature he had very few personal acquaintances, and in Congress his intermeddling would have the appearance of attempting to exert executive influence. He was fully sincere in assuring Paine that he wished to promote his cause, however, for in the next month he forwarded Paine's letter to a member of the Virginia legislature with the request that the latter sound out individual members to find out whether sentiment favored Paine's request. Apparently sentiment did not, for Virginia neither then nor later ever made a gesture in Paine's behalf.

Since Jefferson in subsequent correspondence made no further allusions to Paine's compensation, Paine wrote on the subject to George Clinton, Vice President of the United States, but he also, no matter how favorably disposed toward Paine, was unable to influence Congress. Paine thereupon began thinking of other means of entering the national payroll. In a long letter to Jefferson concerning Napoleon's military successes on the continent (30 January 1806), Paine offered himself as a special envoy to France, whether Napoleon should either engage in a descent upon England or conclude a treaty of peace. In March, when England and France seemed to be ready to come to terms, Paine repeated his desire to negotiate with Napoleon. Jefferson, kind and tactful, explained (25 March) that discussions were needed only with Spain and England, and that qualified American plenipotentiaries were already on the scene.

The refusal of Congress to vote financial compensation and Jefferson's rejection of his proffered services undoubtedly hurt Paine's pride, but realization that thirty years had elapsed since his revolutionary activities softened both blows. A much greater shock came later in the year when Paine was refused the right to vote in New Rochelle by a group of election inspectors. In explaining the circumstances of this disgraceful affair to Joel Barlow, 4 May 1807, Paine characterized the inspectors as Tories who had lived behind the British lines during the Revolution.

These men refused my vote saying to me "You are not an American Citizen." Upon my beginning to remonstrate with them, the chief of them (Ward, Supervisor, whose father and all his brothers had joined the British, but himself not being old enough to carry a musket staid at home with his mother) got up and calling out for a constable said to me "I commit you to Prison." He chose however to sit down and go no further with it.

Ward and his cohorts had denied Paine's citizenship on the grounds that Gouverneur Morris would not reclaim him while he was in prison in France and that Washington "refused to do it." As a matter of historical fact, Morris did reclaim Paine, although in a perfunctory manner—and Washington formally approved Morris's action. Paine prepared to prosecute the inspectors and wrote to Barlow asking for a certificate asserting that he and other Americans in Paris had gone to the Convention to petition for his release. He wrote also to Madison for an attested copy of Monroe's letter to Randolph describing his claiming of Paine as an American citizen and of his liberation as a consequence. Of Vice President Clinton, Paine requested a letter setting forth the influence of his revolutionary writings. According to Mme Bonneville, the trial or hearing actually took place before the Supreme Court of New York; Paine lost; and the costs were borne by his estate. Conway and subsequent legal scholars have made painstaking searches for records of such a case, but absolutely none can be found. The fact remains, however, that Paine's citizenship was denied in the very community where the state government of New York had presented him an estate in gratitude for his patriotic services.

While Paine was living in lodgings in New Rochelle during the spring of 1806, William Carver rode out to see him, urged him to return to the city for the sake of his many friends, and offered him a room in his house at 36 Cedar Street. Paine consented and shortly after moved in with Carver, but unfortunately made no agreement about payment, an omission, with painful consequences. They later engaged in a haggling correspondence over the compensation due Carver, and Carver showed his lack of discretion by making it public.

At the end of July 1806, Paine was striken with a fit of apoplexy, which temporarily deprived him of all sense and motion, and made the people around him take him for dead. He had felt unusually well earlier that day, and after a supper of bread and butter, was going to bed when the fit took him on the stairs. He was so badly injured by the fall that for weeks afterwards he was unable to get in and out of bed without being lifted in a blanket by two persons. Mrs. Palmer, widow of the deistical preacher who lived on the same street, took care of Paine for twelve weeks.

Paine's doctor apparently advised him to leave Carver's, and he looked around in October for other accommodations. He inquired first of Hitt, a baker, on Broome Street, but since the latter's rooms were not then available, he moved in with John Wesley Jarvis, the eminent portrait painter, at 85 Church Street. He arrived on 3 November 1806 and remained until the following April.

He had left Carver's without settling accounts, and on 21 November, Carver sent him a polite but firm letter asking for $150 for his board for twenty-two weeks and that of Mrs. Palmer, his nurse, for twelve weeks.

Paine replied in a querulous letter complaining of the treatment he had received at Carver's. "In no case was it friendly, and in many cases not civil," especially from Mrs. Carver. She had not given him his "tea or coffee till every body else was served, and many times it was not fit to drink." He had been obliged to furnish his own bedding, his room was nothing but a closet to the front room, and Mrs. Palmer had neither a room of her own nor access to a fire when the weather grew cold. Carver also had left him alone on the night he was stricken with apoplexy. Paine affirmed that he had already paid $10 toward his last stay, and he refused to pay any more until Carver presented an itemized account.

Carver's written retort was filled with abuse. He accused Paine of drunkenness and filthiness. He described finding Paine in a tavern at New Rochelle in a most miserable situation. Paine appeared not to have shaven for a fortnight; his shirt was in tatters, nearly the color of tanned leather; and he gave off a most disagreeable smell. Carver had washed him with warm water and soap from head to foot, an operation which had to be performed three times to get him clean. "I likewise shaved you and cut your nails, that were like birds claws." Carver also made irrelevant slurring insinuations concerning Paine's relations with Mme Bonneville. He suggested "some criminal connexion," and bluntly, but equivocally, remarked, "whether the boys are yours, I leave you to judge."

Carver later turned over this correspondence to Cheetham, who published it in his biography of Paine. Mme Bonneville then brought a libel suit against Cheetham for spreading and embellishing these unfounded insinuations concerning the paternity of her children. Cheetham was adjudged guilty, but got off with a nominal fine and a commendation for having written in the cause of religion. Carver later said that his claim against Paine was amicably settled by Paine's friends John Fellows and Walter Morton. Just before Paine's death, Carver wrote to him again, apologizing for his intransigence and seeking a reconciliation. He later claimed to have attended Paine's funeral as a grieving mourner—and until his own death represented himself as Paine's friend and disciple. Carver must at the very least be indicted for insincerity. If before Paine's death, he actually regretted the misunderstanding which separated them, he could hardly a few weeks after have put his scurrilous correspondence into Cheetham's hands, knowing full well that it would be exposed to the public.

With Jarvis, Paine's relations were much happier than with Carver. Although widely separated in age, Paine in his seventies, Jarvis in his thirties, they had much else in common. Both were staunch Jeffersonians; both enjoyed a somewhat Bohemian manner of life, and both were avid talkers. Jarvis was considered "the greatest wit of the age," and Paine had one of the richest funds of personal experience. Although Jarvis spent most of his evenings at social clubs, he often sat until the late hours with Paine discussing Christianity, a future state, the rights of man, and all phases of human relations. One night Paine pressed him to stay at home, offering as inducement an impromptu concert. "I'll sing and you shall sing." "Jarvis overcome by entreaty, but uneasy at his disappointment, waggishly determined a trick on Mr. Paine; and therefore commenced the concert with 'God save the king,' in order to vex the veteran republican." Paine, falling in with his humor, completely ignored the words of the song and asked Jarvis if he would like to know the origin of the music. Paine explained that in the time of George I it had been invented by an "old Jew clothesman," who used it to advertise his wares on the London streets. To render the calling of 'Any old clothes to sell' easy to his lungs, he fit to the phrase the notes which compose the air of "a fine old anthem." When his own turn came, Paine sang "Rule Britannia" in the tremulous tones of his advanced age.

Paine and Jarvis undoubtedly found the winter at their "Bachelor's Hall" mutually agreeable. Jarvis indeed wrote to one of his friends: "I have had Tom Paine living with me for these five months; he is one of the most pleasant companions I have met with for an old man." And thirty years later he still spoke of "their agreeable companionship with much gusto."

When Jarvis once noticed the serving girl reading *The Age of Reason*, he made her stop and give up the book. Jarvis's given name, we must remember, was John Wesley. He explained to the indignant Paine that this simple girl lacked extensive reasoning powers and argued that individuals who cannot reason for themselves would be deprived of all guidance in moral conduct were it not for religious faith. This was a view held, not only by Christians such as Jarvis, but by many deists such as Shaftesbury and Franklin. As an illustration of the principle, Jarvis pointed out of the window to a colored congregation, where a notorious reprobate after being accepted into membership had become a respected member of the community. Cheetham, who tells the story, says that Paine had no reply, except *pish* and *pshaw*, which in view of Paine's vanity and self-assurance is somewhat hard to believe. The New York antiquarian, John W. Francis, related a parallel anecdote showing that Paine exercised more skill in repartee. He had been invited to dinner with a number of the city's intellectuals who had known him during the Revolution. John Pintard, historian and man of letters, publicly remarked, "I have read and re-read your Age of Reason, and any doubts which I before entertained of the truth of revelation, have been removed by your logic. Yes, sir, your very arguments against Christianity have convinced me of its truth." "Well, then," answered Paine, with a sarcastic glance, "I may return to my couch tonight with the consolation that I have made at least *one* Christian."

Toward the end of his stay with Jarvis, Paine published his "Essay on Dream," an examination of passages in the Bible in which dreams are made the foundation of doctrine. Paine asked Jarvis whether he had seen any notices of it in the newspapers. When Jarvis replied that he had not seen even an adverse mention,

Paine attributed the silence of the press to the cunning of his enemies. "They know that if they abuse it, everybody will obtain it." Jarvis replied that if Paine wanted to write a work which would not be abused, but be extremely popular, he should write Paine's "Recantation." He would then enjoy the profits for himself and not leave them to others. "You know the time must soon come, when, like Voltaire and others, you will recant all you have said on the subject of religion." "I do not know," Paine replied, "what I may do when infested by disease and pain; I may become a second child; and designing people may entrap me into saying anything; or they may put into my mouth, what I never said. . . . I don't believe what the priests reported of Voltaire's confession on his death bed." Paine, therefore, declaring himself in perfect health and soundness of mind, solemnly repeated to Jarvis "his belief in his already written opinions."

As a matter of fact, a pamphlet entitled *The Recantation; being an anticipated valedictory address of Thomas Paine* had been published in New York while Paine was still in France. When Paine returned to New York and the author, Donald Fraser, a Scots schoolmaster, heard that Paine intended to prosecute him for forgery, he boldly confessed his trickery and threw himself on Paine's mercy. He explained that he had come from England to fight against the Americans during the Revolution; he had later set up as a fencing master, a clergyman and as a schoolmaster with absolutely no success. As a last resort he had turned author and made more money from Paine's *Recantation* than from all his other ventures. According to Dr. Francis, Paine tolerantly replied, "I am glad you found the expedient a successful shift for your needy family; but write no more concerning Thomas Paine; I am satisfied with your acknowledgment—try something more worthy of a man." Paine, nevertheless, later exposed Fraser's forgery in the *American Citizen* (23 July 1805).

During his last three years in New York City, a period of violent partisan feeling, Paine engaged in a gush of journalistic activity more voluminous than that at any other time in his life. The chief Republican journal at the time was the *American Citizen*, published by the same Cheetham who later wrote Paine's *Life*. A hatter by trade, Cheetham in England had strongly advocated Paine's *The Rights of Man*. During riots in Manchester in 1798 he had been charged with conspiring to overthrow the government and was forced to leave the country. He made Paine's acquaintance in March 1803 after the latter's return from France.

Paine, in the year and a half prior to his residence with Jarvis, published a half dozen pieces in the *American Citizen*, and after September 1806 he contributed five or six each month. Since he wrote under pseudonyms, most of these articles have been unknown to Paine's editors and previous biographers. Although the political issues which Paine raised are now completely dead, these writings illuminate important aspects of his personality, and many of them, particularly those in which he feuded with opposition writers, are filled with satirical vigor and spice even more piquant than that in his previously-known writings.

One of these pieces has been identified by means of a description by a Scotsman, John Melish. When he visited Paine for the second time at Carver's in September 1806, Paine showed him a manuscript copy of a squib, which was later published anonymously in the *American Citizen* 23 September. Melish made a copy, considering the piece "a relic of an extraordinary political character, and as a very good specimen of the acuteness of his mind, and his turn for wit, at the advanced age of 70." Paine's communication satirized a passage by a Federalist writer named Stephen Carpenter, editor of *The People's Friend and Daily Advertiser*, deploring rumors of a peace between England and France. "We will aver," Carpenter had written, "that the sun which dawns upon that event will be the DARKEST that ever rose since the transgression of our first parents brought sin into the world." Paine seized on the word *darkest* as evidence that poor Carpenter had reached a point of insanity beyond all hopes of recovery. "This is the first time that we have ever heard of the sun *shining* darkness: But darkness or light, sense or nonsense, sunshine or moonshine, are all alike to a lunatic."

In a later piece in the *Citizen* (11 October) Paine accused Carpenter of being openly a British emissary because of his proposals that the United States join England in a war against France and Spain. "A man never turns a rogue but he turns a fool, and this is always the case with emissaries." Carpenter had also asserted the existence of terrible discontents in Louisiana and had direfully predicted that Napoleon would take advantage of them to seize the territory. Paine repudiated these alarms by quoting dispatches declaring New Orleans as being in perfect tranquility. Paine pointed out moreover that France had always behaved with perfect honor toward the United States.

Paine used essentially the same arguments in "A Challenge to the Federalists to Declare their Principles" (17 October). The continual aim of the Federalists, he charged, "has been and still is, to involve the United States in a war with France and Spain. This is an English scheme, and the papers of the faction give every provocation that words can give, to provoke France to hostilities."

In the meantime Carpenter replied to Paine in his *People's Friend* by publishing falsified extracts of Paine's article of 11 October. Paine thereupon made a written copy of these falsifications and sent a friend to Carpenter's printing office to force Carpenter to acknowledge or repudiate them. Carpenter after repeated efforts was still not to be found nor could his residence be discovered. Paine thereupon accused Carpenter of deliberately hiding and continued his blast in the *American Citizen* (28 October). "An emissary is always a skulking character. His business is lying and deceiving. He shuns the public and is afraid that every enquiry about him is for the purpose of apprehending him."

A week later (5 November) Paine published a number of extracts from the Philadelphia *Aurora*, charging Carpenter with acting as a British agent. After these extracts Paine observed that Carpenter was now losing favor even with his fellow Federalist editors, some of whom were publishing against him. According to Paine, "the project which this emissary went upon, that of an alliance offensive and defensive with Britain, would have been the ruin of the merchants." These Federalists realized that an alliance with England would mean the end of United States shipping, for all European ports would as a consequence automatically be shut against American vessels.

Subsequently the *Aurora* published further abuse of Carpenter charging that he went under an alias, his true name being Cullen. Paine added to it some unsavory details he had picked up in New York and published the whole as a further letter (19 November).

This man arrived in this city [N. Y.] about four years ago and lodged at a house in which a friend of mine then was. Cullen at that time passed

by the name of MacCullen, and as it often happens to men of his description that when the liquor is *in* the wit is *out*, he often lets himself
our very foolishly. He vauntingly said he had been offered great sums
of money by the English ministry not to write against them. He went to
his room one day when he was in his capers, and dressed himself in an
English regimental uniform, and came to shew himself. (N.B. He has
been a regimental deputy paymaster, and is the son of Cullen the box
keeper of Crow Street Theatre, Dublin.)

Paine denounced the Irishman Cullen with greater fury than
he had denounced the Irishman Edmund Burke, even though the
issues of Federalist propaganda could hardly be compared in importance to those of *The Rights of Man*.

In March of the following year, Carpenter threatened to bring
suit against another Republican newspaper, the *Public Advertiser*,
and Paine triumphantly published a letter (8 April) asserting that
"he will now have to identify himself and prove who he is, and
upon what recommendation he came to America." After repeating
the story of his earlier vain efforts to confront Carpenter, Paine
exulted that he would now know where to find him. Apparently
Carpenter withdrew his bluff, for his paper ceased publication in
August 1807, and Paine never had further occasion to refer to him.

XXVI

The Defense of New York

One of the subjects which kept recurring during Paine's controversy with Carpenter was that of gunboats and the defense of New York. And this bone of contention, strangely enough, was closely connected with an article which had appeared in the *Bien informé* during Paine's French sojourn, presenting a blueprint for invading the United States. As we have seen, Paine's enemies had accused him of drawing up this plan, and he formally denied it in the sixth of his letters to the citizens of the United States (23 April 1803). In November 1806 Federalist papers in Philadelphia and New York revived the charge by publishing a number of questions addressed to Paine similar to the following:

Do you know any thing of a certain memorial transmitted to the executive directory of the then French Republic by an American citizen then in France, inviting them to send over a powerful army to revolutionize America. The memorial, stating among other inducements, that there was a French party and an English party in the United States, and that the army would be joined by the French party here immediately on its arrival?

Paine replied ironically in the *American Citizen* (11 November) that the Federalists were beginning to reform, having descended from the high vice of direct lying to the humane vice of merely asking lying questions. He again denied being the author of the memorial and prepared a series of pertinent questions of his own designed to embarrass the Federalists and vindicate his own record.

During the same month there appeared an article in three New York Federalist papers damning the Jefferson administration for not fortifying the port of New York. The author, probably Rufus

King, made use of the alleged French memorial as evidence of the danger from invasion. Paine retaliated in the *American Citizen* (13 November). "If Rufus King, in case he is the writer of the piece in Cullen's paper of November 4 . . . will say in direct terms what he there insinuates indirectly, that *Thomas Paine invited two or three thousand French troops to plunder the city,* Thomas Paine will honor Rufus King with a prosecution for LYING." All the affectation about fortifying New York, Paine charged, was "a mere electioneering federal bubble." The nation was then no more in danger of foreign invasion than it had been during the administrations of Adams or Washington.

As the issue of national defense continued urgent, Paine wrote several more pieces designed to prove the superiority of small gunboats over traditional ships of the line (*American Citizen*, 7 January 1807). In later essays in another newspaper, *The Public Advertiser,* he attempted to convince his readers of the superior advantages of gunboats in speed and manoeuverability. Initially (11 March 1807) he compared naval vessels to whales; "they must be in deep water, and at a distance from land." They were highly vulnerable to the enemy, for they presented their whole broadside to the object they were firing at, whereas a gunboat fired from its nose and presented only this narrow part. Paine offered gunboats as the only means of defending New York. Fortifications would be futile, he maintained, for a place that cannot be enclosed in a polygon cannot be fortified and New York could not possibly be so enclosed.

Subsequently he denounced cumbersome naval vessels as wasteful as well as ineffectual (4 April). "Navies do not protect commerce," he argued, "neither is the protection of commerce their object. They are for the foolish and unprofitable purpose of fighting and sinking each other at sea; and the result is, that every victory at sea is a victory of loss. The conqueror, after sinking and destroying a part of his enemies fleet, goes home with crippled ships and broken bones. The English fire the tower guns and the French sing Te Deum."

Paine combined economic and strategic arguments in treating the "Comparative Powers and Expense of Ships of War, Gun-Boats, and Fortifications" (*Public Advertiser*, 21 July). He attempted to show that seventy-four gunboats, each with a single gun readily trained upon a target, would have exactly twice the efficient firing power of a regular ship of the line, carrying seventy-four guns, thirty-seven of which must inevitably be pointing in a direction exactly opposite to the target. The cost of the seventy-four separate gunboats ($296,000), Paine demonstrated would, moreover, be much less than the cost of a single ship of the line with seventy-four guns ($500,000). Gunboats, he maintained, required less costly repairs, they were more durable, and could be constructed more rapidly and in greater numbers than ships of the line.

These essays inspired a wag to write the following verses for *The Barber's Shop*, a periodical publication at Salem (reprinted in New York *Evening Post*, 25 September 1807):

> TOM PAINE has exploded the old-fashion'd notion,
> That ships of the line are the lords of the ocean;
> And shewn how a gun-boat, with only one gun,
> *In a calm* can occasion a *first-rate to run:*
> Nay more, he has prov'd (to cut the thing shorter)
> The gun-boat can blow the first-rate out of water!
> Then let nations be told, who *great navies* have arm'd,
> The Sovereign of Ships, is a—*gun-boat becalmed!*

These lines are based on Paine's actual words: "Gun-boats, being moved by oars, cannot be deprived of motion by calms, for the calmer the weather the better for the boat. But a hostile ship becalmed in any of our waters, can be taken by gun-boats moved by oars. . . . And besides this, *gun-boats in calms are the sovereigns of ships.*"

Paine applied his scientific as well as his literary talents to gunboats, for in September he wrote a letter to Jefferson enclosing a model for using two guns in the head of a gunboat instead of one. Jefferson sent the materials to Robert Smith, Secretary of Navy, who considered the project and in turn sent a report to Jefferson offering "the ideas of two practical men" upon it. Unfortunately this report cannot be found either in Jefferson's papers or in the national archives. Since Paine's writings had been uniformly directed against large navies in favor of small craft, however, it is more than likely that the Department of the Navy officially expressed its disapproval of Paine's strategy.

Paine gave detailed consideration in the *Public Advertiser* (1

August) to the important matter of how a defense program was to be financed. As a further contribution to naval strategy, he described a few days later (6 August) the only eligible mode of obstructing the ingress of enemy ships. This was a method proposed by Franklin in 1776 for the Delaware River. It consisted of sinking iron frames with exposed pointed forks so placed as to penetrate and sink any vessel entering the river without a pilot. Two weeks later (18 August) Paine repeated his advocacy of this plan and attacked a rival project to obstruct the North River by means of stone blocks stretching entirely across the channel.

The potential enemy against whom all these defenses were projected was England. Even Federalists by June 1807 had greater fears of England than France. Paine presented a commentary on the political situation in an article "Of the Affairs of England" (1 June 1807) signing it ONE WHO KNOWS ENGLAND. In his interpretation of British history, Paine derided England as a world power somewhat in the manner in which Burke had previously disparaged France. He pointed out that while the King and the Cabinet were at odds with each other, the coalition on the Continent against Napoleon was suffering loss after loss. This meant that England was in imminent danger of invasion, an invasion which its much-vaunted and ruinously-expensive navy could not prevent. Attributing the injuries and miseries the English were suffering to the insane malconduct of his old enemy George III, Paine concluded with a highly amusing burlesque history of the Hanoverian regime.

In 1714 the English nation, for the principles of government were not understood at that time, sent to Hanover for a man and his family, George the first, to come and govern them. The poor man knew nothing about England, he had never been there, knew nothing of its laws, and could not spake [sic] a word of English, and when he got in a passion, which he often did, he used to kick his hat about the room.

His son, George the second, was the same sort of man as to dulness of capacity as his father was but not so peaceable, for the wars of George the first were carried on against his hat, but as George the second thought he knew something of military wars he was often engaged in continental wars in which England as a nation and an Island ought to have had nothing to do; and the present incumbent George the third and *last* has hardly ever been at peace; but he is sly enough to stay at home and set other nations together by the ears, and the poor English have to pay the expense till they have hardly bread to eat themselves. This is the short history of the Guelphs or *Whelps* of Hanover.

Paine continued with this form of ridicule in another squib (24 August 1807) entitled simply "Royal Pedigree."

Later in the year (18 December 1807) Paine published a mock Royal Proclamation of His Mad-jesty addressed to his "dutiful and loyal subjects . . . residing in our provinces in America, commonly called the United States of America." His Mad-jesty's loyal subjects were called upon to combat the "disorderly and disorganizing set of people . . . who do sedulously support, aid and comfort the present *illegitimate form of government.*" In a sense Paine was fighting the American Revolution all over again. He advocated, therefore, in a later article "On the Question, Will There Be War" (15 August 1807) stiff resistance to the British policy of searching American ships and impressing American seamen. He characterized the British nation as a pirate and advocated that it be treated as a pirate.

A letter from Washington had appeared in the *Evening Post* (11 December) asserting that the British did not actually contend for the right of searching national ships and that all cause of war with Britain had therefore vanished. Paine refused to accept this facile denial of reality and protested indignantly against the indifference of the Federalists. Is it nothing to these scoundrels, he asked (14 December), "that three or four thousand of our fellow citizens are impressed from our own merchantmen's service and fight on board British ships of war?" If they themselves were victims they would cry out that the government had no energy, "but since it happens to poor and friendless sailors these federal patrons can see no wrong in it, nor feel any."

Whether writing on questions of military tactics and national defense or on narrower issues of New York state politics Paine consistently followed a pro-French policy. He ingeniously combined his Francophile sentiments with an attack on the Federalist Governor of New York, Morgan Lewis, in a caustic appraisal in the *Public Advertiser* (24 February 1807) of one of Lewis's addresses to the legislature. Paine again heckled Lewis in the spring of the year (26 May) in consequence of the state election in which

Lewis was defeated by the Democratic candidate, Daniel D. Tompkins.

As a balm to assuage the hurt of their election losses, the Federalists issued a proclamation asserting that "all the wealth and all the talents, and all the virtue" were on their side. Paine retaliated (27 May) by denying their possession of all three qualities. The wealth of the state consisted in landed property; according to the constitution only those possessing real property could vote; the Republicans had beaten the Federalists by several thousand votes; therefore the Federalists did not have all the wealth. On the subject of talents, William Coleman, Federalist editor of the *Evening Post*, had declared Rufus King to be the first man in the state. Paine argued that if "shanny-brained Rufus" were their best specimen, the rest must be "as innocent of the crime of talents as a new born babe." Paine found the Federalists' arrogation of virtue their worst offense. To refute it he reviewed their attitude toward Louisiana. Originally they had cried that the western states would be ruined unless we had Louisiana, that its possession by the Spanish would depopulate the West and shut off its commerce. But no sooner had Jefferson engineered its quiet and peaceful purchase than the Federalist faction "tacked about and gave itself the lie full in its own teeth." It howled "that Louisiana was a burthen on the United States—that it was a country of serpents and crocodiles, and not fit for a man to live in." Paine found only one tenable explanation for the Federalist faction—that its leaders were "British agents, or old tories employed as such, to make confusion in the country by any means they can."

Paine began a second blast (30 May) by repeating this accusation verbatim and associating it with changes the party name had recently undergone. From Federalist they had progressed to Federal Republican and, in the last election, to American Party. Paine accused them of acting upon orders from London. Had they won the election, Paine taunted, the ministerial papers would have written in the following style:

We congratulate the friends of Monarchical Government on the important intelligence arrived by express from New York, that the AMERICAN TICKET headed by his excellency Rufus King formerly minister plenipotentiary to the British Court and the friend of the British Monarchy has triumphed over the republican ticket by a large majority.

The Federalists did not take their defeat gracefully, and Coleman in the *Evening Post* complained of the excessive number of
foreigners naturalized since 1807 as though these were responsible
for the Republican victory. The new names *American party* and
American ticket were intended to distinguish the Federalists from
the new arrivals. Paine asked ironically (2 June) why Coleman
did not speak of the *Indian Ticket*, for except the Indians every
man in the country was a foreigner or descended from foreign
stock. "If Coleman's Father was an Indian and his Mother a Squaw
then he is literally of the American Party. He is a full blooded
American, and ought to have stood first on the American ticket
instead of Rufus King who is only a half bred Yankey." Reverting
to a serious tone, Paine asserted that the founders of the Republic
created the representative system of government, "and whoever
is *not* in allegiance to this system as well in principle and theory,
as in form, is a FOREIGNER *whether born in America, or in
Europe, or in any other part of the Globe.*"

XXVII

Feud with Cheetham

The reader has probably noticed that between January and March of 1807, Paine transferred his writing from the *American Citizen* to the *Public Advertiser*. This may have been because Cheetham began to waver in his Republican loyalties, but, according to William Carver, it was because Cheetham altered one of Paine's pieces before publication. Paine had written a reply to a political article in the *American Citizen*, which Carver had personally delivered to Cheetham. When it appeared in print it had been considerably altered, and Paine, highly incensed, summoned Cheetham to answer for it. " 'I Sir,' said Paine, 'never permit any one to alter any thing that I write, you have spoiled the whole sense that it was meant to convey on the subject.' Cheetham replied 'that it was too harsh to appear in print.' " Paine retorted, " 'that was not your business to determine; why, sir, did not you return it to me.' This was the cause that broke up their friendship."

The exact relationship between Paine and his new outlet the *Public Advertiser* cannot be determined. From 1807 to 1808 the ostensible editor was the printer, Jacob Frank, but Paine himself asserted that there were other editors. Paine apparently furnished nothing of his own until March 1807, but thereafter the frequency of his contributions and the presentation of some of them as editorials suggest that he occasionally served as consultant or policy maker.

Although Paine began writing for the *Public Advertiser* in March, he did not directly attack Cheetham until 22 August 1807, when in consequence of an article in the *Citizen* criticizing Paine's article "Of the Affairs of England," Paine unleased a torrent of abuse:

Mr. Cheetham in his rage for attacking every body, and every thing that is not his own, (for he is an ugly tempered man, and he carries the evidence of it in the vulgarity and forbidingness of his countenance— God has set a mark upon Cain) has attacked me on the ground of my political works, and in doing this he has exposed the barrenness of his understanding.

Cheetham had accused Paine of following John Locke, idea for idea, in his writings on heredity and elective government. Paine retorted in a passage highly significant in reference to his own intellectual history, "I never read Locke nor ever had the work in my hand, and by what I have heard of it from *Horne Tooke*, I had no inducement to read it. It is a speculative, not a practical work, and the style of it is heavy and tedious, as all Locke's writings are." Cheetham had also by innuendo cast aspersions on Paine's war record. "I would not," he wrote, "charge with cowardice that gentleman who, in the 'times that tried men's souls,' stuck very correctly to his pen in a *safe retreat*, and never handled a musket offensively." Paine replied by summarizing his very active participation in several military campaigns during the Revolution.

Two weeks later (5 September) Paine published another defense of his career against the fulminations of Cheetham. His title, "Farewell Reprimand to James Cheetham," proved to be somewhat inappropriate since he subsequently published other attacks equally violent. Paine concluded this attack with his most serious denunciation of Cheetham—the accusation that he was deserting his Republican principles for Federalism. He called upon Cheetham to explain "the intimacy between him and the anglo Irish emmissary Cullen, alias Carpenter. . . . He is now giving symptoms of becoming the successor of Cullen."

Paine repeated this accusation verbatim in "Cheetham and His Tory Paper" (26 September) in consequence of an article Cheetham had written attacking the French government. Paine bluntly remarked that Cheetham as an adopted American citizen had no business with such matters. "As a John Bull it is impertinence in him to come here to spew out his venom against France. But Cheetham cannot live without quarreling, nor write without abuse. He is a disgrace to the Republicans, whose principle is to live in peace and friendship with all nations and not to interfere in the domestic concerns of any." Cheetham had accused the French government of oppressing its people under a systematic military slavery. Paine indignantly denied the accusation and retorted that "of all people enslaved by their own governments, none are so much so as the people of England." He insisted that the French nation in all its changes of government had "always behaved in a civil and friendly manner to the United States." It was scarcely sufferable, he concluded, "that a prejudiced and surly tempered John Bull should fix himself among us to abuse a friendly power."

The morning after this piece was published Cheetham sent a message to Jacob Frank, printer of the *Public Advertiser*, demanding that he apologize for publishing it. Paine immediately said to Frank, "Tell Cheetham from me that I am the writer of that piece, and if he has any thing to say, he must say it to me." Paine exposed these facts in a letter addressed to William Coleman, editor of the Federalist *Evening Post*, where it was published 23 October. According to Carlile, Cheetham and Frank had a duel over this issue, but neither suffered any serious hurt.

A curious aftermath of Paine's fracas with Cheetham brought to public attention another letter from Jefferson to Paine and created as much embarrassment for the President as had his earlier letter inviting Paine to return to America on a national vessel. Coleman had visited Paine to talk over Paine's piece concerning Frank and Cheetham. In the course of their conversation Paine happened to drop the remark that Jefferson had just written to him indicating the possibility of a war with England. Jefferson's exact words: "In the mean time all the little circumstances coming to our knowledge are unfavourable to our wishes for peace." On the next day Coleman mentioned this line to two or three of his friends, and put the sentence in writing for one of them, who, proceeding to Philadelphia, had the item printed in the *United States Gazette*, another Federalist organ. When the printed item came to the attention of Cheetham, he published an abusive piece in the *American Citizen* (27 October) insinuating that Paine had forged the letter.

Once more Paine's correspondence had become a political issue. The Federalists decried Jefferson for placing confidence in Paine; Jefferson's advocates denied that the correspondence existed; and Paine's friends asserted that the correspondence was authentic but shed no discredit upon the President.

For some reason, possibly his illness, Paine temporarily allowed his controversy with Cheetham to wane. He was not aroused again until Cheetham in his papers of 29 and 30 December 1807 attempted to prove that a projected embargo act discussed by Congress had not been inspired by any dispute with England but by "some imperious demands on the part of France." Paine (8 January 1808) called his opponent "an idiot in diplomatic affairs," for assuming that since dispatches of Monroe from London, dated 10 October, had not called for an embargo, both Monroe and the Congress believed that an immediate war with England was unlikely. Paine argued that the only reason that Britain had not enforced her threat to seize American vessels going to or coming from France was that she feared retaliation and would suffer more from her bullying than would France.

During the spring and summer of 1808 Paine's illness kept him from writing, but in August he recovered sufficiently to fling a final challenge at the Federal faction and Cheetham (25 August). He asserted that by their anti-French attitude they were going the right way to ruin the country and were such blind politicians that they lacked the discernment to realize it. For the last sixteen years the United States had flourished unrivaled in commerce. Paine warned that this was a temporary state of affairs and would probably change at the end of the European war. Bonaparte would then in all likelihood enforce a rule for all Europe forbidding any article to be brought to any country except those produced "in the country to which the vessel belongs that brings them." By following this plan Napoleon would build up French shipping, commerce and colonies. Paine concluded his blast against the Federalists by once more identifying Cheetham as a Tory emissary and revealing that other groups in New York now held the same opinion.

Can any thing be more unwise and foolish, than the conduct of the federal faction, who are continually abusing and blackguarding France and Bonaparte, and putting them in a fit disposition to cut short American commerce. There is nobody has gone further in this stile of abuse and ignorance than the imposter Cheetham; but he has run his length, and is now posted in every meeting in the city, as a professed British hireling would be. Thomas Paine wrote to J[oh]n F[ellow]s from New Rochelle, three or four years ago, desiring him to show that letter to De Witt Clinton, in which Mr. Paine gave his opinion of Cheetham, that "*in religion he was a hypocrite, and in politics a John Bull,*" that is, an ignorant, conceited, headstrong Englishman; but J[oh]n F[ellow]s, who is not a strong-minded man, wrote Mr. Paine an apology for not doing it. He has since expressed his regret that he did not.

The ward meetings have done exceedingly right in posting Cheetham. . . . I cannot pay the same compliments to the general administration nor to the governor of the state of New York. They still continue Cheetham their printer. This gives an appearance that they encourage him in his abuse of France and the French government. Our professed maxim is "*to live in peace with all nations*"; but this is an indecent violation of that principle.

This was Paine's last known writing. Together with his preceding attacks, it provides a body of abuse sufficient to explain the malice and violence of Cheetham's subsequent retaliatory biography of Paine.

XXVIII

Last Days

Paine spent most of his last two years as an invalid. In April 1807, he moved from Jarvis's to the establishment of Hitt, a baker, on Broome Street, whose rooms had not been available in the preceding fall. Here Paine wrote to Dr. Mitchill his proposal for a constitutional amendment to provide for the removal of unsatisfactory judges. He also published *An Examination of the . . . Prophecies*, a demonstration that the alleged prophecies in the Old Testament concerning the coming of Christ actually refer to contemporary circumstances of the Jewish nation. In February 1808, Paine moved to a small tavern at No. 63 Partition (Fulton) Street near the Bear Market.

From January to July of this year, he wrote a series of letters to the Senate and to the House of Representatives of the United States, making further claims for his services during the Revolution, particularly the reimbursement of his expenses incurred in accompanying Laurens to France, claims which were rejected on the ground that his memorial had been "unaccompanied with any evidence in support of the statement of facts." Mme Bonneville, in relating his grief over this refusal, acknowledged that he should have foreseen this outcome and not exposed himself to it, but, as she explained, he saw his capital diminishing and his expenses daily increasing when he expected, like his ancestors, to live to an advanced age and wanted to leave the Bonnevilles adequately provided for.

In July 1808, Paine went to board with a family named Ryder in Greenwich Village on Herring Street (later No. 293 Bleecker Street). There a New York cartographer, John Randel, remembered seeing him in fair weather, "sitting at the south window of the first story room . . . , the sash was raised, a small table or stand was placed before him, with an open book placed upon it, which he appeared to be reading. He had his spectacles on, his left elbow rested upon the table or stand, and his chin rested between the thumb and fingers of his hand; his right hand lay upon his book, and a decanter, containing liquor of the color of rum or brandy, was standing next to his book and beyond it."

He paid ten dollars weekly until February 1809, after which he paid twenty dollars a week because he required almost constant attendance.

Paine's illness was an outgrowth of the paralytic affection he had suffered in France and his attack of apoplexy in 1806. He grew progressively weak, his appetite declining daily. According to Mme Bonneville, "the want of exercise alone was the cause of his sufferings." During his last months he was confined almost totally to his bed. He had the newspapers read to him and conversed vigorously on politics, although he wrote nothing for publication after his last will, 18 January 1809. Although "he had no disease that required a Doctor, . . . Dr. Romaine came to visit him twice a week." He suffered from a swelling, commencing in his feet and threatening to encompass his whole body. Some one told him he should be *tapped*, but Dr. Romaine and a colleague resolved that the tapping was not necessary. " 'Your belly diminishes,' said the Doctor. 'And yours augments,' said Paine."

During the last twelve months of his life, Paine was anxious to have anybody at all call upon him—even complete strangers who came under the pretext of buying his deistical pamphlets. A curious, but unprejudiced English visitor, T. Adams, who was a friend of Sir Francis Burdett, ascribed Paine's fondness for company to his being "completely deserted by those who formerly had almost deified him." Adams, who visited Paine in the company of three other gentlemen, "found him sitting behind a table, which was necessary to his support, as he had received a paralytic stroke. He was endeavouring to shave himself. . . . One of the gentlemen asked him why he did not get a barber to shave him? He replied, that he could not get one to come from the town, although it was scarcely more than a mile and a half." Adams concluded that since Paine had plenty of money, this circumstance revealed his unpopularity with the mass of people. Paine's appearance, according to Adams, "was that of a man of superior mind. He had been a tall man," and as far as Adams could judge, "well made. His blue eyes were full, lucid, and indicated his true character." His intellect did not seem in the least impaired. "His conversation was calm and gentleman-like, except when religion or party politics were mentioned. In this case he became irascible, and the deformity of his face, rendered so by intemperance, was then disgusting."

The eminent American ornithologist, Alexander Wilson, found him in the fall of 1808 "sitting wrapt in a night gown, the table before him covered with newspapers—with pen and ink beside them." Although complaining of his inability to walk, Paine was eager to converse. He showed a lively interest in Wilson's scientific investigations and subscribed to his *American Ornithology*, then going through the press, after examining a sample copy page by page. Wilson wrote to his collaborator, Alexander Lawson, that "the penetration and intelligence of his eye bespeak the man of genius and of the world."

One of Paine's friends at this time was a Quaker, Willet Hicks, cousin of a soon-to-be-famous preacher, Elias Hicks. On 19 March Paine sent for him to communicate a request that he be interred in the Quaker cemetery. "I am now in my seventy-third year, and do not expect to live long; I wish to be buried in your burying ground. I could be buried in the Episcopal church, but they are so arrogant; or in the Presbyterian, but they are so hypocritical." Hicks passed on the request to his church committee, which denied it. According to Fellows, the Quaker society had no personal animus, but "suggested the probability that Mr. Paine's friends might wish to raise a monument to his memory, which being contrary to their rules, would render it inconvenient to them." Mme Bonneville observed that Paine seemed "deeply moved" at this refusal and considered it foolish. She promised Paine that he would be buried on his own farm. "I have no objection to that," Paine replied," but the farm will be sold, and they will dig my bones up before they be half rotten." Mme Bonneville then admonished him to have confidence in his friends and promised him that his burial place would never be sold. She was as good as her word about keeping the burial plot intact, but destiny nevertheless carried out Paine's prophecy, though the agency, not of his enemies, but of one of his most zealous admirers, William Cobbett, who had been converted from foe to disciple. In 1819 Cobbett dug up Paine's bones and sent them to England, where Cobbett planned to raise a shrine and monument to "the common sense of the great man." English public opinion, however, refused to sanction the project. At his death, the bones passed from hand to hand with Cobbett's other effects, and all trace of them was completely lost.

Despite his frequent visitors, Paine felt lonely at Ryder's and begged Mme Bonneville to accept him in her own household. With some reluctance she consented, renting for the purpose an adjoining house at 59 Grove Street. On 4 May 1809, Paine was carried in an arm chair to his new habitation, a distance of only seventy eight yards. A neighboring mechanic, Amasa Woodworth, sat with Paine on the last two nights of his life. He testified "that some meddlesome persons, taking advantage" of Paine's supposed debility of mind "were very properly refused admittance," but there was absolutely no truth in the report that Paine's friends had kept him plied with liquor to keep him from recanting. A physician who gained access to Paine, James R. Manly, later wrote and testified under oath that Paine was questioned on his beliefs and did not recant. On 5 June Manly asked, " 'Do you believe? or let me qualify the question—do you wish to believe that Jesus Christ is the son of God?' After a pause of some minutes, he answered, 'I have no wish to believe on that subject.' "

On his last night, Mme Bonneville, seeing his end approaching, asked him whether he had felt satisfied with the treatment he had recieved. He could only exclaim, "Oh! yes!" and a few other incoherent words. He spent the rest of the night in tranquility and died in the morning, 8 June, at eight o'clock.

On the next day, Mme Bonneville, her son Benjamin, and a few of Paine's friends escorted the body to New Rochelle for burial.

Mme Bonneville found the scene one to wound and affect any sensitive heart.

Contemplating who it was, what man it was, that we were committing to an obscure grave on an open and disregarded bit of land, I could not help feeling most acutely. Before the earth was thrown down upon the coffin, I, placing myself at the east end of the grave, said to my son Benjamin, "stand you there, at the other end, as a witness for grateful America." Looking round me, and beholding the small group of spectators, I exclaimed, as the earth was tumbled into the grave, "Oh! Mr. Paine! My son stands here as testimony of the gratitude of America, and I, for France!"

XXIX

Recapitulation

H ad Paine ever been elected to a political office in the United
States, his death and burial would probably have been accorded some degree of public attention. Yet even though
in America he had never been more than a private citizen, when we
consider the contribution he had made to the development of the
nation and to the clarification on a world scale of the principal
issues of religion and politics, the personal neglect he suffered in his
last days seems almost incomprehensible.

It has been suggested that the indifference, if not the hostility, of
the public was due in large measure to his deistical writings, but
this explanation is not sufficient. Some Republican propagandists
defended Paine right down the line, including his religious beliefs.
This was relatively easy since it was necessary merely to point out
the equally heterodox views of Franklin, Jefferson and Adams. True,
the Federalists used Paine's deism as a weapon to attack the Jefferson
administration, but there is no proof that this propaganda had any
influence on any but other Federalists. Paine's chief enemies were
appalled by his political, not his religious views. In England, we
must remember, Paine was considered a disciple of the devil for
writing *The Rights of Man* long before *The Age of Reason* was
ever in print.

The real reason for the obscurity which enveloped Paine's last
years was his long absence from the United States. Immediately after
his return from France, he enjoyed a brief flash of notoriety, but
never succeeded in recapturing the wide following he had enjoyed
during the Revolution. He landed in Baltimore almost twenty years
after the Revolution, and public issues had changed. Concern with

317

the fundamental principles which Paine had previously developed and applied in an arena embracing two continents had degenerated into the relatively petty issues of party politics. Paine dedicated himself earnestly to the cause of Jefferson and the Republicans, but the subjects of conflict were so narrow and local that his writing, much of it over unfamiliar pseudonyms, was scarcely distinguishable from that of the scores of minor journalists engaged in routine political controversy. Paine was inevitably engulfed in the mass.

That his close friends were so few is explained by his solitary manner of existence and his undeniably difficult personality. During all his years as a public figure, he lived as an old bachelor. He enjoyed almost no intimacies with family groups, and his social ties were almost exclusively with other men. He was always vain and hypersentitive, and these unendearing characteristics did not diminish with advancing age. He developed also a demanding disposition and untidy habits, which did nothing to increase the number of his friends. To be sure he had faithful followers: Rickman and Thomas Hardy in England; Bonneville and Lanthenas in France; and John Fellows in the United States. But these disciples attached themselves to Paine because of his intellectual achievements rather than his personality.

During his last illness Mme Bonneville attended him out of a sense of loyalty and obligation, and he received the calls of Jarvis, but his other visitors were either neighbors or curiosity-seekers. Jefferson, Monroe, and other Republican chiefs still held him in high esteem, but they had long since lost personal contact. His death was given only scant attention in the New York newspapers. It is not surprising then that Paine's body should have been committed virtually unnoticed "to an obscure grave on an open and disregarded bit of land."

Joel Barlow in a letter to Cheetham, laying a foundation for Paine's biographers, wrote that he should be portrayed "as one of the most benevolent and disinterested of mankind, endowed with the clearest perception, an uncommon share of original genius, and the greatest breadth of thought." This is not, of course, the entire picture. Although Paine was in a sense Barlow's mentor in France, Barlow knew him only slightly and was unaware of the major facets of Paine's career. His whole life was a series of contradictions. Paine was a great humanitarian, but also a great egotist. He could be a true friend, yet was quick to take offense. His forensic writings often reflect personal grievances rather than universal principles. He dedicated himself to great causes, but he was personally lazy. His fundamental honesty did not keep him from accepting clandestine rewards for his propaganda, particularly from both the American government and the French Ministry for his writings on the American Revolution. He never ceased alluding to the free bestowal of his services. Yet after the battle was won he set up an unending clamor for additional financial compensation. His self-sacrificial pen is largely a myth. Yet he made sacrifices for the causes he served. He presented half of his net worth to a subscription fund to bolster credit in 1780; he paid his own expenses to accompany Laurens to France in 1781. In England, he signed over the profits from the sale of *The Rights of Man* to the Society for Constitutional Information; and in France he contributed a large amount for the descent on England. But in private life he was niggardly, particularly in old age when he haggled with Carver over bedding and firewood.

Although frequently portrayed as a ragged philosopher, Paine never belonged to the ranks of the down-trodden poor. Even at the outset, his salary in the English excise was at the least a living wage. When he emigrated to America, Paine immediately met and associated with the literati in Philadelphia and hereafter lived as a gentleman, even though for a brief time he engaged himself as a common clerk. His deal with Morris and Livingston made him financially independent, and his rewards after the Revolution placed him in easy circumstances. Indeed he became a small-scale financier, but apparently lost most of his capital attempting to build his bridge. While serving as a deputy to the French Convention, he had no financial difficulties, and while he was in Luxembourg prison he even had a large sum of cash in his possession. After his release he used up his liquid resources in America—and thereafter lived on the bounty of Madison, Bonneville, Burdett and Bosville. Yet during all these years in France, he was the proprietor of an estate in New York, which he valued at seven thousand pounds. When he returned to the United States, he lived on the income from this farm and died leaving well over ten thousand dollars, a respectable sum at the beginning of the nineteenth century.

The biographer of Paine must inevitably deal with his alleged intemperance. It almost seems that more space has been devoted to this question than to the influence of *Common Sense*. Paine's detractors uniformly describe him as a disgusting inebriate always in the company of a brandy bottle. Opinion is unanimous that brandy was his favorite drink. Paine's admirers tear down the picture of Paine as a tippler, admitting merely that he may have been temporarily driven to drinking because of acute physical suffering as an aftermath of his harrowing confinement in Luxembourg prison.

Probably Paine never completely gave up his drinking, but during his last days it became only occasional, perhaps because of illness and increasing age.

For many years after Paine's death the question of his drinking was involved with the merits of his literary work. His enemies proceeded under the absurd notion that if it could be proved that he was a drunkard, this proof would invalidate his political and religious principles. In the same way fanatical Christians assumed that Paine's deistical principles could be disproved if it could be demonstrated that he had recanted them on his deathbed. This subject also has busied scores of authors, but it can safely be ignored. Paine never wavered in his convictions. And even though he had succumbed to pressure on his deathbed (which he certainly did not do), conversion at such a time of mental and physical weakness would have relatively little meaning. To the degree that Paine's conduct reflects on his religious beliefs, the most significant evidence is his demeanor in Luxembourg prison, when he was in full possession of his faculties and hourly expecting to die. His fellow prisoner, Bond, the English surgeon, confided to Rickman that every night when they parted to be locked up separately, Paine "always expressed his firm belief in the principles" of *The Age of Reason* and begged his friend to "tell the world such were his dying opinions." Since Paine's own deistical creed affirmed existence in a future state, it is somewhat presumptuous of professional Christians to assume that the approach of death would have given him more reason to adopt Christianity. In religion and in every other realm it is Paine's principles themselves which warrant our final consideration. The only means of understanding Paine is through his ideas.

His writings on government, economics and religion are tied together by a unifying theme—the concept of a parallel between the natural universe and the social system, between laws of science and laws of human relations. According to Paine, human progress consists in the discovery of these laws in both realms. His initial statement of the concept appeared in *The Rights of Man*, which he considered to be a presentation of first principles in government. Here he specifically drew the parallel between science and politics and argued that universal principles could be ascertained as accurately and conclusively in government as in nature. Systems and practices not based upon an understanding of first principles, he considered to be manifestations of ignorance or superstition. To him, Burke's *Reflections* represented the wasteful and inefficient system of trial and error in government—criminal as well as stupid since it created human suffering which might have been avoided. Political ignorance to him was worse than scientific—the latter meant merely the absence of knowledge, perhaps the denial of some material comforts, but political ignorance meant the subjection of the common man to an irresponsible aristocracy, the needless misery, poverty and endless toil of the greater part of mankind and the perpetuation of wars and civil strife.

Although *Common Sense* is based on exactly the same concepts as *The Rights of Man*, we cannot be sure that when he wrote it he had already formulated his notion of first principles. The manner of viewing human relations as comparable to natural law may have come to him through contact with French rationalists. Or he may already have developed it during his youth in London when he bought a set of globes and attended the lectures of Martin and Ferguson. At any rate *Common Sense* is an application of Paine's principles of government to the Revolution in America just as *The Rights of Man* is an application to that in France.

Later in his *First Principles of Government* he reaffirmed the existence of natural law in political relations. Here he drew a distinction between absolute principles (such as natural rights and government by election) and optional or relative matters (such as a bicameral or unicameral legislature). Before writing *The Rights of Man*, he evidently considered monarchy or republicanism as optional matters. In his most famous economic work, *Decline and Fall of the English System of Finance*, he exposed a ratio between war and national debt, which he declared to be as infallible as Newton's laws. Finally, in his *Age of Reason*, he applied the same method to religion, seeking first principles of theology. Like other scientific deists before him, he found these to be identical with the laws of mathematics and astronomy, the works and wisdom of God. He was following a well-charted tradition in drawing the parallel between natural law and religion, but struck out independently in extending the notion of first principles to politics and economics.

Most historians have assumed that Paine's great influence came as a result of his journalistic style—the compelling manner in which he wrote. It is worthy of considering whether his matter may not also have been universally appealing—that readers have been attracted by the sense of finality, of an approach to the absolute, in his works communicated by his notion of first principles.

Paine's concepts were revolutionary for his time, it is true, but they also rested on an appeal to a sense of permanence, of the absolute nature of things. In the political realm most of his principles are now considered axiomatic—and for that reason no longer associated with him. That is, of course, his democratic concepts, not his notion of politics as a precise science. The universal acceptance of his principles has paradoxically meant the decline of his popularity, for to the degree that they have been accepted and applied in society they have lost the aura of novelty and individuality. Paine made many mistakes in his career—and some of his applications of principles were grotesque—but his principles themselves have endured and triumphed and represent the most effective vindication of his life.

Acknowledgments

My research in archives in France and England was made possible through a Fulbright grant in 1952-1953 and a sabbatical leave from the University of Maryland in 1954-1955. During the summer of 1958 I had a grant from the Research Council of the University of Maryland.

The institutions to which I must express my gratitude for the use of Paine manuscripts and other facilities include: Bibliothèque Nationale, Archives de France, Ministère des Affaires Etrangères, Bibliothèque Municipale de Nantes, Bibliothèque Municipale de Mantes, Archives du Département de la Seine et de la Ville de Paris, Secrétariat d'état aux forces armées (terre) Vincennes, Public Records Office (London), British Museum, The Royal Society, Customs House Library (London), Northamptonshire Record Office, Sheffield City Libraries, Public Library Rotherham (Yorkshire), Library of Congress, National Archives, New York Public Library, New York Historical Society, Long Island Historical Society, New York State Library (Albany), Thomas Paine Historical Association, American Philosophical Society, Historical Society of Pennsylvania, Library Company of Philadelphia, Minnesota Historical Society, and the libraries of the following universities: Yale, Harvard, Duke, North Carolina, Pennsylvania and Maryland.

Among the many individuals who have given me help and information I am most indebted to Dr. Gilbert Chinard, to Colonel Richard Gimbel of Yale University, and to the staff of the Benjamin Franklin Papers also at Yale: Dr. Leonard W. Labaree, Dr. Whitfield J. Bell, Jr., Mrs. Helene Fineman, and Miss Helen Boatfield. I have also received the advice of W. H. C. Armytage, Esq., David Williams, Esq., Adrian Brunel, Esq., Dr. Howard C. Rice, Dr. James Woodress, Dr. Curtis Carroll Davis, Dr. Melvin J. Friedman, Dr. Rudd Fleming, Dr. Roland N. Stromberg, Mr. Hans Arnold, and Miss Millicent Sowerby. I wish to express my appreciation to these scholars as well as to Mlle Madeleine Griffet, Signora Nelly Pereira Lima, and Mlle Christiane Jorgensen. Finally, Miss Cecily Joan Aldridge graciously helped in preparing the Index.

Notes

Quotations from Paine's *Writings* edited by Philip S. Foner, 2 vols. (New York, 1945) are not identified, but the origin of all Paine quotations from other sources is indicated. Quotations from the standard editions of the writings of Jefferson, Madison, and Monroe also are not documented. All translations from French and German are my own.

INTRODUCTION

Following are the most important previous biographies: George Chalmers, *The Life of Thomas Paine . . . By Francis Oldys* (London, 1791); James Cheetham, *The Life of Thomas Paine* (New York, 1809); Thomas Clio Rickman, *The Life of Thomas Paine* (London, 1819); William Thomas Sherwin, *Memoirs of the Life of Thomas Paine* (London, 1819); Richard Carlile, *Life of Thomas Paine* (London, 1819 [1820]); Gilbert Vale, *The Life of Thomas Paine* (New York, 1841); Moncure Daniel Conway, *The Life of Thomas Paine*, 2 vols. (New York, 1892); Moncure Daniel Conway, *Thomas Paine (1737-1809) et la révolution dans les deux mondes* (Paris, 1900). There is a University of Chicago thesis by Arnold Kimsey King available on microfilm, "Thomas Paine in America, 1774-1787" (Chicago, 1951), valuable for discussions of economic theory.

I. A CIVIL SERVANT

Facts concerning Paine's early life are to be found in Chalmers and in *At the Sign of the Bull, Lewes,* by Walter H. Godfrew . . . *with an Account of Thomas Paine's Residence in Lewes* by J. M. Connel (London, 1924). Paine's recollections of his childhood appear in *The Age of Reason.* The obituary of Mrs. Paine appeared in *Monthly Repository,* III (1808), 517. Henry Adams mentions the Nicholson daughters in

The Life of Albert Gallatin (1879, reprinted New York, 1943), pp. 100-102. Barlow's praise appears in a frequently-published letter to Cheetham, conveniently available in Sherwin, Appendix, pp. xxxiv-xxxviii.

II. "THE SUMMERTIME OF WIT"

Paine discussed his career as an editor in a letter to Laurens, 14 January 1779. Isaiah Thomas cited Aitken in his *History of Printing in America* 2 vols. (Worcester, 1810), II, 346. William Hazlitt confirmed Aitken's testimony concerning Paine's method of composition. Hazlitt failed to reveal the source of his knowledge, but it may have come from a common friend, Thomas Holcroft. "The Plain Speaker," Essay XXIV, P. P. Howe ed., *Complete Works of William Hazlitt*, XII, 275.

III. AN UNCIVIL REBEL

Paine's experiments with saltpeter were published in *Pennsylvania Journal*, 22 November 1775. S. F. Bemis in *The Diplomacy of the American Revolution* (New York, 1935), discovered that Adams's public pronouncements were all subsequent to *Common Sense*. Rush set forth his recollections in *A Memorial containing travels through Life or sundry incidents in the life of Dr. Benjamin Rush* (Lanoraie, 1905), pp. 84-85. William Duane in his edition of *Memoirs of . . . Benjamin Franklin* (Philadelphia, 1818) remarked (p. 360) that Paine told him "that the suggestion of the papers Common Sense was made to him by Dr. Franklin"; and that he communicated the spirit of conversations with Franklin. "He also said that one or two papers were revised by the doctor, but with very few alterations." Franklin's political theory is analyzed by Gerald Stourzh in *Benjamin Franklin and American Foreign Policy* (Chicago, 1954). Noah Webster raised the question of priority in calling for the constitutional convention in *A Collection of Papers* (New York, 1843), p. 169. Adams's criticism of *Common Sense*, 19 March 1776, is printed in *Familiar Letters of John Adams*, C. F. Adams ed. (New York, 1876), p. 146. Paine affirmed the independence of his ideas in the New York *Public Advertiser*, 22 August 1807. An account of the publication of *Common Sense* appears in Richard Gimbel's *Bibliographical Check List of Common Sense* (New Haven, 1956). Another account appears in A. O. Aldridge, "Some Writings of Thomas Paine in Pennsylvania Newspapers," *Am. Hist. Rev.* LVI (July, 1951), 832-838. Paine's letter on copyright, 21 April 1783, is in the New-York Historical Society. His statements on the influence of *Common Sense* appear in Foner, II, 1163. The letter in the British press, *Gazetteer and New Daily Advertiser*, 16 May 1776, may be found in M. W. Willard, *Letters on the American Revolution* (Boston, 1925), p. 274. Lee's letter is printed by E. C. Burnett in *The Continental Congress* (New York, 1941), p. 132. Silas Deane's report is published in Francis Wharton ed., *Revolutionary Diplomatic Correspondence* 6 vols. (Washington, 1889), II, 124.

IV. THE MODERN TACITUS

General Lee's remarks on Paine are recorded in a letter to Rush, 25 February 1776. Lee Papers. *Collections of N.-Y. Hist. Soc.*, 4 vols. (New York, 1872-1874), I, 325. Paine wrote his personal vindication in the *Pennsylvania Evening Post*, 20 April 1776. Wilmer published his description of Paine in *Men and Measures from 1774 to 1809* (Washington, 1809), pp. 8-9. Alexander Graydon described the New York action in his *Memoirs* (Edinburgh, 1822), pp. 184-185. Paine's "handsome puff" appeared in the *Pennsylvania Journal*, 6 November 1776; the account of Washington's retreat, 29 January 1777. The latter was reprinted in Almon's *Remembrancer*, 1777, p. 28, and attributed to Paine by Chalmers. Paine rebuked the Congressional report in *Pennsylvania Packet*, 20 March 1779. The theft of Paine's coat was described by John Hall in a letter, 16 May 1788 (Conway, *Life*, II, 469). Details of the Indian conference are found in U. W. Condit, *History of Easton* (Easton, 1889), pp. 60, 118; Frederic A. Godcharles, *Daily Stories of Pennsylvania* (Milton, 1924), pp. 70-72; *Pa. Colonial Records*, 16 vols. (Harrisburg, 1851-1853), IX, 96, 98, 142. Paine's recollections of King Lastnight appeared in New York *Public Advertiser*, 15 August 1807; of Colonel Sampson in a letter of Dr. Samuel L. Mitchill, *Harper's New Monthly Magazine*, LVIII (April, 1879), 740-755. Paine's election to the Committee of Correspondence of the Whig Society is announced in *Pennsylvania Packet*, 18 April 1777. The accusations against Paine are cited by Adams in his autobiography; by Jay in William Jay, *Life of John Jay*, 2 vols. (New York, 1833), I, 97. Paine described the fall and winter campaigns in a letter to Franklin, 16 May 1778. Biographical information about Kirkbride appears in New York *American Citizen*, 19 March 1803, reprinted from the Trenton *True American*. John Joseph Henry's recollections appear in *Pa. Archives* Second Series (Harrisburg, 1890), XV, 143-149. Paine gave his retrospective account of *Crisis* No. 5 in Letter No. 3 to the Citizens of the United States, December 1802. All official documents of the French diplomats in America are located in the Ministère des Affaires Étrangères in Paris. Most of the correspondence of Gérard has been printed by John J. Meng in *Despatches and Instructions of Conrad Alexandre Gérard 1778-1780* (Baltimore, 1939) and much of that of his successor by William E. O'Donnell in *The Chevalier de la Luzerne, French Minister to the United States 1779-1784* (Louvain, 1938). Professor Meng has also written "French Diplomacy in Philadelphia: 1778-1779," *Catholic Historical Review*,

XXIV (1938). I have worked with the original documents and have also profited from the contributions of Meng and O'Donnell. In subsequent notes I shall refer to the volumes and pages of the original documents, using the abbreviation MEA:EU (États Unis). Gérard described his soliciting of Paine, 25 October 1778, MEA:EU 5:100. Background concerning the Pennsylvania constitution appears in J. P. Selsam, *The Pennsylvania Constitution of 1776* (Philadelphia, 1936). Paine supported it in a series of articles in the *Pennsylvania Packet*, 1, 5, 10, 12 December 1778.

V. THE DEANE AFFAIR

Many of the official documents concerning Deane and Beaumarchais are published by Henri Doniol in *Histoire de la participation de la France à l'établissement des États-Unis d'Amérique*, 5 vols. (Paris, 1886-1900) and by Francis Wharton in *The Revolutionary diplomatic correspondence of the United States* 6 vols. (Washington, 1889). Richard Henry Lee made his statement in a letter to Henry Laurens, 13 August 1779, in *Letters of Richard Henry Lee*, J. C. Ballagh ed., 2 vols. (New York, 1914), II, 120. Paine published his articles in the *Pennsylvania Packet*, the first on 15 December 1778. His letter to Laurens suggesting a link between Morris and Deane is undated. It is described in a sale catalog of Parke-Bernet Galleries, 6 December 1938. The wording of Paine's oath appears in *Journals of the Continental Congress*, VII, 274. Gérard described his relations with Paine in a letter to Vergennes, 10 January 1779. MEA:EU 7:76-78. Later he wrote out a detailed statement of his financial offers, 22 September 1779. MEA:EU Supplément I: 402-403. Gouverneur Morris's remarks on Paine are printed in Jared Sparks, *Life of Gouverneur Morris* 3 vols. (Boston, 1832), I, 201-204. The British comment, a "newsletter" from Andrew Elliot, 14 February 1779, appears in Historical Manuscripts Commission, *Manuscripts of the Earl of Carlisle* (London, 1897), p. 419. Lee's comment appears in his *Letters*, II, 50. The account of Paine's drubbing appears in *Pennsylvania Archives*, 2d series, XV, 144. Another beating is obliquely referred to in *Pennsylvania Evening Post*, 22 July 1779. Paine made a public declaration of his financial arrangements with Gérard in *Pennsylvania Packet*, 14 September 1779. Gérard to protect himself wrote the statement to Vergennes, 22 September. MEA:EU Supplément I:402-403. Gérard, before returning to France, left Holker a series of replies to Holker's questions. His despairing comments on Paine are found in MEA:EU Supplément I:262. Morris replied to Paine in *Pennsylvania Packet*, 9 January 1779. Gérard condemned Paine's interfering with commerce in a letter to Vergennes, 8 August 1779. MEA:EU 9:262-268. Morris replied to the citizens' meeting in *Pennsylvania Packet*, 5 August 1779. The Holker affair is described in the *Pennsylvania Packet*, 3, 8 and 24 July. Gérard's correspondence with Vergennes, with Congress and with the Executive Council of Pennsylvania is found in MEA:EU 9:191ff. Paine's activities in the committee on economic affairs are described in the *Pennsylvania Packet*, 10 July and 11 September. Paine published his satirical article against Rumford in *Pennsylvania Packet*, 14 August. R. H. Lee's comment appears in his *Letters*, II, 99. Modern scholars believe "Americus" to have been Edward Langworthy, a former delegate to Congress from Georgia. Paine published the correspondence between Deane and Peale in the *Packet*, 29 July; Paine made his declaration in the *Packet* 31 July. La Luzerne in a letter to Vergennes, 14 December 1781, mentions his design of employing Paine. MEA:EU 19:355-356. See also Marbois to Vergennes, 7 April 1782, MEA:EU 21:20-22.

VI. STATE CLERK AND DIPLOMATIC AGENT

Paine's letter to Gérard is in MEA:EU Supplément I:399-400. The correspondence concerning Paine's application for a literary pension is printed by William R. Reed in *Life & Corres. of Joseph Reed* 2 vols. (Philadelphia, 1847), II, 155-157. Records of Paine's appointment and activities as state clerk are printed in *Journal of the Pennsylvania Assembly*. Peale's comments are reported by Charles C. Sellers in *Charles Willson Peale* (Philadelphia, 1947), I, 213. La Luzerne's report to Vergennes is in MEA:EU 14:412-413. Paine revealed his connections with the Indiana Company in *Freeman's Journal*, 1 May 1782. La Luzerne commented on *Public Good*, 4 January 1781, MEA:EU 15:26. Paine confided to Robert Morris, 20 February 1782, his intention of establishing a newspaper. He revealed his conversation with Laurens in a letter to the Senate, 21 January 1808. The letter of Sarah Bache to Franklin is in the Yale University Library. Details of the voyage are found in Gardner W. Allen, *A Naval History of the American Revolution* 2 vols. (Boston, 1913), II, 546-547, and in a letter from Paine to James Hutchison, 11 March 1781. The "Rough Sketch of the Life of Commodore Barry" is in the Papers of John Kessler, Minnesota Historical Society. The letter of Jonathan Williams is at the University of Pennsylvania. The published version of Watson's memoirs appears in *Men and Times of the Revolution* (New York, 1856), pp. 108-110; the manuscript version, differing in many particulars, is in the New York State Library, Albany. The Committee of Claims printed a *Report of the . . . Letter and Representation of Thomas Paine* (Washington, 1809). Paine stated in a letter to Franklin, 31 March 1787, about Paris: "I do not feel myself introduced there, for I was in no house but at Passy and the hotel Col. Laurens was at." Paine recounted his voyage in a letter to a committee of the Continental Congress in October 1783. Morris's diary may be consulted at the Library of Congress. Some passages are printed in Jared Sparks, *Diplomatic Correspondence* 12 vols. (Boston: 1829-1830) and Francis Wharton, *Diplomatic Correspondence* 6 vols.

(Washington, 1889). An open letter addressed to Common Sense had appeared in the *Pennsylvania Packet,* 7 December 1782, asking him to write on the plight of the army officers. There is some doubt concerning which writing Paine considered to be *Crisis* No. 10. Between No. 9 (*Pennsylvania Packet* 19 June 1780, with corrections 13 June) and No. 11 (*Packet,* 11 May 1782) appeared the *Crisis Extraordinary* as a pamphlet, dated 4 October 1780, and letters in the *Packet,* 19 February, 28 February, 7 March 1782 and *Pennsylvania Gazette* 3 April 1782. The first three were printed by Sherwin as *Crisis* No. 10, but the last has never been reprinted. Marbois' despatch 7 April 1782 is in MEA:EU 21:20; La Luzerne's 14 May 1782 is in MEA:EU 21:171. La Luzerne's payments are recorded by O'Donnell from private archives, *op. cit.,* pp. 68-69. A. O. Aldridge has written "La Signification historique, diplomatique et littéraire de la Lettre adressée à l'abbé Raynal" in *Études Anglaises,* VIII (juillet, 1955), 233-232. La Luzerne's letter, 27 August, is in MEA: EU 22:162. Harry Hayden Clark discusses Paine's expedition to Rhode Island in *Six New Letters of Thomas Paine* (Madison, 1939).

The denials of Madison and Randolph that Paine was sent by Congress appear in E. C. Burnett, *Letters,* VII, 186.

VII. A BONUS, A BANK, AND A BRIDGE

Paine described his experiment with Washington in the New York *American Citizen,* 27 June 1806. Paine's membership in the American Philosophical Society is discussed in the Society's *Year Book* 1943 (Philadelphia, 1944), p. 72. Paine's conduct at his village fete is recorded by Vale, *op. cit.,* p. 74. Albert J. Beveridge describes Marshall's interest in Paine's behalf in *Life of John Marshall* 4 vols. (Boston, 1916), I, 213.

R. H. Lee expressed his theory in a letter to Washington, 22 July 1784, *Letters of Richard Henry Lee,* II, 291. Paine reported Gerry's conversation in a letter to the Committee of Claims of the House of Representatives, 14 February 1808. Paine's financial theories are treated by A. O. Aldridge in "Why Did Thomas Paine Write on the Bank?" in *Proc. Am. Philos. Soc.* XCIII (September, 1949), 309-315. Rawle's account of the Society for Political Inquiries, widely cited by writers on the period, is found in T. I. Wharton, "A Memoir of William Rawle," *Memoirs of the Hist. Soc. of Pa.,* IV Part I (1840), 57. Charles Biddle's account in his *Autobiography* (Philadelphia, 1883), p. 223, although equally valuable, is virtually unknown. Parts of Hall's journal are reprinted by Conway, *Life,* II, 460-472. Thompson Westcott describes Fitch's visit in *Life of John Fitch* (Philadelphia, 1878), p. 138. Paine's letter to Banks, 25 May 1789, almost identical with one to Sir George Saunton (Foner II, 1040-1050) is in the Royal Society. Someone read it to the Society, 28 May 1789, but it was not published in the *Philosophical Transactions.* Paine gave extracts from Sir Joseph's reply in a letter to Jefferson, 17 June 1789. Montpetit described his bridge in *Prospectus d'un pont de fer d'une seule arche* (Paris, 1783). An iron bridge consisting of one arch of 100 feet in the span with five ribs had been erected in 1779 over the Severn in Shropshire. *National Intelligencer,* 6 November 1801. Franklin's comment was cited by Vale, p. 138. Paine recalled Franklin's advice in his letter to Banks cited above. Moustier's invitation is found in the Jefferson Papers, Library of Congress. Paine recounted his meeting with Littlepage in the New York *American Citizen,* 29 March 1806. The letter of Ethic de Corny is in the Archives du département de la Seine et de la Ville de Paris. A letter from Lafayette to de Corny, 7 April 1788, on Paine's bridge is in Yale University Library. There is a long discussion of Paine's memorandum on rights and laws in *The Papers of Thomas Jefferson,* XIII (Princeton, 1956), 6-8. The editors believe that January or February 1788 is the probable date. Lafayette wrote to Henry Knox, 4 February 1788, that "Mr. Jefferson, Common Sense" and himself were debating the American Constitution "in a convention of our own as earnestly as if we were to decide upon it." Quoted by Louis Gottschalk, *Lafayette . . . (1783-1789),* (Chicago, 1950), p. 374. W. H. G. Armytage describes Paine's bridge building in "Thomas Paine and the Walkers," *Pennsylvania History,* XVIII (January, 1951), 16-30. Paine cited his friend's praise in a letter to Jefferson, 26 February 1789. Gouverneur Morris recorded his impressions of the bridge in his *Diary.* Paine cited the Smyth-Milbanke correspondence in an article on bridge-building in the Philadelphia *Aurora,* 17 June 1803. Comments on the Sunderland bridge appear in Samuel Smiles, *Life of Thomas Telford* (London, 1867), p. 173.

VIII. A POLITICAL BRIDGE

Paine's letter on Anglo-French relations is in the Bibliothèque Publique de Nantes. His address in Paris was Hôtel de Nismes, rue Grenelle, St. Honoré. There is no other clue to the identity of de Brienne's secretary except the *Almanach royal* for 1788, where we read, p. 217, M. Soufflot de Mercy, écuyer, *premier secrétaire.* Paine wrote to Catherine Nicholson Few, 6 January 1789, glorying in his intimacy with the heads of the political opposition. Paine's letter to Walker, 16 January, is in the Rotherham (Yorkshire) Public Library; his letter, 26 February, is printed in Foner. Paine's letter to Washington, not in Foner, is in the Washington Papers, Library of Congress. Gouverneur Morris recorded his interviews with Paine in his *Diary.* The letter of the Baroness de Vasse is in the Yale University Library. Lafayette's letter is printed in *Mémoires, correspondances et manuscrits du General Lafayette* (Bruxelles, 1837), II, 148. Paine described Christie in a letter to Rush, 16 March 1790, now in the Library of Congress. Burke's contemporary biographers were: George Croly, *Memoir of the Political Life* (Edinburgh, 1840), Robert Bisset, *The Life of Edmund Burke* (London, 1798). Thomas W. Copeland described the correspondence between Paine, Jefferson and Burke in *Edmund Burke Six Essays* (London, 1950), pp. 146-189. Paine's letter to Burke, 17 January 1790, is in the Northamptonshire Record Society. It has been published by J. T. Boulton in the *Durham University Journal*, XLIII (March, 1951), 49-55. Paine made his retrospective statement about Burke in a letter to Jefferson, 1 October 1800. Paine reported his conversation with Debrett in a letter to a friend [Thomas Christie?], 16 April 1790. Paine mentioned his agreement with Burke in a letter, 3 August 1790 [to Louis Alexandre duc de la Rochefoucauld?] in the Bibliothèque de Mantes. Paine described his news-gathering in a letter to John Rutledge, 2 June 1790, in the Library of the University of North Carolina.

IX. THE RIGHTS OF MAN

The unavailability of Paine's book was announced in *Morning Chronicle* 24 February 1791; its imminent reappearance and Paine's return to town in *Morning Chronicle,* 7 March 1791. Elbridge Colby prints Holcroft's note in *Life of Thomas Holcroft* 2 vols. (London, 1925), I, xli. Godwin's literary diary is available on microfilm at Duke University. Godwin recollected his dinner with Paine in *Memoirs of Mary Wollstonecraft,* W. C. Durant ed. (London, 1927), p. 62. Hollis's denial is found in *Memoirs of Thomas Brand Hollis* by John Disney (London, 1808). Copeland, *op. cit.,* p. 148, declares this "the most crucial ideological debate. . . ." Burke referred to "little English *piggen riggen*" in a letter to John Gifford, 7 March 1799, published by Gifford in *A Letter to the Earl of Lauderdale* (London, 1800), pp. 145-146. Walpole's comments may be found in a letter to Miss Mary Berry, 4 April 1791; the objectionable passage is on p. 132 of the first edition (in Foner I, 136). The comments of Sir Samuel Romilly are in a letter to Dumont, 5 April 1791, *Memoirs of the Life of Sir Samuel Romilly* 2 vols. (London, 1841), I, 317. The comments of the Earl of Charlemont are in Historical Manuscripts Commission, *Manuscripts of James, First Earl of Charlemont* (London, 1894), II, 204. The comments of La Luzerne are in MEA: Angleterre 577:257-260; those of Otto in MEA:EU 35:376-377. The comments of George Hammond, 1 November 1791, are in Historical Manuscripts Commission, *Manuscripts of J. B. Fortescue* 3 vols. (London, 1894), II, 223. J. C. Hamilton printed Randolph's letter to Madison, 21 July 1791, in *History of the Republic of the United States* 7 vols. (New York, 1857-1864), IV, 515.

X. A REPUBLICAN MANIFESTO FOR FRANCE

Étienne Dumont discusses Paine in his *Souvenirs sur Mirabeau,* J. Bénétruy ed. (Paris, 1951), pp. 145, 175-180. Paine's relations with

Condorcet are explored by A. O. Aldridge in *Revue de littérature comparée*, XXXII (janvier-mars, 1958), 47-65. Paine's presence at the Cercle Social is recorded by Philippe de Harivel in *Nicolas de Bonneville* (Strasbourg, 1923), p. 64. Christie described his experiences with Paine and Stone in the *Morning Chronicle*, 29 June 1791. Information on Du Chastelet is found in *Achille . . . d'Urfé, marquis du Chastelet* (Dijon, 1896) by David de Saint-Georges. Lakanal made his revelation in *Journal des Patriotes de 1789*, 1 mars 1796.

XI. "THE REVOLUTION OF THE WORLD"

The assemblage at the Crown and Anchor was reported in the *Morning Post and Daily Advertiser*, 15 July 1791. Walpole commented in a letter to Miss Mary Berry, 26 July 1791. Information on the societies is given by W. P. Hall in *British Radicalism 1791-1797* (New York, 1912) and by Nicholas Hans in "Franklin, Jefferson, and the English Radicals," *Proc. Am. Philos. Soc.* XCVIII (December 1954), 408-426. That Paine was an honorary member of the Society for Constitutional Information was brought out in the Trial of Horne Tooke together with the dates of his attendance. T. B. Howell ed., *A Complete Collection of State Trials*, XXV, 102. The statement of the Sheffield branch appears *Ibid.*, p. 135. Details on the London Corresponding Society are found in *Memoir of Thomas Hardy . . . written by Himself* (London, 1832). *The Proceedings of the Society of Friends of the People . . . in the Year 1792* (London, 1793) reveals that the group was organized 11 April 1792 (p. 4) and repudiated Paine 12 May 1792 (pp. 30-33). The meeting on 4 November 1791 was described in the *Morning Chronicle* on the next day. A statement that Paine was not a member of the Revolution Society appears in *The Correspondence of the Revolution Society . . . with the National Assembly* (London, 1792), p. 217. Hardy recalled Paine's toast in writing to Paine, 15 October 1807: British Museum. Additional Manuscripts 27:818 ff. 72-73. The controversy over the address to the Jacobins is presented in Thomas Cooper, *A Reply to Mr. Burke's invective against Mr. Cooper, and Mr. Watt, in the House of Commons, on the 30th of April, 1792* (London, 1792). Conway prints the address of 27 May in his French edition of Paine's life, pp. 210-212, but not in the English. He says the manuscript was discovered in London by Dr. Clair J. Grece, but I do not know its present whereabouts.

XII. CONTINUATION OF THE RIGHTS OF MAN

Cobbett asserted Paine's concealment in *Life of Thomas Paine Interspersed with Remarks and Reflections* (London 1796?), p. 37. Chapman's evidence appears in *The Trial of Thomas Paine*, T. B. Howell ed.,

A Complete Collection of State Trials, XXII, 402. Further circumstances of the publication of Part II of *The Rights of Man* are given in the trials of Paine, Tooke and Thomas Hardy. Tooke minimized his relations with Paine in the trial of Thelwall, *Morning Chronicle*, 4 December 1794. Paine's letter donating his profits to the *Society for Constitutional Information* was published in the Philadelphia *Aurora*, 11 December 1802. Paine's arrest was described in *Public Advertiser* 17 April 1792, in *Morning Herald*, 18 and 23 April; the discreet reference to his withdrawal appeared in the *Chronicle* 14 April. The debate in Parliament was reported in the *Morning Herald* 26 May 1792. Mason's letter to J. B. Burges, 13 September, is printed in Historical Manuscripts Commission, *Manuscripts of J. B. Fortescue*, II, 316-317.

XIII. WHERE LIBERTY IS NOT

The Franklin-Paine legend originated with Rickman, but he was careful not to say that the two men were together when they uttered their epigrams. The circumstances of Paine's election by Pas de Calais are described by E. Lecesne in *Arras sous la révolution* 3 vols. (Arras, 1882-1883) I, 280-295. Documents concerning his election by the other departments are found in Archives Nationales, C 180. The appeal of the electors of Puy-de-Dôme was printed in the *Moniteur* 13 Septembre 1792. Details of Paine's arrival in Calais are found in *Paine Insulted at Dover! Letter from Thomas Paine to Mr. Secretary Dundas* . . . (London, 1792). Paine gave the date of his arrival in Paris in an article in the *American Citizen*, 29 March 1806. Frost reported Paine's entrance in a letter to Horne Tooke, 20 September 1792, printed in *The Trial of Thomas Hardy*, T. B. Howell, *A Complete Collection of State Trials*, XXIV (London, 1818), 535. Sessions of the Convention are reported in *Archives Parlementaires* . . . *Première Série 1787 à 1799*, a composite of *Journal des Etats Généraux*, les *Procès Verbaux* et *le Moniteur*. Durand de Maillane discussed the Constitution in *Histoire de la Convention Nationale* (Paris, 1825), p. 25. Perry described the constitution-makers in *Historical Sketch of the French Revolution* (London, 1796), I, 9-10. Brissot's relations with Williams are discussed by Claude Perroud in *J.-P. Brissot, Correspondance et Papiers* (Paris, 1912), p. 305. Paine's letter in the Danton papers is in Archives Nationales, AF II. 49 Dossier 380. Madame Roland described Paine in her *Mémoires*, Claude Perroud ed., (Paris, 1905), I, 269-270. The story of Paine's relations with Fitzgerald and Oswald has been compiled from MEA:EU 587:101,173-177; 588:12-13; Procès Verbal de l'Assemblée Electorale du Département du Pas de Calais C180 Carton II dossiers 58-59 Archives Nationales; L. D. Woodward, "Les Projets de descente en Irlande," *Annales historiques de la Rév. Fr.*, VIII (janvier-février, 1931), 6-7. Rosamond Jacob, *The Rise of the United Irishmen* (London, 1937); Oswald Papers, Library Company of Philadelphia. Paine's memorial entitled "Projet d'Expedition en Irlande" is in Secrétariat d'État aux Forces Armées (Terre), Archives de la Guerre, ou Mémoires et Reconnaissances carton 1420. Other biographical information on Oswald appears in *Pa. Mag. Hist.*, II, 144-145. The civic feast was described in the *Annual Register . . . for the Year 1792*, Part II, p. 153. The gesture of Lord Edward Fitzgerald and Sir Robert Smyth is described by Patrick Byrne in *Lord Edward Fitzgerald* (Dublin, 1955), p. 113. Monro reported to Lord Grenville in September 1792. Oscar Browning ed., *The Despatches of Earl Gower, English Ambassador at Paris* (Cambridge, 1885), pp. 250-268.

XIV. THE RIGHTS OF MAN ON TRIAL

Thomas Walker reported the demonstrations against Paine in *A Review of some of the Political Events which have occurred in Manchester* (London, 1794), p. 65. The particular broadsides described are at Yale University. Edmund Malone reported Erskine's fainting in a letter to the Earl of Charlemont, 22 December 1792, Hist. Mss. Comm. *Charlemont Mss.* II (London, 1894) 209. Brissot's speech was reported in the *Moniteur*, 15 janvier 1793.

XV. A KING ON TRIAL

Paine's reply to Brissot was reported by Gênet in a manuscript published by Conway as an appendix to *Thomas Paine et la Révolution dans les deux mondes*. Bertrand de Moleville praised Paine in *Histoire de la Révolution de France* (Paris, 1802), X, 399.

XVI. A FIREBRAND ON TRIAL

Barère's observations appear in his *Mémoires* (Paris, 1824), II, 297. Paine alluded to Johnson's attempted suicide in his essay "Forgetfulness." The letters of Sampson Perry and Mme Moreau are in Archives Nationales W 269 no. 16. The trial was reported in the *Moniteur* 3 mai 1793. Thibaudeau reported Marat's conversation in *Mémoires sur la convention et le directoire* (Paris, 1824), I, 111. Paine's testimony in Miranda's behalf is published in *Archivo del General Miranda* 15 vols. (Caracas, 1929-1938), XII, 170-172. The police report of Paine's dispute is found in Archives Nationales F [7] 2475 pp. 136-137. John Epps relates the anecdote concerning Wollstonecraft in *The Life of John Walker* (London, 1840), pp. 142-143. Lewis Goldsmith reported Danton's warning in *Antigallican Monitor*, 13 February 1814. The address against the delegates of Pas de Calais and the defense of Jean-Baptiste Personne are in Vol. 66 of *Archives Parlementaires*. Paine reported Morris's dismissal of the sea-captains in a letter to Barère, 5 September 1793. The address of the sea-captains is in the Thomas Paine Historical Association. Paine described his relations with Barère in a letter to James Monroe, 30 Vendémiaire, 21 October 1794. The memorandum proposing Paine as a commissioner is in MAE:EU 38:215-218. Barère's tribute to Paine is in his *Mémoires* (Paris, 1824), II, 137. Paine accused Barère of "signing the warrant" in his third letter *To the Citizens of the United States,* but Barère's signature appears on none of the documents concerning Paine's arrest.

XVII. IN LUXEMBOURG PRISON

Perry's retrospective view of Paine's imprisonment appeared in *Historical Sketch of the French Revolution* (London, 1796), II, 514. Manuel referred to Paine, 13 November 1793. Archives Nationales W 295 no. 246. Paine described his last hours of liberty in "Forgetfulness." Paine described the events of his arrest in an Appendix to Part I of *The Age of Reason*. The petition of the American delegation and the reply of Vadier are given in the *Moniteur* 1 fevrier 1794; the original documents are in Archives Nationales F 7 4774 61. Griffith's journal reporting his participation is in Elizabeth W. Latimer, *My Scrap-Book of the French Revolution* (Chicago, 1898), p. 50. Thomas D. Scoble, Jr., discusses *Thomas Paine's Citizenship Record* (New Rochelle, 1946). The Morris-Deforgues correspondence is in MEA:EU 40:91 and 50:102. Morris's letters to Jefferson, 21 January and 6 March, are printed by Jared Sparks in *Life of Gouverneur Morris* 3 vols. (Boston, 1832), II, 393, 408-409. Luxembourg prison is described in *Mémoires sur les Prisons* (Paris, 1823), II, 137-186. Sampson Perry described Paine's concealment of funds in *Register of Occurrences and Miscellany [of the Argus 1795 & 1796]* (London), pp. 558-561. H. M. Williams reported Paine's conversations with Clootz in *Letters containing a Sketch of the Politics of France* (London, 1795), II, 177. Danton's words are quoted in *Mémoires sur les Prisons*, II, 153. Paine's testimony concerning Jullien is in Archives Nationales W 189 dossier *Jullien* and U 1021 dossier 941. All the documents concerning Paine's imprisonment, including the appeals of Lanthenas and Audibert are in Archives Nationales F 7 4774 61. The appeal of Lanthenas, 5 August, is misdated by Conway.

XVIII. RETURN TO THE CONVENTION

Paine's account in the *Public Advertiser* appeared 17 April 1807 (Foner II, 974-975). Rowan's note to Monroe is in the Monroe Papers, Library of Congress. Rowan wrote to C. A. Rodney about Monroe's election, and Rodney copied his letter for Monroe, 8 May 1817. It also is in the Monroe Papers. Thibaudeau's motion and Paine's thanks are printed in the former's *Mémoires*, I, 108-111. Nodier described Paine in *Souvenirs de la Révolution et de l'Empire* (Paris, 1864), I, 343. Chenier's speech, 3 janvier 1795, is printed in his *Œuvres* 8 vols. (Paris, 1823-1827), V, 180-181. Paine's letter to Thibaudeau is printed in the latter's *Mémoires*, I, 112-116.

XIX. THE AGE OF REASON

Richard Gimbel described "The First Appearance of Thomas Paine's *The Age of Reason*" in *The Yale University Library Gazette*, Vol. 31 (October, 1956). Eaton published Paine's letter in an advertisement in *Morning Chronicle*, 19 December 1795. Sampson Perry made his observation on Watson in *The Argus* (London, 1796), p. 495. William Hamilton Reid, author of *Rise . . . of the Infidel Societies* (London, 1800) commented on the Corresponding Society, p. 3. The standard study of the Theophilanthropists is Albert Mathiez, *La Théophilanthrope et le culte décadaire* (Paris, 1903). Frank MacDermont reports that a wag invented the pun *filous en troupe*. *Theobald Wolfe Tone* (London, 1939), p. 239.

XX. FRIENDSHIP WITH MONROE

Cobbett described Paine's illness in his manuscript biography published by Conway in *Life*, II, 441. Cramer's letter was published by Hermann Tiemann in "Neues aus Paris Anno 1795," in *Der Vergleich* Reihe A, Band 42, (Hamburg, 1955), pp. 177-178. The printing and distribution of *Decline and Fall* may be traced in Archives Nationales AF III, 365 dossier 1763; AF III 374 dossier 1865. The act of the Directory allowing Paine to remain in Paris is in Archives Nationales AF III 369 dossier 1805. Edwards reported Monroe's temporary mistrust of Paine in a letter to Rufus King, 18 August 1796. Charles R. King, *Life and Correspondence of Rufus King* (New York, 1895), II, 80-81. The editor incorrectly identifies Enoch Edwards with his brother Evan. Charles Biddle repeated Paine's comment on his writings and posterity in *Autobiography* (Philadelphia, 1883), p. 310. Correspondence between Monroe and Miranda is printed in *Archivo del General Mirando*, XIII, 163-176.

XXI. AMATEUR DIPLOMAT ONCE MORE

Paine's letter concerning Pinckney is in MEA:EU 46:425-426; the comment on it in MEA:EU 46:427-428. Paine reported the British search for him at sea in *Letter IV to the Citizens of the United States* (Foner II, 927). Paine's letter to Talleyrand is in MEA:EU 48:273 (Foner, II, 1401-1402); Talleyrand's reply MEA:EU 48:277. Marshall reported the overtures of Church in his journal. A photostatic copy is in the Library of Congress. Paine's letter to the commissioners and Marshall's disparaging comments are in National Archives, Department of State Papers

(Pinckney, Marshall, Gerry September 2, 1797-November 24, 1798)
Vol. 6. Paine's criticism of the commissioners and the Directory is in a
letter, 29 May 1798, to an unnamed person, printed in part in an American Art Assoc. Sales Catalog in the New York Public Library.

XXII. RELATIONS WITH THE DIRECTORY

Mme Bonneville related Paine's domestic habits in Cobbett's manuscript published by Conway. Other details appear in George Duval,
Histoire de la littérature révolutionnaire (Paris, 1879), p. 299. The
declaration of François de Neufchâteau is in Archives Nationales AF III
478 pl. 2955 pp. 7-8. Dr. Walker's visits to Paine are described by John
Epps in *The Life of John Walker*, pp. 133-143. The passage from Tone's
Journal is published in *Life of Theobald Wolfe Tone edited by his Son*
2 vols. (Washington, 1826) II, 348. R. R. Crocker's impressions of Paine
appear in Frederick Freeman's *The History of Cape Cod* 2 vols. (Boston,
1858), I, 574. Paine's letter to Sottin is in Archives Nationales F [7] 7300
dossier B [4] 3246. Paine's correspondence concerning May is in Archives
Nationales F [7] 7310 dossier B [4] 4509. The document on invading England
is printed by A. O. Aldridge in "Thomas Paine's Plan for a Descent on
England" in *William & Mary Quarterly* XIV (January, 1957), 74-84.
The patriotic rally is described in *le Bien informé* 26 February 1798; the
St. Patrick's Day banquet in *le Bien informé* 18 March 1798. Edouard
Desbrière quoted the Irish memorial which Paine presented in *Projets
et tentatives de débarquement aux Iles Britanniques* 5 vols. (Paris, 1900-
1902) II, 40, from the original in Archives de la Marine, which now
cannot be located. Paine's hostage plan was printed in *le Bien informé*
27 October 1798. The scheme for attacking the United States was
printed and attributed to Paine in *Porcupine's Gazette*, 13 February 1799;
American Citizen, 1 February 1810; and John Bristed, *Hints on the
National Bankruptcy of Britain* (New York, 1809) 267-271. The police
report associating Paine with Somers is in Archives Nationales F [7] 6152
PLAQ 2 dossier 868 B.P. Paine's letter on behalf of Bonneville is in
Archives Nationales AF III 544 PL 3620 pp. 8-10. Lewis Goldsmith
revealed the relationship between Brune and Bonneville in *Secret
History of the Cabinet of Napoleon* (London, 1810), p. 572. Paine wrote
a congratulatory letter to Brune, 8 Brumaire An VIII (Foner II, 1403-
1405). The police complaint against Paine is in Archives Nationales AF
194 pp. 41-42. Paine reported his interview with Ellsworth in a letter
to Jefferson, 1 October 1800 (Foner II, 1407). Paine's document on
internal improvements is in the New York Public Library. Goldsmith
printed his recollections of Paine in his *Antigallican Monitor*, 27 September, 1 November 1812, and 6 and 13 February, 1814. Yorke's recollections appear in *Letters from France*, II, 337-369. Paine made his
disillusioned remark concerning Napoleon in a letter, 29 September 1801:

typed copy in Thomas Paine Historical Association. Landor's report of Paine's opinion of Napoleon appears in his *Complete Works*, T. E. Welby ed., (London, 1927), VI, 110-111. Landor described Paine to the American artist W. W. Story; Henry James, *William Wetmore Story* (New York, 1903), II, 26-27. Paine expressed his pique to Jefferson, 20 April 1805 (Foner II, 1465-1466) and Jefferson replied 5 June. Lewis Goldsmith in *Antigallican Monitor*, 28 February 1813, reported the largesse of Burdett and Bosville.

XXIII. BALTIMORE AND WASHINGTON

One of Rufus King's friends wrote from Baltimore, 12 November, that "the boarders of the Tavern where he alighted refused to remain in the house if Tom were admitted to the public table. The Tavern where I am, Evans, the best in Town I hear, refused to admit him because the frequenters of it manifested the same spirit." C. R. King, *Life and Correspondence of Rufus King* (New York, 1897), IV, 182. The report of L. A. Pichon is in MEA:EU 55:78. Plumer's social life is described in *Life of William Plumer by his son William Plumer, Jr.* (Boston, 1856), pp. 242-243. Dr. Mitchill described Gallatin's dinner in a letter published in *Harper's New Monthly Magazine* LVIII (April, 1879), 740-755. The dinner at General Dearborn's was reported in the *Aurora*, 17 February 1803. Cutler discussed Paine in a letter to Dr. Joseph Torrey, 3 January 1803, W. P. & J. P. Cutler, *Life and Correspondence of Rev. Manasseh Cutler* 2 vols. (Cincinnati, 1888), II, 119. William Duane's letter is printed in *Proc. Mass. Hist. Soc.* Second Series XX (1907) 279. Levi Lincoln's letter is in the Jefferson Papers, Library of Congress. Information on Madgett is available in the *Moniteur*, 14 Thermidor An III; also in Frank MacDermont, *Theobald Wolfe Tone* (London, 1939), *passim.*

XXIV. NEW ROCHELLE AND NEW YORK

Paine's visit with Driscol was reported in the *Patriot* 24 February; his arrival in Philadelphia in the *Aurora*, 22 February. His reunion with Peale is discussed by Charles Coleman Sellers in *Charles Willson Peale* (Philadelphia, 1947), II, 162. Paine's host is identified in C. L. Rives, *Selections from the Correspondence of Thomas Barclay* (New York, 1894), p. 151. Richard Gimbel discusses Paine's articles in the Hartford *American Mercury* and his relations with Elisha Babcock in *The Yale University Library Gazette*, XXX (January, 1956), 94-107. Fosdick's letter is in the Jefferson Papers, Library of Congress. Vale, p. 146, recounted the story of Paine's apple gathering. Paine wrote about Kirkbride's death to Anthony Taylor of Bordentown, 20 November 1803. Typed copy in Thomas Paine Historical Association. Fellows described

Mrs. Palmer in the *Beacon*, 23 October 1841. Paine's letter in the *Aurora*, 6 March 1804, was shortly after reprinted and refuted by John Cartwright in Vol. II of *Aegis, or the Military Energies of the Constitution* (London, 1806). Bonneville expressed his appreciation of Paine in *De l'origine de la Franc-Maçonnerie* (Paris, 1812). Paine promised to give the Bonnevilles equal treatment in a letter to Fellows, 18 April 1805, in the Thomas Paine Historical Association.

XXV. JARVIS AND CARPENTER

Details concerning Paine's life with Jarvis and Carpenter are presented in Cheetham, Vale, and Harold E. Dickson, *John Wesley Jarvis* (New York, 1949), pp. 97-104. That Paine lodged at the Bull's Head tavern in New Rochelle is shown in a letter of J. W. McDowell, 1 May 1806, in the Pennsylvania Historical Society. The American Antiquarian Society has a photostat of Paine's letter to Barlow, 4 May 1807, only partially reproduced in Foner II, 1488-1489. (London, 1818), p. 62. Carver's letter of reconciliation is in *Works of Thomas Paine* (Philadelphia, 1854), I, XXXVIII-XXXIX. Jarvis described Paine's impromptu concert in *Beacon*, II, (1838) 314. Melish recounted his visit to Paine in *Travels Through the United States of America*. J. W. Francis revealed Paine's verbal repartee in *Old New York* (New York, 1866), p. 140.

XXVI. THE DEFENSE OF NEW YORK

no notes

XXVII. FEUD WITH CHEETHAM

Carver gave his version of the rift between Paine and Cheetham in his manuscript autobiography, *Beacon* IV (1839-1840), 142.

XXVIII. LAST DAYS

John Randel gave his recollections of Paine in "Residence of Thomas Paine" in D. T. Valentine, *Manual* (New York, 1864), pp. 841-846. T. Adams recorded his visit in *Democracy Unveiled; in a Letter to Sir Francis Burdett* (London, 1813), reviewed in *Monthly Review*, LXX (March, 1813), 275-285. Alexander Wilson described his visit in a letter to Lawson, 3 November 1808, in the Harvard University Museum of Comparative Zoology. Fellows offered his explanation of the Quaker refusal in the preface to an edition of Paine's *Theological Works* (London, without date). Randel cited the testimony of Woodworth in *Valentine's Manual* 1864, p. 843.

XXIX. RECAPITULATION

Barlow's letter, first published by John Fellows in *The Theophilanthropist*, has been widely reprinted. A note defending Paine's religion as being that of the most learned men of the age was originally part of the letter, but Barlow "flinched" at allowing this to appear over his name. *Beacon* VII, 67.

Index

343